GOD'S CARESS

GOD'S CARESS

The Psychology of Puritan
Religious Experience

Charles Lloyd Cohen

New York   Oxford
OXFORD UNIVERSITY PRESS
1986

Oxford University Press

Oxford   New York   Toronto
Delhi   Bombay   Calcutta   Madras   Karachi
Petaling Jaya   Singapore   Hong Kong   Tokyo
Nairobi   Dar es Salaam   Cape Town
Melbourne   Auckland

and associated companies in
Beirut   Berlin   Ibadan   Mexico City   Nicosia

Library of Congress Cataloging-in-Publication Data
Cohen, Charles Lloyd
God's caress.
Bibliography: p.   Includes index.
1. Puritans—New England—Religious life.
2. Conversion.   3. Christianity—Psychology.
4. Spirituality—History of doctrines—16th century.
5. Spirituality—History of doctrines—17th century.
6. New England—Church history.   I. Title.
BX9354.2.C64   1986   248.2'0974   85-21843
ISBN 0-19-503973-4

Printing (last digit): 9 8 7 6 5 4 3 2 1
Printed in the United States of America
on acid free paper

To My Wife
CHRISTINE AMBER SCHINDLER

Eshet Chasîdîm
Aggelos tis Agapes tou Theou
Agent of God's Love

Acknowledgments

Studying history makes one aware of the intricate human connections that compose any event; writing history makes one cognizant of how much one's own work depends on what other people do. This book exists because numerous individuals have contributed to it in ways both profound and subtle. My parents did not raise me to be an historian, but they did foster my love of learning and bankroll my first readers. In high school I decided to become an American historian through listening to Edson Scudder, whose renditions of the past and of "Yankee Doodle" on a squeaky desk chair were equally inspiring. I learned something about decisions of conscience from Dr. Milton Miller during the Vietnam War.

A grant from the Mabelle McLeod Lewis Memorial Fund in 1980–81 and grants from the Newburger Foundation in 1981 and 1982 provided both the wherewithal for meat and potatoes, and the confidence that someone else thought the project worthwhile. When the fate of the manuscript (and the career of its author) hung in the balance, an award from the Society of American Historians effected a happy ending.

In the face of frantic requests to locate fugitive materials, overdue books, and misplaced microfilms, the staffs of Doe Library at the University of California, Berkeley, the combined Libraries of the Graduate Theological Union and the Pacific School of Religion, the New England Historic Genealogical Society, the Massachusetts Historical Society, and Memorial Library at the University of Wisconsin-Madison always manifested their guild's gentle competence.

My debt to the community of scholars, visible and invisible, is manifest on every page: one may think for oneself, but never by oneself. More particularly, I owe much to Herbert Phillips, purveyor of exuberant good sense and theoretical acumen; William Simmons, possessed of a Rhode Islander's facility at dissecting New England orthodoxies; and especially Robert Middlekauff, Southern California's token Puritan, who subjected the text to equal doses of justice and mercy. Michael McGiffert, as versed in the covenants as was Robert Rollock, dispatched a number of misstatements. My colleagues at the University of Wisconsin-Madison have provided a most comfortable and stimulating environment; there, Michael MacDonald has treated with tact and candor the mystical bedlam into which my ideas sometimes degenerated.

My dinners with André Mayer always left me with more to think about than I could possibly digest. Steven Lipman could always be counted on to ferry the distraught pilgrim over sloughs of despond. For fifteen years Clive Matson has dispensed a post-graduate education in style, suggesting how poetry can be the language of scholarship. At Oxford University Press, Sheldon Meyer offered patient support for the final revisions; then, neither gilding the lily nor sparing the rod, Leona Capeless dotted all the *i*'s that needed it.

Two people warrant special thanks. My association with Winthrop Jordan has led, on one occasion, to locking a turkey in an oven; more usually, it has afforded the excitement of attending on a mind rigorous enough to illuminate the arcane and eccentric enough to make the obvious compelling discourse on myriad topics. This book is dedicated to my wife because she did not type a single letter of it. Whenever I waltzed with angels on the head of a pin, she flicked us off. Her catholic faith has ravished me—for which blessing (along with allowing me to finish this tome) I thank God.

Madison   C. L. C.
August 1985

Contents

Note on Transcription

Seventeenth-century orthography is wonderful to behold, a salve for every-one who did not win his fourth grade spelling bee. I have retained the original renderings because, in their quaint and entertaining way, they accent the historicity of the sources, an emphasis that reminds us that we are listening to distant voices. Readers unfamiliar with such quirky spelling may be startled at first, but I hope they will not be inconvenienced. At the same time, fidelity to the text has not subordinated clarity; some particularly confusing or ambiguous spellings have been changed (within square brackets). The original punctuation (or lack of it) has usually been retained, and most alterations are indicated by the use of square brackets. The follow-ing instances are the only exceptions: colons at the end of a sentence have been changed to periods, while semi-colons, colons, and periods may have silently been either changed to commas or removed if the phrase or clause they complete is used in the middle of a sentence. In the Geneva Bible and the King James Version words with no equivalents in the original text are set in italic type; this convention has been retained in quotations herein. Book titles retain their original capitalization.

Abbreviations

Unless otherwise indicated, specific references to Bibles in the text are to the editions whose dates and catalogue numbers are given here.

BB The Bishops' Bible (DMH #271, 1602).

Cov. Coverdale's Bible (DMH #84, 1550).

DM Thomas Herbert Darlow and Horace Frederick Moule, eds., *Historical Catalogue of the Printed Editions of Holy Scripture in the Library of the British and Foreign Bible Society*, 2 pts. in 4 vols. (London, 1903–11).

DMH Arthur Sumner Herbert, ed., *Historical Catalogue of Printed Editions of the English Bible, 1525–1961* (London and New York, 1968).

DNB *Dictionary of National Biography*, 22 vols. (London, 1921–22).

Douai The Douai Old Testament (DMH #300, 1609–10).

GB The Great Bible (DMH #62, 1541).

GenB The Geneva Bible (DMH #107, 1560).

IB *The Interpreter's Bible*, 12 vols. (Nashville and New York, 1951–57).

KJV The King James Version of the Bible (1611, repr. [1975?]).

MB Matthew's Bible (DMH #74, 1549).

NEB The New English Bible (1970).

OED *The Oxford English Dictionary*, 13 vols. (Oxford, 1933).

Rheims The Rheims New Testament (DMH #177, 1582).

RSV The Revised Standard Version of the Bible (1977).

Tav.   Taverner's Bible (DMH #45, 1539).

TDNT   Gerhard Kittel and Gerhard Friedrich, eds., *Theological Dictionary of the New Testament*, trans. Geoffrey W. Bromiley, 10 vols. (Grand Rapids, 1964–76).

TDOT   G. Johannes Botterweck and Helmer Ringgren, eds., *Theological Dictionary of the Old Testament*, trans. John T. Willis et al., 4 vols. to date (Grand Rapids, 1977–   ).

Tyn.   Tyndale's New Testament (DMH #19, 1536).

GOD'S CARESS

Introduction

Of making many books on Puritans there is no end, a testimony to their significance in Anglo-American culture. Protagonists in the first great European political revolution, progenitors of several denominations, colonizers of New England, they helped pioneer new civic and ecclesiastical institutions on both sides of the Atlantic. Part of their legacy included the invention of a distinctive religiosity that suffused them with peculiar fervor. To underscore their perfervid spirituality at the outset of this book involves taking a stand on one of the more vexing questions in seventeenth-century historiography, the problem of determining just who belongs within the select circle of Saints. Like the proverbial carrot on a stick, so palpably close but so frustratingly inaccessible, Puritanism seems easy to categorize until one actually takes a step to qualify it; then, it bounces tantalizingly out of reach. Scholars have piled definition upon definition, until some have concluded that no categorization is valid or even called for.[1] Yet to dismiss "Puritanism" as an empty

1. The difficulties of defining Puritanism and the details of this controversy may be traced in Basil Hall, "Puritanism: the Problem of Definition," in G. J. Cuming, ed., *Studies in Church History*, II (London, 1965), 283-96; Charles H. George, "Puritanism as History and Historiography," *Past and Present*, 41 (1968) , 77–104; William Lamont, "Puritanism as History and Historiography: Some Further Thoughts," *ibid.*, 44 (1969), 133–46; Ian Breward, "The Abolition of Puritanism," *Journal of Religious History*, 7 (1972–73), 20–34; Richard Greaves, "The Nature of the Puritan Tradition," in R. Buick Knox, ed., *Reformation, Conformity and Dissent: Essays in Honour of Geoffrey Nuttall* (London, 1977), 255–73; Paul Christianson, "Reformers and the Church of England under Elizabeth I and the Early Stuarts," *Journal of Ecclesiastical History*, 31 (1980), 463–84; and Patrick Collinson, "Comment," *ibid.*, 485–87.

concept will not do. One of its foremost expositors has noted that "'Puritan' is an insistent voice" in the hubbub of the sixteenth and seventeenth centuries, and it is instructive to learn how contemporaries used it. In the decades before the English lobbed cannon balls at each other, they bombarded their religious opponents with epithets.[2] The targets of the moniker "Puritan" were people who looked with distress on the condition of their church and who covenanted together in groups of self-professed godly souls to reform what they considered an intolerable string of abuses. Considering themselves the leaven that would raise the lump of ignorant, indifferent, and false professors through constant pious endeavor, they earned their neighbors' enmity for divisive scrupulosity and hypocritical self-righteous zeal. To friends they seemed militant soldiers in the army of the Lord; to foes, officious busybodies disrupting village camaraderie, but on at least one point all observers could agree: to be a Puritan meant living a life distinctively ardent.[3]

This "intensity" has been variously located in the Saints' "white-hot" moralism, "uncompromisingly" biblical faith, fervent adherence to the Reformed theology of grace, unique capacity to obsessively entertain fantasies of dependence, and programmatic denial of any limbo that secured "indifferent" matters of theology from the demands of Scripture and conscience.[4] Whatever its manifestations, holy passion demanded unrestrained devotion to God's cause, goading the faithful to contemn "*glozing neuters*" who think gospel zeal "a fever in a mans body" and who cultivate "a cold luke warme temper" to suppress it.[5] Puritans were a "hotter sort" of Protestant, and what kept them bubbling was a religious sensibility intimately bound up with conversion, an emotional confrontation with grace borne by the Holy Spirit in the Word. This encounter formed the nexus around which Puritanism developed its strain of evangelical piety, and some have accounted it the movement's "essence."[6] The emphasis is well placed. Few topics so occupied Puritan preachers as did explicating the pangs of the "new birth," and few

2. Patrick Collinson, *English Puritanism* (London, 1983), 7–11 (quotation, 11); Thomas H. Clancy, "Papist-Protestant-Puritan: English Religious Taxonomy, 1565–1665," *Recusant History*, 13 (1976), 227–53.

3. Patrick Collinson, *The Elizabethan Puritan Movement* (London, 1967); *The Religion of Protestants: The Church in English Society 1559–1625* (Oxford, 1982), 141–283; *Godly People: Essays on English Protestantism and Puritanism* (London, 1983), esp. 1–18, 527–62.

4. Marshall M. Knappen, *Tudor Puritanism: A Chapter in the History of Idealism* (Chicago, 1939; repr. Gloucester, 1963), 344; Horton Davies, *Worship and Theology in England*, 5 vols. (Princeton, 1961–75), I, 41; Dewey Wallace, *Puritans and Predestination: Grace in English Protestant Theology 1525–1695* (Chapel Hill, 1982), xi, 29, 37; Thomas Leverenz, *The Language of Puritan Feeling* (New Brunswick, 1980), 107; Collinson, *Elizabethan Puritan Movement*, 127–28.

5. Thomas Hooker, *The Sovles Vocation or Effectval Calling to Christ* (London, 1638), 273, 275.

6. Alan Simpson, *Puritanism in Old and New England* (Chicago, 1955), 2.

activities so engrossed believers as did scrutinizing themselves to discover how far regeneration had proceeded.

On one level, the reasons for this concern are obvious. Puritan theology insisted that the straight and narrow path to heaven traversed the gate of conversion; those whom God had elected to salvation passed through a protracted experience of desperation and relief. To glimpse one's heart beating faster at the sound of the Word and find the terror of God's wrath assuaged by the joy of deliverance signified admission into the Kingdom of Heaven. But conversion also served another purpose, one more prominent in the rhetoric of the godly, and more critical for the creation of a covenanted society. Puritans were preoccupied with the limits of human power. Without faith, they thought, humanity wallows in sinful debility, but conversion changes helpless unregenerates into puissant Saints. The new birth was their initiation into potency, and belief the vehicle of their strength. The dynamism of Puritan activity and the cohesiveness of their community arose from the psychological foundation laid down by the Lord's mercy in regeneration. Puritanism cannot be reduced to merely an affective style, but the pious zeal that stamps it issued directly from a psychological transformation fundamental to the movement. The nature of this experience and its function in the lives of the people who underwent it form the subject matter of this work.

I

The notion that only conversion establishes an authentic relationship to God has resonated in Judeo-Christian thought since the plaints of Amos and Hosea. Dismayed by what they considered the failure of ritual fasting and lamentation to elicit more than superficial penitence, the prophets announced that God demands sin be repudiated at the altar of the heart. What this involves they communicated by investing a word borrowed from common speech—*shûbh*, 'to go back again,' 'to return'—with theological value. True piety consists in consciously turning back from sin to embrace God, reversing one's earlier path. The repentant put themselves under God's will; they trust Him unconditionally and turn from transgression. Conversion reorients one's life course, asking more of the person than lip-service to ceremony or willingness to perform moral obligations. Turning enlists the entire personality; it engages all of one's faculties. A human being who has "missed the mark" in transgressing returns to God through a thoroughgoing self-transformation.[7] Christian Scripture meditates on the Old Testament themes in light

7. W.W. Holladay, *The Root Shûbh in the Old Testament* (Leiden, 1958); G.G. Harrop, "'Returning Unto the Lord'," *Canadian Journal of Theology*, 7 (1961), 239–44; *TDNT*, s.v. "μετανοέω, μετανοια," B. I-II.

of the Christ-event and its eschatological promise. New Testament writers assimilate the significance of *shûbh* to their own vocabulary and affirm the need for a radical personal change. The call to redirect one's ways dominates the Gospel, especially in the preaching of Jesus. God's revelation in Christ discloses conversion's absolute necessity, since only those who repent and believe can enter His Kingdom. Turning is imperative, for on it depends eternal life.[8] Among its central concerns, the Bible teaches that an individual comes to God in reponse to His summons, wholeheartedly moving away from sin. The roles in the process assigned to divine initiative and human capacity are not formally reasoned out, nor is a paradigmatic psychology anywhere displayed, but the invitation to turn is emphatic.

The concept of conversion developed along with Christianity, and at times meanings other than 'inward change' gained primacy. Already in the New Testament conversion implied more than an internal transformation. As "The Way" swept beyond the Jewish community, turning to God involved leaving one's old religious culture and accepting a new ethic; private change impelled public alterations of affiliation and belief. Another sense emerged against the backdrop of the numerous but often nominal conversions the faith inspired as official religion of the Roman Empire: rigorous devotion to Christian principles, especially by leaving the secular world for a monastery. Over several centuries this definition gained ascendance, until Bernard of Clairvaux, one of the few medieval churchmen Puritans esteemed, reaffirmed the significance of the redirective inner experience, at least within the context of choosing and following the monastic vocation. By the late Middle Ages, the interior turn had been linked by Francis of Assisi to mendicant pilgrimage, by Thomas Aquinas to the Eucharist, and by Johannes Tauler to mystical union. It remained for Martin Luther, in whom experience propelled thought with the same explosive velocity as it did in Paul and Augustine, to remove conversion from a small circle of professional discussants and make it the issue for an age. Luther insisted that one must turn from the false righteousness of works to the faith that justifies, and he castigated the Church for neglecting to preach the Word that turns. The importance of conversion was one of the standards under which the Reformation marched.[9]

8. *TDNT*, s.v. "μετανοέω, μετανοια," E, and s.v. "στρέφω," q.v. "επιστρέφω, επιστροφή"; *The New International Dictionary of New Testament Theology*, gen. ed. Colin Brown, 3 vols. (Grand Rapids, 1975–78), s.v. "Conversion."

9. Marilyn J. Harran, *Luther on Conversion: The Early Years* (Ithaca, 1983), 24–53, 189–93; A. J. Nock, *Conversion: The Old and the New in Religion from Alexander the Great to Augustine of Hippo* (Oxford, 1933), 7, 193–211. On Bernard's influence, see Gordon S. Wakefield, *Puritan Devotion: Its Place in the Development of Christian Piety* (London, 1957), 94–95, 101ff, 158; Barrington R. White, "Echoes of Medieval Christendom in Puritan Spirituality," *One in Christ*, 16 (1980), 87.

English Reformers shouldered a banner stitched by Swiss and Rhenish hands, and their theory of conversion bore the label of Strasbourg, Zurich, and Geneva. Although they drew selectively on Luther, patristic writers, and indigenous sources, the first generations of English Protestants learned their lessons from men like Martin Bucer, John Calvin, Heinrich Bullinger, and Peter Martyr, who were fashioning Reformed theology. Their dialogue germinated despite Henry VIII's desire to weed out the newly sprung heresy, flourished when the church under Edward VI cultivated the presence of leading Reformed divines, and sustained itself in prison and exile while Queen Mary sought to wither English Protestantism at the root. Through letter and lecture, conversation and tract, Reformed theology had by the 1550s established itself as the dogma of English Protestantism.[10] Embedded in this thought was an anthropology that dwelt on human frailty and a soteriology that strung together a sequence of steps through which the Holy Spirit turns the soul to God. So enfeebled by the Fall that one can never merit salvation by good works, the individual is liberated from sin's bondage only through the gratuitous gift of faith apprehending Christ the Redeemer and imputing his righteousness to the believer. Grace imparted by the Spirit regenerates the convert and issues forth in a lifetime of sanctified works. Christ's sacrifice applies effectually only to the Elect, who are infallibly called to salvation; they cannot resist grace when it comes, nor can they fall away to perdition. Eternal life depends entirely on God's will carrying out His predetermined election to salvation. These propositions harbor certain expectations about how one turns. Mortal activity lies within God's compass and His inexorable direction of the Spirit to the Elect soul. A person struggles helplessly against sin until He initiates the call. The theory seems to intimate human passivity at the outset of conversion, a position that Reformed apologists rejected, but it posits an end result of unequivocal activity. Grace leads ultimately to heaven but penultimately to a career of holy service regulated by the Moral Law. Turning does not inhere in a single event; it stretches out through a lifetime of faithful discipline.

This formulation of God's redemptive work captured the Elizabethan clergy, and it held sway, despite some brief spats at Cambridge, until a small

10. Wallace, *Puritans and Predestination*, 3–28. On the advisability of using the term "Reformed," see *ibid.*, x–xi, 3–4, and David D. Hall, "Understanding the Puritans," in Stanley N. Katz, ed., *Colonial America: Essays in Politics and Social Development*, 1st ed. (Boston, 1971), 31–50. To say that English churchmen took over Reformed Protestantism does not imply that the English people accepted it so readily; they had to be evangelized into the new faith. See J. J. Scarisbrick, *The Reformation and the English People* (London, 1984), 163–88; Christopher Haigh, "Some Aspects of the Recent Historiography of the English Reformation," in W. J. Mommsen, ed., *The Urban Classes, the Nobility, and the Reformation* (London, 1980), 88–106; and Dewey Wallace, "George Gifford, Puritan Propaganda and Popular Religion in Elizabethan England," *Sixteenth Century Journal*, 9 (1978), 27–49.

but well-placed party headed by Bishop (later Archbishop) William Laud and encouraged by Charles I championed Arminianism, precipitating a major doctrinal struggle. Against the great majority of English divines, who continued loyal to some version of Reformed orthodoxy, the Arminians advanced a more generous view of human capacity in the conversion process and maintained that a justified person can fall from grace. Full-fledged theological disputes rived the dogmatic consensus only in the 1620s, but conflicts within it had often broken out earlier.[11] The perceived uniformity of thought about grace and other issues in the period 1560–1640 has tempted some scholars to homogenize English Protestantism, to aver that little, if anything, separated churchmen who lived comfortably within the established ecclesiastical settlement from those who, dissatisfied with some of its features, yapped at their heels. Rightly pointing to a body of widely shared belief, this view nevertheless minimizes real differences of opinion concerning matters like the authority of Scripture and the nature of the 'true church, and it disallows the possibility that people who agree on a platform may bitterly contest how best to interpret and apply its planks.[12] Just such a dispute opened up in the later sixteenth century regarding the importance of preaching. Widespread agreement that the Church of England sorely lacked a full complement of dedicated preachers did not conceal disparate evaluations of that fact's soteriological significance. To many ecclesiastics, the shortage constituted an institutional embarrassment, bearable because reading homilies and performing the sacraments could sufficiently deliver the Gospel.[13] To others—the Puritans—it represented an artifact of hell. Grace pierces the heart in the sound of sermons, they held, and therefore the paucity of

11. Wallace, *Puritans and Predestination*, 29–111; Nicholas Tyacke, "Puritanism, Arminianism and Counter-Revolution," in Conrad Russell, ed.,*The Origins of the English Civil War* (London, 1973), 119–43.

12. That one should speak of "English Protestantism" rather than of "Puritanism" and "Anglicanism" is the contention of Charles H. George and Katherine George, *The Protestant Mind of the English Reformation, 1570-1640* (Princeton, 1961); see also Charles H. George, "Puritanism as History and Historiography," and Timothy Hall Breen, "The Non-Existent Controversy: Puritan and Anglican Attitudes on Work and Wealth, 1600–1640," *Church History*, 35 (1966), 273–87. Major rebuttals include John F. H. New, *Puritan and Anglican: The Basis of Their Opposition* (Stanford, 1964); John Coolidge, *The Pauline Renaissance: Puritanism and the Bible* (Oxford, 1970); and J. Sears McGee, *The Godly Man in Stuart England* (New Haven, 1976). By the 1620s, at least, real differences regarding conversion did divide the English church, J. Sears McGee, "Conversion and the Imitation of Christ in Anglican and Puritan Writing," *Journal of British Studies*, 15 (1976), 21–39.

13. Davies, *Worship and Theology*, I, 204–7; Patrick McGrath, *Papists and Puritans Under Elizabeth I* (London, 1967), 39, 44–45, 150–53; Ralph Houlbrooke,"The Protestant Episcopate 1547–1603: The Pastoral Contribution," in Felicity Heal and Rosemary O'Day, eds., *Church and Society in England: Henry VIII to James I* (Hamden, Conn., 1977), 81, 84–85, 91, 98; Philip Edgcumbe Hughes, "Preaching, Homilies, and Prophesyings in Sixteenth Century England," *The Churchman*, 89 (1975), 7–32.

preachers, by inhibiting the proclamation of the Word, cheats people of salvation's most essential means. The failure to properly convey the Gospel, thus forestalling conversion, outraged men animated by the biblical urgency to turn sinners to God, so they addressed their knowledge and enthusiasm to the task to evangelizing England. Finding their colleagues insufficiently zealous and the magistracy indifferent, they recruited themselves out of the mass of the clergy and formed a "Spiritual Brotherhood" to advance the cause of grace.[14]

The genius of the Brotherhood manifested itself in their pastoral concern. Adept at enlisting dogmatics in the service of the Gospel, they gained reputations as "practical and affectionate" men who carefully superintended the spiritual development of their flocks. They excelled at dissecting the psychology of religious experience, an expertise compelled by their commitment to sponsoring conversion and by the particular variant of Reformed soteriology they espoused. Reformed theologians prided themselves on the doctrine of perseverance, for it allowed them to comfort Protestants gripped by a most Christian anxiety, "How do I know I am saved?" Pastoral responses drew upon the certainty that Saints cannot backslide because election to eternal life rests in God's unswerving determination to carry out His Decree. Since the Elect never leave the state of grace, those who judge they are chosen can gain an unshakable assurance that they are saved. In predestination lies freedom from qualms that faith will dissolve and damnation ensue. How the unsure attain assurance, however, arrayed one divine against another. For Calvin, assurance is identical to faith, the firm conviction that Christ died for oneself. Faith is knowledge, the apprehension of Christ's redeeming sacrifice thrust on the mind by the Spirit, and to it attaches a confidence in one's salvation rooted in appreciation of the Saviour's universal atonement. Although Christ intercedes only for the Elect—the reprobate reap no benefit from the Passion because they do not believe—he gave himself up for all. Anyone who takes Christ enjoys justifying faith, and since his sacrifice expiates the sins of every person, anyone who apprehends him must perforce be Elect. One need go no further for assurance than to contemplate the Redeemer, for to believe in Christ is to know that one is saved. In directing the faithful to look to Christ for assurance, Calvin leads them away from self-contemplation, counsel that mitigates against his construing the conversion experience psychologically.[15]

14. Irvonwy Morgan, *The Godly Preachers of the Elizabethan Church* (London, 1965), esp. 1–32; William Haller, *The Rise of Puritanism* (New York, 1957), 1–82.

15. R. T. Kendall, *Calvin and English Calvinism to 1649* (Oxford, 1979), 13–28; Gordon J. Keddie, "'Unfallible Certenty of the Pardon of Sinne and Life Everlasting': The Doctrine of Assurance in the Theology of William Perkins (1558–1602)," *Evangelical Quarterly*, 48 (1976), 231–34. Kendall's stand that Calvin taught a doctrine of universal atonement runs against the more usual assertion that he limited the atonement to the Elect, and the matter is very

Assurance is not a sensational perception, so absorption in what one feels and does is irrelevant, even inimical, to establishing it: Christ matters, not the fleeting proprioceptions of self. Reprobates too may enjoy certain feelings or do good works, but these constitute false grounds for hope. Calvin's depiction of the faithful as robust believers little troubled by uncertainty likewise diminishes his curiosity about conversion's inward dynamic. Insensitive to the plight of weak believers, he manifests little interest in telling how one may descry embers of grace when doubt smothers them; allowing that the damned may possess temporary faith, he neglects to explain what signs connote true belief. Puritans learned much from Calvin, but their taste for introspection derived from other sources.

Theodore Beza assumed Calvin's office but not his doctrine, severing assurance from faith and opening up the possibility for a more extensive analysis of religious experience than Calvin thought either necessary or desirable. While concurring with his predecessor that Christ saves only the Elect, who persevere in grace, Beza denied that the Saviour's sacrifice extends to humankind indiscriminately, restricting it to the Elect. As a result, the atonement no longer grounds assurance; a person who trusts that Christ died for oneself cannot secure this belief in a universal redemptive promise. Since Christ's death belongs only to some, hope in the personal efficacy of his sacrifice may in reality be merely a presumptuous wish. Faith is not revealed in the act of taking Christ, for the decree's dark curtain mantles his response; a person on the mortal side of the veil cannot deduce from Christ's death to whom it applies. Having jammed one door to assurance, however, Beza unlatches another. Although faith cannot know itself directly, conscience can detect its presence. By examining one's actions and determining that they proceed from grace, an individual can apperceive saving faith at work and through this realization come to assurance. Good deeds do not earn salva-tion, but they mark its certainty. The promise belongs to men and women who manifest the effects of regeneration in their carriage, and if conscience can certify the signs of grace in deeds, then it may conclude that faith is

---

controversial. The debate and its recent literature may be followed in Mark R. Shaw, "Drama in the Meeting House: The Concept of Conversion in the Theology of William Perkins," *Westminster Theological Journal*, 45 (1983), 45–57, who contradicts Kendall; James B. Tor-rance, "The Incarnation and 'Limited Atonement'," *Evangelical Quarterly*, 55 (1983), 83–94, who supports him; and M. Charles Bell, "Calvin and the Extent of the Atonement," *ibid.*, 115–23, who allows that Calvin can be read to uphold both limited and unlimited atonement, though Bell ultimately sides with Kendall. Bell also asserts that the relation between the atonement and assurance in Calvin's thought is more problematical than Kendall allows, and maintains that it "was not the issue for Calvin that it became for later Calvinism" (121). This last point is most germane. Even if Calvin did subscribe to limited atonement, he did not, as the Puritans did, deduce from it the necessity to anchor assurance in self-examination.

present, oneself elect, and eternal life confirmed. Assurance adheres not to belief, but a syllogism.[16]

The path of assurance, which for Calvin ascends from the believer to the Redeemer at God's right hand, for Beza descends back into the self, a change of direction fraught with implications for thinking about conversion. The emphatic link between grace and works, identifying the performance of holy duties as a pre-eminent sign of election, transforms assurance from a concomitant of faith into an act of perception, and in so doing generates an increased concern with states of mind as indicators of conversion's progress. How does one know one performs for God, that pious acts are in fact executed for His benefit, except by self-scrutiny? Election is revealed not in Christ but in thoughts and affections, the moods and motives that plot the Spirit's passage—in which case it behooves the evangelist intent on breeding Saints to study these internal phenomena and exhibit them for the edification of regenerates who crave assurance and, by extension, of people not yet regenerate who wish to understand how grace proceeds. If such a perspective deflects attention from Christ crucified to the self anatomized, it does have the virtue of elaborating a model that differentiates justifying from temporary faith on experiential grounds. Grace's presence—or absence—can be read in sighs and smiles. Beza's perspective, then, is more conducive than Calvin's to casting conversion in psychological terms, and it was Beza's system, glossed by the theological faculty at Heidelberg, that Puritans appropriated.[17] By the 1580s, preachers like Richard Greenham were expounding conversion as a progression of inner states, and in the 1590s, William Perkins organized these insights systematically.[18] Later Puritans refined the paradigm and explored its nuances more deeply, but by the end of the sixteenth century the Spiritual Brotherhood had clothed Reformed soteriology in a distinctive experiential dress.

The paradigm that Puritans fashioned can be illustrated from the writings of one of the late sixteenth century's most dedicated pastors. Having preached the Word in Wethersfield, Essex, for forty years, Richard Rogers packed a series of sermons on the new birth into a small book because "all that the people know and practise without conversion is nothing." Rogers

16. Kendall, *Calvin and English Calvinism*, 29–38.

17. *Ibid.*, 38–41; Keddie, "'Unfallible Certenty'," 235–36. A few earlier English theologians, like John Bradford, anticipated some of Beza's concerns. The Puritans' debts to and differences with Calvin are assessed in R. T. Kendall, "The Puritan Modification of Calvin's Theology," in W. Stanford Reid, ed., *John Calvin: His Influence in the Western World* (Grand Rapids, 1982), 199–214; Basil Hall, "Calvin Against the Calvinists," in G. E. Duffield, ed., *John Calvin* (Grand Rapids, 1966), 19–37; and Hall, "Understanding the Puritans," *passim*.

18. Ian Breward, "The Significance of William Perkins," *Journal of Religious History*, 4 (1966–67), 113–28; *idem*, "William Perkins and the Origins of Reformed Casuistry," *Evangelical Quarterly*, 40 (1968), 3–20.

wanted his readers to "cleerely see how to trace the way," and, like many of his fellows in the pulpit, he found the way traced perfectly in the experience of the Philippian jailor (Acts 16.19–34). At the time he incarcerated Paul and Silas, the jailor was a pagan, lacking any "sparke of shame or sorrow" for his unredeemed condition. Cruel, capricious, and "drunken" with love of the world, he lived oblivious to his danger until God's earthquake rocked the cell and shook his complacency with terrors that his prisoners had escaped. Ready to kill himself (for malfeasance of duty), the jailor was stayed by Paul, but his "iollity was abated" and "his pride allayed."[19] The frights occasioned by divine wrath initiate conversion, Rogers explained; by "bridling" the rage of the wicked and "breaking" their hearts through affliction, God begins to steer them towards repentance. Fear shocks unregenerates out of their habitual lethargy, facilitating their spiritual growth; just as a log impacted in a "deepe mire" can be easily removed once turning it breaks the mud's grip, so people immersed in the "dregges" of sin can be "loosened from them by some terrour and heart-smart." Whom God would save He must first afflict with sorrow and fear, rendering them broken-hearted and humble. No longer complacent, anxious about the eternal doom they recognize engulfing them, sinners demand, with the jailor, what they must do to be saved. This, said Rogers, comes "neerer the matter" than "all that went before".[20]

In fact, however, the disconsolate can do nothing. Though the jailor was told to "believe and be saved," he had no power to do so, "faith being the free gift of God." One cannot will one's own redemption, nor can any deeds prior to faith merit salvation—"popish doctrine" to that effect is "false and diuellish." Fears do not in themselves guarantee salvation, for "many that God humbleth with his terrors, become not humble indeed," but at the same time "meeken(ing)" is absolutely prerequisite for becoming a fit "vessell" for grace. People brought to such a pass can receive counsel and comfort from godly souls, and while they hover "betwixt hope and fear," faith enters the heart. Rogers identified no explicit sensation with faith's appearance, and in the believer's life the specific instant of translation from doom to grace passes unremarked amidst the wishes and despair of the salvific quest. But over time, the change manifests itself in a characteristic emotional pattern, which Rogers explicated at various points in his tract. A person saved from eternal death for no reason except God's mercy apprehends "the loue of God" bringing "free remission of sin." The Lord saves because He loves the Elect, and the realization of this transcedent favor triggers reciprocating feelings in the Saints.[21] Cognizant of their gift, they love God more than family, friends,

19 Richard Rogers, *Certaine Sermons Preached and Penned by Richard Rogers* (London, 1612), A5[ro], A4[vo], 12, 16, 17–18.

20. *Ibid.*, 18, 19, 24.

21. *Ibid.*, 26, 33, 32, 31, 70.

"or any thing else of the greatest account and reckoning." *Agape* constrains regenerates to labor in God's name, for whereas the fear of God that even reprobates may display stirs up merely a "frothie and rash" desire to obey His commands, the love of God proceeding through faith coupled with assurance of God's favor inspires the purpose "to walke before him in vprightnes and innocencie for euer after." Love to God parallels love to the Saints, which also solicits good works; the Elect minister "mutually" to each other, and, in the process, enjoy "outward and inward peace." Peace mixed with joy "that al sinne is put away" displaces the "feare of hell" that formerly disquieted the heart. Faith brings forth undeceived happiness of being accounted righteous in Christ. Begun in fear and trembling, conversion opens into love and joy.[22]

The elation of entering into grace cannot sustain itself forever. Although conversion regenerates the soul, Saints remain an admixture of godly capabilities mingled with inherent weaknesses, and inevitably the remnants of corruption assert themselves. Joy disappears, "drowned with deepe sorrowes, caused by sinne and afflictions," while the love of Christ, formerly so great, becomes "slaked." Old fervor decays as transgression and hardship take their toll, and the motive to perform God's duties declines. But holy emotions and the works they inspire can be rekindled by "a certaine violence" against oneself and "a wary walking afterward" to prevent recurrences of sloth. Saints dead in the water can reactivate themselves "by more th[a]n an ordinary turning to God againe." Engaged in a vigorous regimen of "watching, praying, hearing, and such other good meanes," regenerates can recover one's wonted joy and restore the love that complies with God's will.[23] In time, as they steadfastly proceed in these graceful exercises, faith grows and fortifies them against relapse. The "first beginning" of grace is only the initial instance of a lifelong routine in which the believer seeks to sustain love, joy, and labor.

Behind Rogers's scheme lies the Reformed theology of grace, rarely breaking the surface of his plain talk. Elsewhere however, it intruded more frequently; a preacher like Thomas Hooker could pass swiftly from gut-wrenching exhortation to learned discourse. Conversion thus obtained two treatments in Puritan pulpits, one intellectual, the other experiential. The first referred to the Spirit's motions as a formula, the second as the fears and exaltations that conduce to holy obedience. Considered in the abstract conversion could be charted precisely, its steps checked off in logical order, but shifting perspective to the flesh made an exact reckoning impossible. The Spirit moves human beings by fits and starts, and God "doth not alwaies keepe one and the same time" in administering grace.[24] The specificity with

22. *Ibid.*, 52, 70, 40, 36.
23. *Ibid.*, 37, 53, 56, 62.
24. *Ibid.*, 29.

which ministers set down the abstract design blurred when they spoke about how people convert. Nevertheless, Puritans did believe that the new birth proceeds more or less predictably, and the patterns Rogers discerned were noticed by his successors on both sides of the Atlantic far into the seventeenth century. This fact demands some attention. Why Puritan ministers stressed the importance of conversion is no mystery—it and it alone affords eternal life—but why they asserted that it was manifested as a special experiential configuration is not so immediately apparent. Reformed soteriology did not in itself demand particular emotional modalities yet, unlike John Calvin, the Spiritual Brotherhood spent more time dissecting the marrow of individual piety than in celebrating the Redeemer's sacrifice. The psychology of Puritan conversion invites a closer look.

II

A society as ruthlessly introspective in the service of self-autonomy as the Puritans were in the service of God has taken some interest in the Saints' spiritual psychology, with results both provocative and problematic. Researching manifestations of a past mentality is tricky business, especially since they are not easily quarried out of the sources, and their ambiguities pose difficult interpretive problems. All historical inquiries proceed at the mercy of their methods, and psychological studies of vanished minds place a premium on methodological precision. Previous investigations of conversion have displayed the strengths and weaknesses of their approaches. Anticipating that knowledge of who converted will illuminate why they did, Philip Greven and Gerald Moran have compiled demographic profiles of men and women accepted into New England churches for which conversion was a prerequisite to admission. Their studies reveal that new members tended to be married people in their twenties and thirties, prompting the conclusion that the new birth signaled one's status as an adult. With matrimony and parenthood, it affirmed a person's maturity.[25] This assertion is debatable, for although converts did pass from one status—"unregeneracy"—to another— "grace"—these categories were not necessarily congruent with "childhood" (or "youth") and "adulthood." No evidence demonstrates that the Saints themselves so equated them. Furthermore, linking conversion so closely to church membership compresses the experience, which cannot be readily

25. Gerald F. Moran, "Religious Renewal, Puritan Tribalism, and the Family in Seventeenth-Century Milford, Connecticut," *William and Mary Quarterly*, 3d ser., 36 (1979), 246–50; Philip J. Greven, Jr., "Youth, Maturity, and Religious Conversion: A Note on the Ages of Converts in Andover, Massachusetts, 1711–1749," *Essex Institute Historical Collections*, 108 (1972), 119–34, esp. 130. Moran (254) notes the need to examine sources of ideas too.

associated with a single discrete occurrence. The new birth was a prolonged process that began years before one joined a congregation and whose impact resonated throughout a believer's life.

Greven and Moran do point up the value of treating conversion as an event that gains significance from its relationship to other occurrences in a person's life course. As much a developmental as an intrapsychic phenomenon, conversion grows out of and functions in response to an individual's history. Recognizing this, George Selement has brought a theory of life stages to bear on Puritan testimonies of religious experience, taking their questing tone as evidence that conversion resolved adolescent identity crises. Selement is right to declare that conversion precipitated a crisis of identity, for salvation demanded renouncing the old self and reconstructing a new one under the Spirit, but he misconstrues his subject.[26] Although in some ways reminiscent of twentieth-century adolescent turmoils, conversion was not exclusively nor even primarily an adolescent phenomenon, as the demographers have shown, and diagnosing Puritans as victims of identity confusion puts them in the wrong ward.[27] If anything, they were plagued by identity certainty— knowledge that they were corrupted sinners worthy of eternal punishment. The central question they posed was not "Who am I?" but "What must I do to be saved?"

Whatever its developmental parameters, conversion did generate power-

26. George Selement, "The Means to Grace: A Study of Conversion in Early New England" (Ph.D. dissertation, University of New Hampshire, 1974), 83–104. Few people know the documents of Puritan religious experience as well as Selement, who (among others) has capably transcribed the notebook in which Thomas Shepard recorded the spiritual narratives of his flock, the single most important source on the subject, but his formulation is not well conceived. Agreeing with psychologist Edwin Starbuck that conversion is essentially a phenomenon of the years between ten and twenty-five, Selement contends that most of Shepard's Saints whose ages during conversion are in any way retrievable experienced a "religious awakening, the first stirrings of introspection . . . before the age of thirty" (89). The span 10–25 is a generous definition of "adolescence," wider than most psychologists today would extend the term; joining pre-pubescents with the biologically mature, children still developing intellectual capacities with fully developed adults, the concept becomes imprecise, and is made even more so by its subsequent extension to the age of thirty. Quite obviously, people who begin to have religious crises at ten are quite different individuals from those who begin at age thirty. In addition, linking conversion to a specific instant—in this case the dawning awareness of unregeneracy—telescopes an extended occurrence. The time between "first stirrings" and the climactic events of calling could be many years; in John Winthrop's case, the initial intimations of God's work took some twenty years to flower (see *infra*, chap. 8). A phenomenon so protracted and complex cannot be easily analyzed as the product of one delimited stage in a person's life cycle. Conversion was an "adolescent" phenomenon only if one defines that term very broadly, and, in any case, its ramifications extended throughout adulthood.

27. Gerald Moran, "The Puritan Saint: Religious Experience, Church Membership and Piety in Connecticut, 1636–1776" (Ph.D. dissertation, Rutgers University, 1974), 154; John Owen King, III, *The Iron of Melancholy: Structures of Spiritual Conversion in America from the Puritan Conscience to Victorian Neurosis* (Middletown, Conn., 1983), 59, 354, n. 116.

ful mental events that beg description, and historians have not had to look far for an appropiate means to study them. Given the similar—though not identical—agenda of Puritanism and psychoanalysis to redirect the lusts and wishes of the unreconstructed self,[28] given too the claims of psychoanalysis to being both a comprehensive theory of human nature that is universally valid and a scientific methodology uniquely capable of probing the innermost wellsprings of human endeavor, engaging depth psychology to interpret Puritan religious experience has made sense to a number of scholars. Their enterprise has achieved mixed results. The most sensitive—and sensible—such treatment, that of Thomas Leverenz, accounts for the peculiar mélange of psychological themes in Puritan discourse by unraveling its emotional knots and setting them against a background of social dislocation. Cadences that summoned people to exercise rigid self-control over their every action but allowed them to enjoy childlike dependence on God's nourishing grace appealed to the "middling sort" whose traditional patterns of life and livelihood were undergoing strain. Listening to preachers expound the work of regeneration, pious audiences coped with the anxieties of change by sharing a common fantasy of being reborn to a "higher" parent infinitely stronger and tenderer than their natural ones.[29] While not convincing in every detail, this argument rightly shows the power of sermons to structure religious feeling, and it reveals Puritan rhetoric as a congeries of opposites whose forcefulness derived from the doubleness of its calls: to self-hatred and self-regeneration, respect for earthly authority and distrust of its prerogatives, initiative before man and submission before God. The religion of the Saints fostered radical voluntarism in the pursuit of mundane objectives as well as absolute obedience to the great Lord who enjoined them. Less certain, however, is conversion's role, presupposed but never clarified. The readiness of people to accept ministerial fantasies of rebirth must have had something to do with the protracted experience of awe and love that signified adoption into His family.

Historians have not always employed psychoanalysis so carefully. Murray Murphey views conversion as a personal transformation, analogous to the resolution of the Oedipus complex, that created a modal Puritan character. By identifying with a threatening authority figure (in this case God) and introjecting His standards, sinners resolved conflicted feelings towards their maker and themselves; love to Christ and the Elect replaced self-love, guilt, fear of the Lord, hatred of Him, and desperation over one's regenerate status. Finely attuned to conversion's emotional complexities, Murphey's explanation is nevertheless susceptible to criticism. It overlooks a critical affection,

---

28. Howard M. Feinstein, "The Prepared Heart: A Comparative Study of Puritan Theology and Psychoanalysis," *American Quarterly*, 22 (1970), 166–76.

29. Leverenz, *Language of Puritan Feeling*, passim.

for in drawing a parallel between the (male) child's fear of castration by his father and the Puritans' fear of God's wrath for sin, it totally misses the importance of God's love in prompting sinners to give up carnal self-esteem. The Saints' conscious longing for *agape* was as much a stimulus to turn as fear was. It recognizes but does not successfully confront the gender-specific implications of an oedipal analysis, which postulates the psychodynamics of superego formation in boys but not in girls. It establishes no connections between the personality that allegedly emerged from conversion and the underlying psychological mechanisms. Since oedipal theory explains only how the superego develops, not how differences in strength arise among individuals, one needs to explain why conversion necessarily produced such highly moralistic people. Finally, it passes over the fact that the Saints' "strong superegos" often antedated conversion. Puritans habitually described themselves as having acted virtuously before grace, even though at the time they imagined their deeds "dead." Faith changed how they regarded their behavior rather than the behavior itself. In this case, psychoanalytic theory muddles an often insightful rendition of the ministerial sources.[30]

Other applications of it have achieved no more success. Michael Reed's, depicting conversion as an oedipal fantasy that energized the personality and simultaneously defended the ego against the forbidden wishes this activation inspired, combines insufficient evidence with reckless speculation that subordinates fact to fancy.[31] Philip Greven's, by far the most ambitious review of colonial religious experience, takes over psychoanalytic theories of personality formation to locate the determinants of adult piety in three modes of raising children. Out of the repressive practices of evangelicals, the more restrained, ego-strengthening ones of moderates, and the relaxed, indulgent

30. Murray G. Murphey, "The Psychodynamics of Puritan Conversion," *American Quarterly*, 31 (1979), 135–47. Murphey's acute description of conversion anticipates several themes taken up here; the problem lies in his theoretical formulation. For instance, he says that "In the conversion experience, the sex of the sinner is irrelevant; hence the same process operates for males and females" (141). I agree; but if this was so, then conversion is really unlike the resolution of the Oedipus complex, and the thesis becomes trivial.

31. Michael D. Reed, "Early American Puritanism: The Language of Its Religion," *American Imago*, 37 (1980), 278–333. Reed's argument is replete with factual inaccuracies (Puritans were hardly "uncomfortable" with the doctrine of predestination, 286), inadequte research (he relies heavily on Perry Miller's exposition of the Covenant, refuted by many scholars, 282–88), and unsupported assertions (there is no rationale for equating the child's love for his mother with the Saint's desire to possess heaven as elements of an oedipal fantasy, 293–94, 303, 333). His enthusiasm for interpreting conversion as an oedipal fantasy runs roughshod over Puritan theology, for he postulates—against all the sources—that Puritans, in desiring to displace the heavenly Father, believed that they could become divine (291, 293, 299–301). On the contrary, they always maintained a radical separation between the Godhead and (even regenerated) flesh. Unlike Murphey, Reed does not raise the issue of the Oedipus complex's gender-specificity, and his casting of conversion in static rather than dynamic terms further obviates the essay's usefulness.

modes of genteel parents developed three corresponding mentalities.[32] Puritans crop up in the first two categories: Thomas Shepard is a self-effacing evangelical, John Winthrop a more autonomous moderate. At times these taxonomies seem arbitrary, for if Shepard's desire to be "melted" into Christ evinces an evangelical temperament, so should Winthrop's identical sentiment.[33] The portrait of the evangelical style, wonderfully evocative of personalities writhing in the throes of constricted self-abnegation, omits the joy that sometimes broke through their ordeal and misses the sense of power that humiliation brought. Part of the study's promise rests on its intention to establish the connections between the way in which parents raised their young and the devotional stances their children adopted, but a flawed research design dooms the attempt. The sources of individual experience are also those that provide information about child-rearing; the people who enunciate their religiosity are the same ones who tell how they raised their own brood.[34] The implied generational relationship between parental guidance and filial behavior breaks down; what correlates are an individual's attitudes towards child-rearing and those towards God. In the end, questions remain. The psychogenesis of emotion is exceedingly difficult to ascertain in historical actors, but even if it could be reached, one would still have to account for other influences. People apprehend what they feel through filters of thought, and if the trials and triumphs of early childhood crucially influence an individual's emotional makeup, they do not by themselves predispose one to connect affections to any specific way of acting. That occurs only when the person learns to connect modes of feeling with certain ideas.[35] A soul raised "evangelically" with no religious training might experience cycles of despair and joy, but they would not be conversions. One cannot turn to God if one knows not a god to turn to.

The psychoanalysis of Puritan religious experience has not achieved all that might have been hoped, in part because it has taxed the theory's powers beyond credibility. Necessarily indirect and unprovable by empirical means alone, psychohistorical propositions are most believable when they show that traditional methods of explication cannot account for some observation, and

32. Philip Greven, *The Protestant Temperament: Patterns of Child-Rearing, Religious Experience, and the Self in Early America* (New York, 1977).

33. *Ibid.*, 85; Robert C. Winthrop, *Life and Letters of John Winthrop, Governor of the Massachusetts-Bay Colony at their Emigration to New England, 1630*, 2d ed., 2 vols. (Boston, 1869), II, 161.

34. Compare, for instance, the treatment of Cotton Mather's parenting (Greven, *Protestant Temperament*, 30-31, 52, 53) and his own experiences (66-67, 76-77, 79, 83-84, 85-86).

35. Suggestive on this point is Sheldon Shapiro, "Quelques réflexions sur la signification psychologique de la prédestination dans la Réforme," *Reveu d'histoire ecclésiastique*, 68 (1973), 823-32; Wallace, *Puritans and Predestination*, ix, xi.

can advance a limited explanation consistent with both the data and with theory.[36] Yet part of the difficulty emerges, paradoxically, from the theory's alluring ability to penetrate beneath the surfaces of self-awareness. Charged to uncover the hidden nature of things, psychoanalysis proposes that subliminal processes determine behavior, that a configuration of unconscious drives established early in life—how early is disputed—molds one's personality, and that symbolic forms encode meanings which people do not consciously grasp. The force of this outlook is, inevitably, to esteem the latent content of human productions over the manifest and to slight the reasons people advance for their behavior.[37] Appropriate, indeed essential, in clinical situations, this attitude may tempt the historian to disregard what people say about them-

---

36. See Saul Friedländer, *History and Psychoanalysis: An Inquiry into the Possibilities and Limits of Psychohistory*, trans. Susan Suleiman (New York, 1978), 26, 121, 122–23; Friedländer thinks of psychohistory essentially as psychoanalytic history. By "limited," I mean an explanation that can be shown to exclude competing psychoanalytic ones; Friedländer (14–16) argues that this is possible, and he proposes four criteria to increase the explanatory plausibility of psychohistorical hypotheses (22–25). This contention assumes, of course, that one accepts the validity of the entire psychohistorical enterprise; David Stannard, *Shrinking History: On Freud and the Failure of Psychohistory* (New York, 1980), does not.

37. King, *Iron of Melancholy*, esp. 1–82, shares this concern. He does not think it helpful to scour Puritan spiritual autobiography for symptoms, and he has some critical things to say about historians who offer reasons—social, cultural, or economic—to explain (or explain away) the diction of Puritan religious experience. The truth of the matter lies open on the printed page, he avers; the text's the thing wherein King would catch the conscience of the Saints. The vocabulary of conversion sprang from a tradition of psychological writing, the Renaissance anatomies of melancholy. Puritan intellectuals appropriated the agonies this literature rehearses into their descriptions of conversion; consequently, the imagery of melancholia structured how individuals articulated their religious trials. King wisely declines to regard the obsessional intonation of conversion accounts as pathological; more troublesome is his analysis of them as purely literary fabrications, thereby clouding both their creation and their significance. He constantly refers to conversion relations as written productions, but they are better understood as documents beginning in speech; their final, written form should not disguise their complex evolution. With this in mind, one can counter King's explanation for how the paradigm of conversion voiced in the earliest narratives shaped subsequent utterances. King reifies the process of transmission, suggesting that the model of experience was passed down by the texts (which were actually squirreled away in private diaries and journals) rather than by the hearts, tongues, ears, and minds of a living community. Finally, he approvingly cites Mikhail Bakhtin's dictum that "*expression organizes experience*," asserting that a textual expression is "capable of creating a person's character" (7). Expression does shape experience, but King's position implies that nothing exists outside of the text. His criticism of those who seek the origins of religious sensibility in social or economic circumstances suggests that one cannot find anything beyond what a text signifies; Puritans may have been melancholic, but this supposition is unimportant compared with the fact that they discoursed melancholically. Such a position seems unduly pessimistic. The documents recording Puritan religious experience were conventionally shaped, but they were not simply conventional. The rhetoric of melancholy is one way of speaking about experience, but it was not the only one available to Puritans, and they accepted it because its syntax best articulated the sensations they felt and wanted to exclaim. Their language reveals real personal experience, not merely a tradition of speech.

selves in order to divine the "real," underlying reasons for their activity. Such procedure is presumptuous, because historical actors knew more about themselves than we ever will, and misleading, because by invoking the superiority of an imposed perceptual system it understates the importance of finding out the "webs of significance" that subjects of historical inquiry spun out. This study proceeds under the suppositions that people live in worlds bounded by the meanings they attach to phenomena, that these meanings are discoverable by learning what people have to say about them, that the discourse between subjects and investigator renders their point of view most intelligibly when conducted in their own tongue, and that apprehending the Puritans' point of view provides the greatest opportunity for understanding the psychology of conversion. "Letting the natives speak," the fundamental postulate of most ethnography, also furnishes a good strategy for meeting with the past. The original experts on Puritan experience were Puritans, a statement less tautological than supportive of an analysis which assumes that the psychological determinants of conversion were not entirely beyond the Saints' ken.[38]

The time has come to put one's method where one's mouth is—or to at least serve up one's guiding principles. The primary task is to make sense of conversion in Puritan terms, a task made easier (though not simple) by the Saints' volubility. Puritans may have thought of themselves as sinkholes of corruption, but sinkholes deserving extended discussion; it is hardly coincidental that a great number of locutions employing "self-" entered into English during the first half of the seventeenth century.[39] Descriptions of religious experience poured forth from pulpit and pew; the tough job lies not in finding them, but in translating them. Translating English texts into English may seem a curious—or spurious—occupation, but any effort to convey the pith of a culture from the "inside out" necessarily involves transferring concepts from the original dialect to the reporter's, a process requiring no less care even though the tongues in question are so similar. Similar, but not identical. The simplicity of Puritan language—the unadorned English of the preachers' plain style mingling with the diction of common speech—disguises its ancient nuances beneath the patina of familiarity. For this reason, I have used word studies and contemporary dictionaries to rub off the accreted meanings of centuries, revealing an utterance's pristine connotation. Much attention has also been paid to the biblical citations that freckle the margins of the ministry's works and punctuate the discourses of laypeople relating their

38. This argument owes much to Clifford Geertz, *The Interpretation of Cultures* (New York, 1973), esp. 1–30, and "On the Nature of Anthropological Understanding," *American Scientist*, 63 (1975), 47–53

39. Marinus van Beek, *An Enquiry into Puritan Vocabulary* (Groningen, 1969), 7–8, 68–70, 117–20; Geoffrey F. Nuttall, *The Holy Spirit in Puritan Faith and Experience* (Oxford, 1946), 7–8.

conversions. Puritans molded their lives to the Good Book's authority, and they were steeped enough in its contents to communicate through casual quotations of chapter and verse. Their scriptural references are compact commentaries that, when expanded, amplify a statement's intension.

How conversion took shape in the lives of the faithful comprises another area of concern. Cultural systems teach people how to perceive, and theology among Puritans had a major impact in shaping experience. Ministers like Richard Rogers articulated models of the new birth, forecasting believers' thoughts and directing them what to feel. Clergy formulated the essential categories of piety, but conversion did not reduce to their definitions alone; ministers had the first word, but not the last. Preacher and parishioner entered into a dialogue about faith, and we better comprehend what conversion entailed by eavesdropping on their conversation. This book's duadic structure—Part I covers the ministry's teaching, Part II the laity's response—emphasizes their mutual importance.[40] Sermons and doctrinal handbooks contain the preachers' position, while the Saints' comments are preserved in some eighty conversion relations, spiritual autobiographies that the early New England churches demanded of prospective members. Unvarnished accounts of personal experience professed before the entire congregation, these narratives open up the lives of common men and women, laying bare the development of grace in ordinary folk. The relations show multiple forces sculpting the experience of regeneration. The ministry's input shows through in the general organization of the chronicles, their content, the numerous allusions to sermon texts, and even in a few snatches of remembered preachments that also manifest how memory amd imagination refashioned the words heard in worship. Family, friends, and strangers touched Saints at times, as did, of course, the persons of the Trinity. The new birth "took place" within individuals, but conversion was nonetheless a communal process, stimulated, nurtured, and directed by the extended network of Puritan society stretching from the regenerated individual to the wider public and ultimately to heaven.

A carefully delineated event (or series of events) so assiduously cultivated by a particular group of people ought to have had more than a random impact on their lives, and conversion did indeed serve a regularized function, as efforts to establish it as a phase of adolescence or a marker of adulthood have implied. The differing norms, values, practices, and institutional forms into which cultures arrange themselves encourage disparate emotional styles, each system eliciting a few characteristic patterns from among the wide range

---

40. This method is partially prefigured in Baird Tipson, "How Can the Religious Experience of the Past Be Recovered? The Examples of Puritanism and Pietism," *Journal of the American Academy of Religion*, 43 (1975), 695–707.

of combinations and intensities that human nature makes possible. At the same time, cultures provide (unless severely stressed) appropriate channels through which these emotive patterns express themselves and influence the social order. Conversion promoted a distinctive pattern of emotionality for a particular end, and, since the Brotherhood frequently reflected on the subject, conversion's function, like its dynamics, can also be analyzed from the "inside out." According to the ministry, there was nothing superfluous about the affections that regeneration churned up; the most desirable set of passions a person could feel, they constituted a new motivational design intended to expedite God's bidding. This new order of affections, coupled with the regenerated mind and will, activated the Saints, preachers said, who diligently worked in their callings. There was nothing quietistic about the new birth, although Puritan devotion had its meditative side;[41] the Elect lined up to labor for the Lord. By its very nature, conversion impelled them to toil and trouble in the world. And it kept them at it. Saints could, and did, re-experience rebirth, which revitalized them for further efforts.

This book, then, is an essay in psychological history, an inquiry into the mental lives of past people that examines their modes of action and the meanings they attached to their behavior. It might also be called an emotional ethnography describing both a configuration of thoughts and affections, and their impact within a particular culture. Drawing on theology and personal testimony, it traces the doctrine of conversion as it evolved in England and America to the middle of the seventeenth century, and reconstructs the religious experience of the New England Saints at the height of Puritanism's influence in America.[42] That experience involved the Elect in a quest for power marked by a progression of doubts and exaltations, a campaign to tap God's potency that eventuated in a mentality of communitarian activism mobilized by complex psychodynamics. Most commentators have assumed that divine wrath impelled Puritan piety, but the Saints knew that God leavened His anger towards them with *agape*. He empowered the Elect because His affection for them overcame His distaste for their sins. Thus, an analysis of conversion must also be a tractate on love.

41. Charles E. Hambrick-Stowe, *The Practice of Piety: Puritan Devotional Disciplines in Seventeenth-Century New England* (Chapel Hill, 1982).

42. I am discussing the mainstream Anglo-American tradition of the Reformed theology of grace as it was explicated by English writers to c. 1640 and by the first generation of American divines; I do not treat developments among English sectarians during the 1640s and 1650s. Focusing on the experiences of first-generation New England was dictated by a combination of desire and necessity. I chose to examine New England because I wanted to lay the foundation for future studies of American evangelical psychology, and because the available sources allow for close investigation of how theology and experience interact. The sources do limit one to the first generation, however; significant numbers of conversion relations from the period 1665–1735 either have not survived or else have not yet been found. Thus there is a gap in the record of personal testimonies until the Great Awakening, which deserves separate treatment.

I

THE CALL
OF THE PREACHERS

Few topics exercised Puritan preachers as conversion did. It united them in proclaiming its necessity for salvation and in holding forth its characteristic program of psychological changes. Part I surveys their gospel of conversion, especially the links they forged between the need for regeneration and the individual's utter inability to achieve it without grace, for the psychology of Puritan religious experience was inextricably bound up with humanity's condition of helplessness under sin. The first three chapters set out this concern, threading among the formal headings of theology. The doctrine of man discovered the causes of impotence, the corruption of the faculties occasioned by the Fall. The doctrine of the covenant, explicating God's instrumentality for administering grace, revealed the contrary mind-sets of the unregenerate and the saved; the former presume they can merit salvation, while the latter divest their efforts of all self-esteem, submitting entirely to the Lord's direction. The *ordo salutis*, the disposition of the Spirit's operations, detailed how grace overcomes corruption and outlined the emotional concomitants of faith. Chapter 4 explicates the psychodynamics and effects of the new birth, the perfervid activism inspired by grace. The ministry's preoccupation with overcoming human weakness governed their paradigm of conversion. The meek may inherit the earth, but the potent will populate heaven.

1

Original Debility

Know thyself. That imperative, inscribed high on the list of Renaissance concerns, animated Puritans as well. It exercised their preachers, who, charged with a desire to induce conversions, extended their study of theology into two broad areas of anthropology.[1] One involved the investigation of how people operate. Puritans organized their understanding around a theory, which might appropriately be called the faculty-humor psychology, that long before the Reformation had become an automatic reflex in the European intellect.[2] The psychology arranged a person's constituent parts into a hierarchical system. A complicated structure of fluids and spirits, dust and eternal stuff, the human being works most efficiently when each part discharges its proper task in obedience to its superior's commands. Puritans borrowed this prevailing wisdom from an assorted array of contemporaries—clergymen, doctors, academics, and courtiers (here denoted collectively as psycholo-

1. By "anthropology," I mean "teaching about the origin, nature, and destiny of man esp[ecially] from the perspective of his relation to God," *Webster's Seventh New Collegiate Dictionary*, s.v. "anthropology."

2. The designation "faculty psychology" is a slight misnomer, since discussions of the humors often accompanied treatment of the soul's faculties. Herschel Baker, *The Dignity of Man* (Cambridge, Mass., 1947), 278, stresses the importance of the humors in Renaissance psychology.

gists)[3]—and they fully absorbed its premises.[4] However, they did not accept it uncritically, for like all knowledge, it had to pass muster with Scripture. Puritans could no more have read the psychology without the Bible than they could have passed an infidel without a shudder, and they tempered science with God's Word, the canon by which all knowledge was ruled. The Good Book offered a competing view. Biblical authors classified the person's parts without ranking them and defined ideal performance as wholehearted engagement in an enterprise. Grafting the two models together yielded a hybrid that combined scriptural concepts with the psychology's categories.

The preachers' analysis of human functioning opened into the second area of interest, the individual's relationship with God and one's capacity to execute properly those activities that retain God's favor. Their conclusions were bleak. With others in the Reformed tradition, Puritans recognized how horribly Original Sin had disfigured humanity and removed all from grace. Since the Fall, error inheres in one's very composition. To William Perkins, one of Puritanism's leading preachers and its first systematizer, "the matter of al heresies, is naturally ingrafted in mans nature," a point "worthy the obseruation of students of diuinitie."[5] It was worthy of the laity's attention too, for constitutional weakness impels sinners to reflect on the extent of their alienation from God and on the likely result of their quest for regeneration. Knelling the death of idle hopes, ministers spotlighted human helplessness and pronounced the awful need to overcome it. From these considerations emerged the fundamental themes that shaped Puritan religious experience.

I

For some two thousand years, Western savants held that the mundane and spiritual spheres intersect at point *homo*, whose activity and well-being depend on the complex interactions of mortal body and immortal soul. Although disputing innumerable details and adopting different nomencla-

3. Paul H. Kocher, *Science and Religion in Elizabethan England* (San Marino, Cal., 1953), 288.

4. Perry Miller, *The New England Mind: The Seventeenth Century* (New York, 1939), 239–79, discusses English and American Puritans, as does Eugene E. White, "Master Holdsworth and 'A Knowledge Very Useful and Necessary,'" *Quarterly Journal of Speech*, 53 (1967), 1–16. J. Rodney Fulcher, "Puritans and the Passions: The Faculty Psychology in American Puritanism," *Journal of the History of the Behavioral Sciences*, 9 (1973), 123–39, and James G. Blight, "Solomon Stoddard's *Safety of Appearing* and the Dissolution of the Puritan Faculty Psychology," *ibid.*, 10 (1974), 238–50, cover American developments.

5. William Perkins, *The Whole Works*, 3 vols. (London, 1626–31), I, 20; Breward, "Significance of William Perkins."

tures, psychologists agreed about the system's basic operations.[6] They began with the body's utilization of the physical world. Four elements—earth, water, air, fire—comprise all matter, in which inhere the four qualities of cold, moisture, heat, and dryness.[7] Composed of these elements and qualities, food is concocted by the liver into four humors: melancholy (black bile), phlegm, blood, and choler (yellow bile); each of them corresponds to one element and its qualities. Humors nourish the body and sustain the heart's natural heat, which communicates the vital power essential for life.[8] Several organs produce spirit, "a most subtle vapour" that the soul uses to carry out its functions in the body. The liver produces natural spirits from blood to effect nutrition and generation, the heart distills them into vital spirits to carry the vital heat, and the brain transforms vital spirits into animal spirits that confer sense and motion through the nerves. The most refined of all, animal spirits facilitate thinking and willing.[9]

By itself the body is an exanimate hulk waiting for the soul to quicken and manipulate it. A "perfect" substance inspirited by God, the soul possesses faculties that direct the body's functions.[10] Like plants, people have a vegetative soul, which imparts the capacities for life, nourishment, and growth; like beasts, they also enjoy a sensitive soul that apprehends objects first through the five external senses—touch, taste, smell, hearing, sight—and then via the interior ones. Enumerated in various ways, the inner wits include common sense, imagination, fantasy, cogitation, and memory. Most faculties have a seat within a particular organ, and the internal senses work within the ventricles of the brain. Alone among corporeal creatures, human beings boast a rational soul with an understanding that can reason and self-reflect.[11] Motive faculties, the appetites, impel individuals to gratify their needs and

6. Fuller treatments include Ruth Leila Anderson, *Elizabethan Psychology and Shakespeare's Plays*, University of Iowa Humanistic Studies, 3 (Iowa City, 1927), the most complete; Lily B. Campbell, *Shakespeare's Tragic Heroes* (London, 1930; repr. New York, 1968), 47–106; E. M. W. Tillyard, *The Elizabethan World Picture* (London, 1958), 60–73; Baker, *Dignity of Man*, 275–92.

7. Sir Thomas Elyot, *The Castell of Helth*, corr. and aug. (London, 1572), folio 2vo; Thomas Walkington, *The Optick Glasse of Hvmors* (London, 1607), 38vo; Levinus Lemnius, *The Touchstone of Complexions*, trans. Thomas Newton (London, 1581), 26ro; Pierre de La Primaudaye, *The Second Part of the French Academy* (London, 1594), 18.

8. [Robert Burton], *The Anatomy of Melancholy*, 6th ed., corr. and aug. (London, 1652; repr. Philadelphia, 1847), Pt. I. Sec. 1. Mem. 2. Subsect. 2; Lemnius, *Touchstone*, 7^{ro-vo}; Timothy Bright, *A Treatise of Melancholie* (London, 1586), 4–5; Philippe de Mornay, *The True Knowledge of a Mans Owne selfe* (London, 1602), 7–10.

9. Burton, *Anatomy*, I.1.2.2. (quotation); Walkington, *Optick Glasse*, 50vo–51vo.

10. Bright, *Treatise of Melancholie*, 40, 42.

11. Burton, *Anatomy*, I.1.2.5, 6, 7, 9–11; La Primaudaye, *Second Part*, 134–35; Andreas Laurentius, *A Discovrse of the Preservation of the Sight*, trans. Richard Surphlet (London, 1599), 73–80; Mornay, *True Knowledge*, 110–17.

preserve their lives. The natural appetite hungers and thirsts for nutriment. The sensitive appetite desires whatever the senses perceive as good and shuns what they conclude is evil.[12] It works by agitating the body, and its movements pass under several names: passions, perturbations, and most commonly affections, "because the soule by them, either affecteth som good, or for the affection of some good, detesteth some ill." When the soul perceives an object it either loves or hates it, and most psychologists derived the other affections from these two primary ones.[13] Will, the rational appetite, also covets good and abhors evil, but unlike the sensitive appetite, it is concerned with universal and immaterial things. How much it must bow to the judgments of the understanding was a much vexed question, but all writers admitted that the will has some freedom of independent choice.[14] The rational faculties are humanity's peculiar glory and its noblest powers; in a well-ordered soul, will commands the inferior appetite, and reason governs the passions.

Spirit knits body and soul together and so makes activity possible. The soul may operate without the body, for it can reason, judge, remember, and discern truth instinctively, but it gains knowledge of the world through its association with the body, and it is this intelligence that prompts the soul to engage the body in some task.[15] At every stage in the complex process of perception, intellection, and actuation, animal spirits carry images (phantasms) from faculty to faculty. Sifting through the material universe, the outer senses in the body's receptors determine the characteristics of tangible objects and convey their findings as images to the common sense, the "judge or moderator" of the inner wits. Common sense composes the jumble of images into meaningful forms and passes them to the imagination (and/or the fantasy), which further examines them and then either stores the phan-

---

12. Th[omas] W[right], *The Passions of the Minde* (London, 1601; facsimile repr., Hildesheim, 1973), 20–22; Anthony Nixon, *The Dignitie of Man* (London, 1612), 46–47.

13. Wright, *Passions*, 14. The primacy of love and hate was held by Bright, *Treatise of Melancholie*, 82–84; Edward Reynolds, *A Treatise of the Passions and Faculties of the Soule of Man* (London, 1640; facsimile repr., Gainesville, Fla., 1971), 39, 74; John Abernethy, *A Christian and Heavenly Treatise: Containing Physicke for the Soule*, 3d ed. (London, 1630), 257. Wright, *Passions*, 2d p. 220, considered love alone the root affection. N[icolas] Coeffeteau, *A Table of Humane Passions*, trans. Edward Grimeston (London, 1621), 32, claimed eleven primary passions. The motions of the will were sometimes called affections or passions: see La Primaudaye, *Second Part*, 202, 238, and Wright, *Passions*, 59. This position is contradicted by Coeffeteau, *Table*, 2–3, and J[ean] F[rançois] Senault, *The Vse of Passions*, trans. Henry, Earl of Monmouth (London, 1671), 17–18.

14. Burton, *Anatomy*, I.1.2.11; Nixon, *Dignitie of Man*, 47–48; Reynolds, *Treatise of the Passions*, 517–19, 537–53; Senault, *Vse of Passions*, 15; Norman Fiering, "Will and Intellect in the New England Mind," *William and Mary Quarterly*, 3d ser., 29 (1972), 515–58.

15. Bright, *Treatise of Melancholie*, 36, 73; Burton, *Anatomy*, I.1.2.2, 10; La Primaudaye, *Second Part*, 237–38.

tasms in memory for future consideration or presents them to the understanding. This faculty discourses "from things knowen to them that are vnknowen," and transforms the cognition of discrete, corporeal entities that it has received from the imagination into awareness of universal and spiritual things. The understanding judges whether the object whose images it has analyzed is good or evil, and then offers its decision to the will. "*Queene*" of the soul's powers, ordaining "what they shall imbrace, & what they shal fly as it pleseth her," will commands the sensitive appetite, stirring the affections that prod the motive power, and the apparatus of "nerves, muscles, cords" lumbers into operation as thought passes into action.[16] Since the body cooperates with the soul in activity, temperament, the disposition of the elemental or humoral qualities, helps determine how an individual reacts. Although it was theoretically possible for a person to enjoy the *temperamentum ad pondus*, the ideal balance of qualities, people in reality are always subject to humoral imbalance and affected by one or more predominant qualities that produce a typical physiognomy and behavioral style.[17] For instance, phlegmatics, whose superfluity of phlegm permeates them with cold and moisture, are normally "sleepye, lazy, slouthfull, drowsie, heauy, lumpish and nothinge quicke at their busynesse."[18] Any act is the product of many inputs.

A number of factors can affect behavior adversely. Burned (adusted) humors raise a "tempest of perturbatiõs" that "destroyeth the braine with all his faculties, and disposition of action"; adusted melancholy instigates causeless terror and fear, unnatural choler mixes madness with rage, and burned blood turns everything into a jest. A too-powerful stimulus can overload the sensory system: in a sudden fear, sometimes "al the blood retiring to the heart choaketh it, and vtterly extingisheth naturall heate and the spirits, so that death must needs ensue thereof."[19] The soul's health consists in "a sweet harmonie betweene all his Faculties, and such an happie subordination of them each to other," but, inevitably, the "sweet harmonie" collapses. Imagination may evoke "chimaeras, antics, golden mountains and castles in the air" with such frenzy that it overturns everything. The passions will do anything to annoy the mind, and may join with the senses, their "ioint-frends" since childhood, to foment outright rebellion against reason's kingdom. Bodily distempers cause similar disruptions. Abundant spirits grown power-

16. The quotations are from Burton, *Anatomy*, I.1.2.7; La Primaudaye, *Second Part*, 162; Coeffeteau, *Table*, "To the Reader," unpaginated; Burton, *Anatomy*, I.1.2.8. See La Primaudaye, *Second Part*, 144–45, 148, 154–62, 174–75, and esp. Coeffeteau, *Table*, "To the Reader."

17. Lemnius, *Touchstone*, 32ro–33ro; Walkington, *Optick Glasse*, 39ro–40ro.

18. Lemnius, *Touchstone*, 111vo.

19. Bright, *Treatise of Melancholie*, 110–11; La Primaudaye, *Second Part*, 261.

ful through overnourishment reject reason, and should a man in such condition chance "to espy any prety wēch or beautifull damsell," the Dutch physician Levinus Lemnius warned, humors and spirits rush to accomplish their tasks, "his priuities undecētly swel, & his mēber of generatiō becōmeth stiffe . . . ." What happens next Lemnius chastely left unstated.[20] Physical malfunctions can be corrected by restoring a more balanced temperament through a regimen of diet, rest, and recreation that properly nourishes the humors and spirits.[21] Curing the soul entails bringing the passions back under reason's sway. With competent direction and self-control, the individual should be able to subdue wayward faculties.[22]

Joining anatomy and physiology with a study of the soul, the faculty-humor psychology drew a comprehensive picture of human behavior. A diagnostic theory, it identified a wide variety of ailments and provided for their relief, yet it often underplayed, if not entirely ignored, the regenerative virtue of grace. In its long history, the psychology had come to be interpreted by both physicians and philosophers, many of whom, particularly the doctors, were engrossed in studying naturalistic phenomena and disregarded their ultimate cause.[23] Psychologists did not forget God, the *primum mobile* who moves the soul,[24] but they did not always advertise the force of His presence. Most discussions intimate that human power emanates from the soul's faculties employing the body's energies and neglect its source in the omnipotent divinity. Puritans had no quarrels with the psychology, which they accepted as the best scientific description of human functioning available, but they were interested in other influences on behavior that psychologists covered only rudimentarily. For these, the preachers turned to their sacred texts.

II

The Bible knows nothing of faculties arrayed in ranks, nor does it dichotomize people into body and soul as the psychologists did. Risen from the dust as flesh (*bâsâr*), inspirited with the breath of life (*rûach*), animated as a living being (*nephesh chayâh*), the individual in the Old Testament is an organism

20. Reynolds, *Treatise of the Passions*, 62; Burton, *Anatomy*,I.2.3.2; Wright, *Passions*, 15–16; Lemnius, *Touchstone*, 14vo.

21. Walkington, *Optick Glasse*, 23vo, 51^{ro-vo}; Elyot, *Castell*, fol. 66vo.

22. Thomas Adams, *Diseases of the Sovle: A Discovrse Divine, Morale, and Physicall* (London, 1616).

23. E. Ruth Harvey, *The Inward Wits: Psychological Theory in the Middle Ages and the Renaissance* (London, 1975), 3, 7–8, 13, 29–30, 31.

24. La Primaudaye, *Second Part*, 598–99.

whose elements completely interpenetrate to create a unified integrity. Hebrews did not distinguish separate loci of psychical and physical activity, instead attributing thoughts and emotions to the entire range of their bodily parts: reins (kidneys) rejoice (Prov. 23.16), bones shake with fear (Job 4.14), bowels sound like harps (Is. 16.11), blood cries out (Gen. 4.10).[25] New Testament anthropology receives its fullest exposition in the Epistles of Paul, who reinterpreted the Hebraic scheme without altering its basic organization of humanity's constituents.[26] As a substantive form, the individual consists of *sarx*, "our mortal flesh" (2 Cor. 4.11), the body and by extension the outward, corporeal state that dictates the original human condition. Flesh as the body is weak, so that "the life I now live in the flesh [*en sarki*]" (Gal. 2.20) is lived in weakness. Central to Pauline, indeed biblical, thought is an intense awareness of how anthropology subserves more general theological concerns. Earthly existence exposes an individual to the dominion of sin, and *sarx* provides the material with which sin catalyzes human wrongdoing: "they that are after the flesh do mind the things of the flesh" (Ro. 8.5), hence they "cannot please God" (Ro. 8.8). One must combat the corruptions that begin in *sarx*, for to live "fleshily" brings death, while to live "spiritually" affords "life and peace" (Ro. 8.6). At redemption, *sarx* will have to die, since "flesh and blood cannot inherit the kingdom of God"

25. Aubrey R. Johnson, *The Vitality of the Individual in the Thought of Ancient Israel*, 2d ed. (Cardiff, 1964); John Chamberlayne, *Man in Society: The Old Testament Doctrine* (London, 1966), 19–37; Glenn E. Whitlock, "The Structure of Personality in Hebrew Psychology," *Interpretation*, 14 (1960), 3–13; H. Wheeler Robinson, "Hebrew Psychology," in *The People and the Book*, ed. Arthur Samuel Peake (Oxford, 1925), 353–82. Against these authors, Robert H. Gundry, *Sōma in Biblical Theology: With an Emphasis on Pauline Anthropology* (Cambridge, 1976), 117–34, contests the assertion that the Bible's formulation of the person's unitary nature denies any distinction between body and soul: "The soul *has* a body and the body *has* a soul and man as a whole *is* both, a psychophysical unity—but a unity, not a monad" (119, 121). The whole man consists in "a unity of parts" (124). See also John William Rogerson, *Anthropology and the Old Testament* (Atlanta, 1979), 46–65, which criticizes the assumption that Hebrew thought necessarily constitutes a "primitive" mentality qualitatively different from modern "scientific" thinking as being founded on an unreliable theoretical basis.

26. Walter David Stacey, *The Pauline View of Man* (London, 1956); Rudolph Bultmann, *Theology of the New Testament*, trans. Kendrick Grobel, 2 vols. (New York, 1951–55), I, 190–352; Bo Reicke, "Body and Soul in the New Testament," *Studia Theologica*, 19 (1965), 200–212; Werner Georg Kümmel, *Man in the New Testament*, trans. John J. Vincent, rev. and enlg. (London, 1963); E. Sadiq, "Man's Nature and Destiny—The New Testament View," *Religion and Society*, 20 (1973), 54–63; Charles Ryder Smith, *The Bible Doctrine of Man* (London, 1949), 133–249; Ernest De Witt Burton, *Spirit, Soul, and Flesh* (Chicago, 1918), 178–207. Disputes about New Testament, especially Pauline, anthropology have raged since the nineteenth century and show no signs of abating. Robert Jewett, *Paul's Anthropological Terms: A Study of Their Use in Conflict Settings* (Leiden, 1971), discusses the historical development of the different interpretations regarding each of the major terms in his chapter sections labeled "the History of Research." The brief summaries given here cannot mirror the complexity of the debate.

(1 Cor. 15.50). Yet Paul rejected the notion that *sarx* itself constitutes an inherently evil element opposed to one's "higher nature." Sin enters through *sarx*, but the entire person sins.[27]

Sarx signifies humanity's frailty, while the spirit, *pneuma*, comprehends divine and human power. A term that can denote the Spirit of God, its divine nature and activity, and the principle of righteousness inspired into the believer, *pneuma* when used anthropologically defines the source of a person's energy, a seat of emotionality, volition, and intellect, one's inward, spiritual side. All people in their natural condition have *pneuma* in this sense, and to this extent the term parallels Hebraic usage, but whereas the Old Testament discovers human beings in the light of their present life, Paul and other New Testament authors discern them in the glare of their future. What a person is always points to what one can become: "if any man *be* in Christ, *he is* a new creature: old things are passed away; behold, all things are become new" (2 Cor. 5.17). Paul's innovation was to insist that those who have faith transmute their ontological status, changing from *sarkikoi*, the fleshly, to *pneumatikoi*, the spiritual. Human nature includes the potential for re-creation by grace. A Christian communes with God's Spirit and experiences the supernatural power that transforms one's own spirit. The person who accepts Christ, whose *pneuma* becomes the "spirit of faith" (2 Cor. 4.13) and thus receives the "fruit of the Spirit" (Gal. 5.22) begins a new life "in the Spirit" (Ro. 8.9), while "The Spirit itself beareth witness with our spirit, that we are the children of God" (Ro. 8.16). *Pneumatikoi* are freed from the compulsion to sin, but the opposing forces of flesh and spirit contend throughout a Christian's lifetime: "For the flesh lusteth against the Spirit, and the Spirit against the flesh" (Gal. 5.17). The spiritual life leads to salvation, the fleshly one to damnation and death.[28]

Preoccupied with the spirit and the flesh, Paul rarely treated *psuchē*, the soul, and he did not hold it in special repute, as did the Greeks. *Psuchē* is the life of the person, an organ of emotion and will that participates in sin as one component of the individual.[29] *Psuchikos* like *sarkikos* describes life in the flesh: "that *was* not first which is spiritual [*pneumatikos*], but that which is natural [*psuchikos*]" (1 Cor. 15.46). At death body and soul separate, a

27. John A. T. Robinson, *The Body: A Study in Pauline Theology* (Chicago, 1952), 17–26. Robinson denies (17) that Paul uses *sarx* in reference to the musculature (or any single part of the body), but Reicke, "Body and Soul," 201, allows such usage in Luke. In some passages Paul depicts *sarx* as an independent force working in the person. However, he never concludes that humanity's materialness renders it inherently evil, Kümmel, *Man*, 60–61, 41–43.

28. Harry S. Benjamin, "Pneuma in John and Paul," *Biblical Theology Bulletin*, 6 (1976), 27–48; Paul Younger, "A New Start Towards a Doctrine of the Spirit," *Canadian Journal of Theology*, 13 (1967), 123–33.

29. Stacey, *Pauline View*, 122–25, but see Jewett, *Paul's Anthropological Terms*, 334–57. Even if Jewett is right that Paul does not use *psuchē* as the seat of emotion and intellect, Reicke, *"Body and Soul,"* 208, finds such use elsewhere in the New Testament.

condition that the Hebrews regarded as terminal but which Christian scriptures ameliorate by promising reunion at the Last Judgment. What happens to the soul in the meanwhile has occasioned some wondrous dogmatic (not to mention poetic) infernos, but the New Testament avoids much speculation and provides no definitive answer.[30]

The New Testament maintains the Old's psychophysical perspective on the internal organs. Paul's term *splagchna* intends both inward parts (or intestines) and sympathy or caring. [31] Christian organs rest notably silent as compared with their unhesitatingly vocal Israelite counterparts, however, and, set against the Old Testament, the New accentuates the psychological and spiritual aspects of the viscera. Although his understanding of the heart, *kardia*, depends on the Hebrew *lêb* (*lêbâb*)—the site of intellect, will, and emotion, and a metonym for the whole personality—Paul referred to it only once in a specifically physical context.[32] *Kardia* denotes the seat of psychological activity, one's center, the intending, purposeful self that may choose either good or evil. Paul appropriated terms from Hellenistic thought to depict some psychological activity, but employed them idiosyncratically. *Nous*, mind, means the thoughts and assumptions that comprise consciousness and govern action. *Suneidēsis*, conscience, denotes both one's knowledge of wrongdoing and the agent of that knowledge.[33] Paul also discriminated between *exo anthropos*, one's outer, corporeal side, and *eso* (or *esothen*) *anthropos*, the inner, incorporeal part that, like *kardia*, intends a person's spiritual center.[34] The heart in Pauline usage normally conveys a spiritual meaning that develops from *lêb* and its physical connotations.

The human being has a body, *sōma*; the term takes in the outer man and the whole person but comprehends more. *Sarx* portends the person in one's

30. Karel Hanhart, *The Intermediate State in the New Testament* (Franeker, Netherlands, 1966); Herman Ridderbos, *Paul: An Outline of His Theology*, trans. John Richard De Witt (Grand Rapids, 1975), 507. For an introduction to the New Testament debate, see Oscar Cullman, *Immortality of the Soul, or Resurrection of the Dead?* (London, 1958), and D. E. H. Whiteley, *The Theology of Saint Paul* (Oxford, 1964), 262–69. On the Old Testament controversy, see Johnson, *Vitality of the Individual*, 89–95, and Gundry, *Sōma*, 119–21, 127–34.

31. William F. Arndt and F. Wilbur Gingrich, *A Greek-English Lexicon of the New Testament and Other Early Christian Literature*, 4th rev. and aug. ed. (Chicago and Cambridge, 1952), s.v. "σπλάγχνον."

32. T. Francis Glasson, "'Visions of Thy Head' (Daniel 2.28): The Heart and the Head in Bible Psychology," *Expository Times*, 81 (1970), 247–48; Stacey, *Pauline View*, 194. The passage is 2 Cor. 3.3, "fleshy tables of the heart."

33. Jewett, *Paul's Anthropological Terms*, chaps. VI, VIII, X, XI, *passim*, esp. 312–13, 447–48 (*kardia*); 367, 327, 450 (*nous*); 419–21, 436–39, 458–60 (*suneidēsis*).

34. Gundry, *Sōma*, 135–37, 156; Ridderbos, *Paul*, 115. In 2 Cor. 4.16 and Eph. 3.16, "inner man" suggests "heart"; in Ro. 7.22, "mind." Hebrews employed a similar locution, A. W. Argyle, "'Outward' and 'Inward' in Biblical Thought," *Expository Times*, 68 (1957), 196–97; Edouard Dhorme, *L'Emploi métaphorique des noms de parties du corps en Hébreu et en Akkadien* (Paris, 1963), 109–28.

weakness, *sōma* as a godly creation. *Sarx* cannot enter the Kingdom of Heaven but *sōma* can, for though *sōma* "is sown in dishonour, it is raised in glory" (1 Cor. 15.43). On the last day "we shall be changed," the natural body "raised a spiritual body [*sōma pneumatikos*]" (1 Cor. 15.52, 44), a real corporeal figure purged of *sarx*: "For this corruptible must put on incorruption, and this mortal *must* put on immortality" (1 Cor. 15.53). *Sōma* defines the connection between believers and Christ—"your bodies are the members of Christ" (1 Cor. 6.15)—and also the church's structure—"For as the body is one, and hath many members . . . so also *is* Christ" (1 Cor. 12.12), further illustrations of how Pauline anthropology always returns to consider humanity's relationship with God.[35]

The Bible posits that the individual is a psychophysical unity with no single supreme faculty. Humanity's makeup, however, is not the center of interest; although its hundreds of scattered observations can be made to cohere, Scripture is hardly a treatise on anatomy. Biblical authors were less concerned with constitution per se than in the quality of performance it allows, and they described optimum effort in reference to the body's principal part. "Wholehearted" endeavor engages will, intellect, and emotion in complete, purposeful harmony; to cry with one's "whole heart" (Ps. 119.145) means to cry with the totality of one's self.[36] This level of execution requires God's support, and the Bible's emphatic theocentrism focuses attention on the divine fountainhead of human ability. Where the First Mover hovers in the background of the psychology, the Good Book's El Shaddai, God Almighty, imposes on all His office as "the strength of my life" (Ps. 27.1). His position is emphasized lexically, for the same words that signify the Deity's power (*rûach, pneuma*) also denominate both what infuses it and its organic residuum within the person. The outcome of the conflict between flesh and spirit depends on the ministrations of a supernatural force, God's Spirit. Since ethical life develops in the context of God's donative potency, behavior must always be evaluated in terms of its possible effect on strength. The import of this did not elude the Puritans.

III

Because the preachers wanted to know how human beings operate, they studied the psychology, and because they could not watch even a sparrow fall

35. Robinson, *Body*, 26–33; Gundry, *Sōma, passim*, esp. 30, n. 1, who disputes that *sōma* is man and restricts it to the corporeal body, which may represent the whole man by synechdoche; Jewett, *Paul's Anthropological Terms*, 279–87; William Nelson, "Pauline Anthropology. Its Relation to Christ and the Church," *Interpretation*, 14 (1960), 22–25.

36. I. Cohen, "The Heart in Biblical Psychology," in *Essays Presented to Chief Rabbi Israel Brodie*, eds. H. J. Zimmels, J. Rabinowitz, and I. Finestein (London, 1967), 41–57, esp. 46–47.

without rushing to the Bible for amplification, they customarily glossed the psychology with Scripture. Their conception of a properly functioning person scrambled these sources. Although the presuppositions that gird the two anthropologies are quite different, Puritans had not lost the sense, inevitably destroyed by the emergence of scientific biblical criticism, that they could address Moses and Paul as contemporaries with whom they shared common assumptions and beliefs. Recognizing no outstanding variations between the theories, they fitted the psychology to the procrustean bed of Scripture, which resulted in some peculiar exegeses. John Downame blurred the biblical term "spirit" trying to identify it as the faculty of reason and understanding. For proof he cited (without quotation) 1 Cor. 2.11 ("For what man knoweth the things of a man, save the spirit of a man . . . ?"), which substantiates his position; Ro. 12.2 ("be ye transformed by the renewing of your mind . . ."), use of which incorrectly assumes an identity in Paul between *pneuma* and *nous*; and Luke 1.47 ("And my spirit hath rejoiced in God my Saviour"), which is immaterial to the point at issue. On the other hand, William Perkins violated the psychology when he held that Ps. 16.7, which he quoted as "My reynes teach me in the night season," establishes that in a sanctified individual the Spirit of God guides the mind, will, and affections, the whole soul.[37] Although Hebrews occasionally imputed a moral sense to the kidneys, psychologists did not attribute much importance to them and scarcely considered them the seat of the major faculties.[38] One expects Hebrew organs to exclaim—but not English ones.

Indecision about the meaning of *spirit* highlights the Puritans' difficulties. In the Bible, the spirit is both the divine breath that empowers the human being and a part of the person that serves God; in the psychology, it is the "subtle substance" that knits body and soul together. Puritans distinguished the two sets of meanings and used both freely, very rarely confounding them.[39] Nevertheless, having retained the biblical signification, they found themselves hard pressed to develop uniform usage, a quandary exemplified by Perkins's efforts to elucidate 1 Thess. 5.23 ("*I pray God* your whole spirit

---

37. John Downame, *The Christian Warfare*, 4th ed. (London, 1634), 1019; Perkins, *Works*, I, 470. Cf. GenB, "my reines also teache me in the nights." Perkins seems to be working from memory. Downame held several posts during his career.

38. But see Lemnius, *Touchstone*, 141ro, where the liver, if "abounding with Bloud, & heated ẇ Wyne, inciteth the Reynes to the desyre of amorous embracements, fleshly cŏcupiscence, leacherous lust, ryot, and lasciuiousness." On the Hebrews, Hans Walter Wolff, *Anthropology of the Old Testament*, trans. Margaret Kohl (Philadelphia, 1974), 65–66.

39. For the only two examples I have located, Richard Sibbes, *The Complete Works*, ed. Alexander B. Grosart, 7 vols. (Edinburgh, 1862–64), I, 156; John Davenport, *The Saints Anchor-Hold* (London, 1661), 121–22.

and soul and body be preserved blameless . . ."). He claimed in one work that the spirit encompasses the mind and memory while the soul includes the will and affections. Elsewhere, uncertain exposition affects the definition. Comprehending the Thessalonians as unregenerate (although Paul addresses them as elect, 1 Thess. 1.4), Perkins took the spirit as "the image of God wrought by the [S]pirit," which since the Fall is "turned to flesh." Here he confused the organ that receives God's Spirit with the new quality of holiness that the Spirit imparts to the faithful.[40] In a third place, he corrected his exegesis, proclaiming spirit "the gift of regeneration, & sanctification," the whole new man in body and soul.[41] The term defied precise denotation. Some ministers thought the spirit coincident with the heart, others identified it with the conscience, and a number concurred that it is "the purest part of the minde and reason," the reasonable faculties that can be "enlightened."[42]

Puritans' most significant adaptation of the psychology involved their gaze[43] at the heart as a material and a spiritual entity. Psychologists considered it a corporal object, locus of the vital spirits and the affections. Pierre de La Primaudaye, scion of a leading French Protestant family and a writer whose interest in problems of faith, election, and God's sovereignty as related to the psychology gives his work a puritanic cast, knew that in the Bible the heart can intend the mind, senses, and affections, but considered it pre-

---

40. Perkins, *Works*, I, 370, 730. He would harmonize 1 Thess. 1.4 with his interpretation by arguing that a minister "in the iudgement of charitie" presumes all hearers elect, and that Paul took this course in the Epistles (I, 709).

41. Perkins, *Works*, II, 45; see also I, 369, where he defines spirit as the "heart and conscience sanctified," and II, 19, where spirit is only the conscience.

42. On spirit as heart, John Forbes, *A Letter . . . for resolving this Question: How a Christian Man may discerne the testimonie of Gods spirit . . .* (Middleburg, 1616), 31, and John Preston, *The Breast-Plate of Faith and Love*, 2d ed., corr. (London, 1630), pt. II, "A Treatise of Effectvall Faith," 50. On spirit as conscience, William Ames, "Conscience with the Power and Cases Thereof," I.iii.7, in *idem, The Workes* (London, 1643), who equated spirit and conscience in Acts 17.16 ("his spirit was stirred in him"), a highly unlikely identification because Paul distinguishes between *pneuma* and *suneidēsis*. Perkins, *Works*, II, 19, and Thomas Shepard, *The Works*, ed. John Adams Albro, 3 vols. (Boston, 1853; facsimile repr., Hildesheim, 1971), I, 254, define spirit as the renewed conscience, but Thomas Hooker, *The Application of Redemption*, books I-VIII (London, 1656), 272, discriminates between the terms. (This volume was bound with books IX-X (London, 1657); henceforth, references will be to *Application*, I-VIII, and *Application*, IX-X.) On spirit as the reasonable faculties, Downame, *Christian Warfare*, 1037, and John Preston, *The New Covenant*, 8th ed. (London, 1634), 415. See also Margaret R. Miles, "Theology, Anthropology, and the Human Body in Calvin's *Institutes of the Christian Religion*," *Harvard Theological Review*, 74 (1981), 307-8, 312.

43. I use the term to mean the act of seeing that implies a system of perceptions determining the act. See Michel Foucault, *The Birth of the Clinic*, trans. A. M. Sheridan Smith (New York, 1973), ix and *passim*.

eminently a physical organ.[44] Puritans recognized the physical definition, of course—"the soul, as far as it understands, is only in the brain; as far as it is the fountain of life, it is in the heart"—but their usual characterization took shape from Paul. According to Richard Sibbes, a leading preacher and promoter of Puritan lectureships in England, the heart is not "the inward material and fleshy part of the body; but that spiritual part, the soul and affections thereof"; therefore, "all the powers of the soul, the inward man, as Paul calleth it, 2 Cor. iv. 16, is the heart."[45] The flexibility of *kardia* permitted preachers several constructions. Heart could designate the most private self imaginable, "the inmost closet of the soul" that only God may search.[46] More usually, it corresponded to soul—"the soul, therefore, is the subject of faith, called 'the heart'"—or to a portion of it, the reasonable faculties, conscience, will, or affections. Steeped in Pauline thought, Puritans referred to the heart primarily as a psychological phenomenon, the inner person.[47]

The preachers also took over the concept of acting wholeheartedly. This idiom, so important in both Testaments and of little consequence to the psychologists, directed how people should conduct themselves towards God: if we come to Him "submitting our selves to be ruled and squared by him in all things, hee shall have our whole hearts to do with us what he will."[48] Behaving in such a fashion is behaving with powerful intensity. When Richard Mather preached farewell to his congregation in Dorchester, Massachusetts (although intimations of his passing were exaggerated, since he did not die until twelve years after the work was printed), he taught that the first Commandment enjoins them to love the Lord "*with all the heart and with all the soul, & with all the mind & with all the strength,*" an idea important enough that he altered his proof text slightly to convey it. Mat. 22.37, the passage cited, mentions the heart, soul, and mind, but omits the reference to

---

44. *Nouvelle Biographie Générale*, 46 vols. (Paris, 1858–78), XXIX, 567–68; La Primaudaye, *Second Part*, 218.

45. Sibbes, *Works*, II, 227; VI, 31; II, 46.

46. John Cotton, *Gods Mercie Mixed with His Justice*, (London, 1641; facsimile repr., Gainesville, 1958), 3. In this passage Cotton equates heart and will, contending that Satan cannot probe them, contrary to Richard Rogers's estimate, *Seven Treatises* (London, 1603), 41, that Satan knows the mind and can judge the will, but does not know our hearts, "for that is proper to God only."

47. Heart as soul: Shepard, *Works*, I, 199, who argues the equivalence from Ro. 10.9 ("thou . . . shalt believe in thine heart") and Mat. 6.21 ("For where your treasure is, there will your heart lie also"); see Thomas Wilson, *A Christian Dictionary*, 2d ed., aug. (London, 1616), s.v. "Heart," def. 3. Heart as one of the faculties: Preston, *Breast-Plate*, I, "Of Faith," 54; Shepard, *Works*, I, 82; William Ames, *The Marrow of Sacred Divinity* (London, 1642), Bk. I, ch. xxvi, par. 30; Downame, *Christian Warfare*, 1033; see Wilson, *Dictionary*, s.v. "Heart," defs. 4-6. John Cotton, *The way of Life* (London, 1641), 50, equates heart and spirit.

48. John Cotton, *The Covenant of Gods free Grace* (London, 1645), 20.

strength.[49] Mather was not unique; Perkins and Thomas Hooker, apotheo-
sized by Cotton Mather as "the light of the western churches," made the same
oversight.[50] So unquestioningly have we assumed the accuracy of Puritan
biblical citation that to find them slurring quotations seems like telling tales
out of school. Yet equivocation has its uses, and offhand slips their significance. Ministers took for granted the idea that a person who performs
wholeheartedly does so with undivided power, and conformed the verse to
their postulate that a fully operational human being is a repository of
purposeful strength.

Familiarity with the faculty-humoral and scriptural conceptions of heart
gave Puritans the opportunity to use both as they saw fit. When Arthur
Hildersam, one of their "patriarchs," allowed that "extremity of worldly grief
will make the minde and heart of man vncapable of heauenly things," which
affliction "so oppresseth the heart, it straighteneth and closeth it so, as it
makes him vnable to profit by the best teacher that shall come vnto him," he
compared the actions of the spiritual heart to those of the physical organ
affected by grief. Hildersam kept the two levels distinct; the spiritual heart is
not the physical one.[51] Ineluctably, however, some preachers linked them:

> Desires are the issues of the heart. Thoughts and desires are the two
> primitive issues of the heart, the births of the heart. Thoughts breed
> desires. Thoughts in the mind or brain, the brain strikes the heart pre-
> sently.[52]

Thoughts and desires issue from the spiritual heart, said Sibbes, but then he
shifted the discussion to material phenomena and interjected between "mind"
and "brain" a conjunction as subtle as the spirit that unites body and soul.
Thoughts in the mind are psychological events. Thoughts in the brain refer to

49. Richard Mather, *A Farewel Exhortation* . . . (Cambridge, Mass., 1657), 20. Mat. 22.37
(KJV) reads "all thy heart, and with all thy soul, and with all thy mind," and the list is identical
in Tyn., Cov., GB, Tav., GenB, BB, Rheims. In this verse Christ is quoting from Deut. 6.5,
which reads "might" instead of "mind," as does 2 Kings 23.25. The parallel passage in Mark
12.30 cites the heart, soul, mind, strength ("power" in Rheims), and Luke 10.27 gives the heart,
soul, strength, and mind ("thoght" in GenB).

50. Perkins, *Works*, I, 32; Hooker, *Application*, IX-X, 306; Cotton Mather, *Magnalia Christi
Americana*, 2 vols. (Hartford, 1853–55), I, 332. The implications are even more apparent in
Thomas Hooker, *The Paterne of Perfection* (London, 1640), 70, where he quotes the verse as
"*Thou shalt love the Lord thy God, with all thy might, & with all thy strength.*" Thomas
Cartwright, *A Treatise of Christian Religion*, 2d ed. (London, 1616), 162, takes Deut. 6.5 as
heart, mind, and understanding, but also lists heart, mind, and strength, referring to an
uncited verse, on p. 163; see also *infra*, n. 57.

51. Haller, *Rise of Puritanism*, 54; Arthur Hildersam, *CVIII Lectures Upon the Fovrth of
Iohn*, 2d ed. (London, 1632), 435.

52. Sibbes, *Works*, 218.

the soul's motions in the body, the idea become fleshy, for brain was always a physical term, as Sibbes demonstrated in a less ambiguous passage:

> The heathen could observe, that God hath framed the heart and the brain so as there is a sympathy between them, that whatsoever is in the understanding that is well and comfortable, the understanding in the brain sends it to the heart, and raiseth some comfort.[53]

This is pure faculty-humor psychology, thoughts traveling from the brain via (understood) animal spirits to affect the corporal heart. The uses of the word *heart* span a continuum from purely spiritual to purely physical, and as the meanings melt together, organ and inner man fuse:

> By the *heart* you must not understand, that fleshly part of the body which is the seat of life, called *Primum vivens, & ultimum moriens* . . . it is meant the will of a man, which lyes in the heart, for as the *understanding* lyes in the head or brain, so the *will* is seated in the *heart*.[54]

No hobgoblin of consistency haunted one of early New England's leading lights; John Cotton banished the physical connotation only to reintroduce it by using the heart as seat of the will in a parallel construction with the head and the brain, material seats of the understanding.

Implicit in these passages lies the profound suggestion that no reference to the heart as the inner man need ever be considered entirely figurative. The polysemy proved inescapable—and essential. Heart can signify the physical organ of the psychologists, Paul's inner man, and something more inclusive too, for ambiguity bound together the strands of biblical and faculty-humoral thought in a way that rigor never could. Exemplar of both material and spiritual life, the heart reminded Puritans that Scripture and psychology stress the integrated functioning of the self's two sides. Humans are most able when they act as what Puritans called the "whole man," inner spiritual core and outer frame, when they can, for instance, hate spiritual enemies with an intention that

> brings the combined forces of confederated power of the whol man & his whol endeavor to destroy the nests of those noysom lusts, what head can contrive, heart desire, hand work, the endeavor accomplish, head, and heart, and hand, desires, endeavors, tears, prayers, in a deadly feud to pursue the spiritual enemyes to their not being.[55]

---

53. *Ibid.*, III, 210–11. The mind was variously defined as: the faculty of reason and understanding, Downame, *Christian Warfare*, 1019; the understanding alone, Arthur Dent, *The Plaine Mans Path-way to Heauen* (London, 1603), 15; the understanding and memory, Sibbes, *Works*, I, 181; one of two special parts of the soul (with the will), Shepard, *Works*, I, 205. Generally, the mind was equivalent to the understanding.

54. Cotton, *way of Life*, 127.

55. Wilson, *Christian Dictionary*, s.v. "Heart," def. 2; Hooker, *Application*, IX-X, 686.

The whole man is the individual performing at peak capacity, in which condition the believer unites with Christ, engages in the act of faith, and responds in regeneration.[56] To love God with heart, mind, and strength means "the whole man yeeldeth simple obedience vnto him, in all the powers both of soule and body." The faculties—understanding, judgment, memory, affections, and will—plus "all the members, parts, and graces of the body," are "wholly employed in the service of God, and in the doing of his will."[57] Here, Holy Writ and Renaissance science meet on common ground. The scriptural locution of heart, soul, and strength merges into the psychology's list of the person's parts, both vocabularies enunciating how body and soul collaborate in the deeds of the preachers' ideal, the whole man walking in the paths of the Lord.[58]

IV

The idea of the whole man related constitution to the potential for activity; ordered faculties working in a well-tempered body are productively engaged. The Bible, however, recognizes the limits that human composition places on achievement. Though one may prove a champion in the earthly realm, the individual consists of flesh (*bâsâr, sarx*) and is ultimately weak. A Psalmist's lament, "my strength faileth because of mine iniquity, and my bones are consumed" (Ps. 31.10), conveys the marrow of biblical anthropology: the human being is an organism whose strength must eventually decline, whose power relates to moral condition, and who sins through impotence. By transgressing, one spurns God, and the Bible construes history as efforts to bridge the chasm sin has opened between frail creatures and the mighty Lord. Christianity has traditionally located the cause of this predicament in the Fall. Since Adam and Eve's expulsion from Eden, humanity lives in a state of degeneration that can only be corrected by grace. Any Christian view of human functioning must decide how badly Original Sin has vitiated the "image of God" (Gen. 1.26–27) in men and women, how wide the gulf

---

56. John Norton, *The Orthodox Evangelist* (London, 1654), 286; Perkins, *Works*, I, 78; Ames, *Marrow*, I.iii.3; Peter Bulkeley, *The Gospel-Covenant*, 2d ed., enlg. and corr. (London, 1651), 265; Hildersam, *CVIII Lectures*, 473.

57. Cartwright, *Treatise of Christian Religion*, 163.

58. Cf. D. R. G. Owen, *Body and Soul: A Study on the Christian View of Man* (Philadelphia, 1956), 196, discussing the unity of the individual in biblical anthropology: "in this context of ideas there can be no 'puritanical' depreciation of, and hostility to, the physical aspects of human existence, with its accompanying exaltation of pure 'spirituality.'" Apart from resurrecting the dead horse that Puritans hated bodily pleasure, flogged by generations of scholarship, Owen accuses "puritans" of opposing the position they supported.

between people and God stretches, and how much a person, infirm and captive to "the law of sin" (Ro. 7.23) can do to cross it.

Psychologists did not attempt to span the gap so much as to ignore it. Where Puritans carefully distinguished between human capabilities in the states of innocence, depravity, and rehabilitation, many psychologists, whatever their denominational affiliations, dutifully noted the fact of Original Sin but proceeded as if regeneration were inconsequential. Thomas Wright, a Jesuit, taught that, since the grace available in baptism overcomes Original Sin, only a "peruerse and wicked will" hinders one from "dooing wel," a condition remedied through self-fermentation: "we see how newe wines, beere, and all liquors worke, by boyling the rawer partes, expelling the dregges, reducing themselves to a due temper, proportionated mixture and perfection: if these insensible creatures, so industriously labour to come to their end, shall not we endeavour to atchiue our end and felicitie?"[59] Alienation from the divine does not sound desperate in a world where mortals and intoxicants can bubble towards the ideal. Such a generous assessment of the unregenerate will's capacities offended Edward Reynolds, who denied that "heathen vertues" and "natural endeavours" could ever compel grace. His own treatise on the faculties, written while he was serving as the Rector of Braunston, Northamptonshire, makes no such claims for "Distorted and Crooked Nature." Having allowed humanity's degeneration, however, Reynolds is in no hurry to revive it, and he begins to sound a little soft on heathen virtues himself. If we are careful "*not to admire Philosophy, to the prejudice of Evangelicall knowledge,*" then "*salvation might be found, in the way of Paganisme,*" an attitude contributive to an impassive study that neither cries out the urgency of regeneration nor explains the process by which grace refurbishes God's Image. Reynolds would like to consider "the Right End, and *Vltimate Felicity*" to which human action leads, but these pertain "to a nobler Science," and hence another book.[60] Grace can wait.

Puritans could not afford this leisurely attitude because it minimized that rift with the Deity attendant upon the damage to the faculties wrought by the Fall. "Man, when he came first out of God's mint, shined most glorious," enthused Thomas Shepard, the pastor of Cambridge: the Creator had

59. Wright, *Passions*, 323, 331, 319. On Wright, see Kocher, *Science and Religion*, 288; Burton, *Anatomy*, I.1.2.8, n. 72. *DNB*, XXI, 1043, denies the book was written by the Catholic controversialist, and attributes it to a Protestant philosophical writer with the same name, but the assertion that baptism removes Original Sin argues for Catholic authorship.

60. Edward Reynolds, *Three Treatises* . . ., 2d ed., rev. and corr. (London, 1632), 249; *idem*, *Treatise of the Passions*, 530, "Preface" (unpaginated), 553. Miller, *New England Mind*, 244, calls Reynolds a "Puritan author," but *DNB*, XVI, 926, accounts him a "moderate Anglican," and see McGee, *Godly Man*, 3.

stamped him with His Image, that "perfection of holiness, resembling God's admirable holiness, whereby only man pleaseth God." Possessing a godlike understanding, affections enamored of the Lord, and a compliant will, Adam could do God's bidding; partaking of His "spirituall vertue," he "was able to know what was needfull, and to will what ever he knew agreeable to Gods will."[61] The dereliction in Eden unhinged this flawless integrity and doomed all Adam's seed to suffer from a congenital defect. In Puritan thinking, Original Sin is a constitutional malfunctioning engendered at conception by which "euery facultie of soule and body is prone and disposed to euill." It "distempers the whole man" and "sets the whole soule out of order." In a favorite image, Hooker compared the impaired faculties to the wheels of a clock pulled by the "poyse and plummet" of corruption into running "the wrong way to the divell-ward, and to the hell-ward."[62] The mind rejects wholesome thoughts for dross, the will chooses perversely, and the affections rage out of control. One's natural inclinations swerve towards sin "as iron is carried to the loadstone," and depraved human nature readily indulges in every possible fault, as Richard Rogers outlined in a description of the heart so notoriously "puritanical" that it verges on caricature:

> ouerspread with vnbeleefe, deceitfull, vnruly, loose, hardned, wilfull, vaine, idle, blockish, cold in goodnes, and without fauour, and soon wearie of it: high, big, proude, disdaineful, selfe-louing, vncharitable, vnkind, conceited, impatient, angry, fierce, enuious, reuenging, vnmercifull, froward and tuchie, churlish, sullen, medling, worldly, filthie and vncleane, louing pleasure more than godlinesse, vnprofitable, repining, earthie, greedie, or couetous; idolatrous, superstitious, vnreuerent, hypocriticall, disobedient to betters, iudging rashlie, hardlie reconciled: and in a word, prone to all euill.[63]

The chasm stretches as wide and deep as imaginations obsessed with God's omnipotence and human depravity could conceive.

---

61. Shepard, *Works*, I, 18–19; Hooker, *Paterne of Perfection*, 9. The phrase originally intended to suggest Adam's position as God's Image, i.e. representative, on earth, exercising dominion over the created world as the subordinate of God, who rules all. Adam's physical and spiritual incidents are secondary, and in Hebrew thought no perfection on his part is implied. Edmund Jacob, *Theology of the Old Testament*, trans. Arthur W. Heathcote and Philip J. Allcock (London, 1958), 166–72; Robert Davidson, *Genesis 1-11* (Cambridge, 1973), 24–25; Bruce Vawter, *On Genesis: A New Reading* (Garden City, N.Y., 1977), 54–59.

62. Perkins, *Works*, I, 20; John Preston, *The Saints Qvalification*, 2d ed., corr. (London, 1634), 42; Thomas Hooker, *The Vnbeleevers Preparing for Christ* (London, 1638), second pagination, 26.

63. Sibbes, *Works*, I, 174; Rogers, *Seven Treatises*, 88.

Implacably, preachers fixed the accountability for such perverseness: "to man belongs all the blame and shame of sin without excuse." God wills the "being" of sin, yet He does not will the act itself. He permits iniquity, but man causes it. Satan does not assume liability either, for though he "tempts man to sin, yet he cannot necessitate man to sin." The Devil "can not compel a man to sin against his will," temptations and torments notwithstanding.[64] The individual chooses to reject God, and Puritans disputed the contravention of human responsibility that medical materialism offered. Physicians often spoke as if the soul either does not exist or plays only a minor role in human operating, and they quickly turned away from speculating about it to contemplate the body's ills. When they averred that "The Splene or Mylte . . . maketh a man exceedingly to delite in talking, laughter, murth, pastime, and wātonnes, mynding no earnest matters, but letting the world slyde," they grounded morality in physiology and denied the importance of self-reflection.[65] Juan Huarte, a Spanish doctor who developed a theory of vocational guidance based on temperament, offered just such an explanation of Paul's character; his blasphemies, persecutions, and struggles with his will show him the victim of corrupted humor:

> True it is that some expound (very well) that this battaile groweth from the disorder which original sinne made betweene the spirit and the flesh; albeit such and so great, I believe also that it springs from the choler adust, which he had in his naturall constitution: for the roiall prophet *David* participated equally of original sin, and yet complained not so much as did *S. Paul. . . .*[66]

Though Huarte admits that Original Sin influences behavior, he eliminates it as a necessary variable. Since the Fall corrupts everyone identically, the decisive determinants must lie in Paul's temperament. To refute writers like Huarte, Puritans refracted the beams of psychological theory through the lenses of Holy Writ. 1 Sam. 16.12 (describing David as "ruddy, *and* withal of a beautiful countenance") satisfied Hildersam that David possessed a sanguine constitution, the best humans could attain. Yet anyone remembering his agony in Psalm 51, occasioned by remorse for his adultery, knows that when David committed "that sweet sin," he lost his cheerfulness and cried

---

64. Norton, *Orthodox Evangelist*, 70, 71; Shepard, *Works*, I, 34.

65. Kocher, *Science and Religion*, 284–305; Lemnius, *Touchstone*, 141[vo].

66. John [Juan] Huarte, *Examen de Ingenios. The Examination of Mens Wits*, trans. R. C. [Richard Carew?] (London, 1594), 148–49; George Mora, "Review of *The Examination of Men's Wits*, (1575) by John Huarte," *Journal of the History of the Behavioral Sciences*, 13 (1977), 67–78. John Preston, *Remaines of . . . John Preston* (London, 1634), 68, attributes Paul's behavior to supernatural strength imparted by Satan.

out.[67] The effects of humors prove insignificant compared with David's conscious response to sin.[68]

Having magnified humanity's distance from God and determined its faulty character, the preachers dashed all claims that one's endeavor can alter the human condition. The line that binds the person to God is anchored at one end in the Lord's omnipotence and secured at the other by one's abject weakness. It is true, preachers admitted, that the unregenerate do retain a pale semblance of Adam's powers, for the Fall does not deface the Image of God entirely. In particular, the conscience, "God's candle," continues to monitor one's actions, "it will shine, and is not easily put out." Relentlessly the preachers intoned how the "entree to godlinesse" consists in a conscience well pricked, "for as long as men are secure," they do not "heartily long for Christ."[69] Yet the fact remains, "you may lead a wounded conscience a good way, but not farre enough." Christ's light stays shut within its walls like "the light of a Starre in a darke night," illuminating itself but nothing else. It wages a thankless struggle against the other faculties, too often facing a rebellious will or "a tumultuous route of vnruly affections" come to drown its voice. Nor does conscience itself escape decay; benumbed, stupid, and seared, it terrorizes when it should comfort and languishes when it should accuse.[70] The "naturall man" cannot rejuvenate himself even with the traces of God's Image that survive because he "*is dead in trespasses and sinnes, Eph,* 2.1" How, asked Hildersam, "can a dead man desire life, or vse any meanes to attaine it?" The question, of course, was rhetorical, as Cotton understood: "we are utterly unable to help our selves."[71]

Only a god who was, to people untutored in Deism, anything but a disinterested watchmaker could realign the gears of the delicately balanced human timepiece gone helplessly awry. He accomplishes this through the agency of the Holy Spirit infusing grace during conversion. Faculty by faculty, sense by sense, the Spirit reorders the soul's powers so they "do now

67. Hildersam, *CVIII Lectures*, 438. On sanguine constitution as best, Walkington, *Optick Glasse*, 57ro, and Lemnius, *Touchstone*, 87vo.

68. Though not entirely irrelevant. The exercise of grace (as opposed to the being of grace) hinges on the body's temperature, Shepard, *Works*, I, 329. Weeping for sin might depend on complexion, and one could grieve without tears, Perkins, *Works*, II, 15. However, if bodily constitution allows one to weep for other things but not for sin, "surely the case is fearefull," Arthur Hildersam, *The Doctrine of Fasting and Praier, and Humiliation for Sinne* (London, 1633), 91.

69. Shepard, *Works*, II, 385; Richard Greenham, *The Works*, ed. Henry Holland (London, 1599), 171.

70. Cotton, *way of Life*, 148; Preston, *Saints Qvalification*, 132; Downame, *Christian Warfare*, 1103 misnum. 1003; Ames, "Conscience," I.xv.2, 6, 8.

71. Hildersam, *CVIII Lectures*, 28; John Cotton, *A Treatise: 1. Of Faith* . . . (Boston, 1713), 6.

ayme at one end, which is the doing of Gods will[.]"[72] The "new man" (Eph. 2.15) born from this labor recovers some of the pristine inclinations to obey God willingly, but the presence of the flesh inhibits complete restoration. Many exegetes have taken Paul's essays at self-control in Ro. 7 as the cries of a sinner anguishing without Christ, but Puritans agreed with Augustine, the Latin Fathers, Luther, and Calvin that the Apostle was speaking about the regenerated Saints. The "body of sinne shal neuer be from vs so long as we liue," they warned, observing that a heart contrary to the Law "is the greatest misery of the saints on earth. Rom. vii. 24."[73] The preachers remained critical of human nature even after regeneration, "For the scum thereof is almost continually boyling and wallopping in vs, foming out such filthy froth and stinking sauor into our mindes," that even a natural man would look on "so loathsome a stie of sinne" abashed.[74] Saints continue to transgress, and although the gap narrows, it never entirely closes during their earthly lives.

Saints err, but their ability to turn against their own wickedness marks a crucial distinction between them and the reprobates. Delivered from the bondage of flesh, they have the competence to will "partly that which is good, and partly that which is euill, as daily experience declareth in the liues of iust mē."[75] The righteous wilfully combat their corruptions, as did the supposed author of the Psalms Puritans so loved. David, in Sibbes's explication of Ps. 42.11, loved sensual things and suffered "a mutiny in his understanding between faith and distrust," a combination of "secret corruptions" that contributed to "discouragement and disquietness arising from faint-trusting in God." A hypocrite, endowed only with common grace, would have submitted passively to these conflicts and clandestinely encouraged them, but David enjoyed the fortitude of true grace and took up against his sin. At times disheartened, "yet by holy indignation against sin he renew[ed] his force, and se[t] afresh upon his corruptions, and gather[ed] more strength by his falls[.]" Striving to conquer his distempers "because they hinder the comfortable intercourse betwixt God and his soul," he yearned to lessen the distance between himself and God and to re-enter communion with Him.[76] Aided by the Holy Spirit, Saints develop the ability to withstand sin through a continu-

---

72. Bulkeley, *Gospel-Covenant*, 246. For the details of the process, Miller, *New England Mind*, 280–99.

73. Donald M. Davies, "Free from the Law. An Exposition of the Seventh Chapter of Romans," *Interpretation*, 7 (1953), 159; Kümmel, *Man*, 50–61; Greenham, *Works*, 269; Shepard, *Works*, II, 18.

74. Greenham, *Works*, 269.

75. Perkins, *Works*, I, 736.

76. Sibbes, *Works*, I, 153–55.

ing process of renewal; backsliding is combatted with renewed vigor. By turning the sinner to God, conversion re-establishes some of the spiritual potency lost in the Fall.

Puritan anthropology climaxes in the person of Israel's second king, the epitome of the righteous man as sinner who challenges his fallibility and realizes his power by yielding totally to the Lord. Humanity's inherent degeneracy makes such submission imperative, and the possibility for revivification through grace makes it desirable. The obedience to God generated by conversion is not thralldom, but rather the actualizing of potential in a creature afflicted with disabling corruptions. The origins of power and of the individual's access to it, spawned by the investigation of human character, was the dominant anthropological issue in the minds of Puritan ministers and congregations. Imbued with the knowledge of humanity's derangement, preachers publicized each person's helplessness, responsibility, and latent power. Puritan sermons never descended into mere invective because they leavened their venomous aspersions on human personality with promises of strength to the godly. The counterpoint of power through redemption insistently accompanied the fortissimo chords of depravity, incompetence, and sin. Images of fleshly and spiritual people, the impotent and the potent, conveyed the central dynamic of Puritan religious experience.

2

Covenant Psychology

Corrupted humanity cannot begin to repair its breach with God until He takes the initiative, and His manner of approach, Puritans thought, has not varied since the days of the Hebrews. The communication of grace takes place in a formalized relationship, the individual "making Covenant with God, and God with him, either at his first conversion, or at other times; of which we read 2 *Sam.* 23.5 & *Psal.* 119.106 & 66.13, 14. & 27.8 & *Psal.* 119.7, 8."[1] These citations manifest something more than Richard Mather's infatuation for the songs he helped to versify in the *Bay Psalm Book*; taken together, they summarize what a covenant involves. God's executive instrument comprising the means through which David enjoys "all my salvation," it is everlasting, "ordered in all *things*, and sure" (2 Sam. 23.5). Pledging God to redeem, it directs David to reciprocate God's favor by enacting His commands, and the king complies: "*When thou saidst* Seek ye my face; my heart said unto thee, Thy face, LORD, will I seek" (Ps. 27.8). He promises to tender "burnt offerings" and "vows" (Ps. 66.13), praise God "with uprightness of heart," keep His "statutes," and perform the Lord's righteous judgments" (Ps. 119.7, 8, 106). Reconciliation with God through the covenant obliges David to ongoing righteousness; its durability notwithstanding, he

---

1. (Richard Mather), *An Apologie of the chvrches in New-England for Chvrch-Covenant* (London, 1643), 3.

must continually effect good works. The emphasis on achievement in return for redemption is the outstanding motif of these texts.

Sadly aware that "right walking" does not happen instinctively, Puritan ministers were anxious to goad their flocks. People need constant prodding from others and, more importantly, from themselves to accomplish especially difficult tasks like obeying the Law. Persistent labor in the holy vineyard requires them to assume a mentality that will compel activity. No one in the lapsed state enjoys this consciousness innately, so sinners must be educated into the proper mind-set. The structure of covenanted accords made them an apposite instructional aid. In the usual compact, one party guarantees to fulfill its obligations if the other side meets a certain requirement. The enthusiasm of a covenantor to uphold commitments may vacillate depending on the duties one must discharge and the profits one anticipates. In the universe of mice and men, response varies with stimulus and reward. The way in which a covenant sets up its liabilities and benefits implicitly models a system of motivation.

In His dealings with human beings, God has found it necessary to extend two agreements, the Covenant of Works and the Covenant of Grace. Each of them holds out eternal life, and each is designed to inspire a lifetime of good works. They diverge, however, in their conditions and stipulations, their assumptions about human capability, and the outlooks they inculcate. The contrasts boil down to one irreducible fact: although both agreements are pacts of salvation, the Covenant of Works perpetuates the ingrained attitudes that, as much as sin, inhibit the successful completion of God's business. Only the Covenant of Grace promotes that way of thinking contributive to someone's implementing the Law while still tainted by Original Sin. Preaching the Covenants did more than inform congregants about the administration of grace; it attempted to instill in them the proper psychology to dispatch the Lord's work.

I

Ministers had several vocabularies—vernacular, legal, and religious—through which they could communicate the niceties of humanity's transaction with the divine. In the daily parlance of early seventeenth-century England, *covenant* intended 'a mutual agreement,' 'a promise to oneself,' 'the terms of an agreement,' and 'the matter agreed upon between the parties.'[2] Puritans extended the word's significance to include "a sacred promise to God to undertake a particular duty or refrain from a specific sin," but it was the first

2. *OED*, s.v. "Covenant," defs. 1–3, 5.

definition that pertained to conversion.[3] Robert Cawdrey, a Puritan lexicographer, connected *covenant* with 'contract,' 'league,' and 'pactation.'[4] All of these synonyms connote some sort of relationship, but dictionaries and word lists of the time group them in two regular clusters: 'contract' corresponds with 'bargain,' 'compact,' and 'pact,' while 'league' connects 'alliance,' 'treaty (especially of peace),' and 'kindred.'[5] The correlations of *covenant* to these combinations varied from writer to writer; the word was associated primarily with 'bargain,' secondarily with 'league.'[6] The analogous Hebrew term also displays a bifurcated meaning, as Thomas Wilson observed: "The word (Covenant) is called in Hebrewe (*Birth* [*sic*]) which hath the signification of friendly parting, and of explayning the conditions of agreement."[7] *Covenant* as a 'mutual agreement' thus conveyed two senses: a relationship connoted by 'bargain' or 'pact' that emphasized the purely contractual nature of the accord, and one denominated by 'league' or 'alliance' that included amicable personal feelings like those associated with family ties, friendship, and peaceful intentions. A preacher tailored his presentation of a covenant by how he remarked upon either its contractual or affective nature.

The English law of contract deepened the term's first sense. As expounded by William West, who, having made his fortune practicing law wrote a highly regarded treatise about it, "A Couenant, is the consent of two or more, in one selfe thing to giue or do some what." The species of consent mattered highly.

3. Van Beek, *Enquiry into Puritan Vocabulary*, 76, and see Thomas Wilson, *A Christian Dictionary*, 2nd ed., aug. (London, 1616) s.v. "Couenant," def. 2.

4. Robert Cawdrey, *A Table Alphabeticall, conteyning and teaching the true writing, and vnderstanding of hard vsuall English words* . . . (London, 1604), s.v. "Contract," "League," "Pactation."

5. T[homas] Blount, *Glossographia, or a Dictionary* . . . (London, 1656), s.v. "Alliant," "League," "Paction"; J[ohn] Bullokar, *An English Expositor* (London, 1616), s.v. "Alliance," "Compact," "Contract," "League," "Pact"; Cawdrey, *Table Alphabeticall,* s.v. "Contract," "League," "Pactation," "Alliance"; Henry Cockeram, *The English Dictionarie* (London, 1623), pt. I, s.v. "Alliance," "Compact," "Contract," "League," "Pact"; John Minsheu, Ηγεμὼν εἰζ ταζ γλῶσσασ . . . *The Gvide Into Tongves* (London, 1617), s.v. "Alliance," "Bargaine," "Contract" (defs. a and b), "League"; E[dward] P[hillips], *The New World of English Words: Or, a General Dictionary* (London, 1658), "Alliance," "Compact," "Contract," "League," "Paction."

6. Cawdrey, *Table Alphabeticall*, s.v. "Contract," "League," "Pactation," and Phillips, *New World,* s.v. "Alliance," "Contract," "League," "Pact," link *covenant* to both groups. Cockeram, *English Dictionarie*, pt. II, s.v. "Couenant," and Minsheu, . . . *Gvide Into Tongves*, s.v. "Bargain" (defs. a and b), "Contract," "Couenant" (def. a), connect it with *bargain*. Bullokar, *English Expositor,* and Blount, *Glossographia* do not give a definition for *covenant*.

7. Wilson, *Christian Dictionary*, s.v. "Couenant," def. 1. Wilson gave additional definitions: 'a promise of obedience to God,' 'an agreement God makes with men for salvation,' 'God's word containing the articles of the agreement between God and man,' 'a promise between married persons,' 'circumcision, the sign of the Covenant,' and 'the tables of the covenant.' The first edition (London, 1612), included 'the sign and pledge of God's Covenant.' Wilson was the rector of St. George the Martyr, Canterbury.

A minor category, "sole consent," vested all responsibility in only one party. A "promise" (*pollicitatio*) and a "bare agreement" (*nudum pactum*), covenants constituted freely by the debtor, created no reciprocal obligation in the creditor and were by themselves unenforceable in Common Law. The predominant instruments in English jurisprudence, however, were contracts, which did impose obligations on both sides and required mutual acceptance before taking effect. Any "error or deceipt" regarding either party's consent to the contract voided the agreement.[8] Both unilateral and bilateral obligations could be constituted in a covenant found in a sealed document, a deed, and if either side failed to execute their commitment, the plaintiff seeking remedy to recover indefinite damages could initiate a Writ of Covenant. The seal provided definitive evidence of agreement, and its existence was critical to the action; without it, the defendant might plead "no covenant" and the action would lapse.[9] Preachers occasionally used this terminology to make a point. John Davenport, the religious leader of early New Haven, had the Deed of Covenant in mind when he said that "miracles were added to the Gospel, as the Kings Seal is unto Charters, or mens seales unto Covenants, for confirmation of faith and assurance," though his analogy fit Puritan theology better than it did the law.[10] God's wonders attest to Gospel truth established independently of them, whereas the "truth" of a Deed of Covenant—the agreement embodied therein—did not legally exist without the seal.

Common speech and law proclaimed to Puritans the essential mutuality of a negotiated bond. "In a Covenant," Thomas Hooker told John Rogers's congregation, the engaged parties spell out the terms of agreement and the conditions of their performance; for example, two men may devise "a paire of Indentures" wherein one consents "to make good the land and to pay thus much rent: the other to let it him thus, and thus." This earthly standard applies to sacred arrangements too. No proprietor appreciates defaulting

8. *DNB*, XX, 1527; William West, *Symbolaeography*, 1st Part, corr. and aug. (London, 1592), Book I, secs. 2–11, esp. 4A, 8A, 9A, 11E. The first edition was published in 1590. It was revised and divided into two parts in 1592, which were reissued separately until 1632. West's definition of *covenant* was quoted in John Cowell, *The Interpreter: or Booke Containing the Significa-tion of Words* (Cambridge, 1607), s.v. "Couenant." Several entries in this volume promoted such an absolute theory of the royal prerogative that it was burned, Godfrey Davies, *The Early Stuarts, 1603-1660* (Oxford, 1952), 12, but Minsheu, . . . *Gvide Into Tongves*, s.v. "Couenant," def. a, quotes much of Cowell's discussion (including West's definition) verbatim.

9. Francis Lyall, "Of Metaphors and Analogies: Legal Language and Covenant Theology," *Scottish Journal of Theology*, 32 (1979), 9–10; W. J. V. Windeyer, *Lectures on Legal History* (Sydney, 1938), 74; A. K. R. Kiralfy, *Potter's Outline of English Legal History*, 5th ed. (London, 1958), 181–82; W. S. Holdsworth, *A History of English Law*, III (London, 1909), 323–26. Minsheu's second definition of *covenant*, . . . *Gvide Into Tongves*, refers to the Writ.

10. John Davenport, *The Knowledge of Christ* (London, 1653), 68–69.

tenants, and Hooker warned the backsliding Dedhamites that the heavenly landlord will call their debts to account at the day of reckoning. William Perkins refused to identify "bare promises" (i.e. the *nudum pactum*), which may be "changed by the makers, or by their successours, if hurts and losses arise," to God's covenant, which binds both sides.[11] Scripture confirmed the reciprocity of holy compacts, once Puritans had reconciled (to their satisfaction) the diverse types the Bible employs. At Sinai and at Shechem, Israel bound itself to God in a covenant whose form, probably derived from Hittite suzerainty treaties, requires the vassal to fulfill conditions imposed by the superior party in order to enjoy the suzerain's continued protection. Blessing and punishment hinge on the nation's obedience. With Noah, Abraham, and David, God executed a covenant resembling the royal grants by which ancient monarchs promised unconditional favor in perpetuity.[12] Less aware than modern scholars of these different motifs and preferring to stress the importance of human activity in upholding God's accords, Puritans overlooked the significance and frequency of the Bible's unilateral parts. Richard Mather did allow that a covenant in Scripture sometimes involves a unilateral divine promise—witness Noah's preservation—but the term is taken "more strictly and properly," for an agreement with a "stipulation of some blessing on God's part" and a "restipulation" of man's duties in return.[13] Mather acknowledged the pre-eminence of bilateral agreements by defining unconditional ones out of existence.

Yet, however closely covenants with God resembled those between human partners, differences remained. God alone initiates the pact, and Thomas Cartwright explained that this reverses normal procedure. Ordinarily, "the weaker seeketh reconciliation at the hands of the mightier. But God (who neither can be hurt or benefited by vs) seeketh vnto vs for place."[14] John Cotton, ever watchful for threats against the doctrine of God's unchallengeable sovereignty, saw danger in making the activities of mortals and the Lord equivalent. Unlike human compacts, which require mutual agreement and consent,

---

11. Thomas Hooker, *The Faithful Covenanter* (London, 1644), 18; William Perkins, *The Whole Works*, 3 vols. (London, 1626–31), II, 242; I, 32.

12. George E. Mendenhall, *Law and Covenant in Israel and the Ancient Near East* (Pittsburgh, 1955); *idem*, "Covenant," in *The Interpreter's Dictionary of the Bible*, 4 vols. (Nashville, 1962), I, 714–23; Delbert Hillers, *Covenant: History of a Biblical Idea* (Baltimore, 1969), esp. 25–71, 98–119; *TDOT*, s.v. "בְּרִית," by Moshe Weinfeld, II, 266–72. Dennis J. McCarthy, *Old Testament Covenant: A Survey of Current Opinions* (Atlanta, 1972), 10–34, 60–78, reviews and criticizes this literature.

13. Mather, *Apologie,* 2.

14. Cartwright, *Treatise of Christian Religion,* 165. Cartwright was a leader of Elizabethan presbyterianism, losing his Cambridge professorship on account of his views.

Gods appointment maketh a Covenant, whether the creature consent to an agreement or no. God sometimes made a Covenant, and established it, not only with *Noah* and his seed, but also with the Fowles and Beasts, and every living creature, that he would never send a flood to destroy them from off the face of the earth, *Gen.* 9.9, 10, 11. And this Covenant was onely an appointment of God, it did not require any consent or agreement of man, much lesse of other creatures, to make it a Covenant. It is therefore a manifest error, to make the agreement or consent on mans part essentiall to a Covenant between God and man.

Peter Bulkeley, the pastor of Concord, in turn thought his colleague's argument captious, complaining that Gen. 9.9 embodies an exception, "more such places I know not any in Scripture." The question "is not how a word may be used upon some speciall occasion; but what is the proper nature of a Covenant," which Cotton had demeaned since "this is not properly a Covenant, where there is not a mutuall obligation and binding of the parties one to another by condition." At Sinai, for instance, Moses twice rehearsed the terms of the Covenant before the Israelites "that they might know what it was which the Lord required of them."[15] Author of the most comprehensive treatment of covenants in early New England, Bulkeley reaffirmed the concept of an agreement with God expressed in contractual terms. At the same time, he shared Cotton's caution. If divine covenants replicate human models too closely, their establishment depends on free human consent, and if individuals can wilfully refuse the offer, God's omnipotence disappears. This far Puritans would not go, and Bulkeley spoke for all when he remarked that "though Gods binding of himselfe to us be free, yet ours is not so to God."[16]

---

15. John Cotton, *The Grovnds and Ends of the Baptisme of the Children of the Faithfull* (London, 1647), 64–65; Bulkeley, *Gospel-Covenant,* 314, 316.

16. Bulkeley, *Gospel-Covenant,* 314. The freedoms of God and Saint within their contracted relationship concerns Greven, *Protestant Temperament,* who finds that differential perceptions of the covenant shaped the experiences of moderates, but not of evangelicals. Following Perry Miller, Greven thinks that God "willingly and freely chose to relinquish His unbounded sovereignty" to establish the "unbreakable" covenant as the means of salvation. The "central paradigm" by which moderates could express "both their awe of absolute power and sovereignty and their assurance that, in practice, such absolute authority would be restrained" (235), it reveals His benevolence and love. The evangelical mentality, on the other hand, "precluded the conception of covenants—binding agreements limiting the exercise of power and authority undertaken by two legally equal parties—since there could be no equality between God and man" (100–101). There are a number of difficulties with Greven's interpretation, beginning with his misconception about how much the Covenant of Grace actually limits God's operations. The holy contract does not bind Him in the sense that it detracts from His absolute sovereignty. It is God's means for applying salvation; He abides by it, but He has freely chosen it and, significantly, He alone decides with whom He covenants. Without grace, the condition of the covenant dispensed by God, no one can enter it. Election remains arbitrary; the conditionality of the covenant motif does not detract from the Lord's freedom to save and reprobate as He wishes. (See Everett H. Emerson, "Calvin and Covenant Theology," *Church History,* 25 (1956), 136–44; John von Rohr,

Man chooses when and how to covenant with his neighbor, but God decides the time, means, and persons with whom He concludes His pacts.

Descriptions of God's covenants had to reflect doctrinal considerations as well as the language of mutual consent; had the preachers insisted on both the absolute applicability of the contractual model and God's all-sufficiency, they would have shredded the utility of the covenant idea. Instead, they took advantage of the word *testament* in certain passages of the Gospel to fashion an alternate theory of covenant that preserved God's independence and human responsibility. The Septuagint, a Greek version of the Hebrew Scriptures translated in the third century B.C.E., rendered *bᵉrîth* by *diathēkē*, which in classical Greek most commonly intends 'last will and testament,' with subsidiary definitions of 'agreement,' 'treaty,' and 'disposition.'[17] The decision to ignore *sunthēkē*, the word more readily meaning 'covenant' or 'treaty,' imparted to *diathēkē* a dual significance alien to *bᵉrîth*, one which the writer of the Epistle to the Hebrews, for whom the Septuagint was the Bible, exploited to elucidate the nature of Christ's sacrifice:

> he is the mediator of the new [*diathēkē*], that by means of death, for the redemption of the transgressions *that were* under the first [*diathēkē*], they which are called might receive the promise of eternal inheritance. For where a [*diathēkē*] *is*, there must also of necessity be the death of the

---

"Covenant and Assurance in Early English Puritanism," *ibid.,* 34 (1965), 195–203.) That so-called evangelicals lacked a conception of a conditional covenant is false; John Cotton, whom Greven classes as an evangelical (8, 9), often preached on it, and he evinces views that would seem to be "moderate." The Covenant has been established to deliver salvation: God "set it down in the court of heaven, being nothing else but an expression of the life of grace." It is enduring: "because Christ hath it in keeping, it shall never be so broken, as to the destruction of the transgressour, *Jer.* 32.40." Through it He donates love: "you may reade, *Jer.* 31.3 where the Lord telleth his people, that *hee had loved them with an everlasting love* (*Covenant of Gods free Grace*, 13–14, 14, 15). Finally, Greven's contentions raise a knotty problem of influence. How can we know if moderate personalities were swayed exclusively, or even substantially, by moderate positions on the Covenant? What does it mean if a moderate influenced an evangelical, or vice versa? Cotton stimulated the conversion of John Preston, deemed a moderate (235; for the incident, Haller, *Rise of Puritanism*, 71), and had a profound impact on the "moderate" John Winthrop, causing him to review his demeanor of twenty years (Allyn B. Forbes et al., eds., *Winthrop Papers*, 5 vols. (Boston, 1929–47), III, 344; Edmund S. Morgan, *The Puritan Dilemma: The Story of John Winthrop* (Boston, 1958), 137). There were different ways of talking about the Covenant of Grace, and Cotton's preaching of it emphasized God's absolute sovereignty more that Preston's did (which is not to say that Preston ignored or even subordinated the issue), but the structures of their theologies do not lead to such radically different casts of mind as Greven suggests. For the period under discussion, it is questionable whether one can distinguish styles of Puritan religious mentality based on distinctive modes of preaching the Covenant.

17. Weinfeld, "בְּרִית," 256; *TDNT*, s.v. "διαθήκη," by Johannes Behm, II, 124–27; James Swetman, "*Diathēkē* in the Septuagint Account of Sinai; A Suggestion," *Biblica*, 47 (1966), 439–44.

[*diathēmenou*]. For a [*diathēkē*] is of force after men are dead: otherwise it is of no strength at all while the [*diathēmenos*] liveth. Whereupon neither the first [*diathēkē*] was dedicated without blood. (Heb. 9.15-18)

Two possible interpretations resonate in this passage, each affecting, and affected by, the word chosen to fill the brackets.[18] The old *diathēkē* the writer has in mind is the agreement at Sinai (cf. v. 19), the epitome of a conditional covenant. Previously (ch. 8.8–11), he has quoted Jer. 31.31-4, where the prophet contrasts the covenant God made when He lead Israel out of Egypt with the new covenant He will write in their hearts. At the same time, the author interprets the agreement in language suggesting a testamentary disposition of the "eternal inheritance" through Christ the testator (*diathēmenos*), whose death alone puts the testament into operation. The multiple meanings of *diathēkē* challenged translators to choose between *covenant* and *testament*.[19] Bibles produced during the initial fervor of printing the Lord's Book in the King's English show a consistent trend, reading *covenant* for *bᵉrîth* in the Old Testament by the mid-sixteenth century while gradually replacing *testament* with *covenant* in the New, but even KJV, the first to favor *covenant* markedly in the New Testament, retained *testament* in Heb. 9.15ff.[20] What is called a covenant in one context is considered a testament elsewhere—most notably in the titles of the Bible's two parts.[21]

Lexicographers sundered what God's epistoler had joined. The mundane world of words defined *testament* as a 'last will' and never equated it with

---

18. The issues of translating this passage—whether *diathēkē* should be rendered *testament* in all verses, only in vv. 16–17, or if *covenant* is always preferable—are famous. James Swetman, "Suggested Interpretation of Hebrews 9:15-18," *Catholic Bible Quarterly*, 27 (1965), 373-90, urges *testament*; supporting *covenant* are G. D. Kilpatrick, "διαθήκη" in Hebrews," *Zeitschrift für die Neutestamentliche Wissenschaft*, 68 (1977) , 263-65, and John J. Hughes, "Hebrews 9:15ff and Galatians 3:15ff: A Study in Covenant Practice and Procedure," *Novum Testamentum*, 21 (1979), 27-96, which gives an extensive bibliography.

19. Petrus Martinius, מַפְתֵּחַ לְשׁוֹן הַקֹּדֶשׁ, *That is, The Key of the Holy Tongve*, trans. John Udall (Leiden, 1593), pt. II, 22, the first Hebrew-English dictionary, translates *bᵉrîth* as "covenant." Minsheu, . . . *Gvide Into Tongves*, associates it with "Bargaine," def. b, and "Testament," not "Couenant." A contemporary study of these lexical issues is John Ball, *A Treatise of the Covenant of Grace* (London, 1645), 1–3.

20. See Appendices A and B, pp. 73–74. BB has "covenant" in Heb. 9.15 only.

21. The interchangeability of the terms in the later sixteenth and early seventeenth century can be illustrated in a short table:

	Heb. 9.4	*Rev. 11.19*
GenB	ark of the testament	ark of the covenant
BB, KJV	ark of the covenant	ark of the testament

'covenant,' 'compact,' 'bargain,' or 'alliance.'[22] A testament in the law disposed of a man's goods and lands after his death, requiring an executor, witnesses, and its own unique procedure.[23] A lawyer who could not tell a *conventum* from a *testamentum* would have been declared *non compos mentis*, if not worse. A minister, however, could equate a covenant and a testament with support of high authority: "The Apostles in Greeke call it [a covenant] (*Diathekee*) a Testament, a testamentall Covenant, or disposing of things by wil at ones death."[24] Covenants, at least some of them, are testaments, yet the two forms are not identical. A testament is "*a covenant, and something more,*" said Sibbes, and he rang out the differences. Its affective character, colored by law and vernacular in the emotionally neutral tones of a bargain inspired by calculations of cooperative self-interest, takes on hues of amity and personal regard because a testament "*bequetheth good things merely of love.*" Testaments confer gifts while covenants enforce reciprocal duties: "In covenants, ofttimes it is for the mutual good one of another, but a testament is merely for their good for whom the testament is made, to whom the legacies are bequeathed."[25] Covenant as testament gave Puritans more flexibility in expositing the meaning of God's compact, His agreement with humanity which is also His disposition of an inheritance mediated by Christ the testator as a free gift to those whom He has designated. Preachers could stress its covenantal or testamental nature, its contractual or affective qualities, according to homiletic demands. In their sermons, Puritans wove a tapestry whose various threads of meaning from common speech, law, Scripture, and Reformed theology overlay one another in complex and sometimes discordant patterns.

II

The first two generations of Reformers conceived of a single divine covenant, but by the 1570s a group of theologians at Heidelberg had recognized two separate parts, ultimately called the Covenant of Works and the Covenant of

22. S.v. "Testament" in: Blount, *Glossographia;* Bullokar, *English Expositor;* Cawdrey, *Table Alphabeticall;* Cockeram, *English Dictionarie*, pt. I; Minsheu, . . . *Gvide Into Tongves;* and Phillips, *New World*, s.v. ("Testamentarious").

23. West, *Symbolaeography*, 1st Pt., II, secs. 675–82; Edward Leigh, *A Philologicall Commentary: or, an Illustration of the most Obvious and Useful words in the Law*, 2d ed., rev. and enlg. (London, 1658), s.v. "Testament."

24. Wilson, *Christian Dictionary*, s.v. "Couenant," def. 1.

25. Sibbes, *Works*, VI, 4.

Grace. Their discoveries passed quickly to the British Isles, where Perkins, Cartwright, and the Scottish professor of divinity Robert Rollock among others publicized them and dug the channels through which Puritan doctrine flowed.[26] According to this thought, God had first established the Covenant of Works with Adam "befor his faule."[27] The invention of an Adamic covenant lacked immediate confirmation from Scripture, for no biblical author knew of a covenant earlier than the one promised to Noah in Gen. 6.18. It found support, however, through identifying the Moral Law (God's precepts commanding godliness and righteousness, summarized in the Decalogue), which expresses the Covenant of Works, with the Natural Law that Paul determined was inscribed in the hearts of the Gentiles (Ro. 20.14–15). Extrapolating backwards educed the conclusion that the first man had received the Moral Law and therefore the Covenant of Works at creation; although it was not concretely recorded until Moses, "the same Law (for the substance thereof) was also written in the beginning in the heart of *Adam* and *Eue*."[28] Similar reasoning insinuated the Mosaic covenant's terms into the otherwise undocumented Adamic pact. Since the Sinai agreement "repeated" or "renewed" the original transaction, it duplicated the form and substance of the earliest compact. Like Israel at Sinai, Adam entered into a conditional covenant with God.[29]

26. William K. B. Stoever, '*A Faire and Easie Way to Heaven': Covenant Theology and Antinomianism in Early Massachusetts* (Middletown, 1978), 81–84, 215, n. 4; Leonard J. Trinterud, "The Origins of Puritanism," *Church History*, 20 (1951), 48–49; Robert Letham, "The *Foedus Operum*: Some Factors Accounting for Its Development," *Sixteenth Century Journal*, 14 (1983), 457–67. Michael McGiffert, "Grace and Works: The Rise and Division of Covenant Divinity in Elizabethan Puritanism," *Harvard Theological Review*, 75 (1982), 463–502, emphasizes the English contribution to the dual covenant theory, and corrects Trinterud in a number of ways. The first English theologian to employ the dual covenants was Dudley Fenner in 1585.

27. Thomas Cartwright, "A Short Chatechisme Mad[e] By M^r. Cartwright," in Albert Peel and Leland H. Carlson, eds., *Cartwrightiana* (London, 1951), 159.

28. Cartwright, *Treatise of Christian Religion,* ch. 14, 74. Wilson, *Christian Dictionary*, s.v. "Law," defs. 2–9, indicates the scope of the term as Puritans used it: 'the Decalogue [the Moral Law], sometimes including God's ceremonial and judicial precepts,' 'the doctrine of salvation in Christ,' 'some [usually the Pentateuch] or all of the books of the Old Testament,' 'keeping the Law exactly,' 'natural instinct [the Law of Nature],' 'legal ceremonies,' the second Table of the Law [i.e. the fifth through tenth Commandments],' and the 'ordinance of Aaron.' In general, it encompasses the "spirituall sence and meaning of the Olde Testament." Finally, the "Law" coequals the Covenant of Works, cf. Cartwright, "Short Chatechisme," 159, and Thomas Shepard, *A Short Catechism Familiarly Teaching the Knowledge of God, and of our Selves* (Cambridge, Mass., 1654) , 15. What a preacher intended is usually clear from the context.

29. Parallels to Cartwright are Robert Rollock, *Select Works of Robert Rollock*, ed. William M. Gunn, 2 vols. (Edinburgh, 1844–49), I, 33–36; [Henry Finch], *The Sacred Doctrine of Divinitie, Gathered ovt of the worde of God* ([Middleburg], 1599 [1590]), 30–32, esp. 30, note a.; [*idem*], *The Summe of Sacred Diuinitie . . .* , published by John Downame (London, [by

The Covenant of Works offers engagingly simple terms coupled with a staggering requirement: God will grant eternal life, if one obeys the Law without a single sin. Total compliance rewards the person with "full blessednesse and perfection of his nature," continuing growth "in all Holinesse, Happinesse, immortalitie." Failure, and the sinner dooms oneself to "the whole curse of the Law," physical death and spiritual subjugation to Satan.[30] Adam must execute the Ten Commandments: love God with heart, soul, and strength, and love one's neighbor as oneself. The Law engages the whole man, prescribing correct performance of all outward religious tasks while charging every faculty to work flawlessly—the understanding to know every duty, the judgment to discern between good and evil, memory to retain these discriminations, will to choose good over evil, affections to love and hate appropriately.[31] These conditions, though onerous, are predicated on the actual circumstances of creation, for a just deity could not possibly have demanded perfect obedience without having made Adam "pure and holy," fully capable of complying.[32] The Covenant of Works presumes humanity's ability to carry it out, a prerequisite obligated by God's rectitude and satisfied by Adam's pristine integrity. In this sense it mimics the Common Law, which required that a contract's conditions "bee possible in deed and in Law, otherwise the agreement is void."[33] Constituted through the human constitu-

---

1621]), 223. Finch was a lawyer with presbyterian sympathies who became Sergeant-at-Arms to James I and was briefly imprisoned in 1621 for writing *The Worldes Great Restauration*, a work that predicted a restored Jewish state that would rule the rest of the world—including England. See Wilfred R. Prest, "The Art of Law and the Law of God, Sir Henry Finch (1558–1625)," in Donald Pennington and Keith Thomas, eds., *Puritans and Revolutionaries: Essays in Seventeenth-Century History presented to Christopher Hill* (Oxford, 1978), 94–117, which identifies Finch as the author of *Sacred Doctrine* and *The Summe*, sometimes ascribed to other writers; and Michael McGiffert, "Who Wrote the Preface and Notes for Finch's *The Sacred Doctrine of Divinity*, 1590?" (unpublished paper), which assigns *Sacred Doctrine*'s marginalia (including the precocious treatment of the dual covenants) to the Kentish minister Josiah Nichols, and credits Downame with writing much of *The Summe*. Perkins, *Works*, I, 32, links the Covenant of Works to the Moral Law, but since his treatment of the Covenant occurs after he discusses the Fall, Jens G. Møller, "The Beginnings of Puritan Covenant Theology," *Journal of Ecclesiastical History*, 14 (1963), 60–61, denies Perkins knows of an Adamic covenant. However, Perkins does say at one point, *Works*, II, 299, that the Covenant of Works was "in nature at creation." On the establishment of the Covenant of Works with Adam and its renewal at Sinai: Sibbes, *Works*, VI, 3; Hooker, *Paterne of Perfection*, 211; Preston, *New Covenant*, 317; Bulkeley, *Gospel-Covenant*, 61–62.

30. Finch, *Summe of Sacred Diuinitie*, 225–26.

31. Thomas Cartwright, "A Methodical Short Catechism," in John Dod and Robert Cleaver, *A Plain and Familiar Exposition of the Ten Commandments* (London, 1609), separate pagination, Bb[ro]; Cartwright, *Treatise of Christian Religion*, ch. 14, 74–75; see Perkins, *Works*, I, 32, 49; Ball, *Treatise of the Covenant*, 10–11.

32. Rollock, *Select Works*, I, 34.

33. West, *Symbolaeography*, 1st Pt., I, 7B.

tion, the Covenant of Works asked no more of Adam than he could in all fairness undertake.

Restating the theory of humanity's original completeness with a corollary that connects human power and activity to salvation moved Puritans beyond the immediate purview of Genesis, which does not explicitly correlate Adam's composition with his actions in Eden. The Yahwist[34] saw no need to locate Adam's capacity to obey in some supposed perfection. Puritans found substantiation of their position in two of Paul's remarks on the inadequacies of the Law. In Gal. 3.12 and Ro. 10.5, Paul appeals to Lev. 18.5 ("Ye shall therefore keep my statutes, and my judgments: which if a man do, he shall live in them") to argue that anyone seeking righteousness through the Law must perform the Law perfectly. Taken in context, he contends for the superiority of faith above the Law and the insufficiency of the Law to save—justification issues from faith, not works, and the Law cannot overcome the power of sin. The Apostle would never concede the possibility of salvation without faith in Christ, and he did not speculate on Adam's prelapsarian character, but Puritans could conceive the case, rapidly made hypothetical, in which a person endowed with superior powers inhabiting a world where sin does not challenge the Law could achieve salvation without Christ. Detecting in Paul's Epistles the provisions of the Covenant of Works, preachers fashioned them into the conditions by which Adam in innocence could merit eternal life and identified the human capacity for gracious action as an issue of special concern at the very outset of history.[35] Because the perfection that enabled Adam to earn eternal life depended on his continued obedience to the Law, anything that diminished his capability to carry out his task endangered his salvation.

A motivational logic to compel Adam's perpetual performance inheres in the covenantal stipulations. If he obeys, he merits a blessing; prospect of future gain encourages suitable behavior. Adam's success depends on how effectively he can sustain his labors, for he can expect no clemency from God should he fail. The Covenant of Works institutes a contractual arrangement similar to a business deal or an agreement to pay off the hired help: the Lord

34. Most biblical scholars subscribe to some form of the "Documentary Hypothesis" that identifies four major sources of Pentateuchal material. The Yahwist (J) is considered a Judean writer of the 9th or 10th century B.C.E.; he consistently employs "Yahweh" for the divine name.

35. Proofs varied: Lev. 18.5, Gal. 3.12—Cotton, *way of Life,* 228; Lev. 18.5, Gal. 3.12, Ro. 10.5—Hooker, *Paterne of Perfection,* 208; Lev. 18.5—Cartwright, "Methodical Short Catechism," Bb[ro]; Gal. 3.12—Bulkeley, *Gospel-Covenant,* 57; Ro. 10.5, Gal. 3.10 (the inverse of v. 12—"Cursed *is* every one that continueth not in all things which are written in the book of the law to do them")—Finch, *Summe of Sacred Diuinitie,* 223, 225; Gal. 3.10—Sibbes, *Works,* VI, 3. Texts were not always cited: Shepard, *Works,* I, 348; Cotton, *Covenant of Gods free Grace,* 12.

will "reward" Adam when he finishes his chores, "for *to him that worketh wages is due of debt*, Rom. 4.4"[36] Having grounded the covenant on equitable principles, God manifests no especial concern for His creature outside the letter of the Law, which "propounds the bare iustice of God, without mercie."[37] Beyond the initial amicability with which the participants entered the pact—"God made this covenant with man, as one friend doth with another," Rollock said—the Lord shows Adam little emotional support.[38] He may be Adam's friend, but the man cannot plead for His mercy or appeal to His love to mitigate the curse if he breaks the covenant. Governing with lawyer-like exactitude, God grants no favors except those explicitly contracted for:

> *Adam* being under a covenant of workes, he finds acceptance with God no longer than his worke is found perfect before him. All his personal indowments, excellent gifts, and the image of God which was stamped upon him, by which he was but little inferiour to the Angels, all these could procure him no favour or acceptance any longer then his worke was right; because hee was under the Covenant of Workes, his person is accepted according to his worke.[39]

The Covenant of Works takes its nature from the 'contractual' significance of the word *covenant*. God countenances Adam for what he does, not for who he is.

What Adam himself thought about his ability to fulfill the covenantal conditions went forever unrecorded, but the preachers inferred that he had felt confident about his abilities, a trait that passed to his descendants: "Adam and his posterity were to be saved by his doing: 'Do this and live;' work, and here is thy wages; win life, and wear it. Hence all his posterity seeks to this day to be saved by doing; like father, like son." Shepard's brief essay into convenantal social psychology predicts that people facing the same conditions will react in identical fashion. Anyone encouraged to work for salvation will do so, and it should surprise nobody, he implies, that they persist despite Adam's conspicuous (and hasty) failure. Men display the same self-reliance in everyday affairs—a bankrupt peddler prefers to "follow his old trade with a less stock" than to learn a new one or live upon another's help—and this quality carries over to the spiritual life. Humanity's ingrained disposition accounts for this tendency, since even "innocent, much less corrupted nature," makes people refuse to give up their own works; attitudes imprinted into the human system convince them that they can successfully meet the

36. Hooker, *Application*, I–VIII, 96.
37. Perkins, *Works*, II, 299.
38. Rollock, *Select Works*, I, 35, "note" in margin.
39. Bulkeley, *Gospel-Covenant*, 78–79.

conditions.[40] We know from our own experience, Rollock observed, that we try to will the good, "Hence it comes that even to this day all the world, following nature, seeks to be justified by good works." Yet these instincts betray us, a point Cartwright made with catechistic bluntness. "Q. Is any man habull to keepe the lawe? A. No not in ye least poynt." Behind this terrible reply lie the effects of the Fall. As described by Hooker, Adam's nature gave him strength to keep the Covenant, "and if he had done that which hee had power to doe, hee might have been blessed for ever, and we all in him," but now that the Fall has enervated everyone, "the sinner is neither able to fulfill the Law, and so to purchase mercy for himselfe; nor to satisfie for that which is done amisse."[41] The Covenant of Works postulated a human creature strong enough to carry it out, but sin vitiated the Image of God and rendered man incapable of complying.

To dramatize the human predicament, God renewed the Covenant of Works at Sinai. Though the consequences of Adam's failure loom over human affairs, people disregard, or more charitably, fail to recollect their plight:

> You might remember that *Adam*, when he was in innocency and perfec-
> tion, was much stronger than you, yet did not keepe the Law; but, because
> that was easie for people to forget, the Law was given againe by Moses
> upon Mount *Sinai*, that the *Lord* by that meanes might re-minde you of
> the Commandement, and of your sinnes, and of the curse belonging to
> you. . . . [42]

At Sinai, God restated the conditions of the old agreement in drastically altered circumstances. He had made the pact in the secrecy of Adam's righteous heart, but, parlaying at the holy mountain with sinners, He orchestrated a display of divine pyrotechnics so devastating that "we are not able to see these fires, these burnings, we are not able to see this and live."[43] Weak-kneed and trembling, the Israelites desired an intercessor, Moses, for they could not face the Lord directly. In Puritan theology Moses at Sinai prefigured the role of Christ as the mediator of the Covenant of Grace, while, as

---

40. Shepard, *Works*, I, 99–100.

41. Rollock, *Select Works*, I, 261; Cartwright, "Short Chatechisme," 159–60; Thomas Hooker, *The Sovles Hvmiliation* (London, 1637), 129.

42. Preston, *New Covenant*, 385. The idea that the Covenant of Works had been renewed at Sinai, although the Decalogue had there been publicly revealed for the first time, reinforced the association of the Moral Law with the Natural Law. It also protected the temporal primacy of the Covenant of Works against an argument from Gal. 3.17 that the Law was "four hundred and thirty years" after the Abrahamic covenant, hence subsequent in time to the Covenant of Grace. Publishing the Law at Sinai did not reestablish the Covenant of Works, and therefore did not abrogate the Abrahamic Covenant of Grace. However, Gal. 3.17 was not held to discredit the original donation of the Covenant of Works to Adam.

43. Preston, *New Covenant*, 385, and see Cartwright, *Treatise of Christian Religion*, ch. 13, 82.

giver of the Law, he also signified "the hardnesse and disability of mans heart to performe the Law."[44] God originally established the Covenant of Works as a means to grant eternal life, but at Sinai He reveals the Law to be a "ministration of death" in Paul's words (2 Cor. 3.7), at least as far as reprobates are concerned.[45] They cannot plead ignorance of their obligations, for the Law allows "no cloak for their sin," and it hardens their hearts against Christ.[46] Paul also designated the Law a "schoolmaster *to bring us* unto Christ" (Gal. 3.24), and it educates the Elect before faith to their fallen estate, making one "sensible for his own inability to redeem himself, and unworthiness to be redeemed from the wrath of God," fit to hear "glad tidings." Destroying specious self-confidence, the Law prepares people to hear the Gospel, otherwise "contemned."[47]

The Covenant of Works describes more than the manner in which God administers the world or executes His decree.[48] A datum of the real world, it is at one level humanity's ontological condition, and on another a state of mind. Since Adam, mankind under the Covenant of Works lives in the flesh unable to reach God by satisfying its obligations, yet individuals believe that they must do good works to gain eternal life and complacently suppose that they still can. The Covenant's stipulations rate unceasing effort highly, encouraging the now erroneous assumption that persistent work suffices to earn a fit reward. Published externally in the Covenant, this outlook was internalized by Adam when God wrote the Law on his heart and has since passed to all humans through the inheritance of acquired attitudinal characteristics. Humanity's psychological set, at creation perfectly congruent with its power to act in the Covenant, now blinds it to the Covenant's failure to serve its needs. In a secular world, imprecise perception of one's situation goes by many names. No social scientists, Puritans called it sin.

Preachers had to alert the unregenerate to this state of affairs, and their rhetorical strategy for doing so took shape from divine example. By bruiting the Law at Sinai, God demanded of humanity the impossible. The conditions tendered to Adam remain—mankind must obey God's codes flawlessly—but nobody can do this. An individual must please the Lord, for the fate of his or her immortal soul is at stake, but no one can properly respond. Because the

44. Wilson, *Christian Dictionary*, s.v. "Moses," def. 3.

45. See Preston, *New Covenant*, 319, and Finch, *Sacred Doctrine*, 30–31, note a.

46. John Cotton, *A Treatise of the Covenant of Grace*, 3d ed., corr. (London, 1671), 70.

47. Cotton, *Treatise of the Covenant*, 69; John Preston, *A Liveles Life*, last ed. (London, 1633), 35.

48. The Covenant of Works fell under assorted theological headings: God's special government, a branch of His efficiency working through Providence, Ames, *Marrow*, I.vi.1; ix.1; xi.1, 9; the execution of God's decree, Perkins, *Works*, I, 31–32; effectual calling, Rollock, *Select Works*, I, 33; the kinds of righteousness, Finch, *Sacred Doctrine*, 30.

Fall has rendered them incapable of unsullied righteousness, humans are damned whether or not they try to obey. They can hardly elect to change their circumstances; none escape from the Covenant and its curse even if they flee "as a Bondslave runnes from his Master, as farre as it is in his power."[49] The contradictions of living under the Covenant of Works after the Fall thread throughout Puritan discussions, the strands loosely coiled until a preacher knotted them together: "Though now in the estate of corruption, no man attains life by the covenant of workes, yet this so comes to passe, *not because the covenant is changed, but* because *we are changed*, and cannot fulfill the condition, to which the promise is made."[50] This theological noose replicates a kind of communication pattern known as the double-bind. A double-bind message contains two or more levels of contradictory meanings that are not explicitly differentiated in a situation where the receiver cannot ask which reply is appropriate and must somehow respond to both. When the receiver strongly desires to respond because the sender is an influential person in one's life, and when the option to not reply does not exist, double-bind theory predicts a rising level of anxiety on the part of the respondant.[51] Unveiling the Covenant of Works exposed congregations to conflicting signals ("I command you to obey and I know that you cannot") from God, the ultimate "significant other." The preachers fully expected the covenant to agitate their hearers, inducing affections of fear, enmity, and fright.[52]

Repeated double-bind communications can elicit neurotic and psychotic behavior. Puritans did not become schizophrenic, although their detractors sometimes depicted them as melancholic madmen, the seventeenth-century equivalent.[53] A counselor may confront a patient with a "therapeutic double-bind" to force new responses in the interests of health;[54] similarly, the

49. Preston, *New Covenant*, 319.

50. Bulkeley, *Gospel-Covenant*, 56.

51. The pioneer statement of the double-bind is Gregory Bateson et al., "Toward a Theory of Schizophrenia," *Behavioral Science*, 1 (1956), 251–64. The theory was initially conceived to redefine schizophrenia as a strategy of coping with contradictory stimuli, and to locate its etiology in certain family settings. (This paper is reprinted in Bateson, *Steps to an Ecology of Mind* (New York, 1972), 201–27. See also Bateson's later papers, *ibid.*, 229–78. A very critical review is A. S. Schuham, "Double Bind Hypothesis a Decade Later," *Psychological Bulletin*, 68 (1967), 409–16. Some experimental evidence suggests that the double-bind does induce anxiety, anger, and confusion in "normals": E. K. Smith, "The Effect of Double-Bind Communication on Anxiety Level of Normals," *Journal of Abnormal Psychology*, 85 (1976), 356–63; Bob Helm et al., "Experiencing Double-Bind Conflict: A Semantic Differential-Assessment of Interaction Perceptions," *Journal of Research in Personality*, 10 (1976), 166–76.

52. Preston, *New Covenant*, 318; Cartwright, *Treatise of Christian Religion*, ch. 13, 82; Shepard, *Works*, II, 52; Finch, *Sacred Doctrine*, 30, note a.

53. John F. Sena, "Melancholic Madness and the Puritans," *Harvard Theological Review*, 66 (1973), 293–309.

54. Bateson, *Steps*, 226.

preachers evoked the terrors of the Law to direct their listeners towards salvation. Mercifully, God offers to the fallen another covenant, founded on a different appreciation of human ability, but those who trust to themselves do not enter into it. Of necessity, then, "the covenant of works is taught to shew us our failing, that seeing our own disability to perform what the law requireth, we may be forced to the new covenant of grace."[55] Release from the old agreement occurs in accepting the facts that unaided efforts to obey the Lord's statutes simply draw sin's binding tighter, and that God frames the new relationship with different conditions. This insight does not come gently, for the Law as a schoolmaster wields a heavy rod. Giving up self-confidence involves denying the postulates inherent in soul and body, one's innate inclination to satisfy the Natural Law. To approach the Covenant of Grace, "a man must be quite stript of selfe-worthinesse, and of all those wretched principles of nature, whereby he would live of himself," in short he must "despaire of himselfe, hee must see himselfe utterly lost and undone."[56] Contrary to what the Covenant of Works posits, a sense of helplessness leads to grace.

III

All men and women deserve damnation; yet not all are damned. God glorifies His mercy by saving the Elect. To do this, He must offer a new covenant, for mankind since the Fall lies disabled by sin and cursed by the Law, unable to save itself through the Covenant of Works. First, however, someone must reconcile the two sides, friends until sin made "a breach between God and man, then strangenesse and enmitie followed, God is estranged from us, and we are enemies unto God, so that without a Mediator, wee can never come to be united into Covenant againe."[57] Jesus Christ, in whom divine and human nature unite, undertook the task "to make intercession and peace between God offended, and man offending." Christ obeyed the Law unfailingly, thereby fulfilling the condition of the Covenant of Works, but he had to die in any case for "no good works of our own, or of any mediator for us," could change the fact that humanity deserves chastisement for breaking the agreement. God's justice "required the punishment and death of the offender, or

---

55. Sibbes, *Works*, VI, 5.

56. Thomas Hooker, *The Sinners Salvation* (London, 1638), 21, 20. For attribution of this work to Hooker, Sargent Bush, Jr., "Four New Works by Thomas Hooker: Identity and Significance," *Resources for American Literary Study*, 4 (1974), 5, 23–25. Cf. Perkins, *Works*, I, 70.

57. Bulkeley, *Gospel-Covenant*, 62.

certainly of some mediator in his stead."[58] By successfully performing the Law and by sacrificing himself under the curse, Christ wholly discharged the Covenant of Works, and because he did so for the Elect's sake, Christ redeems them from the Law and its penalty. His death satisfied God's justice, and his righteousness merits "a new grace and mercy of God for us."[59] As mediator, Christ established the foundation on which God raised the Covenant of Grace.[60]

Conceived before time, the Covenant of Grace entered history prior to the Incarnation. Puritans thought that the Christ-event had bisected the pact into the old covenant, "which in types and shadowes prefigured Christ to come, and to be exhibited," and the new one declaring him "already come in the flesh, and is apparently shewed in the Gospel."[61] Typological analysis such as Perkins employed in this passage related persons and events in the Hebrew Scriptures, the "types" or "figures," to their Gospel analogues, known as "antitypes." In such manner Preston proved that the Jews had expressed the Covenant of Grace through ceremonial sacrifices, ablutions, and incense offerings, types that signified Christ's death, sanctification by the Spirit, and the "sweete" works of the Saints.[62] God extended the Covenant to a number of Israelite worthies, although they had understood its significance darkly and had glimpsed Christ only through a veil. Successive revelations defined the old covenant more clearly, until the new one, which surpassed it in strength, clarity, extent, and intelligibility, superseded it. Nevertheless, Israelites under the former compact enjoyed the same salvation in Christ; the two dispensations "both agree in substance, they differ onely in the manner of the ministration."[63]

Searching for the origins of the Covenant of Grace, Puritans once again discovered an agreement ancillary to any covenant the Bible mentions, a pact effected with Adam immediately after the Fall. Their reasoning made use of

---

58. Rollock, *Select Works*, I, 52, 53.

59. *Ibid.*, 53–55, 38; Norton, *Orthodox Evangelist*, 303–5. Rollock maintains that only Christ's passive obedience—his death—satisfied God's justice; Christ's active obedience—his works—caused his passion to be satisfactory and meritorious. Norton held that justification is by both Christ's passive and active obedience.

60. Perkins, *Works*, I, 165; Ames, *Marrow*, I.xxiv.17; Ball, *Treatise of the Covenant*, 265.

61. Perkins, *Works*, I, 70. The old/new covenant dichotomy usually referred to the two dispensations of the Covenant of Grace, although it sometimes intended the Covenants of Works and Grace, as in Ames, *Marrow*, I.xxiv.13–22.

62. Preston, *New Covenant*, 326.

63. *Ibid.* All Puritans asserted the Covenant of Grace extended into the Old Testament. On the periodization from Adam to Abraham to Moses to Christ: Sibbes, *Works*, VI, 4; Ames, *Marrow*, I.xxxviii-ix; Bulkeley, *Gospel-Covenant*, 112–81; Ball, *Treatise of the Covenant*, 36 and *passim*.

an exegetical tradition, pioneered by Irenaeus in the second century, that took Gen. 3.15—"And I will put enmity between thee (the serpent) and the woman, and between thy seed and her seed; it shall bruise thy head, and thou shalt bruise his heel"—as the *Protoevangelium*, the beginning of the Gospel.[64] Mary is considered "the woman," and Christ is "her seed."[65] If one accepts this construction, and, beginning with some of the early fathers, many theologians have not, the sense of the passage seems to predict unceasing enmity between the rival seeds and challenges orthodox Christian belief that Christ will triumph over the serpent, Satan. Davenport, for one, countered this unacceptable conclusion by remarking on an important anatomical distinction:

> His (Christ's) heels or footsteps, not his head, was [*sic*] pierced when he was *crucified, through infirmity, and put to death concerning the flesh, but was quickened by the spirit, and liveth through the power of God*, 2 *Cor.* 13.4, 1 *Pet.* 3.18. But he pierced the serpents head, when *through death, he destroyed him that had the power of death*, the *devill*, Heb. 2. 14. being the *Sonne of God manifested for this purpose, that hee might destroy the workes of the devill*, 1 Joh. 3.8. [66]

Christ triumphs by devastating Satan's head, the body's noblest part according to the faculty–humor psychology, while himself suffering wounds only to lesser members. Most preachers did not bother to fix a proof, simply transmitting the interpretation both their Catholic and Protestant contemporaries favored.

The theory of the *Protoevangelium* emerges from the actual wording of Gen. 3.15—Christ is the "seed of the woman"—while a specifically covenantal interpretation necessitated a more drastic reading. Covenants as Puritans understood them require the parties to exchange mutual stipulations and pledges, whereas in Gen. 3.15 God speaks to the serpent (see v. 14) and not to Adam, his ostensible partner in the pact. To avoid what amounts to a

---

64. Vawter, *On Genesis*, 83–84; see Sibbes, *Works*, VII, 197, #120; Preston, *Liveles Life*, 39; Cartwright, *Treatise of Christian Religion*, 170.

65. A corruption of the Vulgate lead to a dispute between Catholics and Protestants over the mariological significance of Gen. 3.15. Vulgate reads *ipsa conteret*, translated by Douai "she shal bruise," which according to Catholics meant that Mary gains the victory over Satan. *Ipsa* is not supported by either the Hebrew or Greek manuscripts, and Protestant Latin translations give *Ipsum*; the error probably did not originate with Jerome (Vawter, *On Genesis*, 83; E. F. Sutcliffe, "Jerome," in G. W. H. Lampe, ed., *The Cambridge History of the Bible*, II: *The West from the Fathers to the Reformation* (Cambridge, 1969), 98–99). Other English Bibles read "that seed" (Tyn., Tav.), "the same" (Cov., GB), "he" (GenB), "it" (BB, KJV). The mistake became a weapon in the Protestant arsenal against "papist" perfidy, but though Puritans challeged popery at the drop of a mitre, they remained strangely quiet on this subject when explicating the Covenant of Grace, usually sticking to the business at hand.

66. Davenport, *Knowledge of Christ*, 34.

covenant by eavesdropping, Puritans either treated the event briefly—the covenant was "reuealed and deliuered" to our first parents, propagated by "lively voice," "given to *Adam* in Paradise" in some undescribed manner[67]— or fantasized that God in fact did speak directly to Adam and Eve:

> It is true, saith hee, the Serpent is your enemie and hath overcome you: But, saith he, you shall not be slaves to him, and captivated to him for ever; But you shall resist him, and be enemies to him, *I will put enmitie* betweene the Serpent and the Woman, and you shall fight together, there shall be a warre, the Serpent shall afflict you, and hurt you something, but thou shalt overcome him, and bruise his head, thou shalt be the death of him, thou shalt have the victorie over him.[68]

Preston rewrites Scripture so that God addresses Adam and Eve, the "you" whom the enemy has "captivated" and who will resist him. The phrase "I will put enmity," directed at the serpent in Genesis, now prefaces God's forecast of humanity's final triumph over evil, "thou shalt be the death of him." The passage progresses further with the preacher recasting God's monologue into a conversation as Eve bemoans "Alas, I am weake," prompting the Lord to mention the seed which, contrary to what Preston has just said about humanity's own prowess, shall "overcome him for thee."[69] What the Yahwist intended as a proclamation of the serpent's punishment for having deceived Adam and Eve turns into a dialogue establishing the Covenant of Grace.

Puritans accounted for the absence of either a covenantal pledge or the word *covenant* in Gen. 3.15 by denoting God's prediction of humanity's victory a 'promise,' meaning "The word of God, giuen or plighted vnto men, for the performance of some good, or for remouing some euill, spiritual or bodily." God makes many promises, Wilson explained, but "Gods Promise"—the upper case *P* is significant despite the notorious vagaries of seventeenth-century capitalization—is twofold:

> first Legall, when hee passeth his word for the giuing of eternal life, and other temporall good things, vpon condition of fulfilling the Law. Leuit. 18, 5. Eph. 6,1. *This is the first commandement with Promise.* Galat. 3, 12. *Do this and liue.* Secondly, Euangelicall; when he passeth his word for the giuing of Christ, and together with him, remission of sinnes, righteousnesse, and eternall life, as also the blessings of this life, vpon condition of beleeuing the Gospell.[70]

---

67. Perkins, *Works*, I, 164; Ball, *Treatise of the Covenant*, 23; Mather, *Apologie*, 26.

68. Preston, *New Covenant*, 352; see Sibbes, *Works*, VI, 4; Bulkeley, *Gospel-Covenant*, 113.

69. Preston, *New Covenant*, 352-53.

70. Wilson, *Christian Dictionary*, s.v. "Promise," def. 3, note following def. 4. The citation to Eph. 6.1 should be to v. 2. See also s.v. "Couenant," def. 2.

Wilson does not call these particular promises covenants, but they parallel Perkins's description of the Covenants of Work and Grace as "legall" and "euangelicall."[71] Moreover, they adhere to the conditional form of the covenants, convey the same benefits, and the proof texts Lev. 18.5 and Gal. 3.12 identify the legal promise as the Covenant of Works. Sibbes voiced the equivalence and its historical significance: in the time span from Adam to Abraham, "the covenant of grace was called a promise of the blessed seed."[72] Like its companion, it comes to the present from humanity's earliest experience.[73]

The Covenant of Grace phrases the Gospel message as the terms of an agreement whereby God holds out eternal life to all who have faith in Christ, "believe and live" in homiletic shorthand.[74] God answers faith by granting righteousness because "after the breach of the covenant of works, that one first original justice, as they call it, was quite lost"; and without this grace, imputed from Christ the mediator, "we can not possibly stand before the tribunal of God." Saints next receive eternal life, "begun" on earth, "per-

---

71. Perkins, *Works*, II, 392–93.

72. Sibbes, *Works*, VI, 4. Ames, *Marrow*, I.xxiv.11; Preston, *New Covenant*, 353; Bulkeley, *Gospel-Covenant*, 118; Cartwright, *Treatise of Christian Religion*, 81; John Cotton, *Gospel Conversion* (London, 1646), 29–30.

73. Locating the Covenant of Grace in Eden did not carry the same implications as did grounding the Covenant of Works in Adam. The first covenant fit into the scheme of human perfection and subsequent deterioration; it could only have existed from creation. Logically, the Covenant of Grace could have been given at any time to any fallen person; initiating it with Abraham, while perhaps causing exegetes to wonder at the fates of righteous men like Enoch and Noah who lived before its announcement, did not alter its character. Cotton could dispense with an Adamic origin, *Covenant of Gods free Grace*, 12, though elsewhere he says God published it to Adam and Eve, *Treatise of the Covenant*, 211. On the other hand, announcing the Covenant of Grace in Eden granted a certain symmetry to God's actions which helped prove, according to Bulkeley, that God had made a covenant with man as well as with Christ. Furthermore, the promise in the *Protoevangelium* paralleled the one made to Abraham, helping to establish that Christ mediated the old dispensation as well as the new, *Gospel-Covenant*, 35–36, 118. Perkins, echoing Calvin (*Commentaries on the First Book of Moses called Genesis*, trans. Rev. John King, 2 vols. (Edinburgh, 1847–50) I, 170–71), took "seed of the woman" as a collective noun, "Christ with all the elect whome the Father hath giuen vnto him, who shall bruise the Serpents head, & *tread Satan vnder their feet* Rom. 16.20," and, culling from Genesis twin genealogies of the saved and the damned seed, dashed the idea that the Covenant of Grace includes everyone, *Works*, I, 164. Perkins forced the proof—every contemporary English Bible reads "your" instead of "their" in Ro. 16.20—and later preachers took "seed" in the singular, but a good Puritan could always find a text to support the doctrine of particular election and supply others without disparaging the Adamic covenant's reality. See Ames, *Marrow*, I.xxxviii.14; Bulkeley, *Gospel-Covenant*, 118; Preston, *New Covenant*, 352–55. Ball, *Treatise of the Covenant*, 38–39, agrees with Perkins.

74. Examples of proof texts: Rev. 2.10 (cited v. 20)—Perkins, *Works*, II, 393; Acts 16.30–31, John 3.16–18—Cartwright, *Treatise of Christian Religion*, 167; John 3.15–16, 5.24, 11.25–26—Hooker, *Faithful Covenanter*, 10; John 3.16, Ro. 3.22, 1.17—Shepard, *Short Catechism*, 16.

fected" in heaven. Incapable of perfect rectitude themselves, they enter the Covenant of Grace "vnder the condition of faith, that is to say, If we beleeue in Christ, who hath done it for vs."[75] The Covenant of Grace places a condition on the believer's obtaining his or her reward which functions differently than that of the Covenant of Works. Inclusion in the first covenant comes by birth, the lot of being human; the condition determines if one receives eternal life. The condition of the second compact regulates entrance into the agreement itself; Adam's sin descends to all, but his reconciliation with God does not. At creation Adam received grace "for himselfe and his posterity," in the Fall he transgressed "not only for himselfe, but for all his posterity," yet it "cannot be prooved" that he received the Covenant of Grace "for himselfe and for all mankinde."[76] Those without faith live permanently under the Covenant of Works; only the Elect enter the Covenant of Grace, publicized to all but established with few.

Characterizing faith as a condition disguised the fact that the Covenant of Grace does not conform to the same mold as does its predecessor, in which, although God makes the agreement possible by creating Adam perfect, no benefits accrue until he performs. A covenant is not merely a covenant when, like the Covenant of Grace, "it hath partly the nature & properties of a testament or will. For it is confirmed by the death of the testatour."[77] Both Common Law and the Bible, notably the frequently cited passage in Heb. 9, contended that only the testator's death activates the provisions of a testament, hence the "Covenant or Testament" God in Christ made with His people "is of no force, till the Testator be dead, *Heb.* 9.15, 19."[78] The

---

75. Rollock, *Select Works*, I, 39; Finch, *Summe of Sacred Diuinitie*, 307. Concerned that calling faith a condition might imply that man can achieve it through his own efforts, later Puritans clarified the term. Norton, *Orthodox Evangelist*, 227–28, distinguished between a proper condition, which goes before its consequence, and an improper condition, "whose performance by the Covenantee, is absolutely undertaken for; and irresistibly wrought by the Covenantor, and not left in suspense upon the Covenantee, to be performed by his own strength. Faith is a consequent condition, not an antecedent condition." See also Ames, *Marrow*, I.xxiv.19; Ezekiel Culverwell, *A Treatise of Faith*, 2d ed., corr. and amend. (London, 1623), 147; Cotton, *Treatise of the Covenant*, 37–38. The discussion really concerns the meaning of a condition; Puritans concurred that God bestows faith freely without regard to man's merit, and that one must have faith to enter the Covenant of Grace.

76. Perkins, *Works*, I, 165.

77. Perkins, *Works*, I, 70. The Covenant of Works could be called a testament on the basis of Gal. 4.22ff, which Puritans took to refer to the two covenants: Perkins, *Works*, II, 299 (a commentary on Gal. 4.24); Wilson, *Christian Dictionary*, s.v. "Testament"; Bulkeley, *Gospel-Covenant*, 54, 71. KJV was the first English translation to substitute "covenants" in these verses. However, Puritans ignored the implication, designating only the Covenant of Grace as a testament.

78. West, *Symbolaeography*, 1st Pt., II, 675D; Cotton, *way of Life*, 454. Other citations of Heb. 9 occur in Ames, *Marrow*, I.xxiv.12 (v. 16); Finch, *Summe of Sacred Diuinitie*, 309 (vv. 15–17); Bulkeley, *Gospel-Covenant*, 317 (vv. 16–17); Preston, *New Covenant*, 368 (cites Heb. 9, paraphrases v. 16).

Covenant of Works operates by virtue of humanity's existence; the Covenant of Grace takes effect through a mediator. The testamentary nature of the latter accord changes the dispensation of God's blessing. A last will and testament "is not for the testators, but for the heires commodity," Perkins pointed out, so in the Covenant of Grace "we doe not so much offer, or promise any great matter to God, as in a manner onely receiue."[79] Where the Covenant of Works only rewards effort, the Covenant of Grace bequeaths "*a Legacy*," and "Inheritance" that believers obtain freely from the testament's terms. These benefits include salvation and, in direct contradistinction to the Covenant of Works, the condition of the covenant itself. The Lord requires human beings to believe, "but here is the privilege, that the Lord as he makes the condition with the soule, so also he keepeth us in performing the condition"; God demands faith and bestows it too. The Lord gives faith before faith can be there, Cotton said, "it is the fruit of the spirit that Faith is wrought in the soul.[80] People do not earn salvation by deeds; they receive it, and the means to it, as a gift.

While reprobates languish under one covenant, the regenerate participate in another that releases them from having to attain salvation via their own efforts. Positing contradictory means to achieve identical ends, the two covenants exclude each other: "The same Soule that is saved by the Covenant of Grace, cannot be saved also by the Covenant of Works."[81] Nevertheless, the donation of faith by divine legacy in no way obviates the task of believers to perform good works. Adam broke the first agreement but God never annulled His injunction to keep the law. Under the second covenant, the godly escape deserved reprobation for transgressing the law, while continuing in their obligation to obey it: we die "to the *covenant* of the law," Cotton held, "though not to the cōmand of it," freed from the curse but not the condition. Superseded by faith, the law in Rollock's words becomes "the rule of the works of grace."[82] Enjoined to fulfill the commandments, Saints at the same time enjoy the security that, unlike Adam, they need not perform them perfectly to ensure eternal life. When, inevitably, they sin against the covenant, Christ makes good the break; the "*Surety*" who answers for the Saints' defaults, he stands between them and the worst consequences of their sins.[83] Christ's mediation never falters, and those who have violated the covenant can always repair their mistakes by returning to him. Translating the law into

79. Perkins, *Works*, I, 70.

80. Cotton, *way of Life*, 454; Hooker, *Sovles Vocation*, 40–41; Cotton, *Treatise of the Covenant*, 36.

81. Hooker, *Sovles Hvmiliation*, 128.

82. Cotton, *way of Life*, 229; Rollock, *Select Works*, I, 37.

83. John Cotton, *Christ the Fountaine of Life* (London, 1651), 38.

a guide for the regenerate, the Covenant of Grace teaches "new obedience" through the old code while promising that imperfect performance does not jeopardize salvation if one believes and atones: "the Couenant of grace is not broken asunder by many transgressions, so long as we follow God in a way of faith and repentance."[84]

The Covenant of Grace commands obedience like the Covenant of Works but encourages it through a motivational system that reverses the latter's imperatives. The Covenant of Works rewards completed accomplishment after the fact; its successor promises the benefits before the deed. The difference devolves from the composite nature of the Covenant of Grace, a concord phrased in contractual language while embodying the intentions of a last will: "God's covenant now is such a testament, sealed with the death of Christ, made out of love merely for our good . . . and though he requireth conditions, requireth faith and obedience, yet he himself fulfilleth what he asketh, giveth what he requireth, giveth it as a legacy[.]" Where the Covenant of Works demonstrates God's probity, the Covenant of Grace issues from His charity, revealing his "iustice and mercie."[85] The Lord's emotional involvement with humanity, largely absent from the Covenant of Works, manifests itself in the loving gift of faith dispensed in an agreement precisely the opposite of a contract:

> I [the Lord] doe not use to deale with my Children, as men do with their servants, that I should give them worke to doe, and when they have done it, I should give them wages, then they would come and challenge it at my hands by way of debt: No, saith the *Lord* this is an inheritance, and you are my sonnes, and you shall have it given you freely, and given you as it becomes a Father to give it, so you shall take it [.][86]

The covenant is a parent's present, not a worker's wage, freely given to those God includes in His family without regard for the merit of previous work. The first covenant left Adam in the status of "an honourable Servant," but the Covenant of Grace transforms "the child of wrath" into "the child of God by grace and adoption." The Lord accepts the Saints for who they are, not what they do.[87]

With gracious solicitude, God through the Covenant of Grace removes two of the impediments preventing the individual under sin from performing good works. Humanity's weakness requires that "power must proceed from god who hath made all thynges to his owne glory." Assuming human po-

---

84. Perkins, *Works*, I, 70; Bulkeley, *Gospel-Covenant*, 91 misnum. 83.

85. Sibbes, *Works*, VI, 4; Perkins, *Works*, II, 299.

86. Preston, *New Covenant*, 365.

87. Ball, *Treatise of the Covenant*, 26.

tency, the Covenant of Works "gives us duties to perform, but no strength wherewithall, the other affords both." The former covenant leaves a man "to stand by his own strength; But in the Couenant of Grace, God undertakes for us, to keep us through faith."[88] God gives regenerates power to do what they could not accomplish before, at least in part. Saints in grace do not evolve into supermen. Humans are still mortal; the flesh lives, and they err. However, God relieves the Elect of the necessity to be perfect; whatever sins they commit, His affection keeps the bond intact: "no sin can possibly break that knot and covenant which so firm and resolute love hath once knit." God's love rather than regenerates' new-found might dissolves the double-bind, for even the godly cannot obey the Law entirely. Instead, the Lord's mercy removes the onus of perfection. The Covenant of Grace promises that intention is more important to Him than actual achievement: "God accepts at our hands *a willing minde*, and of childe-like indeavours; if wee come with childe-like service, God will spare us.[89] As long as Saints strive to do their best, God will overlook their shortcomings.

The Lord's newly revealed stance precipitates a new attitude in the Elect. Chosen to receive faith, empowered by the Holy Spirit, secured from the burden to attain perfection, they change their perceptions of God, themselves, and their duties. The psychology articulated by the Covenant of Grace takes hold as regenerates awaken to the graciousness of their new situation and the opportunities it brings. When he views the Covenant of Grace, Preston commented, a new man "lookes not on it now as an enemy, as hee did before upon the Commandement, but hee sees in it much love, and much friendship towards him." He apprehends the affectual qualities of the covenant, and, understanding that God accounts his devotion sincere even "though there be not a perfection of obedience, now hee begins to change his opinion, both of *God* and of all his Lawes and precepts[.]" A mere comma between "obedience" and "now" marks the critical insight that salvation does not require perfection. This is the psychological moment that the covenant celebrates, one's realization that grace removes the pressure from the necessity to perform. John Cotton might have paused at this point to sound a paean of praise to God's wondrous gift, but his convert hurries on. Gracious knowledge alters one's perceptions of the Law and of the self; touched by the Lord's compassionate kindness, the Saint magnifies God's goodness and condemns oneself, believes the covenant promises and "growes up in loue towards *God*." Unregenerates try to gain salvation through their own works; a Saint dispenses with them and closes with the Lord in faith. Then the Spirit

---

88. Cartwright, "Short Chatechisme," 172, Cotton, *Covenant of Gods free Grace*, 12; Bulkeley, *Gospel-Covenant*, 80.

89. Shepard, *Works*, I, 309; Cotton, *Covenant of Gods free Grace*, 12.

"writes the Law in his inward parts," establishing "all those graces that give him strength" to perform his tasks. Able now to fulfill the Law, the Saint "becomes not onely applicable to the Commandm[en]t but is ready to delight in it." Moved to obedience by the conviction that God loves him despite his frailty, such a man is truly a "new creature."[90]

IV

Passing from covenant to covenant transmits an important insight: confidence fueled by God's love produces good works more effectively than does reliance on one's own abilities. New creatures appraise themselves more realistically than they did previously, casting off the delusion that they are Adam and recognizing their limits. Buoyed by the Lord's loving tolerance and forgiveness of their mistakes, they perform the Law from preference rather than from a sense of obligation. Preachers decried the instinctive attitude, generated by the Covenant of Works, that seeks regeneration through deeds. The experience of humanity shows that this mentality is faulty, not because it is inherently bad—God, after all, had inspired it in Adam—but because it does not succeed. If the motive to work for salvation had been strong enough, there would be no need for the Covenant of Grace, since human beings would still be toiling in paradise fulfilling all God's commands. That Adam failed is an historical fact, and a psychological one too. In effect, the preachers said, all people are Adams, acting as if they can obey the Law, like him condemning themselves to futility. The first man had reason to labor for grace, since he originally did have the requisite power, but after the Fall such an attitude misrepresents reality. Puritans had not heard of "neurotic" behavior, but they described it: the constant efforts of unregenerates to accomplish what they cannot while thinking that they can. People who expect themselves to be perfect demand the impossible. Having exposed the fallacy of the old attitude, Puritans preached the Covenant of Grace to bring their congregations into another frame of mind, a willingness to have faith and depend on God. Renouncing self-confidence effectuates a psychological salvation, release from the impulse to achieve perfection. One can work as hard as one can, err, yet still please God if the heart is right, the intentions good, and the work done in faith. A person who trusts in God admits weakness and gains strength, asks less of oneself and accomplishes more.

90. Preston, *New Covenant*, 345, 342–43.

APPENDIX A

		Appointment	Bond	Covenant	League	Testament	[Note]
Tyn.	(1530)[b]	2	14	1		9	
Cov.	(1535)[a,b]		3	22			Omits first ref. in 17.19.
Tav.	(1539)[a]	1	14	3	1	7	
GB	(1540)[a,b]		11	8		6	Omits Eng. wd. in 9.13.
MB	(1549)[a,b]	2	14	1		9	
GenB	(1560)[b]			26			
BB	(1602)[b]			21	4		Omits Eng. wd. in 9.13.
Douai	(1609)[a]			22	4		
KJV	(1611)[b]			26			

VERSES: 6.18; 9.9, 11, 12, 13, 15, 16, 17; 15.18; 17.2, 4, 7 (twice), 9, 10, 11, 13 (twice), 14, 19 (twice), 21; 21.27, 32; 26.28; 31.44.

SOURCES: Tyn. (DMH #4), in Luther A. Weigle, ed., *The Genesis Octapla: Eight English Versions of the Book of Genesis in the Tyndale-King James Tradition* (New York, 1965); Cov. (DMH #18); Tav. (DMH #45); GB (DMH #53), *Genesis Octapla*; MB (DMH #74); GenB (DMH #107), intro. Lloyd E. Berry (Geneva, 1560; facsimile repr., Madison, Wisc., 1969); BB (DMH #271); Douai (DMH #300); KJV (DMH #1995), *Genesis Octapla*.

a. Cov. and Tav. did not translate directly from Hebrew. MB is a printing of Tyn., and is not an original translation. GB revises MB (1537). Douai translates the Latin Vulgate.

b. GB is the 1540 revision of the 1539 original. MB is a 1549 reprinting of the 1537 original, which prints Tyn. (1530). BB is the 1602 reprinting of the 1569 revision of the Old Testament, originally 1568. Tyn., Tav., GenB, BB, Douai are the first editions. KJV was not revised (except in private translations of small issue and little impact) until the late nineteenth century, when the Revised Version (RV) was proposed. The edition was printed in 1873.

OED, s.v. "Covenant," def. 7, note, claims that "The 16th c. English versions used *covenant* entirely in O.T. (including the Psalter)," a statement modified by the above table. In Genesis, only GenB and KJV use *covenant* exclusively. KJV renders *bᵉrîth* 270 times as *covenant* and 17 times as *league; testament* does not appear in the Old Testament (except as the title).

APPENDIX B

WORDS TRANSLATING *DIATHĒKĒ* IN THE NEW TESTAMENTS OF EARLY ENGLISH PRINTED BIBLES

		Testament	*Covenant*	[*Note*]
Tyn.	(1535)[b]	31	5	Omits English word in 1 Cor. 11.25. Reads *tabernacle* in Heb. 9.1.
Cov.	(1535)[a]	31	5	Omits English word in Heb. 8.13. Reads *tabernacle* in Heb. 9.1.
Tav.	(1539)	31	5	Reads *promise* in Ro. 11.27. Omits English word in Heb. 9.1.
GB	(1540)[a,b]	34	5	Adds second *testament* in Heb. 9.17.
MB	(1549)[a,b]	32	5	Reads *tabernacle* in Heb. 9.1. It follows Tyn. (1534) in reading *testament* in 1 Cor. 11.25, omitted by Tyn. (1535).
GenB	(1560)	27	10	Omits English word in Heb. 9.18.
Rheims	(1582)[a]	33	0	Translates Latin *testamentum* literally in all places. Omits English words in Heb. 8.7, 13; 9.1. Omits second reference in Heb. 9.16, 18.
BB	(1602)[b]	18	20	Omits first reference in Heb. 8.9 and adds a second *testament* in Heb. 9.17.
KJV	(1611)	14	23	Omits second reference in Heb. 9.16.

VERSES with *diathēkē* or plural: Mat. 26.28; Mark 14.24; Luke 1.27, 22.20; Acts 3.25, 7.8; Ro. 9.4 (pl.), 11.27; 1 Cor. 11.25; 2 Cor. 3.6, 14; Gal. 3.15, 17; 4.24 (pl.); Eph. 2.12 (pl.); Heb. 7.22; 8.6, 8, 9 (twice), 10; 9.4 (twice), 15 (twice), 16, 17, 20; 10.16, 29; 12.24; 13.20; Rev. 11.19. Verses having English word without Greek equivalent: Heb. 8.7, 13; 9.1, 16 (second reference), 18.

SOURCES: Same as Appendix A, with the following exceptions: Tyn. (1534, DMH #13), in *The New Testament, Translated by William Tyndale, 1534*, ed. N. Hardy Wallis (Cambridge, Eng., 1938); Tyn. (1535, DMH #15) in Luther A. Weigle, ed., *The New Testament Octapla: Eight English Versions of the New Testament in the Tyndale-King James Tradition* (New York, 1962); Rheims (DMH #177).

a. Cov. did not translate from the Greek. GB revises MB (1537). MB prints Tyn., and is not an original translation. Rheims translates the Latin Vulgate.

b. Tyn. (1535) is Tyndale's final revision of the 1525 and 1534 editions. GB is the 1540 revision of the 1539 original. MB (DMH #74), the version used here, is one of two 1549 editions of MB; it edits and prints Tyn. (1534), see Charles C. Butterworth, *The Literary Lineage of the King James Bible* (Philadelphia, 1941), 150–51. MB (DMH #75) prints Tyn. (1535). BB is the 1602 reprinting of the 1572 revision of the New Testament, originally 1568. Other sources are first editions, except KJV.

The figures given in *OED*, s.v. "Covenant," def. 7, note, are misleading. Tyndale (1534, 1535) introduced *covenant* into the New Testament five times, not six as is stated. GenB did not extend this to 23, but to 10. KJV gives 23 readings of *covenant*, not 22. *OED* correctly notes 14 readings of *testament* in KJV, but KJV changes the GenB reading from *testament* to *covenant* 14 times (not 3) and reverts one time (Rev. 11.19) from *covenant* to *testament*.

3

The Way of Salvation, the Power of Faith

Humanity dreams of strength but lives in enfeeblement. No one can enter into the Covenant of Grace or do any godly work unless and until the Holy Spirit at God the Father's direction applies the benefits of Christ's redemption apprehended through faith. The mechanics of the Spirit's proceedings particularly interested the Reformers, and from numerous passages in the New Testament, most notably Eph. 1.3–14 and Ro. 8.29–30, they and their descendants pieced together the logic of its behavior.[1] In the *ordo salutis*, the "way of salvation," theologians catalogued the motions of the Spirit translating sinners from doom to salvation, the names of its works sounding a rhymed checklist of grace: vocation, justification, adoption, sanctification, glorification. Acted on by God and acting through faculties newly regenerated, Saints turn from bondage in Satan to freedom in Christ. "Turning" is what Puritans called "conversion," a topic preachers never tired of expounding, and their treatment of it swung far from merely explicating the *ordo*'s stages.[2] Impressed by the invigorating qualities of grace, they spoke of the new birth as the antidote to human incapacity. Conversion is the process by

---

1. Louis Berkhof, *Systematic Theology*, 4th ed., rev. and enlg. (Grand Rapids, 1941), 415–17.

2. The meaning of "conversion" varied. It was often synonymous with "regeneration," the rehabilitation of the faculties; both of these terms were also equated with some part or all of "vocation." See Ames, *Marrow*, I.xxvi.19; Norton, *Orthodox Evangelist*, 271, 282; Hooker, *Sovles Vocation*, 348; Perkins, *Works*, I, 613–14; John Cotton, *The Way of Congregational Churches Cleared, 1648*, in Larzer Ziff, ed., *John Cotton on the Churches of New England*

which Saints emigrating to the Kingdom of God finally gain the power to accomplish His Law.

The dialectics of the "way of salvation" imply nothing about believers' subjective responses to the Spirit, but since Puritans ministered to human beings, not abstractions, they hung on the bones of the *ordo* a body of experiences. People who turn to God undergo a characteristic series of emotions, an "affective cycle" that begins before faith and stretches beyond the actual moment of its implantation. Incipient Saints feel the stirrings of sorrow over sin intensify into hatred of it, which occasions the despair of perceiving one's incapacity to achieve salvation. As an awareness of faith emerges, despondency passes into joy, peace of conscience, and love of God. The affective cycle evidences the Spirit's presence, giving proof of election, and it testifies to that transformation in the ability of believers to fulfill God's commands which is regeneration. The affections that accompany conversion reflect the changing circumstances of a Saint's sufficiency. Contrition and humility associate to the status of helplessness, while joy and love connote potency. The events of conversion forge these links between energy and emotion for the first time, and once learned, reliving them stimulates renewed feelings of strength. Saints may lose their sense of vitality, but they can restore it, preachers said, by recapitulating their prototypical experience, the original work of the Spirit transfigured into habit. Acts of self-humiliation increase strength and joy. The *ordo salutis* explains how Saints receive the power of faith, and it models the development by which the psychological type depicted in the Covenant of Works becomes and remains the type described by the Covenant of Grace.

I

Before the beginning was God, and in the Puritan imagining of time and fate, His will dictates the history of all creation. Salvation depends utterly on the Lord's decree, His "firm decision by which he performs all things through his almighty power according to his counsel." The decree insofar as it concerns

---

(Cambridge, Mass., 1968), 205. Conversion occasionally denoted the whole scope of the Spirit's activities, Perkins, *Works*, I, 454; II, 294. The definition of these terms was not fixed in the seventeenth century; in twentieth-century Reformed theology they are more sharply demarcated. James L. Shields, "The Doctrine of Regeneration in English Puritan Theology, 1604–1689" (Ph.D. dissertation, Southwestern Baptist Theological Seminary, 1965), 194–97; Berkhof, *Systematic Theology*, 419, and Part Four, *passim*. Occasionally there were anomalies in the *ordo*'s order: Perkins sometimes reversed justification and adoption (cf. *Works*, I, 81–82, 368, with I, 358; II, 18). So did Cotton, *Treatise of the Covenant*, 23, 124–25. Shepard, *Works*, I, 247–51, distinguished reconciliation from justification, which precedes it, and adoption, which follows.

human beings is called predestination, and through it God determines that some, for reasons known only to Himself, are elected to eternal life, and others (the majority, Puritans thought) reprobated forever, all of which redounds to His "speciall glory."[3] The Elect come into the world foreordained to salvation, but they do not inherit their predestined faith at birth. During the interval between their nativity and their entrance into the Covenant of Grace, God's knowledge of them courses secretly like "a river under ground" and they live indistinguishable from the ungodly mass.[4] The Lord beckons sinners to Him whenever a preacher rehearses the drama of humanity's fall and possible redemption, but a future child of God may, and most likely will, rebuff the call at first. The best preaching does not in itself guarantee conversion; crowds of people "resorted daily" to hear Jesus himself in the flesh yet "could not be conuerted by him." The reason is as plain as the nose on a reprobate's face, and as close as the corrupted faculties that lurk just behind it. "The Elect of God haue no better hearts, by nature, than the worst of all the Reprobate haue," and until the Lord pleases "to open their eares, and incline their hearts, they are euery whit as backeward and vntoward as the worst."[5] Before they believe, Saints-to-be, like other unregenerates, are unwilling to give up their transgressions, and before Christ enters into spiritual union with such a soul, it must be cut off from its love of wrongdoing. While the soul is "in the state of Nature, under the command of sin, and Power of Satan," it cannot be implanted in Christ because in that case it would be "in Hell and Heaven at the same time" serving "two contrary Masters"; the Elect must be called from Satan and so be "prepared" before they receive faith and Christ. Sinners cannot properly hate their misdeeds unaided, but the Holy Spirit, its "irresistible power" working a detestation of evil in the soul, disannuls the rule of iniquity and averts the soul from it.[6] Preparative work readies a person for faith. Simultaneously, it initiates the affective cycle of conversion.

Preparation precipitates a personal crisis whose features Puritans reconstructed from a wide range of biblical sources. The expression "to prepare the heart" derives from the Old Testament, where the Hebrew idiom employing *kûn* and *lêb* (heart) occurs 13 times. Understood primarily as 'to prepare' or 'to ready,' *kûn* could also intend 'to establish' or 'fix': "we must keepe our

3. Ames, *Marrow*, I.vii.2; xxv.3. Cf. Perkins, *Works*, I, 15, 16. Reprobates are those who are fated for damnation; unregenerates are those whose faculties have not been sanctified by grace. All reprobates are unregenerates, but not all unregenerates are reprobates; the Elect are predestined to salvation, but they are unregenerate until their calling. See Kendall, *Calvin and English Calvinism*, 4, n.3.

4. Sibbes, *Works*, V, 433.

5. Hildersam, *CVIII Lectures*, 325 misnum. 305, 326.

6. Hooker, *Application*, I–VIII, 156, 161; IX–X, 680.

hearts prepared or fixed," commented Cotton on Ps. 57.7, "the word [kûn] signifies both."[7] 'To fix' carried the sense in English of 'to fasten,' 'make sure,' hence "to prepare the heart" meant 'to make the heart ready beforehand' with the implication of preparing for a purpose, directing it to fasten securely on some object.[8] In the Old Testament, the phrase has the exclusively theocentric connotation of a worshipful attitude unrelated to specific liturgical contexts, a piety whose psychological features are not apparent.

The concept that the heart is prepared for Christ applies this idiom to a New Testament experience prototypically represented by Paul's confrontation with the Law.[9] "I had not known sin, but by the law," he claimed, "when the commandment came, sin revived, and I died" (Ro. 7.7, 9). The Law induced in him a new awareness of sin and a kind of spiritual death; as a result, he abjured salvation by the Law and sought it in Christ alone. Paul is upholding the merits of the Law even as he pronounces it incapable of redeeming, but Puritans took these remarks further, in effect dogmatizing his life. Since the Law exposes error and confronts sinners with their inexcusableness, the Elect face the same predicament as did Paul. The preachers cited his own words for proof: "the Law is said to bee a *Schoolemaster to drive men to Christ* [cf. Gal. 3.24]," echoed John Preston, "first, there must be the Law before Christ can be had; for else, although we should preach the Gospell, it would be contemned."[10] How does a sinner live through the death of sin in preparation? Paul is not a theologian of conversion experience, and preachers sought examples elsewhere, most notably the Prodigal Son. Though the Prodigal hears no sermon and makes no remarks about the Law, to Puritans he nevertheless epitomized the person in preparation. John Norton, who systematized early New England's thinking about conversion, pointed out that "In him we may see the conscience of sin," followed by a

7. Cotton, *way of Life*, 207; Martinius, . . . *Key of the Holy Tongve*, II, 66, s.v. "בון"; Minsheu, . . .*Gvide Into Tongves*, s.v. "Prepare," "Readie." English Bibles translated with *prepare* in a majority of cases, while employing 14 different terms in all.

8. Bullokar, *English Expositor*, s.v. "Fixe," "Fixed"; Cockeram, *English Dictionarie*, pt. I, s.v. "Fixe," "Fixed"; Cawdrey, *Table Alphabeticall*, s.v. "Fixed."

9. *Preparation* has several definitions in Puritan theological discourse. While signifying the preliminaries to faith, the subject discussed here, it also refers to the activity of the Saints as they renew themselves for God's work or ready themselves to meet Christ in glory. See Perkins, *Works*, I, 733; Wilson, *Christian Dictionary*, s.v. "Prepare," defs. 2, 4; Cotton, *way of Life*, 207; Shepard, *Works*, II, 70; Sibbes, *Works*, IV, 175.

10. Preston, *Liveles Life*, 35. Paul, of course, did not call his experience "preparation." Ames, *Marrow*, I.xxvi.12, connects Ro. 7.7 and the term, but such an explicit relation is rare. The notion of preparing the heart passed so easily into Puritan vocabulary that the term usually did not require a text, although Ro. 7.7ff was often used to identify aspects of the preparatory process. Proof that the Law prepares for Christ rests on Gal. 3.24 and other verses. Cf. Perkins, *Works*, I, 70; Hildersam, *CVIII Lectures*, 15; Finch, *Summe of Sacred Diuinitie*, 30, note a.

growing awareness of his lost estate and a resolve to seek Christ. Desperate on account of having fallen away, the Prodigal prepares to submit to his father's (i.e. God the Father's) will.[11] The same pattern appears in other New Testament stories and in the lives of the Elect themselves.

A review of three representative preachers shows that Puritans agreed on the essential framework of preparatory experience even while contesting subordinate issues. William Perkins, Elizabethan Puritanism's most comprehensive theologian, approached the subject by the numbers, as he did so much else, precisely enumerating faith's prerequisites. First comes knowledge of the Law and Gospel, for one cannot have faith ungrounded in Christianity's fundamental doctrines. Reprobates may reach this level of understanding and attain the general faith that accompanies it, but the Elect achieve more because "God is their *schoole-master*," an adaptation of Gal. 3.24 to emphasize the ultimate source of Saintly wisdom. Second, Christ through his Spirit effects a sight of sin that satisfies the high standards of cognition preachers expected. The "vilest wretch in the world can generally and confusedly say, *he is a sinner*," but a person sees sin effectually only when he or she perceives both the particular evils for which one is responsible and their consequences to oneself, "that ougly taile of the curse of God, that euery sinne draweth after it." Third follows sorrow for sin, denominated "the *spirit of bondage to feare*" because the enlightened sinner "is smitten with feare and trembling, through the consideration of his hellish and damnable estate." Perkins's reformulation of Paul's phrase from Ro. 8.15 gives it a psychological reading and reassesses the audience addressed. Paul in his Epistle adverts to contradictory ontological conditions, freedom of life in the spirit compared with the bondage of life in the flesh, and he assures believers as he looks on Christians' former captivity that they have become God's children and do not return to the slavery of sin. Perkins, in contrast, understands a mental disposition, "paine and pricking in the heart" elicited by a sense of God's displeasure and the damnation it warrants, so he stands with the unregenerate to advise them that their shudders anticipate faith. In Puritan thinking the "spirit of bondage" normatively identifies either the affections God's Spirit induces in reprobates undergoing preparation or the Holy Spirit itself as it perturbs them, in both cases evoking the fears occasioned by God's fierce indignation over sin.[12]

---

11. Norton, *Orthodox Evangelist*, 138. Cf. Rogers, *Seven Treatises*, 13; Hooker, *Sovles Hvmiliation*, 7, which work takes Luke 15.14–18 for its text.

12. Perkins, *Works*, I, 363–64. Other preachers who define "spirit of bondage" as a psychological state are Norton, *Orthodox Evangelist*, 131, and Wilson, *Christian Dictionary*, s.v. "Spirit of feare," *sub* "Spirit." Wilson's wording, taken from 2 Tim. 1.7, is eccentric among Puritans. The phrase refers to the Holy Spirit in Bulkeley, *Gospel-Covenant*, 361; Richard Mather, *The Summe of Certain Sermons Upon Genes: 15.6* (Cambridge, Mass., 1652), 4; Forbes, *Letter*, 53; Shepard, *Works*, I, 169; Preston, *Remaines*, 40. The difference seems to have gone

Fourth, the individual reaches the state of holy desperation, giving up "all hope euer to attaine saluation by any strength or goodnes of his owne," vilifying himself and acknowledging he deserves "ten thousand damnations." To the "Many" who think that "melancholike passion" rather than God's anger inspires sorrow for sin, Perkins exhibits David, "who by all coniectures was least troubled with melancholy, and yet neuer any tasted more deepely of the sorrow and feeling of Gods anger for sinne th[a]n he did," concluding that the two afflictions, which may "concur together," manifest strikingly opposed symptoms and cures.[13] A heart this troubled has been humbled sufficiently; faith enters it and, through the illumination of the Spirit, the Gospel promises encourage one to hunger and thirst after grace, to crave pardon "with vnspeakable sighs, and in perseuerance."[14]

---

unremarked, and did not affect the theology of preparation; in fact, Perkins, *Works*, I, 457, seems also to have taken the second position, and both Preston, *Saints Qvalification*, 109 misnum. 129, and Shepard, *Works*, I, 275, also took the first. Both interpretations, and others, are current; see C.E.B. Cranfield, *A Critical and Exegetical Commentary on the Epistle to the Romans*, 2 vols. (Edinburgh, 1975–79), I, 396; Matthew Black, *Romans* (London, 1973), 118; Charles Kingsley Barrett, *A Commentary on the Epistle to the Romans* (New York, 1957), 163. However intended, Paul conceived the spirit of bondage as a phenomenon continually existent before faith; Puritans restricted it to a limited time period in preparation: "The state of bondage was alwayes until faith: the Spirit of bondage signifieth the sensibleness [i.e. perception] of that bondage. We must distinguish between the state of bondage, and the Spirit of bondage," Norton, *Orthodox Evangelist*, 131. Norton calls the condition of slavery to sin a "state," reserving the term "spirit" for conscious awareness of it.

13. Perkins, *Works*, I, 365.

14. Perkins, *Works*, I, 79–80, compared with 365. Perkins abbreviates the fourfold path in *The Golden Chaine* (I, 79), where the first step is knowledge of the Law alone, and in *Cases of Conscience* (II, 13), where God initially gives the "outward meanes of salvation," but departs from it somewhat in *A Graine of Musterd-Seede*, which omits explicit mention of the Spirit's role, the necessity of doctrinal knowledge, and holy desperation: "Beginnings of preparation . . . are the accusations of the conscience, by the ministery of the law, feares and terrors arising thence, compunction of heart [cf. the third "hammer," I, 79], which is the apprehending of Gods anger against sinne" (I, 638). Perkins moves on to consider "beginnings of composition," which comprise, Norman Pettit claims (*The Heart Prepared: Grace and Conversion in Puritan Spiritual Life* (New Haven, 1966), 64), a second stage of preparation in which a reprobate (*sic*, see *supra*, n. 3) "begins to prepare himself for saving grace with the help of the Spirit. Not yet effectually converted, his thirst for grace and his anticipation of the covenant promises allow him to play a part of his own." Pettit, however, is misled by assuming that Perkins employs *conversion* to indicate one's entrance into grace, whereas in this instance he offers a peculiar definition: it "is not the change of the substance of man, or of the faculties of the soule, but a renewing and restoring of that purity and holinesse, which was lost by mans fall, with the abolishment of that naturall corruption that is in all the powers of the soule" (I, 637). What Perkins here labels "conversion" is what he and other Puritans ordinarily call "sanctification," defined in *The Golden Chaine* as a process "whereby such as beleeue, being deliuered from the tyrannie of sinne, are by little and little renued in holinesse and righteousnes" (I, 83; cf. Wilson, *Christian Dictionary*, s.v. "Sanctification," def. 4) This identification is further cemented when Perkins mentions "foure seuerall workes of grace in euery childe of God: his vnion with Christ, his adoption, iustification, and conuersion." In this list of the Spirit's works

Thomas Hooker was adamant enough about the necessity of fitting the soul for Christ to issue the most compendious treatment in Puritan literature. Where Perkins disposed of it within a few paragraphs, Hooker's most thorough presentation covers approximately one thousand pages—and remains unfinished. "Scripture never enough expresseth the love that is between sinne and the soule," he warned, an attraction so intense it requires the Lord to pluck unregenerates from their corruptions by a "Holy kind of violence."[15] Preparation involves contrition and humiliation, which loosen a person "from his sin" and then "from himself." Contrition begins when the Spirit of Bondage—a title of the Holy Spirit rather than a mental state, as for Perkins—works through the Law to expose one's misdeeds, scattering the "fogs" of the mind so one "sees himself and his sin and he sees God and Christ, as the *sun of righteousness* shining gloriously in his Eyes," a pun with Mal. 4.2 that Puritans repeatedly employed, unfortunately. So illumined, the understanding apprehends sin "in its own Nature," causing the judgment to "reflect upon his own follies and corruptions."[16] Faculty-humor psychology dictates that intellectual perception stimulates an affectional response; Perkins notes that sorrow for sin follows sight of it, and Hooker likewise finds that a sorrow for sin "*rightly set on*" pierces the heart of a truly affected sinner. [17] Acts 2.37, on which both Perkins and Hooker ground their proof of contrition's effects, relates how the Spirit "pricked" the hearts of the 3000 who heard Peter's Pentecost sermon, but since Hooker wants a more powerful image to convey the force of the Spirit's work, he goes behind the English text to the "Original," where the Greek word "implies more than bare pricking." Untranslatable by an exact English equivalent, it means "*a shivering and pulling all asunder.*" In the Septuagint it often stands for a Hebrew root that signifies a piercing, "as when the body of a travelling [i.e. travailing, laboring] woman is wounded with the sorrow of Childbirth," hence it suggests "a work of sound

---

according to the "order of nature" (I, 637), "conversion" occupies the place normally accorded to "sanctification." Thus Conclusion II, "*The first materiall beginnings of the conuersion of a sinner, or the smallest measure of renewing grace, haue the promises of this life, and the life to come*" (I, 638), refers to events that take place in Saints, not in unregenerates; it counsels them how to recognize the signs of grace. It is under this heading that Perkins takes up beginnings of composition, which are the same as beginnings of conversion and, through the apposition in Conclusion II, equivalent as well to "the smallest measure of renewing grace." Renewing grace "is not common to all men, but proper to the elect" (I, 638), hence the same must be true of "beginnings of composition." In other words, "beginnings of composition" have nothing to do with works before faith, but are those early steps by which the regenerate, still unsure of their grace, can gain comfort in their election. Perkins does not advance a two-tiered theory of preparation.

15. Hooker, *Unbeleevers Preparing*, 2d pagination, 6; *idem*, *Application*, I–VIII, 349.

16. Hooker, *Application*, IX–X, 15, 41, 42 misnum. 22, 53, 75.

17. Perkins, *Works*, I, 364; Hooker, *Application*, IX–X, 358.

sorrow" that parts the soul from sin.[18] Hooker's descriptions of a terrified sinner rival the most forceful Puritan expressions, and with reason. Having himself suffered "the just *wrath* of Heaven" with "unusual degrees of horror and anguish," he spoke from personal experience in evoking the armies of indignation with which the Lord "besigeth" the contrite. Such pangs eventu-

18. Hooker, *Application*, IX–X, 323. Hooker's investigation of the underlying text affords a rare glimpse at a preacher's technique and purpose in making word studies. The analysis as presented consists in offering a definition of the "word in the Original" that is then deepened by comparison with the usage of various authorities; much of the process must be re-created because Hooker does not disclose any of the words or verses that figure in his thinking. The word in Acts 2.37 is *katenugēsan*, from *katanussō*, and Hooker's initial rendering, "a shivering and pulling asunder," is inaccurate, for he describes a coming apart whereas the root of *katanussō* was understood to mean 'to prick,' 'pierce,' 'bore,' John Baret, *An Alvearie or Quadruple Dictionarie* ([London], 1580), s.v. "bore," "prick"; Minsheu, . . . *Gvide Into Tongves*, s.v. "Pricke." Some of the "Antients," Hooker says, rendered it as "so to prick as to pierce and enter, dig on every side, to pierce not overly, but quite through the soul"; a marginal note refers to Cyprian. (I have been unable to locate this reference; Cyprian, Bishop of Carthage in 248–58, does not seem to have discussed Acts 2.37. See Alexander Roberts and James Donaldson, eds., *Ante-Nicene Christian Library: Translations of the Writings of the Fathers Down to A.D. 325*, 24 vols. (Edinburgh, 1867–72), XIII: *The Writings of Cyprian, etc.*, vol. 2, 529). Comparison with other New Testament passages is precluded because *katenugēsan* is "found only in this place," but since "the Seventy Interpreters used it often," contrast with the usage of the Greek Old Testament is possible. Rather than evaluate the meaning of *katanussō* by collating its meanings in the Greek text, Hooker determines which Hebrew roots the Septuagint translates with it. One of them is *âtsab*, understood as 'to be troubled,' 'grieved,' and as 'sorrow,' 'heaviness' (Martinius, . . . *Key of the Holy Tongve*, II, 112, s.v. עָצַב). Forms of *âtsab* appear twice in Gen. 3.16, where God punishes Eve for her share in the Fall: "I will greatly multiply thy sorrow [*itsbônêkh*] and thy conception; in sorrow [*bᵉetseb*] thou shalt bring forth children[.]" The Septuagint translates this verse with a different word (*lupas, lupais*), but it does render "and the men were grieved [*vayit'atsbû*]" in Gen. 34.7 with *katenugēsan*; it is this connection between Gen. 3.16 and 34.7 that prompts Hooker to associate Eve's primal pain with the grief of contrition. Hooker's method puts scholarship at the service of "powerful preaching" in the best tradition of the Puritan plain style, which submerged displays of learning and artifice to promote the bare truth of God's Word. Refraining from any mention of Greek and Hebrew, he employs his erudition for the sole purpose of documenting, through a scrupulous appeal to the text, how the Bible displays the duress of contrition. At the same time, the intent is homiletic, not lexical; the Septuagint translates *katanussō* with "several words in several places," only one of which is deemed relevant. Interestingly, he pursues the analysis for descriptive ends alone; omitting mention of the proof texts in Genesis, he passes up an opportunity to relate contrition and Original Sin. The lack of reference notes makes it impossible to ascertain the particular books employed; the following works, with which Hooker was likely to be familiar, were used to replicate his study: Τῆς Καινῆς Διαθήκης Ἅπαντα Εὐαγγήλιον . . . (Paris, 1550), DM #4622, Robert Estienne's third edition of the Greek New Testament, the basis of the "Textus Receptus" for English biblical translation until the late nineteenth century; *Novvm Iesu Christi Testamentvm, Græcè & Latinè* ([Geneva], 1590), see DM #4650–51 and note, Theodore Beza's fourth minor version, Estienne's text with a few revisions; Henri Estienne, ed., *Concordantiæ Græcolatinæ Testamenti Novi*, 2d ed. ([Geneva], 1624), the preeminent concordance to the Greek New Testament text; Conrad Kircher, *Concordantiæ Veteris Testamenti Græcæ, Ebræis, vocibus respondentes* . . . , 2 vols. (Frankfort, 1607), the first published concordance to the Septuagint; Ἡ Παλαιὰ Διαθήκη . . . *Vetus Testamentvm Ivxta Septvaginta* (Rome, 1586 [1587]), DM #4647, the "Sixtine Septuagint," used by translators of KJV and normative through the nine-

ally separate the sinner from one's errors: "Fear troubles his sin, sorrow loosens it, hatred abandons it."[19] Detesting what it once loved, the soul turns from its bond with iniquity.

Contrition alerts unregenerates to their damned estate, but preparation is only half-complete. Rather than turning immediately to God and Christ, distressed sinners look to their own abilities for relief. Congenital corruption, "old *Adams* nature," inspires mistaken self-reliance, which necessitates humiliating them until they completely accept their helplessness and submit wholly to God. An eagle-eyed conscience picks over every action and spies weaknesses; it tells the soul confident of its ability to pray about "his barrennesse, and deadnesse, and roaving thoughts, when hee doth pray, and how insufficient, he is to pray," concluding "you have formerly contemned prayer: and now you cannot pray." The Lord must "weary us" of self-confidence until the sinner sees "hell fire flashing in his face, and that he cannot succour himselfe"; only then will one admit "I know that all the meanes in the world cannot save mee." Abased and ashamed, the humbled soul "lyes at God's foot-stoole" totally at the Lord's disposing.[20] Perkins at this point judged a person ready for faith, and accounted the fervent thirst for Christ one of its works, but Hooker considers "spirituall thirst" a special work of the Spirit "in a humble and contrite heart" that points to future faith.[21] A soul in preparation turns towards God; in fact, it already enjoys some saving qualities. Many a man "thinkes that he must first be in Christ, before he can have any grace," but this is untrue; "the Lord workes some grace upon us to bring us to himselfe, as the worke of preparation and vocation, this is a saving worke of Christ." Reprobates may have a legal preparation, a "plashing" of the soul that does not completely cut it off from sin, but the Lord works evangelical preparation in the Saints that fits them for grace and "can never miss."[22] Preparation in those who will be regenerate connects infallibly to succeeding graces and therefore deserves to be called saving; though a soul undergoing evangelical preparation does not yet "partake" of faith and Christ, nevertheless "he shall

---

teenth century; מקראות גדולות [*Mikra'ôth Gedôlôth*], 4 vols. (Venice, 1524–25; facsimile repr., Jerusalem, 1972), DM #5085, the Second Rabbinic Bible, Jacob ben Chayyim's work, which constituted the standard printed Hebrew text of the Old Testament well into the twentieth century; *Biblia Sacra Hebraice, Chaldaice, Græce, & Latine*, 8 vols. (Antwerp, 1569–72), DM #1422, second of the great polyglots, which includes a Hebrew text of the Old Testament and a version of the Septuagint.

19. Mather, *Magnalia*, I, 333; Hooker, *Application*, IX–X, 367, 678.

20. Hooker, *Sovles Hvmiliation*, 14, 23, 29, 81–82, 123.

21. [Thomas Hooker], *Spiritual Thirst: A Sermon Preached upon John 7.37* (London, 1638), 10. For attribution of this piece to Hooker, see Bush, "Four New Works," 5, 18–23, 25.

22. Hooker, *Sovles Vocation*, 344–45; *idem, Application* I–VIII, 152.

be everlastingly saved and redeemed[.]" A truly thirsting soul can take comfort because it is "heire of all Gods saving graces here," and will possess the Kingdom of Heaven "as surely as if thou wert invested therein already, and wert now singing praises to the Lambe."[23]

Hooker's position drew fire from John Cotton, who prefaced his remarks with professional politesse. Though "Reserving due honour to such gracious and precious Saints, as may be otherwise minded," Cotton himself could discern no saving qualifications in a Saint "till he have union with Christ." To suppose otherwise prejudices "Grace and Truth" by implying that the soul "may be in the state of Salvation before Christ," and by overestimating the competence of unregenerates to "bring forth good fruit" before being "grafted into Jesus Christ."[24] Cotton did not disparage preparatory activity as such, however, agreeing with his colleagues that God must separate a sinner from the love of iniquity before He can work faith in the heart. The Lord "prepareth" His people through a "double work of his Spirit," first cutting off "the Seed of *Abraham* from all worldly intanglements and delights" by the Spirit of Bondage, which fixes the danger of sin on their consciences and worries them with "fear of damnation." Having cited Ro. 8.15, standard proof of the Spirit's accusatory role, Cotton establishes an original text to illuminate its second work by seizing on Mal. 4.1, "behold, the day cometh, that shall burn as an oven; and all the proud, yea, and all that do wickedly, shall be stubble." Associating "day" with "spirit"—the rationale is not readily apparent—he arrives at the designation "Spirit of Burning" and locates its activities in the ministries of John the Baptist and Christ (Mat. 3.9; 6.2, 5, 16), contending it burned up "all the Hypocrites like stubble; and the beauty of their works were blasted by it." In a sinner already troubled by the Spirit of Bondage, the Spirit of Burning destroys trust in Abraham's Covenant and all confidence in self-sufficiency, humiliating the unregenerate by blasting (Cotton's favorite verb) the illusion that passes for faith. People by nature conceive they can do whatever God requires, and only when the Spirit of Burning makes one realize that such thoughts are fictions is the soul fit for Christ.[25]

23. Hooker, *Sovles Hvmiliation*, 166; *idem, Spiritual Thirst*, 71–72. Cf. John Rogers [of Dedham], *The Doctrine of Faith*, 3d ed., corr. and enlg. (London, 1629), 126–28, 157–58, 225–30, 362–68, 374–79. Rogers was Hooker's mentor, and Hooker wrote the book's preface.

24. Cotton, *Treatise of the Covenant*, 35; *idem, Gospel Conversion*, 2–3; cf. *idem, Way of Congregational Churches*, 271.

25. Cotton, *Treatise of the Covenant*, 14–15, also 119–20. Cotton's use of the word *prepare*, his mention of the Spirit of Bondage, and the description of the Spirit's humiliating work clearly show his essential agreement with other Puritans that the soul passes through preparatory states that antecede calling. See also his remarks about the ministries of the Law and the Gospel, *Spiritual Milk for Boston Babes in Either England* (Cambridge, Mass., 1656), 7–8, and about taking the covenant, *A Sermon Preached at Salem, 1636*, in Ziff, ed., *Cotton on the Churches*, 49, 51, 60–61. The point must be insisted upon, because it is often asserted that he

Cotton's exposition proceeds along stereotypical lines—the Spirit's "double work" corresponds quite closely to Hooker's "contrition" and "humiliation"—but the variation in nomenclature and the absence of preparatory "thirst" suggest a difference in treatment, one more tactical than dogmatic. Hooker's thoughts are for his flock, his terms refer to human reactions, and he is always concerned to reassure sinners that their trials have a soteriological purpose. The doctrine of saving preparations attempts to secure the insecure against terrors that might make them "choose not to be th[a]n to be so miserable."[26] Legal preparation is a possibility so cursorily entertained that it appears inconsequential. Cotton, in contrast, has God in view first, his categories pertain to Spiritual acts, and he is far more willing to let unregenerates face bondage and burning unsure of the outcome. With almost cavalier insouciance to the worries of would-be Saints, he proclaims that they (and their minister) know only after the fact if fear has led to faith because preparation can go for nought. The Spirit may burn "and yet leave the soul in a damnable condition, for ought I know; and such as many a soul may be in, and yet never come to enjoy saving fellowship with Jesus Christ."[27] He leaves no possibility for an unregenerate to spark the flame of specious self-confidence with hopes that humiliation leads infallibly to grace.

In all discussions, preparative experience follows the same pattern. Differences of detail merely strike variations on the theme of a sinner whose increasing anxiety culminates in pride's collapse. The process begins with the comprehension of basic Christian premises, discovered in Scripture and the heart. Those nescient of these principles—and such folk were numerous in

---

denounced preparation's utility, discounted human initiation of it, and even denied its existence, thereby putting himself at odds with his fellows: Perry Miller, "'Preparation for Salvation' in Seventeenth-Century New England," in *idem, Nature's Nation* (Cambridge, Mass., 1967), 60–67, 72, 74; Pettit, *Heart Prepared*, 129–30, 138–39; Frank Shuffleton, *Thomas Hooker, 1586–1647* (Princeton, 1977), 247; Alfred Habegger, "Preparing the Soul for Christ: The Contrasting Sermon Forms of John Cotton and Thomas Hooker," *American Literature*, 41 (1969), 346; Richard Etulain, "John Cotton and the Anne Hutchinson Controversy," *Rendezvous*, 2, 11 (1967), 10. Cotton did not gainsay the necessity for every Saint to be prepared for faith, as the above quotations demonstrate; sin's hold on the soul must be destroyed. He did reject human initiative in these activities, but this position fairly isolated him, for preachers routinely held that preparation is first of all the work of the Spirit, to which one responds: "the soul may have a good work wrought upon it, and be the receiver of it though not the Author of it," Hooker, *Application*, I–VIII, 151; see *infra*, 86–87, and Lynn Baird Tipson, Jr., "The Development of a Puritan Understanding of Conversion," (Ph.D. dissertation, Yale University, 1972), 329–30. Cotton did dispute the matter of saving qualifications with Hooker, and on this point Hooker held the minority view, see *infra*, n. 35. An excellent discussion of the definitions of preparation and its place within the constellation of issues surrounding human participation in conversion is Stoever, *'Faire and Easie Way,'* 192–99 (see 194–95, 198–99 for Cotton).

26. Hooker, *Application*, IX–X, 368.

27. Cotton, *Treatise of the Covenant*, 120.

Puritan England[28]—do not escape damnation; God justly condemns them for their ignorance of the inbred Natural Law and for "that habituall Infidelitie whereby they would have resisted" the Gospel even had they met it.[29] A little knowledge becomes a dangerous thing if it inspires merely casual piety, which mistakenly assumes that living the Golden Rule and parroting creeds "no doubt" suffice for salvation.[30] Properly applied, Christian knowledge shatters this complacency by translating the new apprehension of one's estate into remorse, fear of God's displeasure, and hatred of sin. As the Covenant of Works displays, however, a person in contrition presumes the ability to gain grace, and therefore must be made "sensible of his owne nothingnesse," the degradation of vanity brought intimately in touch with its own fatuity. Awareness of weakness finally stills ungodly quibbles: "then doe wee lay our hands on our mouthes, and dare not answere."[31]

II

The preacher's task was to instigate humiliating self-inquiry in a soul by nature disinclined to do so, a project they hoped to stimulate with insistent reminders of humanity's inability to ready itself for faith. Divine will initiates and controls preparation, the work "is Gods and not ours." To suggest otherwise traduces His majesty and elevates human potential to fantastic heights. "It is a sottish conceit to think that we can fit ourselves for grace," chided Sibbes, "as if a child in the womb could forward its natural birth." Direction must come from the Holy Spirit. Sinners follow in its stead: it is the Spirit, Shepard said, that works the "secret virtue" in convicting a man of sin, that "shakes the soul" in compunction and "hews the roughness and pride of spirit off," in humiliation.[32] Unable to begin and sustain the process, the soul in preparation cannot claim its achievements deserve consideration for grace. The best intentions notwithstanding, an unregenerate's good works weigh nothing in salvation's balance. Catholics, Arminians, and their ilk claim that such performances warrant and receive the Lord's mercy, but they are mistaken; since Adam broke the Covenant of Works, in no sense do human beings earn salvation.[33] Puritans denied that preparation could be a "merito-

---

28. Keith Thomas, *Religion and the Decline of Magic* (New York, 1971), 159–66, and see Perkins, *Works,* II, 665.

29. Rogers, *Doctrine of Faith,* 506–9.

30. Dent, *Plaine Mans Path-way,* 25.

31. Hooker, *Sinners Salvation,* 19; Greenham, *Works,* 97 misnum. 93.

32. Perkins, *Works,* I, 733; Sibbes, *Works,* VII, 189, #45; Shepard, *Works,* I, 136, 148, 177.

33. Norton, *Orthodox Evangelist,* 130, 165–66, 169; Hildersam, *CVIII Lectures,* 28; Cotton, *way of Life,* 182; Shepard, *Works,* I, 163.

rious cause" of conversion. Vocation depends only on God's will; the "dignity, honesty, industry, or any indeavor" of those called is irrelevant.[34] Deeds done without faith are "but glistering sins" that do not satisfy God or accrue salvific merit. For this reason, most of Cotton's New England colleagues shared his disquietude that Hooker's doctrine of saving qualifications yielded too much credit to preparatory works. The best actions of unbelievers "are painted sins" that God does not accept, Norton rejoindered.[35] The tenet's arch-apostle agreed with this dogmatic point. Saving qualifications are "not my fruit, nor can I be said to do any thing to please God by them," Hooker allowed, but he thought the proposition compatible with effective preaching. Again, Norton demurred. While supporting his peers in their duty "to hold forth the increase of hope, according as the preparatory work doth increase," he cautioned that the disputed doctrine invites the soul to think itself "in a safe way when it is in a perishing condition," hindering "kindly humiliation" by "exempting" it from self-prostration.[36] Both parties acknowledged that the Lord bestows salvation independently of whatever unregenerates accomplish, but controverted the issue of how best to drive them into recognizing the fact.

Norton worried about not humbling sinners enough, but he knew—all Puritan ministers knew—that they sometimes succeeded too well. Effective evangelical technique balanced rigorous use of the Law to alarm unregenerates with timely recountings of the Gospel to nurse them along, a theoretical equipoise easily upset as the reactions of very real human beings required weighting now one side more heavily, now the other. A superfluity of the Gospel contributes to laxity, while an overdose of the Law leads to despair.[37] "It is dangerous," Sibbes confessed, to "press" some spirits too much and too long, "because they may die under the wound and burden before they be

---

34. Sibbes, *Works*, VI, 522; Ames, *Marrow*, I.xxvi.6.

35. Shepard, *Works*, I, 240; Norton, *Orthodox Evangelist*, 174, and more generally, 163–93. On the existence of saving qualifications, Hooker, not Cotton, was the odd man out among the triumverate of the first generation's most renowned soteriologists, for Shepard too rejected the doctrine, *Works*, I, 170–71. That Cotton enjoyed widespread support was noted in 1637 by an unidentified observer reporting to England on the doctrinal debates then agitating Massachusetts. Among the topics was "Whether there be any saving preparation in a Christian soule before his unyon with Christ," and the writer claimed that this was "only Hookers position, the rest of the Ministers do not concurr with him: Cotton and the rest of the contrary opinion are aginst him and his party in all[,]" "3. Propositions wch haue divided Mr. Hooker & Mr. Cotton, in Newe-England," Colonial Office Papers, 1/9, fol. 159ro, Public Record Office, London, on Library of Congress Microfilm #Ac. 10,741, reel 4. Edmund S. Morgan, *Visible Saints: The History of a Puritan Idea* (Ithaca, 1965), 97, n. 58, is confusing in his assertion that Cotton's view was defeated, for he also cites this letter; if Cotton commanded a majority, why did he lose? In fact, this particular tenet of his was not cried down.

36. Hooker, *Application*, I–VIII, 151; Norton, *Orthodox Evangelist*, 166, 190.

37. Perkins, *Works*, II, 664–66; Rogers, *Doctrine of Faith*, 68–69; Greenham, *Works*, 11; Shepard, *Works*, I, 160–61.

raised up again."[38] Holy desperation unleavened by hope metamorphoses into consternation that inhibits rather than furthers the goals of preparation. Sinners properly readied for faith respond to fears of damnation and cognition of weakness by hungering for Christ and resolving to spare no effort or means to reach him. The despondant misconstrue their situation and choose an unproductive course. Magnifying appropriate anxiety, they overreact to perceived debility and paralyze themselves. Despair cuts off the "sinewes" of comfort, enervates "the meanes of grace," and "plucketh up a mans endevours as it were quite by the rootes."[39]

Reeds overly bruised need corrected perceptions to restore their incentive, and they were told to stop exaggerating their dismay. Acute horrors of conscience and fears of damnation may well belong to the normal preparative process: "GOD workes sometimes after one manner, sometimes after another."[40] Terrors should be kept in perspective. God affrights some suddenly and violently, others more gradually, and the intensity of the former case may make it appear more filled with pain than the latter when in the long run it is not. In addition, "melancholy and the temptation of Sathan" vex people already distraught with legitimate concerns, heightening their woes.[41] Any of these reasons, the desperate should remember, may account for their distress, and they ought also to keep in mind that God upholds His own against all dread. In every instance, He secretly maintains incipient Saints as they pass between "insensible blockishnesse, and desperate madness or dissoluteness"; even those troubled by the devil and bile "doe well at last." Manage your fears, preachers counselled, and though your errors appear too great to forgive, sustain your efforts towards redemption despite their inadequacy. The Lord can save the most stubborn sinners, a fact to check the "desperate discouragement" of those who, finding "no power in theselves, no succour in the meanes," think it "an impossibilitie" to receive mercy. God is all-sufficient and can provide, so labor to the "utmost" to get it.[42]

The loss of natural self-confidence and the attitude of hopelessness incumbent to preparation detour some persons into "dark disputes of election and predestination," fortune-telling, in other words.[43] Overwhelmed by the decree's absolute determination of their destinies and lacking any signs of

---

38. Sibbes, *Works*, I, 47.

39. Hooker, *Sovles Vocation*, 122.

40. Preston, *Breast-Plate*, II, 82.

41. Rogers, *Doctrine of Faith*, 87.

42. Rogers, *Doctrine of Faith*, 83, 87; Thomas Hooker, *The Sovles Preparation for Christ* (London, 1632), 6–7, 11.

43. Sibbes, *Works*, IV, 182.

faith, they hope to prove their sainthood by divining their fate. The practice, preachers warned, is forbidden, because "that way is unlawfull and thou medlest with that which belongeth not to thee"; inexpedient, in that one must inevitably "loose thy selfe" in "such curious speculations"; and hurtful, since the attempt to penetrate God's deepest mysteries distracts from pursuing Christ.[44] As Norton put it, a drowning man does not refuse lifelines until he can ascertain how his rescuer is disposed towards him, yet unregenerates who scan the decree behave this foolishly.[45] They must learn, said Puritans, to discriminate between God's whole will and those elements of it He wishes to make known. His volition is essentially "one and the same," but He chooses to publicize only parts of it.[46] "The secret things are for the Lord; the revealed belong to us," a shorthand form of Deut. 29.29, became for Puritans a motto of God's decision to disclose some particulars and hide others.[47] The fate of a living non-believer belongs to His secret will, indeterminate to mortal ken until such time as the person dies. Saints come to know they are chosen after they are called, but before Faith no "speciall certaine difference betweene sinners" singles out the sheep from the goats. None in the state of unregeneracy can tell if they are predestined for heaven or hell, and they sin if they conclude that they are damned.[48] What God does open to human view, most notably in the black letter type of His holy book and from the white-garbed throats of His diligent messengers, are His commands. The decree "determineth what shall be done," but God's revealed will, the Law, exhibits "what is the duty of man to do, or leave undone." The Law, not the decree, is "the rule of life," and it is by this standard that one discovers if he or she is elect.[49]

The unregenerate were warned that God's secret decree defeats all attempts to discover it, told that His revealed will demands that they have faith, and urged to seek Him out. "If I knew that I were elected, or that Christ died for me, then I could believe," complains a sinner in Sibbes's caricature; the minister, immediately citing Deut. 29.29, replies that one's "duty" is to "yield

44. Hooker, *Application*, I–VIII, 81 (quotations); Norton, *Orthodox Evangelist*, 84.

45. Norton, *Orthodox Evangelist*, 84–85.

46. Perkins, *Works*, I, 723.

47. Ezekiel Culverwell, *Time Well Spent in Sacred Meditations, Divine Observations, Heavenly Exhortations* (London, 1635), 150. Cf. Perkins, *Works*, I, 724; Sibbes, *Works*, V, 403; Hooker, *Application*, I–VIII, 81.

48. Culverwell, *Treatise of Faith*, 179. There are rare exceptions. Those who, enlightened by the Gospel and in full knowledge of what they do, blaspheme the Spirit and deliberately set themselves against it, commit the unpardonable sin against the Holy Ghost (cf. Mat. 12.32). They cannot be redeemed, and their condition is known. Perkins, *Works,* I, 106–7; Norton, *Orthodox Evangelist*, 84.

49. Norton, *Orthodox Evangelist*, 92, 80. Cf. Perkins,*Works*, I, 723–27; Shepard, *Works*, III, 90–92.

obedience, and in yielding thereof, thou shalt find the fruit of Christ's redemption, that thou art one for whom he gave himself." God's command is clear, perform it.[50] Hooker confuted musings about election with the same text, but where Sibbes attempts to stimulate activity with reverberations from the revealed will alone, Hooker first bounces his call off the silence of the decree. Whether God will save an individual or not remains the province of "his owne free will," so forget about it: "that he Leaves to him[self], So do thou[.]" Turn, instead, to Christ, who has purchased your redemption.[51] Hooker reminds his audience that election is both unpredictable and predetermined in order to contrast the uselessness of worrying about it with the purposefulness of executing the command. Then he tells them to look to Christ. Shepard took another tack. Sibbes and Hooker directed attention to the certainties of the revealed will, but Cambridge's pastor was willing to employ the motivational possibilities of incertitude. Faced with the whine of the perplexed—"it may be Christ hath not redeemed me, nor shed his blood for me; therefore why should I go to him?"—he turns the question against itself. "It may be," that God has redeemed you, "may be not." Admittedly, the probabilities look grim. God elects but few, and the odds calculate at 1000 to 1 against, but salvation is not a gamble. The only rational course is to act, for those who prepare have everything to gain and nothing to lose; if beseeched, the Saviour may be merciful, and in any case "it is better to die at Christ's feet than in thine own puddle." The outcome is unsure, but since the alternative is damningly clear, linger not in helplessness.[52] Preachers tried to transmute stagnation into movement.

At the other extreme, indifference to the decree corrodes the will to prepare as surely as does obsession with it. For libertines, exhortations to seek Christ clash against assertions of humanity's weakness and the doctrine of limited election. If no human acts conduce to grace, the argument runs, none can inhibit it; God's will alone disposes Sainthood, and human efforts are irrelevant. One may live however one wishes, awaiting the call wherever one fancies. Grace flowers in the Elect regardless of how Saints-to-be might parch it, and fails to germinate in reprobates no matter how assiduously cultivated. Preachers answered "That Diabolical Sarcasme" and its threat to preparatory work by reasserting God's injunctions to refrain from sin, elucidating the means of grace, and upholding human responsibility in the process of salvation.[53] People are not free to disregard the decree without penalty

---

50. Sibbes, *Works*, V, 403.

51. Hooker, *Application*, I–VIII, 81.

52. Shepard, *Works*, I, 54–55. Cf. Rogers, *Doctrine of Faith*, 63–65. Shepard's odds-making is in *Works*, I, 45, and Hooker agreed, *Spiritual Thirst*, 28–29.

53. Norton, *Orthodox Evangelist*, 83.

because God has clearly prescribed how to behave. The Law instructed Adam to serve God's will, and though mankind fell, its duty remains. Like the desperate, libertines make the secret will "the rule of their liues," and by neglecting the revealed will they sin.[54] Unregenerates must perform their duties if for no other reason than that God obliges them to, and they must avoid what He forbids. People are judged by God's *"evident"* truth, and though lacking inherent power to repent and believe, a sinner "hath ability to abstaine from the things, by the which he provokes God to anger." The unsaved should continue to labor because the Lord condemns transgression, and also because "Good duties are good in themselves, although, coming from thy vile heart, they are sins." Obeying the Law lessens sin and may even accrue worldly benefits as well.[55]

The assumed irrelevance of personal comportment, Puritans continued, falsifies how God operates. The imputation that grace comes irrespective of time and place fails to consider that God, having subjected His power to His will, works in an orderly and regulated manner. The Lord's "absolute" power can effect all possible things, but He does not accomplish everything that He possibly might; omnipotent but not omnivolent, "God can do whatsoever he pleaseth, yet God is not pleased to do whatsoever he can." He voluntarily limits His "ordinate" power, by which He achieves what He has actually decided to do. The ways of the Lord are circumscribed by the decree, knowable according to the revealed will, and consistent because "God having freely bounded himself, changeth not, being immutable."[56] The Lord's essential incommutability ensures that His methods, including the application of Christ's redemption to fallen humanity, do not vary once laid down. The circumstances of faith are predictable because God dispenses it specifically through the preaching of the word, the "onely ordinary meanes" of attaining it. The Lord has ordained preaching, sanctified it, and "set it apart to call the soule."[57] Puritanic preoccupation with running to sermons evolves from this central fact of divine mechanics, that God uses the spoken word as the vehicle through which the Spirit bestows preparatory and then saving grace. There were, of course, exceptions; the Lord may have bound Himself, but Puritans did not dare to box Him in. God can always supersede the natural order, and he saves "infants and ideots," whose defective faculties make it impossible for them to apperceive the word normally, in an "extraordinary" manner.[58] He

54. Hooker, *Application*, IX–X, 306; Perkins, *Works*, I, 724.

55. Preston, *Saints Qvalification*, 180, 225; Shepard, *Works*, I, 32. Hooker, *Application*, IX–X, 306–7, makes the point about worldly benefits.

56. Norton, *Orthodox Evangelist*, 19. Cf. Perkins, *Works*, I, 11, 13; Ames, *Marrow*, I.vi.16–20; vii.4.

57. Perkins, *Works*, I, 363; Hooker, *Sovles Vocation*, 63.

58. Downame, *Christian Warfare*, 1111.

can, if He wants, "worke above meanes," or employ an alternative ordinance like prayer or meditation, but in the "common course," preaching is the means that conveys grace.[59] The implications for human activity are clearcut. Grace catches the Elect in certain postures: it will not find them lolling in a meadow or prostrate in a tavern, but seated on hard church benches. "They which are ordained to life euerlasting cannot but heare the word," and conversely, those who do not hear it are *ipso facto* doomed.[60] Sinners come to grace, not vice versa, and they are enjoined to "meete the Lord where he hath appointed."[61]

Libertinism's charge that predestination renders one's actions inconsequential confounds a distinction between efficacy and effort that Puritans affirmed. To say that the soul cannot save itself and that actions have no *merit* for its coming to faith does not mean, they maintained, that one is totally *passive* in the process. An unregenerate cannot earn salvation, but does play a necessary part in bringing it about. Grace does not operate without human participation. The propositions that support this claim descend from rarified strata, the theology of implementing the decree. Having eternally determined "the infallible future being of whatsoever is besides himself," to quote Norton, God in time carries out the "great designe" precisely as He has willed. The execution of the decree, God's efficiency, consists of "many transient Acts," which come about through the concurring efforts of God and the creature (i.e. any created entity).[62] Their collaboration takes place in accordance with a causal hierarchy that presupposes the Lord's all-sovereignty. God, "the first and universal Cause," guides the creature, or second cause, "moving upon, co-working with, and assisting" it in its operations. Dependence on the Prime Mover is absolute; should He "ceaseth his assisting influence, the creature ceaseth to act."[63] Nevertheless, God does not proceed alone. Although in the order of causes "the first is more worthy th[a]n the second," and although the action of the second cause is an "effect" brought about by the "influence" of the first, yet "as the second cause cannot produce such an effect without the first Cause, so the first Cause will not produce such effects without the second cause[.]" An act's manifest character

59. Hooker, *Sovles Vocation*, 63. Cf. Cotton, *Treatise of the Covenant*, 123; Perkins, *Works*, III, 2d pagination, 167; John Davenport, *God's Call to His People To Turn unto Him* (Cambridge, Mass., 1669), 6. On the superiority of preaching above the other means, Perkins, *Works*, I, 709–10; Rogers, *Doctrine of Faith*, 54–58.

60. Perkins, *Works*, I, 709.

61. Rogers, *Doctrine of Faith*, 58. Cf. Shepard, *Works*, I, 106; Hooker, *Vnbeleevers Preparing*, 1st pagination, 47, 121.

62. Norton, *Orthodox Evangelist*, 51, 101; Stoever, *'Faire and Easie Way'*, 87–90.

63. Norton, *Orthodox Evangelist*, 91, 106, 107, and see 52. Cf. Ames, *Marrow*, I.vii.38, and ix.2, 5–6, 25–26; Perkins, *Works*, I, 723–24.

assumes the qualities imparted by the creature. The incidents of phenomena transpire through the agency of the second cause, which is why Norton could point out that "God causeth the burning of the fire, yet we do not say God burneth, but the fire burneth." Fire burns because God, the "efficient" cause, determines and generates it; it burns hot rather than cold because the "formal" cause, fire itself, donates the power to heat.[64] In the role of formal efficients, creatures are substantively involved in their own actions; their participation matters despite God's supreme direction of their affairs. Furthermore, God's use of second causes as the instruments of His efficiency does not violate their integrity as actors. Advancing His ends in a fashion peculiarly consonant with the creature's makeup, God, "offereth no violence, nor changeth the nature of things, but governeth them according to their own natures;" the sweep of His will "sweetly ordereth" the world.[65] It does not disturb the normal functioning of the human faculties; consequently, people can exercise their free choice. The relationship between first and second causes guarantees that God determines the will only insofar as it "determineth it self." The will under God's "Motion" makes exactly the same decisions as it would without His superintendence. Notwithstanding "our weak capacities" to comprehend how necessity and liberty coexist, "Man acts as freely, as if there were no decree; yet as infallibly, as if there were no liberty."[66] He cannot go against the decree, but he can, and does, freely exercise his will in fulfilling it. Human beings, then, are subordinate yet autonomous agents, and it is both consistent and salutary to encourage them to prepare. Sinners have the capacity to "waite upon God in the meanes," and may be cajoled to put down their mugs, pick up their ears, and move from the tavern to God's ordinary, where grace, not beer, is served: "as long as the parts and members of your bodies and the faculties of your soules continue, as long as your understanding and memories indure, why cannot you bestow your bodies to come to Church as well as to goe to the Alehouse?"[67]

The duties of the command, the availability of means, and the formal efficiency of second causes ground the argument for the soul to prepare, and preachers hymned the praise of fitting oneself for faith in harmonies that held out the possibility of reward for purposeful work. At the same time, the notes clashed against the chorus of human inadequacy, and it is easy to see why preachers troubled themselves so much about strengthening the motive of

64. Norton, *Orthodox Evangelist*, 107–8, 110.

65. *Ibid.*, 114. Cf. Sibbes, *Works*, IV, 248; Perkins, *Works*, I, 15; Preston, *Saints Qvalification*, 459.

66. Norton, *Orthodox Evangelist*, 114, 115, 76. Cf. Sibbes, *Works*, I, 205–6; Perkins, *Works*, I, 740.

67. Hooker, *Vnbeleevers Preparing*, 1st pagination, 120–21.

sinners to prepare. Puritan evangelism asked them, with straightfaced and earnest concern for their immortal souls, to work towards an end they cannot possibly achieve on their own. That the fruits of laboring for a good estate lie totally beyond mortal hands, and that one cannot know while one is preparing whether the effort will be effectual or not, profoundly disconcert the expectations of natural men and women, certain that good acts yield good results. The preachers' rhetoric contradicted the strongest psychological instincts of unregenerates, while Arminianism and libertinism offered escape from the anxiety Puritans promised. Arminianism allows for unregenerates to contribute to their salvation; God chooses the Elect on the basis of having foreseen their meritorious deeds. Libertinism admits humanity's helplessness but absolves people from the necessity to perform. Puritans rejected both, for anxiety in the unregenerate is exactly what they wanted to induce. All sparks of self-confidence must be blasted away so that sinners crave Christ, for they experience humiliation only in trying to save themselves by actually doing preparatory work. At some moment, people who have been praying, meditating, following the Law, heeding the Gospel, and listening to sermons realize that their efforts have been completely futile. Trying to save themselves, they comprehend they cannot. Preachers held out the rewards of preparation so that unregenerates would come to know its terrors; the purpose of encouraging them is to humble them. Shepard, one of Puritanism's most caustic practitioners of this art, pointed out what the preachers had been doing all along: "The Lord doth purposely command thee 'to plow up thy fallow ground,' that thou mightest feel thy impotency so to do, and come to him to take it away."[68] Any expedient that lessens holy despair leads from faith, because humiliation is the fulcrum to Christ: the deeper the nadir to which one descends, the more resolute is the spring up to grace. A person believes in Christ when he or she stops believing in oneself. The paradox of laboring for preparation is that to receive faith, one must fail to get it, and that in having failed, one succeeds.

III

Cut away from its love of sin, the prepared soul awaits regeneration. The various works by which God translates it from unregeneracy to grace occur together at a single moment in time, but conceptually, in the "order of nature" as Puritans put it, they necessarily follow each other in a fixed sequence. Saving faith is wrought in vocation, or calling, which severs the Elect from the reprobate and transforms them into Saints. The offer of Christ

68. Shepard, *Works*, I, 173.

in the Gospel's promises, hitherto ineffectually perceived by the corrupted faculties, now penetrates the heart, which believes in him as the means of salvation. Faith makes possible the union of Christ and the Elect, which accords believers the benefits that come from apprehending him and sets the foundation for their possessing everything they need "to live well, and blessedly with God."[69]

The first grace takes away the punishment of eternal death that sinners incur for transgressing the Law. Although Saints have erred as readily as any, God forgives their trespasses. Bound into a "spirituall relation" with Christ by faith, they are justified—accounted righteous—for the Saviour's sake. The Father imputes the Son's perfect righteousness to believers, absolving them from condemnation and reckoning them "righteous unto life." He further dignifies and honors the faithful by adopting them into His family. Justification and adoption are "relative" changes that alter the believer's status in an instant; their physical consequences issue in sanctification, the lifelong process of restoring the faculties from the "filthinesse of sin, to the purity of Gods Image." Under the Spirit's mortifying and vivifying motions, remnants of sin that held sway over body and soul fade, while the Image of God marred by Adam's Fall recovers its pristine holiness. Culminating in glorification at the Final Judgment, renewal of the whole man during earthly life brings Saints closer to eternal perfection.[70]

Salvation's keystone, without which the edifice of justification and the other graces tumbles down, is faith. An "understanding grace," the mind's "assent" to Christian knowledge, faith credits the belief that Christ can redeem "poore sinners," but it encompasses more than intellection.[71] A reprobate may enjoy "naked knowledge of God" or hold with the promises "for a time," one may also entertain a "certaine and sure perswasion" that God works wonders and confidently expect some marvelous good thing, but these faiths—"historical," "temporary," "miraculous"— soon prove counterfeit.[72] Reason's "generall asent" to the truth of Scripture "may be without any life," lacking the "force" to justify. Trust that one will receive a future good is not faith, but rather presumes the "true and proper confidence" in God that alone grounds such expectation.[73] Saving faith presupposes "intellectual

69. Ames, *Marrow*, I.xxvii.1; xxvi.2.

70. *Ibid*, I.xxvii.6, 3; xxix.4; and more fully, I.xxvi–xxx.

71. Sibbes, *Works* I, 245; Rogers, *Doctrine of Faith*, 20; Rogers, *Seven Treatises*, 8.

72. Wilson, *Christian Dictionary*, s.v. "Faith," defs. 4, 6, 5, 10. An early Puritan like Perkins occasionally denoted faith a "speciall perswasion" of salvation, thus, like Calvin, equating faith with assurance. Ames thought calling faith a persuasion useful in combatting Catholic teachings on the subject, but he and his generation preferred to separate the perception of faith from faith itself. Cf. Perkins, *Works*, III, 2d pagination, 2; Ames, *Marrow*, I.xxvii.19; xxviii.24; Shepard, *Works*, I, 319, 191–93; Bulkeley, *Gosepl-Covenant*, 364.

73. Ames, *Marrow*, I.iii.16; xxvii.15; iii.13.

faith" but involves a more profound "trusting upon Christ" that passes beyond the understanding to embrace the other faculties too.[74] Ezekiel Culverwell's definition may serve as representative: "*a beliefe of the Gospell, whereby I receiue Christ offered vnto me in the same,*" the assent of mind and judgment accompanied by "consent with our heart and will."[75] Faith forges a bond between Christ and the believer that takes the Son into one's deepest self and opens the door to salvation.

To convey faith's complexities required Puritans to use a rich and varied vocabulary. From one perspective, it is a thing, the "eies" and "ears" that apperceive Christ, the "feet" that approach him, the "hand" that applies his benefits.[76] When called a "vertue," "faculty," "disposition," or "habit," it becomes an "inherent principle" that activates the soul.[77] The "engine" whereby one goes to God, faith also functions as the "channels and conduit pipes of grace," the "vessel" that conveys spiritual life.[78] Conceived another way, it comprises the soul's "answer" to God's call and hence denotes an action: "resting" on Christ's "amiablenesse," "receiving" mercy, the "coming of the whole soul to Christ" and its motion between the "two extremes" of emptiness and death to life and fullness.[79] Both a noun and a gerund, faith is what apprehends Christ and the apprehending itself, a cause of grace, its instrument, and the foremost grace of all, "our life," Ames said, as well "an act of life."[80] It is all of these things, and it is incompletely understood without reference to them all.

Faith is wrought in manner congruent with one's inability to accept Christ unaided. The Gospel, perceived by the senses as the sounds of preaching, communicates only a "light flash" to the soul unless the Holy Spirit concurrently regenerates the faculties as they digest the Word.[81] Faith permeates all the powers, but its "first beginning" lies in the will, into which God infuses "a habit or quality of holinesse," that allows it, however imperfectly, to choose good with the intention of serving Him. Likewise imbued with renewing

---

74. Bulkeley, *Gospel-Covenant*, 364.

75. Culverwell, *Treatise of Faith*, 12, 16.

76. Henry Smith, *The Sinners Conuersion* (London, 1594), [A6]ᵛᵒ; Preston, *Saints Qvalification*, 332; Shepard, *Works*, II, 61; Bulkeley, *Gospel-Covenant*, 297.

77. Ames, *Marrow*, II.v.11; Perkins, *Works*, I, 79; Preston, *New Covenant*, 358, and *Breast-Plate*, I, 48; Norton, *Orthodox Evangelist*, 263.

78. Hooker, *Sovles Vocation*, 320; John Preston, *Riches of Mercy to Men in Misery* (London, 1658), 150; Sibbes, *Works*, V, 359.

79. Mather, *Summe,* 13; John Preston, *The Onely Love ot the Chiefest of Ten Thousand: or an heavenly Treatise of the divine Love of Christ* (London, 1640), 20; Hooker, *Sovles Vocation,* 349; Shepard, *Works,* I, 319; II, 317.

80. Ames, *Marrow*, II.v.19.

81. Hooker, *Sovles Vocation*, 35.

grace, the understanding assents to the evidence of Gospel truth, but it is the will, the "Queene of humane acts," where the habit of faith resides and that leads the soul to God.[82] The infixion of faith depends entirely on the "irresistable" work of the Spirit implanting it exclusively into the Elect, and the soul has "no more causal power thereunto, th[a]n a dead body hath unto life," cooperating as a "meere passive receiver."[83]

Incorporating the habit alone does not sufficiently complete the impartation of faith, for the intromitted principle comes to fruition only in activity. The habit "unavoydably" elicits a response in which the Saint "doth now wholly leane upon Christ as his Saviour."[84] This act of faith effectuates the union that grounds justification; to believe, Richard Mather thought, "is that act of the soul, of the will especially," whereby a person relies on Christ "that in him he might be justified and saved." God does not forgive sins until sinners cast themselves on the Redeemer.[85] The habit is God's promise that ushers one into the Covenant of Grace, and the act is the condition one must fulfill to enter it.[86] A believer goes to Christ as an active participant in his or her own salvation, an "efficient co-working cause." The mind apprehends Christ's righteousness and presents its image to the will, whose gracious potential actualizes into movement.[87] Empowered and enlivened by the habit, the faithful for the first time in their lives possess wills that can, in part, will

---

82. Ames, *Marrow*, I.iii.22; John Preston, *The Position of John Preston . . . Concerning the Irresistibleness of Converting Grace* (London, 1654), 5, 12. Kendall, *Calvin and English Calvinism*, perceives a drift in Puritan thought toward a voluntaristic conception of faith.

83. Norton, *Orthodox Evangelist*, 230, 257.

84. Ames, *Marrow*, I.xxvi.28, 26.

85. Richard Mather, *Summe*, 18. Cotton's demurral on this point, in which Anne Hutchinson and her followers concurred, constituted a major issue during the Antinomian Controversy of 1636–38. (This crisis, which fractured Massachusetts Bay and especially the Boston church, involved the efforts of the colony's magistrates and ministers to arrest the spread of Hutchinsonian heterodoxies. For a fuller account, see *infra*, Chapter 8.) Boston's teacher thought that union is accomplished by the habit of faith "but before the act of faith" (*Way of Congregational Churches*, 227), the soul remaining passive in the operation, and he considered the union so wrought sufficient for justification (*Gospel-Conversion*, 41; see also *Treatise of the Covenant*, 22–23, 37). In Cotton's scheme, the act of faith "chiefly" justifies believers only as a consequent effort that puts forth "daily beleeving on the name of Christ for daily pardon," a quotidian revitalizing of the Saint's righteousness (*way of Life*, 334–35, and see *Treatise of the Covenant*, 173). To Cotton's colleagues, this position overthrew the fragile balance they had established between divine omnipotence and human instrumentality, subverting the rationale for human participation in conversion and opening the door for fatalistic libertinism. Some fifteen years after the passions stirred by the affair had subsided, Norton, in a book Cotton prefaced, attempted to reconcile Cotton's doctrine with orthodoxy: depending on one's angle of vision, union is by habit, by act, or by both (*Orthodox Evangelist*, 289).

86. Preston, *New Covenant*, 389–90, and see 358–59. Cf. Bulkeley, *Gospel-Covenant*, 317, 332–33; Shepard, *Works*, I, 309.

87. Norton, *Orthodox Evangelist*, 260 (quotation); Preston, *Breast-Plate*, I, 15.

well. To the Arminian "cavill" that the irresistible infusion of grace turns human beings into stones, "acted and moved by another," Puritans like Preston rejoined that although people indeed cannot resist the granting of the habit, the will's self-propulsion evidences human engagement, "from whence it is that the Scriptures doe exhort us to turne our selves, and circumcise our hearts, and so forth."[88] Momentously, human initiative shares in accomplishing both union with Christ and every subsequent gracious act.

Faith comprises the most critical transformation a person undergoes, and not only because it portends life eternal. If salvation was the goal the preachers ultimately had in mind when they dinned the new birth, they more often dwelled upon the power faith supplies to bring it about. The problem of unregenerates lies in their incapacity to perform saving acts, a condition remediable only if they somehow obtain the vigor to close with the Lord. That ability, Puritans assumed, "must come of God through Christ," transferred in the agency of the Holy Spirit and administered through the Covenant of Grace: its "power" makes a man "a living creature to *God*, which before he was not."[89] The way to power is clear if sinners will take it, which they do by believing. Faith affords two-fold vitality—a "power inherent" that enables them to act, and a "power assisting" drawn continually from the Godhead.[90] Through the ingenerated power of faith, they come to God. Then, in the course of Christian conversation, Saints exercise their ability to perform godly acts, utilizing their faith to accrue the necessary might. "You are to expect and look for power from the Lord Jesus in the use of means," Shepard advised, "For faith fetches all from Christ." Hooker echoed that faith "goes to fetch that spirituall power from God, which we lost in Adam."[91] The natural man lacks potency for spiritual tasks, but the regenerate make use of "the power of Christ" to do those good works that Preston celebrated in a litany of strength:

> if you have the Spirit, you shall finde your selves able to keepe downe your lusts, have power and abilitie to sanctifie the Sabbath, power to pray, power to heare, power to conferre, power to meditate, power to love, power to obey, all above nature; a power to forsake life, and libertie, riches, and honour, pleasure, and all things if they come in competition with Christ. . . .[92]

Quickened by "a new soule of life and power," Saints achieve God's designs. For Preston, and for Puritans in general, power defined Protestantism's chief

88. Preston, *Position*, 2, 16, and *passim*.
89. Mather, *Apologie*, 26; Preston, *New Covenant*, 343.
90. Bulkeley, *Gospel-Covenant*, 353.
91. Shepard, *Works*, II, 58; Hooker, *Sovles Vocation*, 335.
92. Rogers, *Seven Treatises*, 93; Preston, *Remaines*, 143.

characteristic: "what is grace, what is that you call Christianity else, but to do that which another man cannot doe?"[93] Regeneration reverses the helplessness of the ungodly as the Elect flex their spiritual muscles. Conversion links believers to an infinite potential; the bonds of union are, as it were, so many wires carrying energy from a divine dynamo.

Faith is power, a power that draws upon power, and so a Saint's awareness of his or her own powerfulness correlates with the perception of one's belief. A lack of correspondence between the way faith is implanted and the mode of experiencing that phenomenon, however, renders this perception problematic. While preparatory works occur in a sequence and are usually experienced as such, faith and its accompanying graces are introduced "in an instant," but are apprehended over time as a process. Nothing in seventeenth-century Puritan theory compares to the precision with which John Wesley and his contemporaries ticked off the exact moment of their coversions; the preachers thought it "somewhat hard to say the very time when faith is wrought." Christ comes suddenly "though thou knowest not at what time," and a Saint may even "be in covenant, and knows it not."[94] Puritans adumbrated a series of events the faithful pass through, but faith could not be isolated at any especial point, and the progression did not quite attain preparation's specificity. For Perkins, knowledge of the Gospel precedes hope of pardon, hungering and thirsting after Christ, and an approach to the throne of grace to confess sins and crave pardon, all capped by a heartfelt persuasion "whereby euery faithfull man doth particularly apply vnto himselfe those promises which are made in the Gospel." Bulkeley discerned a deep consideration of blessedness, which leads to a longing desire to enter the Covenant, terror over sin, meditation yielding a resolve to go to God, a watchful observance as He responds to the plea for grace, and a range of reactions depending on God's reply. At last, the Lord grants promises of hope that the soul embraces happily. In Downame's more abbreviated scheme, the "firme resolution to chuse Christ alone for his Saviour" succeeds upon the initial hunger and thirst for righteousness.[95] These analyses miss preparation's climactic denouement, the despairing acknowledgment of helplessness; faith's apotheosis occurs after death. There is no unique, certifiable happening coincident with the perception of strength, but faith can be gauged

---

93. Downame, *Christian Warfare*, 1127; Preston, *Breast-Plate*, III, "Of Love," 204.

94. Norton, *Orthodox Evangelist*, 282; Rogers, *Doctrine of Faith*, 126; Thomas Hooker, *The Soules Implantation* (London, 1637), 115; Shepard, *Works*, I, 320. On the other hand, vocation need not be a secret. The relief from God's displeasure so impresses the regenerate that, in Hooker's opinion, they can recount that "in such and such a manner and by such means [God] was pleased to work my heart to his own terms" (*Application*, IX–X, 352).

95. Perkins, *Works*, I, 79–80; Bulkeley, *Gospel-Covenant*, 337–44; Downame, *Christian Warfare*, 1097.

from its results. "True obedience" to God's Word furthered by "conscionable use" of all fit means manifest its effects, deed piled upon good deed to frame an edifice of sanctified works.[96]

Faith also knows itself by a reflex act "whereby we are fully perswaded, and doe beleeve that we doe beleeve." The conscience, cognizant of a person's belief and having recognized "true grace from the shew of it," ratifies one's blessed estate, and the Holy Spirit confirms it.[97] Saints may come to assurance of salvation by substantiating the presence of any single gracious work. The *ordo*'s elements, "like inseparable companions, goe hand in hand," and a soul confident of one may "infallibly conclude" it has interest in the rest.[98] Assurance crowns a Saint's earthly experience. Attempting to describe it, John Preston, a preacher of considerable volubility and poetic imagination, reached the limits of the describable: "it is a certaine divine expression of light, a certaine unexpressible assurance that we are the sonnes of *God*, a certaine secret manifestation, that *God* hath received us, and put away our sinnes," a phenomenon so "extraordinary" that, without the corroboration of "some Christians that did feele it, and know it, you might beleeve there were no such thing."[99] Assurance builds on the objective certainty that God does not disinherit His adopted children. The decree fixes forever the salvation of the Elect, for the Covenant of Grace, once established, "can never be disannulled or broken off." The gospel promise of eternal life is given to faith, and the habit of faith, one's power to believe and enter the Covenant, "cannot be utterly lost."[100]

Saints persevere in grace—"once blessed," Cotton said, "always blessed" —and it was one of the Puritans' great grievances against Catholics and Arminians that they disputed the doctrine of perseverance and disallowed the possibility of assurance, a position "injurious" to God, Bulkeley snapped, "uncomfortable" to Saints.[101] On the contrary, preachers said, "God commands us to beleeve, and not to doubt," for doubting is a sin, a weakness to be "withstood and overcome"; true faith "excludeth" it. Believers should strive to attain absolute trust that they are saved, "else you will fear death and hell that follows it."[102]

---

96. Culverwell, *Time Well Spent*, 274.

97. Norton, *Orthodox Evangelist*, 326; Ames, *Marrow*, I.xxx.15.

98. Perkins, *Works*, II, 18.

99. Preston, *New Covenant*, 400–401.

100. Bulkeley, *Gospel-Covenant*, 76, 276.

101. Cotton, *way of Life*, 335; Bulkeley, *Gospel-Covenant*, 275.

102. Perkins, *Works*, III, 2d pagination, 4; Culverwell, *Time Well Spent*, 83; Hildersam, *CVIII Lectures*, 333; Shepard, *Works*, II, 281. Thus it is misleading to infer, as does Mary Cochran Grimes, "Saving Grace Among Puritans and Quakers: A Study of 17th and 18th Century

The affections that faith engenders are a third indicator of its presence. They vary from account to account, and no one compiled an authoritative list, but a number received frequent notice. Humiliation does not disappear with grace, but now it inspires purposeful self-criticism in place of despair: "the more you can hate and abhorre your selves, the more you are improved thereby." The fright with which unregenerates regard the punishing Lord of justice transmutes into a "reuerent feare" against transgressing God's will.[103] Fear and trembling monitor the Elect's actions; with "much strength," they rule themselves and walk in righteousness.[104] Humility and awe place the Saints at God's disposal, making them tractable and eager to serve Him. Imbued with "such an earnest desire and care to please God with," a Saint is "willing to deny his own will," and subject himself entirely to the Lord's yoke. In return, God encourages the believer with the hope of mercy, and hope, looking towards His "unspeakable compassions," makes it "clear and certain" that the regenerate already possess His glory.[105] All of these affections, even fear, are pleasurable by their connections with faith, and descriptions of the three most frequently mentioned often trumpeted the superlative. Faith calls forth a "sincere" love for God that extends to fellow Saints, and the Elect cleave to Christ with such intensity—"many times they are almost besides themselves"—that they gladly follow Christ into the grave, "yea into prison[.]"[106] Happiness at having received the Spirit's benefits, most manifest during spiritual exercises, is "no slight nor flitting joy," but, on the basis of 1 Pet. 1.8, an *"vnspeakable and glorious"* transcendence that mingles with sublime peace and comfort.[107] Unparticularized, "peace" referred to the soul's reaction when assurance of God's love, pardon, and salvation "banisheth feare and terrour," but it was generally understood as pertaining to the peace of conscience, which "passeth the understanding of a man to conceive, *Phil. 4.7.*"[108] Regeneration establishes a new emotional life.

Conversion Experiences," *Quaker History*, 72 (1983), 21, that it was "impossible" for a Puritan to know if s/he was saved, a "mystery" compounded by the anxiety necessarily attendant to grace. A Saint could not know definitively if someone else was saved, but could determine his/her own election with certainty, and, as one grew in grace, doubts over salvation would diminish.

103. Preston, *Saints Qvalification*, 30, 31; Laurence Chaderton, *An Excellent and godly Sermon, most needfull for this time* . . . (London, 1578), [D.v.]ro.

104. Preston, *New Covenant*, 380.

105. Culverwell, *Time Well Spent*, 274; Bulkeley, *Gospel-Covenant*, 345; Shepard, *Works*, II, 150.

106. Ames, "Conscience," II.vi.22; Hooker, *Sovles Vocation*, 257, 260.

107. Downame, *Christian Warfare*, 1120.

108. Rogers, *Doctrine of Faith*, 260; Cotton, *Christ the Fountaine*, 102. Nothing in the Epistle demands or even encourages the interpretation Puritans gave Phil. 4.7. Paul is concerned with a perfectionist heresy threatening the Philippian church, and the subject of conscience never

The passions of grace complete the affective cycle of conversion, an "order of emotion" that, commencing with confidence in one's own abilities, passes through sorrow and despair on the way to comfort and hope. Peace, love, and joy are not usually ascribed to Puritans, yet according to the preachers, every Saint experiences them. To a limited degree, affections distinguish the *ordo*'s various works from each other. Peace of conscience follows forgiveness of sin through justification, and sanctification manifests itself in the zeal to accomplish God's commands, but these (and other) associations evince formulae rather than reality, samples of the theologian's art that ministers did not expect life to reproduce. Since vocation and the other graces are wrought simultaneously in an imperceptible instant, arrogating one affection to a specific work was a procedure somewhat arbitrary and never exact. The same affection might indicate the operation of several works: unspeakable joy, to cite one case, witnesses to faith, justification, adoption, and the first fruits of glorification.[109] Some preachers located the same affection in several works, as when Perkins listed the love of God as part of adoption on one occasion and of sanctification on another.[110] Gracious affections constitute an aggregation of passions that coexist in regenerates. The person who loves God and rejoices in peace of conscience also fears the Lord, gives thanks for His gifts, and desires to please Him. John Cotton, in fact, proposed that sanctification combines affections in ways "not to bee found in nature," joy and grief, for example, or joy and sorrow.[111] That any of these emotions may connote a particular part of the *ordo* is less important

---

figures. In the immediate context (ch. 4.4–7), Paul tells them to rejoice in the Lord, forbear, and make their requests known to God, extending assurance that "the peace of God, which passeth all understanding, shall keep your hearts and minds through Christ Jesus." The passage does not suggest (though it does not deny) that Paul sought to assuage emotions of guilt. Calvin, for one, offered no such interpretation; see *Commentaries on the Epistles of Paul the Apostle to the Philippians, Colossians, and the Thessalonians*, trans., ed., and collated by John Pringle (Edinburgh, 1851), 120. Puritans did conceive alternative readings—Ames, *Marrow*, I.xxx.23, cited it to support the proposition that peace is a quieting of the mind deriving in part from deliverance from evil and in part from the presence or hope of good—but the normative exegesis connected God's peace with that of the conscience: Perkins, *Works*, I, 84. Greenham, *Works*, 1st p. 97, Preston, *New Covenant*, 422, and Hooker, *Application*, IX–X, 441, quote Phil. 4.7 without explicitly citing it, while Downame, *Christian Warfare*, 1116, and Sibbes, *Works*, IV, 167, quote the verse while appealing, incorrectly, to others. The preachers could ground their hermeneutic on GenB's marginal gloss to Phil. 4.7. (The identical process is at work in the treatment of Ro. 5.1, where both GenB's gloss and Calvin (*Commentaries on the Epistle of Paul the Apostle to the Romans*, trans. and ed., John Owen (Edinburgh, 1849), 187) refer to conscience. See Perkins, *Works*, I, 369: Norton, *Orthodox Evangelist*, 324; Shepard, *Works*, I, 247; Cotton, *way of Life*, 314.)

109. Rogers, *Seven Treatises*, 55; John Cotton and John Wilson, "To The Christian Reader," in Mather, *Summe*, unpaginated; Forbes, *Letter*, 57; Ames, *Marrow*, I.xxx.21.

110. Perkins, *Works*, I, 369, 84.

111. Cotton, *Christ the Fountaine*, 119, 110, 113.

than the certainty that they issue from the donation of power in faith and that they register this all-important metamorphosis. Where contrition and terror noise one's helplessness to oneself, love and joy whisper new-found strength. The affective cycle of conversion betokens the changing status of a Saint's potency.

IV

Puritans took the new birth in John 3.3 literally; Saints begin their spiritual life with infantile capacities. The "new borne babe in Christ," so recently regenerated, "feeles it selfe in a cold and naked condition, and thereupon feels its owne weaknesse and hunger." Neonate Saints, their little faith often compared, on the basis of Mat. 17.20, to a grain of mustard seed, lack assurance that God has forgiven their sins; desiring mercy, they pray God for pardon and "strength to leaue them."[112] Weak faith does take hold of the promises effectually and is perfectly competent to grasp the covenant, but it often falters in performing its duties: "a weake hand is able to receive as well as a stronger," Preston alleged, "but a stronger can doe more worke."[113] Children mature, however, and so does faith. Although the godly never outgrow their absolute dependence on the Lord, by degrees they attain to strong faith, "which overcomes all difficulties, & proceeds freely in its course," belief filled with assurance. As faith increases the other graces keep pace: the regenerate ripen into Christian "middle age," wrestling with "courage against our sinfull lusts," finally evolving into experienced Saints whose grace guides them most "constantlie" of all. Time withers the body; grace improves with age. Young Christians, Sibbes reported, make " a great expression" of zeal with their superior natural strength, but elderly Saints "grow more in strength and stableness, and are more refined." Not carried by youth's "full stream," still they are "more stable and judicious, more heavenly-minded, more mortified." Faith reaches its apex in senescence.[114]

Spiritual growth requires the constant exercise of faith. Increased assurance and facility in godly duties develop through practice, and only through practice; no blessings attach to dormant potential. "The habit serues but for the act," Preston commented, "*God* rewards not men according to the habits they haue, but according to their workes."[115] A life lived in faith means a life

---

112. Cotton, *way of Life*, 6; Perkins, *Works*, I, 366.

113. Preston, *New Covenant*, 415. Cf. Bulkeley, *Gospel-Covenant*, 338; Perkins, *Works*, I, 641.

114. Ames, "Conscience," II.vi.15; Rogers, *Seven Treatises*, 115; Sibbes, *Works*, VII, 222–23, #311.

115. Preston, *Breast-Plate*, II, 130.

lived by faith, trust in God and thoughts of Christ inhering in every operation; ideally, "every particular act" a Saint commits coincides with "a distinct
act of faith." Even Thomas Shepard, as demanding a mentor as can be found
among the professional taskmasters who manned Puritan pulpits, admitted
that such perfect correspondence "can not be," but he insisted that in "every
fit season" the soul "ought to look up to the Lord for life and fresh strength."
Saints renew themselves, recurring to faith as the source of gracious power,
and should they lag, "thence comes all the deadnesse of heart," Cotton
warned, "that is in many of the best of Gods servants, by not putting their
faith to exercise in this kinde." Conscience dulls, the sweetness of pardon
vanishes, and "experienced" Christians return to the throes of souls "that
never yet knew what assurance meant."[116]

The Elect defend against spiritual deadness and raise their faith to consistently higher levels by re-enacting the actions and affections associated with
coming to believe. The experience of conversion takes place repeatedly, a
circumstance alluded to by the phrase "first conversion" to designate the
inceptive happening. "First" presupposes additional conversions, iterations of
the earlier event, as in Richard Mather's evocation of God and man making a
covenant "either at his first conversion, or at other times[.]"[117] Reliving the
humiliation and desire that accompany infusion of the habit augments faith.
Shepard told his congregation not to rest smugly on faith attained, "Be
always converting, and be always converted . . . more humble, more sensible
of sin, more near to Christ Jesus; and then you that are sure may be more
sure."[118] If belief wanes or good works pale, "labor a new Conversion, *i.e.*
renew and act over the work of Conversion," Hooker urged:

> The Disciples were called, and so converted, truly, savingly humbled, and
> yet they must renew and act over again these first impressions of the
> powerful operations of the Spirit of God, be broken hearted, loosened
> from thy lusts as at the first, be abased and brought to nothing in thine
> owne sence and apprehension as at the first, be drawn to Christ as at the
> first; and there is more reason and greater necessity of this, than men are
> readily aware of.[119]

---

116. Shepard, *Works*, II, 58; Cotton, *way of Life*, 314–15.

117. Mather, *Apologie*, 3. Cf. Hildersam, *Doctrine of Fasting*, 89; Cotton, *Christ the Fountaine*, 50, among others. The phrase "first regeneration" is used in the same sense, Culverwell,
Time Well Spent, 42; Perkins, *Works*, I, 736.

118. Shepard, *Works*, II, 632.

119. Hooker, *Application*, IX–X, 377–78. Hambrick-Stowe, *Practice of Piety*, has also called
attention to the Saints' continuing recapitulation of an initial religious experience. He demonstrates that a wide variety of cultural practices, from public events such as covenant renewal
ceremonies to family devotions to the most closeted performances of meditation, led believers
through what I have labelled the affective cycle of reconversion.

Saints believe by denying their own power, and they revitalize faith by recapitulating their primary denial.

Reconversion notwithstanding, the course to Christian maturity never runs smoothly. Paul's struggle in Romans 7 to control his refractory will epitomizes godly life, the preachers thought, and in Gal. 5.17, they read the etiology of the Apostle's inner conflict: "the flesh lusteth against the Spirit, and the Spirit against the flesh." The flesh, as Puritans understood the term, refers to "the natural corruption or inclination of the minde, will, and affections" against the Law, and the spirit is a "created quality of holiness" in the same faculties wrought by the Holy Spirit. Sainthood divides a person, the *"old man"* still under Satan's dominion sharing space with the *"new man,"* two opposed impulses directing the individual towards or away from sin. Saints accumulate a measure of comfort from discerning this "self-combat," which demonstrates that "sin hath no quiet possession in thee," but the flesh induces pernicious effects that far outweigh its benefits.[120] It can cause the Elect to apply the promises "falsly", and to "presume of Gods loue and our owne saluation," taking blessings for granted and forgetting responsibilities. A few may lapse into "some great sinne," equivalent to Noah's drunkenness, David's adultery and murder, or Peter's denial of Christ.[121] A feeling of faith—knowledge acquired by the external senses that one believes—often disappears, leading a Saint to "thinke, yea appeare to others, that the life of the spirit is not in him," and to despair over his estate.[122] For these and other reasons, even regenerates with the "strongest faith" do not always retain their assurance of salvation, acceding, despite admonitions to the contrary, to "doubts and some distrust."[123] The flesh cuts into the daily strength Saints draw from faith, and gracious work declines as believers drift from the source of their power. The presumptuous forget their dependence on God and revert to trusting their own skills. Gross sinners turn from the covenant. Those who miss the feeling of faith wonder if they ever really believed, and since duties "spring from assurance," loss of certainty dampens the motivation to fulfill the commands.[124] Corruption enervates faith as it gains the upper hand, for the sway of sin is impotence.

120. Perkins, *Works*, I, 469; Downame, *Christian Warfare*, 1018, 1019; Sibbes, *Works*, V, 406.

121. Downame, *Christian Warfare*, 1098; Perkins, *Works*, I, 377.

122. Greenham, *Works*, 449. "Feeling," in the technical vocabulary of the faculty-humor psychology, defines the power by which the soul gains knowledge of objects by apprehending qualities with the external senses, [Stephen Batman], *Batman vppon Bartholome, His Booke De Proprietatibus Rerum* . . . (London, 1582) , 15ro. A "feeling" constitutes a datum acquired by the senses from their experience of the material world. Cf. *OED*, "Feeling," defs. 2b, 3; John C. English, "The Puritan Doctrine of Christian Initiation," *Studia Theologica*, 6 (1969), 162.

123. Hildersam, *CVIII Lectures*, 333.

124. Sibbes, *Works*, V, 453.

Saints repel the flesh by repenting, which turns them away from sin and ameliorates its baneful effects. Repentance includes "godly sorrow for sinne, wherein the soule humbleth it selfe before God, and commeth home to him," as well as "an vtter condemning & misliking of that sin which we haue left," but the most encompassing definition points to an intense reversal of thought and action that engages the entire personality, "a thorough change of the whole man," whose soul and body "are turned a quite contrary way; the heart is turned out of the way of sinne, into the way of holinesse."[125] Only the godly have the capacity and the grace to accomplish this feat. Hypocrites may reform under the spur of "seruile feare and terrour of conscience," confusing "a temporary restrayning of their corruptions" for the Spirit's work, and unregenerates preparing for faith, in Norton's opinion, manifest "legal repentance," certain "inward workings" of the Spirit "that do dispose to a change," but genuine repentance embraces righteousness with that heartfelt intensity achievable only by "such an one," said Perkins, "as is in the sight of God regenerated & iustified, & indued with true faith."[126] God initiates repentance through the work of the Spirit in "the ministery of the Gospel," but man plays an active role. The Spirit "convinceth our conscience" that a Saint's ways are evil and refocuses attention on the dangers of sin. A natural conscience "cannot change the will," but a regenerate one can, and, properly alarmed, it directs the will to seek the good.[127] Empowered by its gracious habits, the will complies, and the repentant sinner reverts to godly ways. The soul's response is not automatic, for Saints can choose to ignore the Spirit and defer repentance, a practice the preachers inveighed against. The "gales of grace" blow intermittently at God's good pleasure, "therefore take the advantage of the present motions of the blessed Spirit," Sibbes counselled, "The longer we live in any sin unrepented of, the more our hearts will be hardened."[128] Responding with alacrity when the Spirit enlightens the soul, regenerates avoid the condemnation that sin can "fasten" upon them, and re-establish the connections to God's might attenuated by the flesh. Casting themselves upon His mercy, they reconfirm their "hold of God's strength."[129]

In the order of nature, repentance follows justification and sanctification; in the order of time, it synchronizes with infusion of the other graces; in

125. Paul Baynes, *A Letter Written by M*^r^. *Pavl Bayne . . . Effectually instructing, and earnestly prouoking to true repentance, loue, and new obediance* (London, 1617), 4; Greenham, *Works,* 178; Preston, *Remaines,* 167. Cf. John Preston, *The Fulnesse of Christ for Us* (London, 1640), 18–19; Wilson, *Christian Dictionary,* s.v. "Repentance," defs. 3, 4; Arthur Dent, *A Sermon of Repentaunce* (London, 1583), A5^ro^—[A6]^ro^.

126. Downame, *Christian Warfare,* 1106; Norton, *Orthodox Evangelist,* 153–54.

127. Perkins, *Works,* I, 456; Sibbes, *Works,* VI, 213; Preston, *Remaines,* 25.

128. Sibbes, *Works,* VI, 212.

129. Thomas Hooker, *The Sovles Exaltation* (London, 1638), 194; Cotton, *Gods Mercie,* 71.

practice, it begins with sadness and ends with a plea for power. Perceiving their past sins, Saints grieve for having committed them, so that repentance "riseth of a godly sorrow in the heart, as *Paul* teacheth, 2 Cor. 7.10."[130] What the Apostle named "the sorrow of the world" Puritans interpreted as self-concerned grief, more troubled by earthly afflictions or fear of God's punitive wrath than for sin itself. In contradistinction, a soul truly humbled with godly sorrow mourns "not so much in respect to himselfe," as in respect "to God, because [H]e is offended and dishonoured by his sinne."[131] Other affections accompany godly sorrow—hatred of sin compounds with an "earnest desire, and setled purpose" to avoid future sin and obey the commands.[132] Wanting to atone and to live godly lives, Saints conduct, in Perkins's schema, a "diligent and serious examination" by the conscience "for all manner of sins," using the Moral Law as the rule. Having determined the nature and extent of their transgressions, the Elect confess to God, arraigning themselves before the "barre" of His judgment, setting forth the indictment, and finally acknowledging that they are "worthy of euerlasting death, hell, and damnation." The verdict of conscience elicits a prayer for pardon, called "Deprecation," in which the guilty are to plead for favor and ask for mercy in a manner that must have been the most demeaning that Perkins could conceive. Like cripples and lepers who beg on the street, Saints must "vnlap our legges and armes, and shew the sores of our sins," crying for pity "that wee may finde mercie at Gods hands, as they get almes at the hands of the passengers." A final prayer asks for "grace and strength" to walk "in newnesse of life." In repentance, as in conversion, self-abasement anticipates the reward of power.[133]

Repentance is a fruit of faith that abets the growth of godly life. When the flesh blocks the progress of faith and hinders its operations, repentance hastens to remove the impediments. If Saints fall into some gross sin or presume salvation and slacken in duties, repentance counteracts the effects; should they lose assurance or the feeling of faith, the difficulty can be traced back to some sin and expunged. Repentance clears the obstacles to renewed faith, and, with reconversion, forms a second means for generating increased power. The two methods resemble each other in their function of furthering spiritual growth, their repetitive quality, the role Saints play in each, and the experience undergone. Repentance recurs, by definition: "Ordinary repentance is that, which euery Christian is to performe euery day," Perkins said, and in Ames's estimation, it is not "true and sound" when it "doth not

130. Perkins, *Works*, I, 455.
131. Hildersam, *CVIII Lectures*, 137.
132. Ames, "Conscience," II.viii.8, 9.
133. Perkins, *Works*, I, 458, 462, 463.

virtually [i.e. in strength] continue, and is actually renewed as often as need is, from the time of conversion to the end of life."[134] Satan never sleeps, and Saints must "Renew your repentance and faith in the blood of Christ daily," to neutralize sin's temptations.[135] In both reconversion and repentance, though not, of course, in preparation, one gains strength partly through the merit of one's own good deeds. To be sure, according to Preston, a person cannot "doe any action" without God's concourse, and in tasks requiring more strength than they can muster Saints "hath need" of God's "speciall supervenient helpe," but grace does enable them to improve themselves: "we maintaine Free-will in the Regenerate, and as farre as thou art Regenerate, thou hast Free-will, thou mayst doe more than thou doest." The power of the regenerated will allowed preachers to make a direct appeal for reform, a significant homiletic shift from the practice of motivating unregenerates to activity in order to bring home their incapacity: there is a "continuall wasting of strength" in the soul that necessitates the daily renewing of union with Christ, said Preston, therefore "the more you doe this," the more "you shall finde new strength comming to you[.]"[136] The same thinking and technique underlie the alarums to repent when the Spirit affords the chance. The experience of repentance duplicates the first part of the affective cycle of conversion (repeated in reconversion), for it parallels the same downward spiral from sorrow to humiliation that heralds the infusion of faith. Preparation begins with contrition and repentance with godly sorrow, affections similar enough for John Rogers to remind that contrition is "a preparative act fitting a man to Faith," repentance a "consequent" grace, and that confounding the two absurdly suggests that one can please God before faith.[137] The end result is conscious self-depreciation and the desire for closure with God. In one sense, repentance truncates the conversion experience; the preachers generally omitted mention of the joy, love, and peace of conscience attendant on conversion, and Greenham's characterization can serve as a motto: "repentance beginneth in vs, continueth and endeth with sorrow."[138] In the final analysis, though, repentance and reconversion are similar enough to consider them versions of a single process of self-renewal for spiritual growth, a reiterated experience of weakness transubstantiating into power. By incessantly going "out of themselves" to God, Saints grow in faith, assurance, and strength.[139]

134. Perkins, *Works*, I, 458; Ames, *Marrow*, I.xxvi.33.

135. Davenport, *Saints Anchor-Hold*, 107.

136. Preston, *Saints Qvalification*, 474, 460, 488, 489.

137. Rogers, *Doctrine of Faith*, 125.

138. Greenham, *Works*, 178.

139. Cf. Baird Tipson, "The Routinized Piety of Thomas Shepard's Diary," *Early American Literature*, 13 (1978), 64–80.

V

Puritan thinking about the *ordo salutis* filters through an overriding concern with humankind's generic infirmity, the corruption, inherited from Adam, that makes good works impossible and sin inevitable. Through the virtue of faith, implanted in vocation, Saints have their sins pardoned, the corrosion of God's Image reversed, and salvation assured. Faith draws power from God and enables them to perform works that please Him. Conversion brings about a real change in the soul, a new disposition wrought by the Holy Spirit regenerating the faculties and imparting spiritual capabilities. The constitutional and ontological transformation of the Elect parallels a psychological change equally far-reaching: they stop trusting their own strength and rely entirely on God's. The dispensation of faith, preachers explained, has nothing to do with human merit, and its nature renders unaided efforts to achieve it impossible. Not simply an assent to gospel promises or the persuasion that one believes, although including the former and inspiring the latter, faith is first of all a supernatural habit that the soul receives passively before it can act. Conversion occurs only after a period of preparation has eliminated all confidence in one's own abilities. Self-sufficiency associates with reprobation, self-deprecation with grace, and within the affective cycle, faith succeeds upon despair of ever attaining it. Consequently, the power of faith corresponds to admitting one's powerlessness, and the strength of Saints correlates directly with their humiliation, a prescription that, from Puritan mouths, sounds too earnestly scriptural ever to be accounted Orwellian: *"our way to be stong is to be weake*; weake in our selves, that we may be strong in the power of [God's] might."[140] Self-confidence returns in the guise of dependence on God, self-reliance through submission.

In its own terms an explication of the Holy Spirit's redemptive motions and the human reactions to them, the way of salvation constitutes a system through whose publication Puritans sought to ensure continuing labor in the Lord's service. The theory of conversion promotes a modal personality that can fashion feelings of humiliation into confidence of strength whenever activity falters. The phenomena of infusion teach the mechanism: as Saints pass through contrition and humiliation to peace, joy and love, they experience coming to power for the first time. Once incorporated and mastered, this repertoire of affections becomes available when the sense of power disappears. In such situations, spiritual deadness or loss of assurance signals that faith is weakening and instigates repentance: Saints review their lives, take note of sins, and humbly cast themselves upon the Lord. Reaffirming one's weakness solicits recovery of strength, and sense of power returns, its concomitant affections reappear, and godly work resumes. The *ordo*, then, is

---

140. Bulkeley, *Gospel-Covenant*, 286.

a construct for motivating activity, and it is wonderfully self-regulating. When adversity casts a Saint down, deprecation comes easily, and with it renewed strength. The more insidious danger is prosperity. Puritans ran the risk that assurance of faith, rooted in the absolute perseverance of the Saints, would slide into presumption, and they worried about having little to worry about: "the more wee grow in gifts, the more to hunger, the more to complaine of our vnworthines, the more to bee humbled in our selues, the more meekly to iudge of others: when wee are most quiet with all things, then to thinke our selues least quiet, and then most to feare our selues."[141] Like an electric motor, which creates kinetic energy as its armature rotates from terminal to terminal whose polarities constantly change, Puritans prevented the stasis of godly work by spinning between complacency and doubt; doubt spurs the desire for assurance, which encourages deeds that increase faith, but assurance edges into presumption and inspires doubt. In theory, at least, the engine of Puritan activity, once engaged, never shuts off.

141. Greenham, *Works*, 22.

4

The Saints Zealous in Love and Labor

A Puritan sloth is as hard to imagine as a Puritan humorist. The Saints have been called many things since the sixteenth century, but seldom if ever have they been accounted lazy. From Ben Jonson's caustic caricature of Zeal-of-the-Land Busy, ready to intrude his opinions on any subject, to Michael Walzer's portrayal of them as the indefatigable pioneers of modern radical politics, observers have readily acknowledged their "extraordinary activism."[1] To link this industry with the ethic of striving that lies at the heart of Puritan thought is easy, for the preachers always spoke of the godly life as arduous. "I say shew your grace, shew your regeneration, by being new creatures, by doing more than others," Preston urged, and he practiced what he preached. Chaplain to Charles I, Master of Emmanuel College at Cambridge, participant in Puritan parliamentary politics while commuting between lectureships at both Lincoln's Inn and Trinity Church in Cambridge, Preston forced several careers into the less than two decades between his conversion and his death in 1628 at the age of forty from consumption probably exacerbated by exhaustion. "[H]e never (by his good will) rested that day since God was truly known unto him untill [his death]," wrote his first biographer, "God gave him therefore now an everlasting rest."[2] Few

1. Michael Walzer, *The Revolution of the Saints: A Study in the Origins of Radical Politics* (Cambridge, Mass., 1965), 3–4, 313, also 12–13, 18, 306–7, 318.

2. Preston, *Breast-Plate*, III, 205; Irvonwy Morgan, *Prince Charles's Puritan Chaplain* (London, 1957), 18, 76, 109–15, 117–24, 202–3, and *passim*; Thomas Ball, "The Life of Doctor Preston," in Samuel Clarke, *A Generall Martyrologie . . . Whereunto are added,The Lives of Sundry Modern Divines* (London, 1651), 520.

people more fully exemplified the Puritan ideal that pious performance is the thanksgiving for the gift of eternal life.

It was axiomatic among Puritans that unregenerate humanity could never duplicate such sustained achievement in God's name. Their faculties corrupted in consequence of Adam's fall, natural men and women lack both the facility and the mental stamina necessary to perform righteous deeds continuously. Ability to do the Lord's bidding is realized only by means of a double transformation during conversion. Through a physical attraction of the soul, people sunk in sin receive power by and in faith. Acts of compliance with the commandments, previously tainted by corruption, now take on the sanctity of righteous deeds. However, this revitalized capacity to perform is useless without energetic efforts to employ it: "when faith lyes still in the heart, and is not stirred and moued, nor shewes it selfe in the fruits of it, this we say is ineffectuall faith; whereas faith should be in the soule . . . shewing it selfe by motion, by action, by doing somewhat or other."[3] Without the believer's inclination to use it, the soul's newly engineered machinery would remain silent, but, while regenerating the faculties, the Spirit concurrently restructures the Saint's thoughts and feelings into a new motivational system. The mentality of wilful obedience in subordination to God's loving mercy, exhibited in the Covenant of Grace, replaces the confidence, already subverted by preparatory humiliation, that one can perform good works on one's own. Conversion is also a change of mind, which preachers explicated in hopes of encouraging Prestonian achievement. Descriptions of the psychodynamic by which regenerates come to labor for the Lord thread disjointedly, but insistently, throughout Puritan literature. The theology of conversion adumbrates a psychology of work.

I

The classic study of Puritan enterprise belongs to Max Weber, who discerned a causal relationship between the value that certain Protestant denominations placed on the methodical practice of piety, and the energetic, calculating spirit he considered the genius of capitalism and of Western civilization generally.[4] Inspiration to toil diligently at one's worldly calling, he argued,

---

3. Preston, *Breast-Plate*, II, 26.

4. Max Weber, *The Protestant Ethic and the Spirit of Capitalism*, trans. Talcott Parsons (New York, 1958 [orig. 1930]); see also Weber, "The Protestant Sects and the Spirit of Capitalism," in Hans H. Gerth and C. Wright Mills, trans. and eds., *From Max Weber: Essays in Sociology* (New York, 1958), 302–22. Herbert Lüthy, "Once Again: Calvinism and Capitalism," reprinted in S. N. Eisenstadt, *The Protestant Ethic and Modernization: A Comparative View* (New York, 1968), 87–92, suggests that what Weber finally meant by "spirit of capitalism" is the

came first from religious motives, and then attached itself to the accumulation of goods that eventually became its guiding rationale. The prolonged debate over the methodology, scope, accuracy, and implications of the thesis may obscure the fact that it first of all investigates the roots of a specific devotional behavior. The proposed historical connection between pursuing one's vocation for God and performing it for mammon depends initially upon the convincing exhibition of purposeful work's psychological origins in religious belief. Weber examines four Protestant theologies to demonstrate how their doctrines fostered "innerworldly asceticism," a positive orientation towards mundane industry, but Calvinism, which he handles as a virtual synonym for English Puritanism, bears the greatest analytic burden. Weber points out both its demanding, totally rationalized ethical universe—a "more intensive" religious valuation of moral action "has perhaps never existed"— and the "systematic self-control" that such a design requires.[5] Calvinist/ Puritan theology committed believers to a lifetime of sustained effort in God's service, and the doctrine of predestination promoted a mentality fitted to discharge the tasks at hand. The idea that God's ineffable and arbitrary decree alone determines a person's fate must have spawned "a feeling of unprecedented inner loneliness" within the individual. No one or thing can help humanity achieve salvation, for the apparatus of priests and sacraments through which the Catholic Church dispenses grace crumbled under the "magnificent consistency" of Calvin's baleful logic. Its disappearance exposed man to an "intercourse" with God "carried on in deep spiritual isolation," a solitude that necessitated restructuring the process by which believers apprehend their estate. Because "the most important thing in life" for a Reformation soul was "eternal salvation," because "the after-life was not only more important, but in many ways also more certain, than all the interests of life in this world," the desire to attain the knowledge that one is saved must "have forced all other interests into the background."[6] The Elect cannot come to this awareness through institutional mediation. Instead, they achieve the assurance of salvation by observing their actions. The signs of grace manifest themselves daily as the Saints carry out the regimen of God's commands, for assurance attends upon "intense worldly activity . . . as the most suitable means."[7] Obeying the Law, the faithful realize that they are saved. Puritan-

---

governing structure of Western society's attitudes, a rationality powerfully inimical to impulsive, spontaneous, instinctual action that generates the pattern of all occidental culture, not merely its economic aspects. Cf. Benjamin Nelson, "Weber's Protestant Ethic: Its Origins, Wanderings, and Foreseeable Futures," in Charles Y. Glock and Phillip Q. Hammond, eds., *Beyond the Classics? Essays in the Scientific Study of Religion* (New York, 1973), 78–80.

5. Weber, *Protestant Ethic*, 116, 115.

6. *Ibid.*, 104, 106–7, 109–10.

7. *Ibid.*, 112.

ism mandates activity by its dogmatic emphasis on fulfilling the commandments for the greater glory of God, and it stimulates effort by promising that such labor can satisfy the all-consuming need to attain certainty of grace. The motive to work emerges from the wish to ascertain one's election.

An examination into the way ideas structure how people behave, the *Protestant Ethic* asserts that belief-systems direct action. Puritanism, the case in point, articulated exacting rules of conduct and, by establishing them as the means to gratify believers' deepest longings, promoted prodigies of moral service. Sibbes confirms Weber's insight that, in the preachers' thinking, the motive to enhance one's confidence of election encouraged good works: "The sense of assured hope cannot be maintained without a great deal of pains, diligence, and watchfulness . . . Therefore we should labour to put our graces into exercise."[8] Nevertheless, the exposition proves vulnerable on several counts. The relationship between the motive to work and assurance is reciprocal, not unidirectional. Works attempt to satisfy the desire for assurance, while experiencing the certainty of salvation in turn promotes godly labor.

---

8. Sibbes, *Works*, VII, 212, #242. A contrary evaluation of Puritan thinking is Robert M. Mitchell, *Calvin's and the Puritan's View of the Protestant Ethic* (Washington, D.C., 1979), 54: "Works do not produce faith or assurance of election." Mitchell further contends that "there was not the great desire or need for assurance. Once again, this is not to say there were not some who had doubts about salvation, but ' . . . these appear to have come only from the hypersensitive and were thus not an important part of the normal English [*sic*] Puritan life . . .'." This devaluation of the importance of assurance would have surprised John Downame, who thought certain knowledge of the Spirit's indwelling "the greatest question, and the waightiest and most important case of conscience, that can bee propounded or knowne of vs" (*Christian Warfare*, 1113; cf. Perkins, *Works*, I, 421), and Marshall M. Knappen, the authority partially quoted (see *Tudor Puritanism*, 394). To complete Knappen's sentence is to refute Mitchell: "While these appear to have come only from the hypersensitive and were thus not an important part of the normal Puritan life, there were enough of them to give the Puritan pastors many troublesome hours." (It may be added that the frequent advice on how to obtain assurance indicates that more than "hypersensitive" Saints had doubts about their estate.) Knappen immediately goes on to confirm the link between assurance and effort that Weber surmised: "The usual solution was to go over the details of the Christian experience, minimizing its requirements in dealing with tender consciences, and finally to resort to a rather un-Protestant, but nonetheless effective, common-sense doctrine of works." Although there were various methods of achieving assurance, "good works were the most common prescription." They constitute "a sure evidence" of election (*ibid.*). Puritan divines were acutely aware that assurance can fade, and they declared works a means to increase it. Mitchell's error on this point proceeds from what can only be called a distaste for Weber's essay delivered in a tone of captious indignation. Although his monograph contains some valuable correctives, and on numerous issues accords with what will be said here, it seems inspired by an ideal of removing any possible connection between Puritanism and what Mitchell sees as a secular (one wants to say unholy), individualistic, grasping spirit of capitalism. This perspective results in misrepresentations of Weber's thesis (he does not equate the Protestant ethic and the spirit of capitalism, as Mitchell implies (62–63)). It also overidealizes the Puritans (there is some justice in Weber's claim that they distrusted spontaneous amusement (*Protestant Ethic*, 166–67), even though one can agree with Mitchell (50) that they did not abjure worldly pleasure enjoyed in moderation).

"The assurance of a confirmed Christian doth increase his alacrity and diligence in duty, and is always seen in his more obedient, holy, fruitful, life,"
proclaimed Richard Baxter, the pastor of Kidderminster, "he is never so
fruitful, so thankful, so heavenly, as when he hath the greatest certainty that
he shall be saved."[9] Weber's evidence that Puritans valued the methodical
exercise of one's calling draws heavily on Baxter, whose output testifies to
Puritan industry (the Wing *Short Title Catalogue* groans with over 180
separate titles), but whose theology departs from Weber's ideal type of
Puritanism on a critical issue. The Westminster Confession of 1647, whose
"authoritative words" served as Weber's source on the subject,[10] enshrine
what is sometimes called "double predestination," a construction that makes
God responsible for the decrees of both election and reprobation. Admitting
the former, Baxter threw out the latter. Against those who insisted that
Christ's redemption, though sufficient in itself for all, does not belong to the
predestined damned, he held that it has a universal intent and applies to any
who choose it. Christ may save even individuals who, though ignorant of the
Gospel, live exemplary lives. Since Baxter did not subscribe to the *decretum
horribile*, yet upheld the doctrine of assurance, his advocacy of work becomes
harder to understand as a prescription to relieve spiritual loneliness induced
by the decree. This minor difficulty is symptomatic of a broader issue, for it
raises the question as to whether Weber properly appreciated the function of
predestination in Puritan homiletics.[11]

That God foreordains a person to heaven or hell for no other reason than
to manifest His glory is an arresting idea, and it grabbed Weber sufficiently
for him to call predestination Calvinism's "most characteristic dogma."[12] This
evaluation overstates its significance. Calvin did not accord it primary dogmatic importance, nor did the preachers single it out for special emphasis in
sermons.[13] Other topics—faith, justification, sanctification, to name a few—

9. Richard Baxter, *Select Practical Writings of Richard Baxter*, ed. Leonard Bacon, 2 vols.
(New Haven, 1831), II, 64; cf. Preston, *Breast-Plate*, II, 72.

10. Weber, *Protestant Ethic*, 99.

11. Hugh Martin, *Puritanism and Richard Baxter* (London, 1954), 132–37. Weber, *Protestant
Ethic*, 258, n.1, recognizes Baxter's position, but does not discuss the ramifications for his
argument. Robert S. Paul, "Weber and Calvinism: The Effects of a 'Calling'," *Canadian
Journal of Theology*, 11 (1965), 28, makes a similar point.

12. Weber, *Protestant Ethic*, 98.

13. Wilhelm Niesel, *The Theology of Calvin*, trans. Harold Knight (Philadelphia, 1956), 159–
69; John T. McNeill, *The History and Character of Calvinism* (New York, 1954), 201–2;
François Wendel, *Calvin: The Origins and Development of His Religious Thought*, trans.
Philip Mairet (London, 1963), 263–84; New, *Anglican and Puritan*, 15–19, 33, 77; but see also
Haller, *Rise of Puritanism*, 83, 85; Coolidge, *Pauline Renaissance*, 115–16; and esp. Wallace,
Puritans and Predestination, passim. Predestination assumed increasing importance in the
doctrinal controversies of the seventeenth century, but sermons designed to inspire conversion
do not reflect this.

received much more attention. Weber contended that predestination aggravated fears about election, and people who speculated that they were reprobate did fall into despair. The preachers, however, warned against investigating the mysteries of the decree: "dark disputes of election and predestination, at the first especially, let them go."[14] To assume that one is doomed is sinful and derogates from the task of examining one's sins, which are real and terrifying enough. The sinner's conclusion that because God reprobates many, He reprobates me, is a *non sequitur*. Confronted with the plaint that Christ, the means of redemption, "is not intended for all, therefore not for me," Shepard challenged, "how doth this follow? How dost thou know this?" and riposted that "he is offered unto all, and therefore unto thee."[15] Puritans always stressed that the free offer of Christ opens the possiblity that one can be saved, and they steered away from the potentially unnerving implications of predestination.[16] On the other hand, they found much about it to advertise. Troubled by predestination's "extreme inhumanity," Weber did not imagine that it could serve as a counsel of cheer.[17] The doctrine of election makes possible the corollary that Saints will never lose their title to grace. If one's election is not certain, then one's salvation is not certain, but since God's eternal purpose does not change, those whom He elects persevere. In consequence, one may "*in conscience*" be assured of salvation because the "*foundation of God*, that is, the decree of God's election, *stands firme and sure*: so as those which are elected of God shall never fall away."[18] Predestination as it sounded from Puritan pulpits gave reason for the Saints to rejoice in the plenitude of God's mercy—"That man is blest whom God hath from all

14. Sibbes, *Works*, IV, 182. Cf. Norton, *Orthodox Evangelist*, 84; Hooker, *Application*, I-VIII, 81; Preston, *Breast-Plate*, I, 11; Bulkeley, *Gospel-Covenant*, 264.

15. Shepard, *Works*, I, 49. Cf. William Gouge, *The Workes*, 2 vols. (London, 1627), II, 112–13, and Mitchell, *Calvin's and Puritan's View*, 45–46, though the statement that Gouge "illustrates the idea of universal atonement effectively," is imprecise. What Gouge does proclaim is the universal *offer* of Christ, which is sufficient to save all (and only all those) who believe. The normative Puritan position (at least before the English Civil War) limited the efficacy of Christ's sacrifice to the Elect and rejected its universal applicability: "wee doe very willingly acknowledge that Christ dyed for all (the Scripture averring so much;) but we utterly deny, that he dyed for *all and every one alike in respect of God*, or as well for the damned as elect, and that effectually on Gods part. For let us weigh wel the words of christ [*sic*]: *I never knew you; depart from me yee workers of iniquity*." Perkins, *Works*, II, 621, also 609, 621–26, 628.

16. See Samuel Eliot Morison, *The Intellectual Life of Colonial New England* (New York, 1965 ed.), 11–12, who, however, goes too far in denying that the New England Puritans were "predestinarian Calvinists."

17. Weber, *Protestant Ethic*, 104.

18. Perkins, *Works*, II, 18, 21; cf. Shepard, *Works*, II, 351–53.

beginnings chosen"—and compelled their gratitude: "This life is too short, and spirits that dwell in flesh too inferior, to express their thankfulness for the Love of God, that unbosometh it self unto his Elect in the doctrine of the Decree." It was not designed to scare them into activity.[19]

Weber's valuation of worldly activity—"It and it alone disperses religious doubts and gives the certainty of grace"—overemphasizes the importance Puritans attributed to the particular calling as evidence of assurance, and it oversimplifies the psychological process through which believers come to know they are saved.[20] The importance of the worldly calling, preachers explained, lies in its relationship to one's general vocation in Christianity; the ultimate end of labor is to serve and glorify God.[21] The goal of assurance was rarely mentioned in this context. Furthermore, acts done in the particular calling are only one avenue among many to assurance; prayer, meditation, and regular religious observance figure much more prominently. In one list of means, Baxter noted laboring to strengthen faith, subduing inward corruptions, frequently exercising faith, doing all possible good in the world, escaping lapses into sin, examining the heart, and escaping error about the signs of grace.[22] Only the fourth item, doing good in the world, necessarily implies mundane activity; the rest are essentially spiritual, internal acts. Weber did not elaborate upon the mental complexities of how the Elect come to assurance, although he pointed out that assurance derives from an act of self-reflection: "It was through the consciousness that [the Saint's] conduct, at least in its fundamental character and constant ideal (*propositum obœdientiæ*), rested on a power within himself working for the glory of God . . . that he attained the highest good towards which this religion strove, the certainty of salvation." The crux of the matter lies in how one comes to this consciousness. For Weber, the answer is through the perception of one's good works, "indispensable as a sign of election," but there is more to be said.[23] While admitting that obedience can signify the presence of grace, Puritans also warned against taking duties at face value, for the most seemingly gracious acts may be a gilded shell covering a rotted soul. The nature and intent of the

19. Greenham, *Works*, 63; Norton, *Orthodox Evangelist*, 100; Mitchell, *Calvin's and Puritan's View*, 40–41, 46–47.

20. Weber, *Protestant Ethic*, 112.

21. Perkins, *Works*, I, 756–57; Cotton, *way of Life*, 437–38; Shepard, *Works*, I, 221; Sibbes, *Works*, VI, 521. See Robert S. Michaelsen, "Changes in the Puritan Concept of Calling or Vocation," *New England Quarterly*, 26 (1953), 319–25.

22. Hildersam, *CVIII Lectures*, 343–44; Shepard, *Works*, II, 399–400; Richard Baxter, *The Life of Faith* (London, 1670), 506.

23. Weber, *Protestant Ethic*, 114–15.

actor count even more than do the deeds themselves: "the workes of men (of what dignitie soever) are not to be esteemed by the shew and outward appearance of them, but by the minde and condition of the doer."[24] A tree, to use a favorite Puritan image, is known by its fruits; but the tree, to push that image to the brink, knows the character of its sap through a serious inward investigation. Assurance of salvation hinges upon knowing that one has been regenerated, knowledge accessible by intensive introspection. In Baxter's account, the self-examination that leads to assurance (or to the discovery that one is not yet regenerate) involves a trial as to "whether there be such an act as Belief, or Desire, or Love to God, within us, or not?" a trial of the moral sincerity of one's acts; judgment of "the habitual temper or disposition of our Hearts, by the quality of their Acts;" and a conclusion. The examiner who determines that he believes "in Spiritual sincerity" or "Loves God" sincerely "is a Regenerate Man." A deed must be done with love to God; "It is not the action, but the love in the action," that matters most, said Sibbes.[25] Recognition of this accomplishment within oneself is a sure sign of election.

The importance of godly love points out Weber's unwillingness to consider Puritans as emotional beings. Throughout the *Protestant Ethic*, he presents them and their intellectual precursors as bloodless personages animated only by ideas. Calvin is supposed to have derived his doctrine of the decree "not, as with Luther, from religious experience, but from the logical necessity of his thought," an inference that ignores the profound effects Calvin's own conversion had on him. The Hebrews in the Old Testament, rightly seen as influencing Puritan attitudes, are said to have expressed their "God-fearing but perfectly unemotional wisdom" in the Psalms, a valuation of the Psalter that every portion of it contradicts. The Puritans, Weber held, suppressed "the whole emotional side of religion," proving antagonistic to all its "sensuous and emotional elements."[26] Such a description, fair enough in regard to their iconoclasm and anti-ritual bias, misrepresents their perspective on the affections and on religious experience. The affections compose part of the Image of God constituted in Adam at creation; like all the other faculties, they have been corrupted by the Fall, but no special opprobrium

24. Perkins, *Works*, II, 17.

25. Richard Baxter, *The Saints Everlasting Rest*, 7th ed., rev. (London, 1658), 404vo–405vo; Sibbes, *Works*, IV, 198.

26. Weber, *Protestant Ethic*, 102, 123, 105. Kai Erikson evinces a similar attitude in his appraisal of justice in Massachusetts Bay, *Wayward Puritans* (New York, 1966), 189–90. For the effect of Calvin's personal experience on his doctrine of conversion, Alexandre Ganoczy, *Le Jeune Calvin: genèse et évolution de sa vocation réformatrice* (Wiesbaden, 1966), 271, 286–304.

attaches to them for this.[27] Affections are an "infinite blessing," concluded William Fenner, who devoted an entire book to their study. Without them, *"we should be like stocks and like senseless stones,"* incapable of piety regardless of the mind's enlightenment: "If a mans reason be never so good, he knowes hee is bound to repent, and be godly, and obey; yet if he have no affections thereto, he goes *like a Chariot without wheeles*[.]" Affections are *"good chanels for grace to run downe in,"* and, in the opinion of Sibbes, the focus of religious life: "Religion is more in the affections of the soul than in the effects and operations."[28] The experience of conversion would be meaningless to Puritans bereft of its emotional concomitants, the grief and fear of preparation that give way to unspeakable joy and surpassing peace. Distrustful, like their contemporaries, of passions completely unchecked by reason, the preachers insisted on emotion's rightful place in human functioning. Affections are mainstays to the life of faith, and they figure prominently in the Puritan psychology of work.

Scholars have charged that Weber, who concentrated on mid-seventeenth-century Puritanism, missed the lengthy development of its doctrines. The same type of criticism may be lodged against his understanding of individual growth. Weber begins his investigation with the person already regenerate; there is no sense of a psychological maturation acccompanying passage into the state of grace. In Puritan works, that passage is well marked. Before the Spirit regenerates them, the Elect undergo a crisis of belief: overcome by their perceived incapacity to serve God justly, they despair of ever being saved. Upon entering the Covenant of Grace, they rejoice in love, and, having been infused with spiritual strength through faith, celebrate their eternal life with godly works. During the process of conversion, through the mutating relationship of person to God and the emotional vicissitudes that attend upon the change, the real motive to work develops. The *Protestant Ethic* remains a lively springboard for inquiry into religious life; references to Weber in thousands of footnotes every year constitute a unique encomium. So much of twentieth-century scholarship lies under his shadow and in his debt that to praise him is superfluous and to bury him impossible. His thesis respecting the Puritan psychology of work, however, can be amended. The desire for assurance plays at most a secondary role in motivating godly activity. Rather, it is love that makes the Saints go round.

27. Perkins, *Works*, I, 17, 21; Shepard, *Works*, I, 19; Preston, *Saints Qvalification*, 63–68; John Rogers, *A Treatise of Love*, 2d ed. (London, 1632), 25.

28. William Fenner, *A Treatise of the Affections; Or, The Soules Pulse* (London, 1642), 66, 67, 68; Sibbes, *Works*, VI, 98. Fenner preached at Sedgley, Staffordshire; an itinerant for several years after being removed for Puritanism, he eventually took the pulpit of Richford, Essex.

II

The motive to work, Puritans thought, develops with regard to God's affections.[29] The deity the preachers knew looks passionately over His creation, and the decisions people make elicit His emotional response. To unregenerates, whatever their good intentions, that reaction must ultimately be unfavorable. Sin places man under guilt, "the binding of the Sinner to undergoe just punishment for his fault," and exposes him to God's chastising wrath.[30] A person becomes aware of one's guilt and of the Lord's revenging anger through the agency of His "vicegerent and chiefe officer," conscience.[31] Whether a faculty or an act—Puritans divided on the question—conscience is the ultimate earthly arbiter of human affairs, judge, plaintiff, witness, and executioner in the mind's high court.[32] It evaluates an individual's acts and condition, presenting "the judgement of man upon himself as he is subject to Gods judgement" in the manner of a logical discourse that assumes the form of a "practical syllogisme":

> *He that truly believeth in Christ shall be saved*: My conscience telleth me this is Gods word. But I believe truly in Christ: My conscience telleth me this also. *Therefore I shall be saved*. And so also on the contrary side.[33]

To summarize Ames's exposition of how conscience performs, God has planted in every person a habit, *synteresis*, that apprehends His Law as it is naturally written in the heart and further revealed in Scripture. God's goodness conserves in fallen man "the knowledge of many things which wee ought to doe or shun," and these principles of moral action, assented to through the operation of *synteresis*, generate the syllogism's major premise. A reflexive act of reason reviewing "our action, or estate, as it hath respect to that *Law* which Conscience giveth," produces the minor premise. The conclusion is reached in the "application," by which "Gods Commandement and mans fact

29. Puritan ministers did not conceive of God's affections as merely human faculties writ divine. The Lord's essential indivisibility precludes His having qualities in the same sense that His creatures do, so that it was meaningless to think of Him loving or hating as people do. The phrase "God's affections" could be taken as a figurative locution evincing His incommensurability. Such niceties were probably lost on the average listener. Cf. Ames, *Marrow*, I.iv.62; Finch, *Summe of Sacred Diuinitie*, 21.

30. Ames, *Marrow*, I.xii.2.

31. Hooker, *Soules Preparation*, 123.

32. Conscience a faculty: Perkins, *Works*, I, 517; William Fenner, *The Souls Looking-glasse* (Cambridge, 1640), 230; Wilson, *Christian Dictionary*, s.v. "What conscience is," p. 85. Conscience as act: Ames, "Conscience," I.i.1–6. Sibbes, *Works*, III, 209, irenically declared it the soul reflecting upon itself, a faculty, and an act, "we need not wrangle whether it be this or that."

33. Fenner, *Souls Looking-glasse*, 32. For the designation "practical syllogism," Perkins, *Works*, I, 547, and Ames, "Conscience," I.vii, p. 15.

THE SAINTS ZEALOUS IN LOVE AND LABOR 121

are mutually joyned together" to "passe sentence on him." As the conclusion warrants, conscience excuses one from guilt and absolves the individual from punishment or accuses and condemns. Absolution inspires joy and confidence; condemnation induces shame, sorrow, fear, anguish, and despair. At some time in the life of every Saint, and in the lives of many reprobates as well, contemplation of one's estate prompts the following train of thought:

> He that beleeveth not in Christ, is subject
>   to the wrath of God:
> But I beleeve not in Christ:
> Therefore, I am subject to the wrath of God.[34]

Tried and found wanting, the sinner confronts the anger of the Lord.

No greater evil can befall a wrongdoer than to suffer a troubled conscience. The wrath of God is burdensome, "so terrible that no man or angel is able to abide it." The idea that one can tolerate it is an illusion: consider, said Hooker, a man subject to all the world's diseases, all the torments that can be devised, all the creatures in heaven and earth conspiring against him, and all the devils in hell punishing him, "you would think this man to be in a miserable condition. And yet all this is but a beame of Gods indignation." Divine vengeance strikes a "seruile and slauish Feare" in the hearts of sinners who only wish to obey God because they dread His punishments.[35] Superadded to these terrors, the affections aroused by the recognition of guilt increase the sinner's distress. A pricked conscience is "fierce and furious, full of folly and desperate madnesse." A man so roiled proceeds aimlessly, for conscience "breedes such hurly burlies in him, that when it is day he wisheth for night; when it is night he would haue it day, his meate doth not nourish him, his dreames are fearfull to him, his sleepe oftimes forsaketh him." Speaking, he is not eased; silent, he is still disquieted; "the light doth not comfort him, the darknes doth terrifie him."[36] At worst, the conjunction of guilt and wrath whip conscience to desperation, "Gods most powerfull meanes to torment the Reprobate," and in a recurrent image, taken from Is. 66.24 and its quotations in Mark 9.44, 46, 48, preachers compared the conscience of the wicked to "a worme, that most sharply biteth and gnaweth their hearts for ever."[37] "Hell is begun in an ill conscience," advised Sibbes,

34. Ames, "Conscience," I.ii.1; vii, p. 15; ix.4; x.4, 10; xi.1–7; xv.17.

35. Fenner, Souls Looking-glasse, 175; Hooker, Soules Preparation, 56; Wilson, Christian Dictionary, s.v. "Feare," def. 6.

36. Cotton, way of Life, 143; Greenham, Works, 238.

37. Ames, "Conscience," I.xv.25. The "worm of conscience" often describes the torments of the damned in hell (cf. Davenport, Saints Anchor-Hold, 72; Perkins, Works, I, 112, 465; Shepard, Works, I, 28, 43; GenB, note 1 on Is. 66.24), but it could be extended to include the pains living reprobates suffer that give them a foretaste of perdition (cf. Ames, "Conscience," I.xv.25; xi.7; Fenner, Souls Looking-glasse, 36, 37, 149, 243). That Puritans imagined the

and heaven begun in a good one.[38] Excusal from guilt and freedom from eternal punishment bring about the peace that passes understanding and occasions the unspeakable joy that Puritans celebrated. A sinner will do anything to drive away the mind's harbingers of hell and live at ease.

The efforts generated by horrors of conscience and fears of punishment rest on the sandy bottom of human disability, fickleness, and self-concern. The strength of the unconverted conscience "will set men a-doing," Shepard allowed, "yet this is but a principle of nature, not an inward principle of life, whose property is to seek the subversion of corrupt nature, as natural conscience seeks the garnishing of it and the actions thereof."[39] Without gracious habits that gyrostatically return a Saint to the straight and narrow path whenever one veers from it, a hypocrite lacks the constant purpose to execute God's Law. Restrained by the natural conscience "because it is as a barking dog, that keeps the theefe [from] robbing," he will steal away to sin if he can, or else he places good works at the disposal of caprice. "If conscience be still, he omits duties; if conscience cry and stir, he falls to duties, and so hath his good mood as conscience has its fits." Sudden resolutions "to reforme this and that, and to do this and that particular," vanish like "*the morning cloud, and as the early dew*," for they rest on a passing work of the Holy Spirit exciting self-love "for a time."[40] Unregenerates obey the commands to pursue their own interests instead of God's. They complete their duties "not for any love or liking of that which is good, but because they would please and satisfie conscience, which otherwise will not suffer them to be quiet." Uninspired by the love of grace and the hatred of sin that animate the godly, an unregenerate "performs holy duties, not because he will use

---

conscience disturbs the soul like a worm eating the body represents another appropriation of Hebraic imagery to the assumptions of Occidental anthropology. The author in Isaiah had in mind corpses that had been denied proper burial decaying in the Valley of Hinnom (i.e. Ge Hinnom = Gehenna = hell; see Roger Norman Whybray, *Isaiah 40–66* (London, 1975), 294); the language refers to physical deterioration and implies no psychological event. Hebrews in any case could not have conceived the workings of "conscience" outside the context of the actions of the organic heart (*lêb*). The quotations in Mark 9 (recent translations drop vv. 44 and 46 while retaining v. 48; see RSV, NEB) also refer to physical doom. The logic of Western thought is evidenced by Calvin, who, while presuming the soul/body dualism, could separate the conscience from the physical heart. Since worms do not spontaneously generate from earth, he reasoned, the passage cannot intend corporeal objects and must be given a "metaphorical" reading. "The plain meaning, therefore, is, that the wicked shall have a bad conscience as an executioner . . . ," *Commentary on the Book of the Prophet Isaiah*, trans. William Pringle, 4 vols. (Edinburgh, 1850–53), IV, 439. (Calvin did not treat the passages in Mark in his *Commentary on a Harmony of the Evangelists, Matthew, Mark, and Luke*, trans. William Pringle, 3 vols. (Edinburgh, 1845–46), II, 334–39.)

38. Sibbes, *Works*, III, 216.

39. Shepard, *Works*, II, 286, 287.

40. John Preston, *The Law Ovt Lawed* (Edinburgh, 1631), B[vo]; Shepard, *Works*, I, 22; Davenport, *Saints Anchor-Hold*, 70 (cf. Hos. 6.4), 71.

them, but because he must use them; there is no quiet else."[41] Anguish and dread do not motivate the consistent toil that marks saintly activity, for labor ceases when they are averted.

Fear can not sustain work according to Puritan theory, but it does help the Elect in the early stages of conversion develop proper attitudes. The godly on their way to grace experience "the dreadful wrath of the Eternal, [that] like the mighty waves of the Sea, overwhelm and sink the soul of the sinner in desperate discouragement." Although full horror of conscience, the prickings that spurred Judas to suicide, may not afflict them, "for this vexation is not absolutely needfull," humiliation must.[42] Saints in preparation find their sins exposed, their hearts affrighted, and their deficiencies made plain. Reprobate rationalizations no longer comfort. Although activity may satisfy the consciences of the damned, Saints-to-be eventually acknowledge that their works can neither save them nor appease their troubled consciences, for they have grasped the nature of their sins too keenly to clothe themselves in "fig leaves of common honesty."[43] Fear and sorrow for transgression lead to humiliation, the sense of one's absolute dependence on God, and thus serve an instrumental function. Gripped by holy despair, elect sinners give up on their own abilities to attain grace and place all their trust in the Lord. Through the process of coming to believe, they learn how to achieve truly good works. Trepidation leads them to discover that Saints act not from fear, but from love.

III

Even the anger with which God consigns the damned to hell does not obscure His charity. Through the love that emanates from His own being, Puritans believed, "God approoueth first himselfe, and then all his creatures as they are good," embracing the entire natural order with infinite "delight."[44] The Lord's affection attests to His fundamental concern for the world that He made, but it does not extend to every entity in like measure and degree. "God

41. Fenner, *Souls Looking-glasse*, 71; Shepard, *Works*, I, 22. This argument contradicts Karl H. Hertz, "Max Weber and American Puritanism," *Journal for the Scientific Study of Religion*, 1 (1962), 192, who concludes that "fear and trembling" are the principal affections that account for the intensity of activity. Hertz offers a second spur, the desire to evidence grace by outward works, but does not bring conversion, the transformation of believers from helplessness to potency, or God's love into his discussion.

42. Hooker, *Application*, IX–X, 367; Preston, *Remaines*, 42.

43. Shepard, *Works*, I, 22.

44. Perkins, *Works*, I, 12, and see Wilson, *Christian Dictionary*, s.v. "[Loue] Referred to God," def. 4.

doth loue all his creatures," Perkins affirmed, "yet not all equally." Reprobates enjoy that "common love" whereby God "freely gave unto us so
excellent a Being after his own Image," a gift "unspeakably above what is
unspeakable," but insufficient to preserve them from perdition. A "special
love" differentiates the Saints from "our fellow sinners" and ushers them
"unto an estate more happy th[a]n that was miserable which we had deserved."[45] "Special love" comprehends two distinct phenomena. It defines the
divine "purpose and decree, to choose some vnto saluation by Christ"; in
other words, "Gods special Love is his Will to bestow all saving good upon
us."[46] The phrase also signifies the "effects" of God's decision, the execution
of His salvific intent through "the donation of Christ," and the "fruits of this
love, expressed in peculiar operations upon the soul and in the soul." By
"peculiar operations" Shepard and his colleagues understood the actions of
the Spirit applying the virtues of Christ's sacrifice in vocation, justification,
and the successive works of the *ordo salutis*.[47] Regeneration, then, is the
"declaration" of God's love.[48] The Saints are elected because God cares for
them, and they discover in converting that His wrath has given way to a more
affectionate disposition. These circumstances have important implications
for the Puritan psychology of work. One's willingness to labor for God grows
in light of His special love, its rationale, and its qualities.

The reasons why God loves the Saints proceed from the nature of His
caring and from His position as the all-sufficient, all-determining first cause.
Divine *agape* differs in essence from the passion of men and women, for
mortal love cannot initiate itself. Puritans grouped the affections in regard to
their relationship with objects considered as good or evil, and, by this
criterion, love is the motion of the will "*whereby it turnes and inclines to
some good, which it apprehends to be agreeable to its own nature.*" Love
pursues the good as it is perceived by the senses to be present, desiring "the
preservation of what it loves," and union with the beloved object, "that they
may draw neerer one to another."[49] A loving response in human beings
requires the proximity of a proper stimulus: "The loue of the creature
followes the goodnesse of a thing: because he seeth it is good, therefore he
loues it." God, however, operates under no such constraints: "the Creator

45. Perkins, *Works*, I, 108; Norton, *Orthodox Evangelist*, 99.

46. Wilson, *Christian Dictionary*, s.v. "[Loue] Referred to God," def. 5; Norton, *Orthodox
Evangelist*, 226.

47. Shepard, *Works*, II, 208; cf. Wilson, *Christian Dictionary*, s.v. "[Loue] Referred to God,"
def. 6, and Norton, *Orthodox Evangelist*, 226.

48. Perkins, *Works*, I, 76, 77, 81, 83, 92.

49. Preston, *Onely Love*, 6, 7. Cf. Hooker, *Sovles Vocation*, 60, and *Soules Implantation*, 172;
Fenner, *Treatise of Affections*, 129.

first loues the creature before it be good: and hence it comes, that it is good, because he loues it."[50] *Agape* transforms the character of the object it takes in, and therefore depends upon no prior quality inherent in the thing. It causes, rather than responds to, human sanctity: "Christ loves not first because men are holy, but that he may make them so."[51] God could not possibly love the Saints if He acted in human fashion, for their sin and corruption render them unworthy of concern, but His charity towards His own can and does accommodate their iniquity. Sin does not deter God's affection in spite of the fact that man hardly warrants it; "God hath loved man, that deserved no such thing from him, man his enemy, man unthan[k]full, *Ro.* 5.8." He loves the Elect solely "for [H]is own sake," since "no good in thee moved him to love thee"; although "Others make love for their own ends," the Lord "hath no need of thee, or of thy love."[52] *Agape* exists solely as a consequence of God's decision to glorify Himself through it, and it attaches to the Saints for no other reason than that He so wills.

The qualities of God's "unspeakable" love defeat attempts to take it in: "We may apprehend the love of God, but we cannot comprehend it." The act of election almost defies belief. Commenting on a passage from the First Epistle of John, Cotton fancied his scriptural namesake wondering "at the marvellous and incredible love of God, that he should vouchsafe to stoop so low, and honour us so much," debasing Himself "to take up such earthworms as we be from the Dung-hill."[53] Believers "stand amazed at that endlesse and boundlesse love of the Lord Jesus Christ," reaching "from everlasting to everlasting; from love in choosing us, unto love in glorifying of us." *Agape* is inviolable, "no sinne of Gods Elect how hainous soeuer, [can] cause God to hate or reiect them."[54] The perception of it fades if God chooses to toughen the Saints through affliction or if Satan malevolently discourages them about their estate, but the affection remains unchanged. A worried believer may "think the Lord loves you not, because you do not always feel his love, nor know his love," but, Shepard reassured, He loves "notwithstanding all our sins."[55] The gratuitous manner of its dispensation further shows the greatness of the gift. Tendered by virtue of God's will alone, His love is

---

50. Perkins, *Works*, III, 2d pagination, 224.

51. Shepard, *Works*, II, 537.

52. Ames, "Conscience," II.xiii.4; Shepard, *Works*, II, 79, 46.

53. Rogers, *Doctrine of Faith*, 260; Sibbes, *Works*, VII, 217, #281; Cotton, *Christ the Fountaine*, 228.

54. Hooker, *Sovles Exaltation*, 305; Sibbes, *Works*, VII, 187, #24; Hildersam, *CVIII Lectures*, 96.

55. Shepard, *Works*, I, 253.

priceless because, preachers claimed, it is "free."[56] These attributes make obvious the transcendent satisfaction and security *agape* promises, since its flawless character precludes the fickle treacheries that inhere in mortal passion. "A lyon," said Preston, "will suffer a man to play" until, at whim, it will "rend him in peeces; so I say, the love of a Prince may be, and the love of men may be." God does have a lion's "strength," and the faithful are indeed "weake creatures subject to him, but hee hath that constancie in him, that when hee loves once, it is alwayes perfect, and unchangeable."[57] God's love compares to no earthly affection.

A number of signs indicate God's love towards an individual. Perkins believed that the loves of the Elect for their brethren and for God demonstrate its presence. Ames recognized, among other manifestations, the pursuit of righteousness, and the performance of pious duties. Cotton, however, hesitated to accord human works primary status as evidence. "Even in nature," he argued, "children doe not first come to know their parents, either by their love to their brethren, or by their obedience to their parents; but from their parents love descending on them." Early New England's leading theologian of the Holy Spirit, Cotton found the surest proof to be the Third Person giving "sensible experience and knowledge of Gods love to us," its incursion into the heart affording a Saint sensate intelligence of "what God hath done for him."[58] Puritans agreed that, however apprehended, God's love affects a profound impact on the soul. Many Saints, stirred with "sweet incklings, and intimations" of His mercy, "begin to bee light headed, because they are so ravished therewith, they are alwayes cleaving thereunto, insomuch that many times they are almost besides themselves." The verb *ravish*, carrying the sense of 'to transport with rapture,' 'to fill with ecstasy,' stands out in Puritan depictions of *agape*'s effects.[59] To be ravished by God's "infinite loue" is to be "in a little heaven," swept away in "admiration" and "wonderment" at His mercy, "swallowed vp with a sea of his loue."[60] The feeling of it may

56. Bulkeley, *Gospel-Covenant*, 407.

57. Preston, *Breast-Plate*, III, 149–50.

58. Perkins, *Works*, II, 20–21; Ames, "Conscience," II.xiii.9–12; Cotton, *Gospel-Conversion*, 20; *idem, Christ the Fountaine*, 237.

59. Hooker, *Sovles Vocation*, 257; *OED*, s.v. "ravish," def. 3c. The earliest use of this definition was during the fourteenth century. The early English dictionaries do not take note of this meaning, giving only the senses of 'to rape,' 'deflower,' 'take away by force': Cawdrey, *Table Alphabeticall*, s.v. "Rauish"; Minsheu, . . . *Gvide Into Tongves*, s.v. "Rauish"; Cockeram, *English Dictionarie*, II, s.v. "to Rauish a Maide", " a Rauishing"; Blount, *Glossographia*, s.v. "Rauishment"; Phillips, *New World*, s.v. "Rauishment, or Rape." Bullokar, *English Expositor*, gives no definition.

60. Downame, *Christian Warfare*, 1124; Shepard, *Works*, III, 375; Perkins, *Works*, I, 319. Shepard uses *admiration* with the now archaic signification of 'wonder,' 'astonishment,' 'surprise,' a sense of marvel stronger than that commonly conveyed by the word's more

disappear—"God is gone again, and the soul loses it"—but just as mature Saints arrive at the subjective certainty of faith, they can also enjoy a firm and lasting persuasion that God loves them.[61] "Those that God means to honour and use in any great employment," Sibbes asserted, "oftentimes before he gives them the full assurance of his love." Hooker held the "well-grounded evidence and assurance of Gods Love in Christ" to be the "highest top of a Christians comfort." The certainty of receiving *agape* itself catalyzes a profound reaction; "it is such a joy," thought Preston, "as will raise the heart, basely to esteeme of all earthly things, and to walke in Paradise as it were."[62] Experiencing God's love surpasses anything the Saints have ever known.

The apprehension of *agape* inspires reciprocal affection. A ravished heart is "inflamed with vnfained loue" towards God and Christ, for the "sense of the Lord's love hath kindled that love to the Lord again, as that it abundantly loves Christ." The love wrought from God, said Hooker, "always draws the soule unto Gods love againe."[63] Divine charity is the *sine qua non* of the Elect's affection. "His love of us is the cause of our love to him," preachers said, "We love him because he loved us first."[64] The nature of the affective faculties determines that God's act must precede the human response. Human beings love by casting their affection on an object conceived as good, so if His lovingkindness "is not set on upon the soule," then "the heart cannot be affected with it." When "a present good" stirs the heart, "then this love comes to God againe, Gods love affecting the heart, and setled upon it, it breeds a love to God againe."[65] In consequence, the capability of individuals to love God rests necessarily on the fact of conversion. They love God because God has loved them and, through His love, saved them. All creatures benefit from the deity's general love, but only His elected children delight in the special charity that enflames their souls. Many come to have "some good will, and affection, and love to the Lord," yet never seek him because they have "not tasted abundantly of the Lord's mercy, grace, and love."[66] The reprobate never entertain the divine affection that ravishes the heart, and, though they may wish to love God as fully as do the Saints, their corrupted

---

modern meaning of 'agreeable surprise,' *OED*, s.v. "admiration," defs. 1, 2; Cawdrey, *Table Alphabeticall*, s.v. "Admire"; Bullokar, *English Expositor*, s.v. "Admire"; Cockeram, *English Dictionarie*, I, s.v. "Admire"; Minsheu, . . . *Gvide Into Tongves*, s.v. "Admire"; Phillips, *New World*, s.v. "Admirable"; Blount, *Glossographia*, s.v. "Admiration."

61. Shepard, *Works*, III, 375.

62. Sibbes, *Works*, V, 397; Hooker, *Application*, IX–X, 33; Preston, *Remaines*, 284.

63. Downame, *Christian Warfare*, 1124; Shepard, *Works*, II, 335; Hooker, *Sovles Vocation*, 241.

64. Sibbes, *Works*, V, 88.

65. Hooker, *Soules Implantation*, 174–75.

66. Shepard, *Works*, II, 335.

natures prohibit their loving well. The Saints' passion is a "grace above nature," possible only for a sanctified soul: "We had as good look for honey in an hornets nest, or in a serpents den, or sweet fruit from a crab-stocke, as love from an unrighteous man." It flows from the *pure heart, true faith, and good conscience* of the regenerate. In Preston's estimation, the Lord infuses "a habit of Love within, answerable to the Commandement without."[67] The Saints cannot love properly until they are renewed, and their affection results from the Lord's free gift.

The nature of the beloved object and the context in which the Saints express their affection reveal the uniqueness of godly love. True "natural love" includes, according to Sibbes, a high esteem for the object, desire to be joined to it, contentment in the thing, and a desire to please the party loved; the Lord's excellency inspires the Saints to deepen these feelings beyond the norm. Since God determines what good comes to us, "we love him more than our selves," Preston averred, "because our good depends upon him, more than on our selves." He is, in fact, the greatest good, deserving the greatest affection. "He that prizeth any thing more in love, or delights in any thing more with joy, than in Christ," Hooker scorned, "is not worthy of Christ."[68] Genuine passion disposes itself to seek God's honour and to please Him "in euery thing." Time after time the preachers struck the note that God is to be loved without limit. Love's measure, said Perkins, "is to loue him without measure," and across the years Shepard echoed, "it must be a dear love, a spring of running love without measure."[69] The sentiment carries with it a sense of self-deprecation—"let God bee honoured, though I bee disparaged"—and self-sacrifice: "if our hearts be truly set upon Christ we are content to have him, though wee should never see good day with him." God must be treasured "absolutely for himselfe," without reference to any "gifts and rewards" that may accrue.[70] Profound and selfless, the ardor of the Saints is also extremely activistic, for to love God entails the performance of His commands. Propelled by the purpose *to serve and please him in all things*, the love of the faithful comes to fruition in executing the divine will embodied in the Law: "Love is the fulfilling of the Law; and not to love the Lord, is, not to keep the Law."[71] The Law convicts reprobates of their

67. Hooker, *Paterne of Perfection*, 110; Perkins, *Works*, III, 2d pagination, 490; Preston, *New Covenant*, 379, and see *Breast-Plate*, III, 51.

68. Sibbes, *Works*, IV, 182–88; Preston, *Onely Love*, 10; Hooker, *Soules Implantation*, 162.

69. Perkins, *Works*, I, 274, 319; Shepard, *Works*, II, 72.

70. Hooker, *Sovles Vocation*, 252; Cotton, *Christ the Fountaine*, 53; Perkins, *Works*, I, 274; Bulkeley, *Gospel-Covenant*, 406–7.

71. Preston, *Onely Love*, 18, 25; cf. Bulkeley, *Gospel-Covenant*, 126; Hooker, *Paterne of Perfection*, 113; Sibbes, *Works*, IV, 190.

degeneracy, and it affrights the Elect preparing for grace, but it leads the Saints to set forth their love in work: "it is not talking, but doing, and that out of love, which is the end and scope of the law." To characterize the essence of godly love, Puritans thought "not of an abstracted love and affection, but of love in our places, and callings, and standings, love invested into action."[72]

As the evangelical rule for right living, the Law prescribes what to do in love. Divided into two tables—duties of "holiness" to God and "righteousness" to man—it commands the Saints to love the Lord above all else and to direct some of that affection towards others.[73] Human beings are intermediaries in whose service the divine itself is served: "God wil haue our neighbor, in respect of loue, to be in his roome & stead: and in the loue of our neighbour, with whom we conuerse, will he be loved of vs."[74] The most extreme formulation of this idea advocates a life of mundane labor becoming the pivotal expression of godly love. "All our travaile in Religion, to know God, to beleeve in him, to love and feare him, and all our prayers, excercises in the Word, and the like, are referred to this, to doe all good to our neighbour in our severall callings," wrote Ezekiel Culverwell under the heading "Love" in his book of meditations.[75] The Law obliges Saints further to apply themselves wholeheartedly in prosecuting this affection. The charge to love the Lord with all one's might (Deut. 6.5) demands that "all the powers of the whole man" be brought to bear, and requires that the Elect cede Christ more than "a little scanty desire, and few lazy wishes, but love him with all thy soule, and with all thy strength, and say, I will love thee dearly, Oh Lord my strength."[76] The concept of the whole man who obeys the command to serve his neighbor in love unites the constitutionally vital human being as conceived by Puritan anthropology with the social role mandated by the Law. Perfervid godly love is inseparable from participation in social life, specifically in the performance of one's chosen task:

> Scripture saith, we must love God "with all our mind, with all our heart, with all our power and strength," Deut. vi.5; that is, in our particular

---

72. Shepard, *Works*, I, 277; Sibbes, *Works*, IV, 194.

73. Shepard, *Works*, I, 275; cf. Sibbes, *Works*. IV, 181.

74. Perkins, *Works*, I, 704; cf. Bulkeley, *Gospel-Covenant*, 126; Hooker, *Paterne of Perfection*, 113; Chaderton, *Excellent and godly Sermon*, D.iiii.ᵛᵒ.

75. Culverwell, *Time Well Spent*, 206–7.

76. Perkins, *Works*, III, 2d pagination, 490; Hooker, *Sovles Exaltation*, 307. In context, Perkins does not think that fallen man can ever love God this completely (cf. Cartwright, *Treatise of Christian Religion*, 163; Rogers, *Treatise of Love*, 14), and that the highest degree that the Gospel contemplates is "standing in an vnfained will, and true endeauour, to loue God, with all the heart, all the strength, and all the powers." Hooker, however (and see Sibbes, *Works*, IV, 190, 195) speaks as if the Elect can fulfill the injunction.

places. To make it clear. When we speak of love to God, we speak of love to him in our particular callings.[77]

Saints love with a similar intensity, but they dress their passion in fittings appropriate to their occupational station: "It is not enough for thee to love the Lord, but thou must love him with thy might. The might of a rich man, of a Magistrate, of a Scholler, or whatsoever thou art."[78] By citing employment in a particular calling as an epitome of godly love, Puritans gave the scope of their affection the widest possible range. Its original focus on the deity expands to take in the world.

Society is the ground on which the Saints parade their obedience, and the force that energizes their performance is godly love engendered by the apprehension of *agape* redeeming and regenerating them. Love "is the affection that stirs up the duty, and stirs up the affection fit for the duty; it stirs up to do the thing, and to do all in love." The "whetstone to obedience," it makes the Saints "thinke nothing too much or enough which they can doe or suffer for [God's] sake; whereby they are moued to make an holy vse of all they know" to practice "all which hee loueth and requireth."[79] No other inclination, no matter how sincerely feigned, can replace it. "An hypocrite cannot love the Lord, he may do the outward works, he may hear the Word, and be diligent in his calling," Preston allowed, "But here is the difference, he doth not this out of love. This is that distinguishing character which distinguishes a Christian; as reason doth a man."[80] The inability of unregenerates to act from the principle of true love points to their failure to convert. Saints can genuinely respond to *agape* because, as new creatures, they act from the infused habit of faith. Their love "is a most operative affection stirred up by faith. Indeed, all our Christian graces are set a-work by faith in Christ." The Saints' activity follows upon belief—"All obedience comes from love. Love is the keeping of the law. This affection is stirred up by faith"—and it was this gracious sequence that preachers had on their lips when they expounded the final clause of Gal. 5.6, "faith which worketh by love" (KJV).[81] In Preston's exegesis, "you have a chaine here consisting of these three linkes; faith which when it is right will beget love, and love when it is right will set you on worke;

77. Sibbes, *Works*, IV, 194–95. The precise quotation is "with all thine heart, and with all thy soul, and with all thy might" (KJV). This passage is the source for Mat. 22.37, and was sometimes confused with it in evaluations of human potency (see *supra*, 38, n. 49). In the present case, Sibbes doubles the references to "might," but there is a basis in the verse for his exaggeration.

78. Preston, *Onely Love*, 151.

79. Sibbes, *Works*, IV, 181; Fenner, *Treatise of Affections*, 68; Downame, *Christian Warfare*, 1115.

80. Preston, *Onely Love*, 114–15.

81. Sibbes, *Works*, V, 368.

faith which workes by love." To Shepard, "Faith is our feet whereby we come to Christ, love is our hand whereby we work for Christ."[82] Regeneration sets the affections on their proper objects, making obedience possible.

Love actuates performance, and it also accounts for the accompanying fervor. Anything done for God is best done ardently, Puritans held, and they despised a tepid approach to faith: "be something, appear in your colours," either Saint or devil, Hooker dared, the Lord "hates and abhors a lukewarme Laodicean foole that is of no side, because he is not sincere hearted of any side."[83] True sincerity is an absolute commitment to promote God's glory in all actions and things, to "contend in his cause with much striving, being zealous for him, and for the defense of his Word, Truth, Gospel, Kingdome, and whatsoever concerns his honour," standing out "to the utmost." Saints should execute all their duties with zeal, the "highest degree" of their obedience, for God "hateth and reiecteth" all service not rendered from "chearefull loue, and earnest zeale of his glorye."[84] Agreeing with contemporary psychologists and moral philosophers, Puritans distrusted excessive affections, those passions and perturbations that disrupt the soul's normal functioning and sweep away the rule of reason and will. The preachers, however, admitted one case in which "exceeding affection is not over-exceeding," the "ecstasy of zeal upon a sudden apprehension of God's dishonour, and his cause trodden under foot." On such occasions, though the Christian be carried on "a spring-tide of affection," the stream "runneth in the due channel," abetting "the cause of Christ and the good of souls."[85] By one reckoning, zeal was categorized as the intensification of any emotion, the "INcrease of affections; as of griefe, ioy, hatred, loue," but some preachers favored the theory that posited zeal as the transmutation of an original amatory impulse. Zeal compounds "loue, and anger or indignation"; it is ire that "proceeds from love to the Lord." Since anger seeks to clear away hinderances to a person's purpose, zeal seeks unity with the Lord in love while removing every "impediment" to the expression of that love.[86] The Saints endeavor to keep their beloved from disrespect, driven by an affection that

82. Preston, *Breast-Plate*, III, 186; Shepard, *Works*, II, 61.

83. Hooker, *Sovles Vocation*, 278–79, explicating Rev. 3.16.

84. Bulkeley, *Gospel-Covenant*, 397; Ames, "Conscience," III.vi.1.

85. Sibbes, *Works*, I, 159, 160.

86. Wilson, *Christian Dictionary*, s.v. "Zeale," def. 1; Perkins, *Works*, III, 2d pagination, 365; Preston, *Breast-Plate*, III, 87–88. Cf. La Primaudaye, *Second Part*, 320–24; Reynolds, *Treatise of the Passions*, 106. William Fenner demurred from other opinions. "*Bonaventura* and other of the Schoole make it onely of *love* [cf. Wilson, *ibid.*, def. 7, which refers to the "most earnest loue of God for yᵉ good of his church and his owne glory," a specification def. 1 lacks; Chaderton, *Excellent and godly Sermon*, D.iiii.ᵛᵒ; also Minsheu, . . . *Gvide Into Tongves*, s.v. "Zeale"]; *Ludovicus Vives* makes it to be compounded of two affections, indignation and pitty

may inspire, as with Moses, a "holy rage" in someone otherwise "unparalleled for meekness."[87]

The Saints, though they love God, fear Him "at all times," and, unlike hypocrites, do not cast off their apprehension when the "thunder" and "lightning" of some temporary judgment have passed.[88] The character of their trepidation distinguishes it from a reprobate's dread. The "holy affection" restrains regenerates from vice and constrains them to well-doing "for desire to glorifie God." They fear to offend Him because He grants them "mercy," because they stand in "awe" of Him, because "true reverence" succeeds upon the perception of His love, kindness, and power.[89] The reprobate fear the Lord's punishments, but the faithful fear to displease Him for His sake. God, though He loves the Elect, continues to chastise them. Freed from the curse of eternal death due every sin, Saints are still obliged to obey the Law; "many times" they feel His displeasure when they transgress. Their consciences are "very much troubled when the Lord is thus angry with them." A Saint may experience a horror of conscience resembling the terror that distracted Judas, but in the worst times a "root of comfort" remains to console and sustain them. Even when "so drunken with wormewood, that it may make them not to know what to doe; yet in all this griefe the fire of Gods love is not quite extinguished, but there are some sparkes thereof remaining under these ashes."[90] Like a loving father, the Lord sometimes finds it necessary to be wroth with His children for their own benefit.[91] The fears of the godly have an adjunctive significance in the Puritan psychology of work. Infused by the Spirit, gracious awe motivates good deeds. "I will put the affections of feare into they heart," said Preston, assuming the Lord's voice, "then thou shalt easily feare me, and keepe my Commandements." A regenerate "is partly mooued vnto obedience, by the feare of Gods iudgements, and

---

[no Puritan seems to have held this]. Others to be mixed of *anger* and *love*: this is not so; for zeale is a high straine of all the affections." Alleging Gal. 4.18 ("it *is* good to be zealously affected always in a good *thing*" [KJV], in his behalf, Fenner took zeal to have a general significance, and, citing Deut. 6.5, equated it with the whole might of the soul. "Zeale is, when the heart raises up it's affections with all it's might on a thing," *Treatise of Affections*, 143–44, see also 20. Fenner recognizes a component of anger, the "whetstone to zeal" (68), and, turning to 2 Kings 10.16, allows that love may be termed zeal "in the Scripture" (157). Most Puritans related zeal to love in one way or another.

87. Sibbes, *Works*, I, 159.

88. Hildersam, *CVIII Lectures*, 420.

89. Wilson, *Christian Dictionary*, s.v. "Feare," def. 5; Perkins, *Works*, I, 84; Dent, *Sermon of Repentaunce* [B6]^{vo}; Ames, "Conscience," II.ix.6.

90. Cotton, *Treatise of the Covenant*, 76; Fenner, *Souls Looking-glasse*, 179; Preston, *Remaines*, 43.

91. Bulkeley, *Gospel-Covenant*, 215; Fenner, *Souls Looking-glasse*, 179; Sibbes, *Works*, VII, 226, #328; Preston, *Saints Qvalification*, 138; Cotton, *Treatise of the Covenant*, 76.

ought so to be," Hildersam thought, for the flesh would hardly obey "without this curbe; nor would bee forward to any good duties without his spurre." The remnants of corruption must be kept in line. Still, the principal ingredient in the Saints' determination stems from affection, not terror: "The regenerate mans obedience grows chiefly from a loue to God: yea, from such a loue as growes from Faith."[92] If the old man in the Saints responds to the stick, the new man grabs eagerly for the carrot; the preachers never questioned who or which was more productive.

IV

The inability of unregenerates to do godly duties figures conspicuously in Puritan thinking, and provides the starting point for their psychology of work. Life in the flesh is lived in weakness, and the despair experienced in humiliation testifies to the profundity of one's desire to escape one's helpless state. The miracle of conversion answers these desperate wishes for power in a way that, according to the preachers, makes the Saints God's willing workers. The Lord gives believers the power of faith purely from love for them. It is free. They cannot earn it, but they do not have to. Power is a manifestation of God's love, and the sensation of this love that redeems and energizes them gratifies the Elect. In response, they love God and perform in His service. As they obey the commands, they become even more aware of *agape* and eventually achieve full assurance of this grace. Intermittently, the conviction fades, but Saints can recover it by examining themselves to make sure they still perform out of love to God, and by continuing to do His duties. Work and love reinforce each other. Evidence of God's love motivates the Saints to work, and the absence of evidence initiates efforts to regain it. The more the Saints love, the more duties they can perform, and through so doing, they feel, with more certainty, the inexpressible caress of *agape*.

No wonder the preachers expected the godly to labor so hard in the fields of the Lord.

92. Preston, *New Covenant*, 380; Hildersam, *CVIII Lectures*, 480.

II

THE CRY
OF THE FAITHFUL

These are the names of the godly of Cambridge: Sparrowhawk, Fessenden, Griswald and Errington, Cutter, Stedman, and Cane. They gave voice to the Spirit in accounts of conversion, and their relations, with others from Wenham and Chelmsford, supplied the answers to the ministry's call, the convert's contribution to the dialogue of faith. Taking up the social setting in which the narratives were given and the patterns of social intercourse they portray, Part II establishes the interactive web in which people were enmeshed; exploring common themes and unique statements, it descries the Elect conforming to shared structures of experience and creating their own. One focus is on the normative and idiosyncratic aspects of conversion, another on how it affected the individual and society. Chapter 5 examines the milieu of giving a relation, the interchange between confessor and congregation that knit the Saints together. Chapter 6 looks at the multiple influences on a person's experience, particularly the impact of sermons. Chapter 7 details the correspondences between cultural ideal and actuality; analyzing four relations intensively, it underscores their concern with helplessness and power. The dimensions of Puritan piety form the background against which Chapter 8 essays a case study of how conversion functioned. Following the actions of John Winthrop, the first governor of Massachusetts, when he was feeling especially weakened and oppressed, it demonstrates the convergence between what Puritans said conversion effected and what it really accomplished. One man's cry unites the preachers' theory with the flesh.

5

Joining the Society of Saints

In seventeenth-century New England, the private audience between God and a believing soul was often broadcast to an attentive public. Before a person could join a particular church and be permitted to take communion, he or she had to present a personal "*confession, & declaring of Gods manner of working upon the soul*," to the congregation.[1] Commencing with the earliest recognitions of sin and the dawning realization of one's innate depravity, the applicant for admission recounted a lifelong struggle against the flesh and detailed the emerging conviction that faith, although entirely unmerited, had been granted by a gracious God. If this spiritual autobiography convinced the assembled church members that regeneration had occurred, the confessor entered into covenant with the church. The sounds that carried through meetinghouse air from thousands of throats have long since been stilled, but the *cris de coeur* of which they were the oral expressions have left some written trace. At Cambridge during the late 1630s and early 1640s, Thomas Shepard took down the confessions of fifty-one people; John Fiske wrote

---

1. "The Cambridge Platform, 1648," in Williston Walker, *The Creeds and Platforms of Congregationalism* (New York, 1893; repr. Boston, 1960), 223. The practice of requiring a conversion relation from all prospective church members was established in Massachusetts, Connecticut, and New Haven during the 1630s and seems to have spread to Plymouth at some later date. A form of it was carried to Rhode Island by the Hutchinsonian refugees. Morgan, *Visible Saints*, 92–105, 58–63, 109–10; Patricia Caldwell, *The Puritan Conversion Narrative: The Beginnings of American Expression* (New York, 1983), 45–80.

twenty-one more into the church records of Wenham and Chelmsford for two decades after 1644; and Michael Wigglesworth recorded in his personal journal six conversion relations made at Cambridge and Malden in the mid-1650s.[2] The jottings of these three ministers register the religious experiences of the Puritan laity.

Register—but how precisely? The documents are secondhand compositions. Inevitably, some alterations of material resulted, and the evidence inheres in the records themselves. Most of the narratives do not give the impression of being verbatim transcripts.[3] Clauses often replace complete sentences, and phrases appear abridged. All of the relations that Fiske recorded employ the third person, as do two of Shepard's.[4] The length of the statements suggests that some matter has been compressed or omitted. According to Thomas Lechford, an adversative but accurate observer of Massachusetts Bay around 1640, a conversion relation required "sometimes a quarter of an houre long, shorter or longer"—often much longer, crediting various allusions to "extravagant, enlarged discourses" that were "wearisome and uncomely."[5] In their present form, the surviving relations are not so

---

2. George Selement and Bruce C. Woolley, eds., *Thomas Shepard's "Confessions"*, in *Publications of the Colonial Society of Massachusetts*: 58: *Collections* (1981), *passim* (henceforth cited as Shepard, *Confessions*); Robert G. Pope, ed., *The Notebook of the Reverend John Fiske, 1644–1675*, in *ibid*.: 47: *Collections* (1974), *passim* (henceforth cited as Fiske, *Notebook*); Edmund S. Morgan, ed., "The Diary of Michael Wigglesworth," in *ibid*.: 35: *Transactions 1942–1946* (1951), 426–44 (henceforth cited as Wigglesworth, *Diary*).

3. The rough character of the relations is more apparent in the original of the Shepard text, "The Confessions of diverse propounded to be received & were entertayned as members," New England Historic Genealogical Society, Boston, than in the much more readable modern version. Wigglesworth recorded his relations in shorthand, which probably accounts for their length and completeness as against those of Shepard. Fiske also employed shorthand, but for some unknown reason, his records are generally shorter than those of the others.

4. Fiske, *Notebook, passim*; the narratives in Shepard, *Confessions*, are those of Edward Hall and Francis Moore. Eight other statements, those of Elizabeth Luxford, née Olbon, George Willows, John Sill, Joanna Sill, Nathaniel Sparrowhawk, Mary Sparrowhawk, née Angier, Mrs. Crackbone, and Ann Errington, shift from the third person to the first person. On occasion, as here, the published *Confessions* put a married woman's maiden name in the title of her relation. The married name is used in this work, with the maiden name indicated at the woman's first appearance.

5. Thomas Lechford, *Plain Dealing, or News from New England*, ed. J. Hammond Trumbull (London, 1642; repr. Boston, 1867), 23, 130; Shepard, *Works*, II, 631. Shepard allows that some relations are long-winded but defends the utility of the practice. The length of conversion relations became an issue during the debates between Presbyterians and Congregationalists in the 1640s on the merits of their respective systems, and defenders of the New England Way admitted, tacitly and explicitly, that some narratives extended too long. See Mather, *Apologie*, 29–30; John Allin and Thomas Shepard, *A Defense of the Answer made unto the nine Questions or Positions sent from New-England . . .* (London, 1648), 189. No one mentioned, however, how long was "too long." Lechford ran afoul of the Bay authorities on several counts, most notably for heterodoxy; see Trumbull, "Introduction" to *Plain Dealing*, xx–xxvi, xxx–xxxvi.

verbose. By far the longest, that of John Collins, takes only some twenty minutes to read aloud, while the great majority need fewer than fifteen.[6] If Lechford's testimony is correct, and there seems no good reason to question it, then one may wonder why the extant relations are shorter than the supposed average. Even if he were mistaken, and only a few minutes normally elapsed, some of the narratives still appear strikingly brief. Mrs. Greene's statement can be spoken in fewer than twenty seconds; those of Hannah Brewer, Robert Daniel, and Elizabeth Batchelor do not require forty-five.[7] Perhaps these and other confessors did not give a full relation, so that what survives is a literally accurate account of what they said, but the suspicion that something is missing lingers.[8] Two of Shepard's records halt in mid-sentence. Fiske admitted to having condensed and paraphrased speeches: he recorded the "sum" of Edward Kemp's relation, and noted the "substance" of what both Henry Farwell and John Rogers of Watertown said.[9] Words have dropped out of the confessions.

Nevertheless, the documents speak primarily in the tones of their subjects rather than in those of their compilers. They are free from purposive redaction. Numerous inaccurate biblical citations stand uncorrected. Taken down

6. Wigglesworth, *Diary*, 426–32; for the name John, *ibid.*, 347. He was the son of Martha and Edward, at one time Shepard's deacon; Shepard recorded both of their relations. See James Savage, *Genealogical Dictionary of the First Settlers of New England*, 4 vols. (Boston, 1860–62), I, 435.

7. Shepard, *Confessions*, 118, 141, 60–61; Fiske, *Notebook*, 8–9. For the name Elizabeth, Clarence Almon Torrey, comp., "New England Marriages Prior to 1700," 12 vols., bound photostat (Boston: New England Historic Genealogical Society, n.d.), I, *sub* Batchelder.

8. Selement and Woolley, "Introduction," 23, conjecture that Mrs. Greene may have been "fearful and bashful," which cut short her statement, and they point out that she was accepted on the strength of her friends' testimonies. In this case, the evidence of activity by church members may help to account for a relation's brevity, but shortness does not always correlate with members' response. In Fiske's *Notebook*, the only source to mention regularly if someone testified in the applicant's behalf, the shortest recorded relation, Batchelor's, elicited no testimony, but some longer ones did (cf. 45, 90). Questions directed at the confessor follow Batchelor's and Daniel's narratives, but not Brewer's; moreover, a single question succeeds John Collins's relation, the longest of all (Wigglesworth, *Diary*, 432). Nothing can be inferred as to why a particular relation is short from the presence or absence of testimonies and/or questions.

9. Shepard, *Confessions*, 212 (William Ames), 92 (Barbara Cutter); Fiske, *Notebook*, 94, 145, 100. See also his comment on Ann Kemp's relation being in "this line" (95); for the name Ann, see Torrey, "New England Marriages," VII, *sub* Kemp. She was Edward Kemp's wife. John Rogers was a member of the Watertown church, and he is called John Rogers of Watertown to distinguish him from his namesakes, the preachers of Dedham and Dublin. He gave a relation to the church at Wenham and took communion at Chelmsford but appears to have remained a member at Watertown, Fiske, *Notebook*, 100, 120. There were at least two men with this name at Watertown, and it is unclear to which Fiske refers; see Savage, *Genealogical Dictionary*, III, 561–62; Charles Edward Banks, *Topographical Dictionary of 2885 English Emigrants to New England, 1620–1650* (Baltimore, 1957), 42, 49. The incompleteness of Cutter's relation is not well rendered in the published version, which uses a period where an ellipsis is preferable.

solely for pastoral reference, the narratives betray no attempts to tamper with their content or to alter them for polemical interest.[10] Their unpolished appearance chronicles the spontaneity of the original event and the excitement of preachers trying to keep pace with confessors. Words or phrases are duplicated and repeated, figures in lists of numerals are missing, and the gender of a few pronouns is incorrect.[11] Abbreviated these records may be, and they lack the hems, haws, pauses, and stutters that must have characterized the actual performances, but everything about them cries out their origins in the utterances of ordinary men and women straining to articulate the most important happenings of their spiritual lives.

The narratives record personal histories interpreted through the filters of Scripture and Puritan teachings. Subsequent chapters investigate the various influences on an individual's experience of saving grace. However, the conversion relations open up another dimension of experience as well. Products of interpersonal encounters, they have resulted from a public occurrence. Documents of social intercourse as well as of personal discovery, they remind us that thinking of conversion as simply a private affair narrows its significance. The dialogue between God and believer also involved conversations between men and women. In this way, Puritan religious experience constituted a profoundly social phenomenon.

I

The public conversion relation formed part of the procedure by which New England Saints distinguished a church—a covenanted company of truly professing believers bound together in "worship" and "mutuall edification"— from the rest of the congregation. Every such gathering, the particular Visible Churches, were supposed to be as congruent as possible with the Invisible Church, the all-inclusive body of God's Elect, hence the need to carefully

10. Patricia Lee Caldwell concurs, "A Literary Study of Puritan Testimonies of Religious Experience from the 1630s to the 1660s, Including a Critical Edition of Thomas Shepard's Manuscript, 'The Confessions of diverse propounded to be received & were entertayned as members,' from the First Church of Cambridge, Massachusetts, 1637–1645" (Ph.D. dissertation, Harvard University, 1979), 344. This is not the case with the narratives published by John Rogers (who will subsequently be identified with Dublin, to distinguish him from Dedham's minister). Hoping to "encourage others over into *Ireland*," he contracted and paraphrased those relations he found least interesting, אֹהֶל *Ohel or Bethshemesh. A Tabernacle For the Sun* (London, 1653), 392.

11. To note but three inaccurate citations: Batchelor spoke of Jer. 4.1 as coming from chapter 3, Fiske, *Notebook*, 8; John Collins referred to Is. 63.20, a non-existent verse, Wigglesworth, *Diary*, 427; Richard Cutter mistook Jer. 3.4 for v. 5, Shepard, *Confessions*, 179. For reference to missing numerals and redundancies, Selement and Woolley, "Introduction" to the *Confessions*, 27–28, and for the incorrect pronouns, Shepard, *Confessions*, 50, 52.

monitor who joined them. Maintaining that the doors to a church were not so capacious "that all sorts of people good or bad, may freely enter therein at their pleasure," the Bay Colony Puritans had, by the late 1630s, devised a method to separate the wheat from the chaff.[12] Candidates initiated the process by "mak[ing] known their desire" to one or more of the eldership, a board composed of both ministers and laymen.[13] After scrutinizing the New Testament for evidence from the primitive churches, the theorists of early New England congregationalism had decided that a fully officered church included a pastor to exhort, a teacher to instruct in doctrine, and one or more lay ruling elders to perform a variety of administrative tasks. Complementing this body was the deacon, who kept the treasury.[14] Hooker preferred the candidate to deal exclusively with the ruling elder, "for it's peculiar to his Office to lead the action of Admission," but ordinarily the pastor also participated in testing those who presented themselves for membership. At Wenham and Chelmsford, Fiske and his deacon conducted the interviews, an unusual arrangement brought about by the failure of those churches to institute the position of ruling elder.[15] During this hearing, held at an elder's house "or some other place appointed," and sometimes attended by interested church members of both sexes, the board queried applicants about their "*knowledge* in the principles of religion, & of their *experience in the wayes of grace*, and of their *godly conversation* amongst men." The screening might reveal a person to be less prepared for admission than he or she had thought, and should the questioners find any "wounded," they were to labor "by love

---

12. "Cambridge Platform," 205, 221–22.

13. Thomas Welde, *A Brief Narration of the Practices of the Churches in New-England* (London, 1651), 8. Cf. John Cotton, *The Way of the Churches of Christ in New-England* (London, 1645), 54; Lechford, *Plain Dealing*, 18–19.

14. "Cambridge Platform," 210–14; John Cotton, *The Doctrine of the Church*, 3d ed., corr. (London, 1644), 2–4. Theory allowed for an "ancient widow" or "deaconness" to administer charity, but the post was virtually never filled. Most congregations could afford only a pastor or a teacher, and in practice, the positions were equivalent. David D. Hall, *The Faithful Shepherd: A History of the New England Ministry in the Seventeenth Century* (New York, 1974), 95–96.

15. Thomas Hooker, *A Survey of the Summe of Church-Discipline* (London, 1648), Pt. III. ch. i. p. 4; Edward Johnson, *Wonder-Working Providence of Sions Saviour in New England*, ed. J. Franklin Jameson (New York, 1910; repr. New York, 1967 [orig. London, 1654]), 217; Don Gleason Hill, ed., *The Record of Baptisms, Marriages and Deaths, and Admissions to the Church and Dismissals Therefrom . . . in the Town of Dedham, Massachusetts. 1638–1845* (Dedham, 1888), 20 (henceforth cited as *Ded. Recs.*, II); Mather, *Magnalia*, I, 554; Fiske, *Notebook*, 17, 186; Harold Field Worthley, *An Inventory of the Records of the Particular (Congregational) Churches of Massachusetts Gathered 1620–1805*, Harvard Theological Studies, 25 (Cambridge, Mass., 1970), 152, 665. The office of ruling elder declined in importance as the century progressed, and by 1700 was nearly defunct. Increase N. Tarbox, "Ruling Elders in the Early New-England Churches," *Congregational Quarterly*, 14, n.s., 4 (1872), 401–16.

and patience to heal them and ripen them."[16] If the interview concluded positively, the ruling elder "in convenient time" informed the church of the applicant's interest at a public meeting, charging it to probe into the individual's conduct and report unseemly carriage to the board. Candidates had to settle every accusation that surfaced, since unsatisfied complaints sufficed "to stay the proceeding for the present," but matters could be "clered up either by ye innocency of ye p[ar]ty appearing or manifestation of repentance."[17] Personal grievances against the applicant were resolved in private; public offenses required public acknowledgment of fault.[18] Church members were allowed "due space" to press their examinations, and months might pass before inquiry ceased. Nearly a year elapsed between the day Sarah Fiske was first propounded as a prospective member and the time she finally persuaded doubters to let her proceed.[19] Only after these preliminaries, which had already featured a confession of experience before the elders, was the individual ready to make a public conversion relation.

During either a weekday meeting or the latter portions of the Sunday afternoon service, the ruling elder called the applicant to recount a spiritual history before an audience that ordinarily included members and non-members.[20] Urged to make repentance and faith "visible before the whole Congregation," a candidate reported the "manner" of his or her conversion, how the Spirit, working through the agency of the preached word, had brought one out of "that natural darkness, which all men are by nature in and under," and indued one with saving knowledge.[21] Some speakers proceeded

16. Lechford, *Plain Dealing*, 18–19; Cotton, *Way of the Churches*, 54; Welde, *Brief Narration*, 8. Hooker criticized the practice of admitting lay spectators to the preliminary hearings (*Survey*, III.i.5), but it persisted. Lonna M. Malmsheimer, "Daughters of Zion: New England Roots of American Feminism," *New England Quarterly*, 30 (1977), 486, avers that women "did not participate in conferring church membership," and Hall, *Faithful Shepard*, 101, states that they did not join in the trial of a candidate. Although women could not vote for members ([Richard Mather], *Church-Government and Church Covenant Discvssed* (London, 1643), 60), they were sometimes present at screenings, and, in Wenham and Chelmsford, at least, testified on behalf of applicants: Lechford, *Plain Dealing*, 19; Fiske, *Notebook*, 61, 106–7, 186. Cf. Mary Maples Dunn, "Saints and Sisters: Congregational and Quaker Women in the Early Colonial Period," *American Quarterly*, 30 (1978), 585–95, who speaks of women playing an active role in church governance for New England's first thirty years.

17. Lechford, *Plain Dealing*, 19; Hooker, *Survey*, III.i.5; *Ded. Recs.*, II, 20.

18. Lechford, *Plain Dealing*, 20.

19. Welde, *Brief Narration*, 9 (quotation); Lechford, *Plain Dealing*, 21; Fiske, *Notebook*, 20, 42. For the name Sarah, Torrey, "New England Marriages," V, *sub* Fiske.

20. Cotton, *Way of the Churches*, 70; Welde, *Brief Narration*, 9; Lechford, *Plain Dealing*, 22–23; *Ded. Recs.*, II, 20; Fiske, *Notebook, passim*. On the audience: Cotton, *Way of Congregational Churches*, 262; Lechford, *Plain Dealing*, 20; Mather, *Church-Government*, 7; Fiske, *Notebook*, 5, 6, 18, 20, 21, 32. A contrary statement is in *Ded. Recs.*, II, 25.

21. B. Richard Burg, ed., "A Letter of Richard Mather to a Cleric in Old England," *William and Mary Quarterly*, 3d ser., 29 (1972), 92; Johnson, *Wonder-Working Providence*, 217.

extemporaneously, while others responded to inquiries the officers posed. Hooker and his elders tendered certain "probatory questions" unless a person could speak comfortably "unto edification[,]" and in a case at Chelmsford, Fiske, Deacon Edward Kemp, and a lay brother "drew . . . out" Henry Farwell's relation by "divers" queries.[22] Those who delivered their confessions spoke "in the midst of the Assembly, or some convenient place," but not everyone addressed the gathering directly.[23] When Sarah Cotton joined the Boston church in 1633, her husband, soon to become one of congregationalism's leading apologists, requested that she not be asked to make an "open" declaration of her beliefs, "which he said was against the apostle's rule, and not fit for women's modesty." Wish gave birth to doctrine. Postulating

22. Mather, *Magnalia*, I, 349 (quotation), and see II, 68; Fiske, *Notebook*, 145 (quotation); John Cotton, *A Coppy of a Letter of M.* *Cotton of Boston* . . . ([London], 1641), 5; John Norton, *The Answer To the Whole Set of Questions of the Celebrated Mr. William Apollonius . . .*, trans. Douglas Horton (Cambridge, Mass., 1958 [orig. London, 1648]), 41; Allin and Shepard, *Defense*, 191. Morgan, *Visible Saints*, 106, takes the "probatory questions" as part of a private examination, but Cotton Mather, Morgan's source, is describing a public event. Hooker, he says, asked applicants "to make before the whole church a profession of a repenting faith," either by a relation or by answering queries. Selement and Woolley, "Introduction," 23–24, and in their introduction to the relation of William Andrews, 110, misrepresent the procedural differences between Hooker and Shepard on three counts. They imply that Shepard, like Hooker, asked probatory questions, but no evidence sustains the claim. They allege that Hooker "examined his Hartford candidates in the privacy of his study," whereas Shepard required a relation "before the entire Cambridge congregation," but this assertion confuses two separate steps. Both Hooker's *ruling elders* and Shepard's (perhaps in his presence) conducted private screenings in the weeks *before* the relation: Hooker, *Survey*, III.i.5; Allin and Shepard, *Defense*, 194. Finally, they suggest that Hooker was willing to dispense with an "explicit relation of faith for church membership; a candidate qualified, he wrote in 1645, if he either lived 'in the commission of any known duty' or could give 'a reason of his hope in God.' " Good behavior could be sufficient for membership, a point drawn from the *Survey* as quoted in Morgan, *Visible Saints*, 107 (who cites III.i.6 instead of III.i.5), but one that garbles the quotation and misreads its import (neither of which faults can be blamed on Morgan). Hooker says that if a person "*live not in the commission of any known sin*, nor *in the neglect of any known duty*, and *can give a reason of his hope towards God*," there is reason to believe that he manifests "something *of God and grace in the soul*," and is therefore "fit for Church-society." Hooker contends for a charitable disposition in judging candidates, not for admitting them without a confession. That he did require a statement of a person's experience to be given in public is apparent from Cotton Mather's account (noted above), Hooker's own declaration that, after passing through the preliminary testing, an applicant gives "*some reason of his hope* in the face of the Congregation" (*Survey*, III.i.5), and Increase Mather's report of a manuscript in which Hooker defended the practice of confessing one's experience on the basis that "if Christians are bound to give an account of the grounds of their hope to persecutors, much more to churches that shall desire it" (*Magnalia*, II, 70). What Hooker did not demand was that this account had to be narrated freely by the candidate. Those who "were able or wishing to do it" (*ibid.*, I, 349) he permitted; the others were coaxed and coached by the officers' questions. In addition, women had their relations read; see *infra*, n. 24. What this adds up to is an attempt to lead applicants through a confession of faith with a minimum of attendant "performance anxiety."

23. Lechford, *Plain Dealing*, 20.

women's "feebleness," their "shamefac't modesty and melanchollick fearful-
nesse," New England churches allowed the "weaker sex" to deliver their
relations in private and to have one of the elders read or summarize them in
public. However, the practice was not entirely gender-specific. Some women
pronounced their narratives themselves, and among the "feabler sort of Ewes
and lambes" whom the clergy feared to "overdrive . . . lest they should
miscarry," walked brethren who betrayed the same timorousness ascribed to
their sisters.[24] At the performance's close, church members desiring clarifica-
tion of some point or seeking to explore further a topic inadequately covered
interrogated the applicant. "How came you to see your sin?" someone
quizzed John Sill, who replied that "Seeing myself only a bare hearer, I saw
my vileness." Sill's answer seems to have sufficed, for Shepard recorded no
further inquiries, but other candidates had to field numerous questions before
their inquisitors ceased.[25]

Having exposed the secret moments of grace in the heart, applicants
moved to display its effects on the mind. In a statement professing "what they
do believe concerning the Doctrine of Faith," candidates reviewed major
tenets of Reformed theology and indicated their wholehearted assent. Persons
judged "weake" answered questions posed by the elders, a procedure that

24. The quoted material is: John Winthrop, *Winthrop's Journal "History of New England",
1630–1649*, ed. James Kendall Hosmer, 2 vols. (New York, 1908; repr. New York, 1959), I, 107
(henceforth cited as Winthrop, *Journal*); Hooker, *Survey*, III.i.6; Thomas Welde, *An Answer
to W. R. His Narration of the Opinions and Practices of the Churches lately erected in New-
England* (London, 1644), 19, 48. See also Lechford, *Plain Dealing*, 22–23; Fiske, *Notebook*, 4,
6, 8, 9, 151; Johnson, *Wonder-Working Providence*, 217; "Cambridge Platform," 223; Richard
C. Simmons, ed., "Richard Sadler's Account of the Massachusetts Churches," *New England
Quarterly*, 42 (1969), 424 (henceforth cited as Sadler, "Account"). Robert A. Rees, "Seeds of
Enlightenment: Public Testimony in the New England Congregational Churches, 1630–1750,"
Early American Literature, 3 (1968), 24, claims that the practice of letting women give a
private relation was the "first innovation" in a campaign to liberalize the admission requirements, but the custom seems to have originated out of deference to women's supposed
weakness. Although public conversion relations may have existed in Massachusetts as early as
1630 (Roger Clap, *Memoirs of Capt. Roger Clap* (Boston, 1731), 8), they were as yet very
uncommon when the Cottons stepped off the boat, and John's contention that his wife's
infirmity obligated a private statement of faith antedated their widespread institutionalization
by a few years. In 1633 there was no strict standard to "liberalize." Moreover, it is unlikely that
Cotton, the leading proponent of a system designed to keep the reprobate out of church
fellowship (Hall, *Faithful Shepherd*, 96–98), was thinking of this practice as a way to make
entrance standards more lenient. Lyle Koehler, *A Search for Power: The "Weaker Sex" in
Seventeenth-Century New England* (Urbana, 1980), 51, erroneously asserts that only women
gave private relations. (He also thinks that private confession was a "practical benefit," but
does not explain why. Dunn, "Saints and Sisters," 593, dates the advent of private relations for
men from the 1660s, but they existed earlier in both theory and practice.

25. Shepard, *Confessions*, 48. Cf., for example, Fiske, *Notebook*, 44; Wigglesworth, *Diary*,
439–40. According to Norton, *Answer*, 42, questions were to be funneled through elders, the
church's "mouthpiece," but the interrogation of Nicholas Wyeth, Shepard, *Confessions*, 195–
97, suggests that, in his case, church members addressed the speaker directly.

amounted to public catechizing, while more competent or self-assured individuals voiced their credos in a "solemne speech."[26] The contents probably varied from place to place. Cotton attempted to establish a core of essential dogma in October 1640, declaring that continued ignorance of any one of twelve fundamental articles excludes one "from the fellowship of the Church." Many of these principles, like the doctrine of the Trinity, belonged to virtually all shades of Christian opinion, but others, like the tenth—God justifies freely "according to his truth, not by works"—marked out a more clearly sectarian stance.[27] Only two personal professions of faith seem to have survived from early New England, and both differ from Cotton's putative standard. Six of the twenty headings John Davenport discussed take up Christ's nature and offices, a topic Cotton only briefly covered, and five more concern church structure, knowledge Cotton thought inessential for church membership. By contrast, Henry Dunster, a future president of Harvard, skipped quickly through Christology and ignored ecclesiology in order to expand upon seven ways by which God strengthens faith.[28] Seeking

26. Richard Mather, *Church-Government*, 23 (quotation); Lechford, *Plain Dealing*, 23 (quotation); Fiske, *Notebook*, 29; Cotton, *Coppy*, 5; "A relatō in w^t man^n any psons are received into the congregaiōns of New England," Colonial Office Papers, 1/9, fol. 166ro, Public Record Office, London, on Library of Congress microfilm #Ac. 10,741, reel 4. Many of the descriptions of admissions procedures place the conversion relation before the profession of faith, but see Welde, *Brief Narration*, 9; Norton, *Answer*, 35–36; Shepard, *Confessions*, 156–64; "A relatō," 166ro. Both professions and catechisms condensed theology into systematic outlines, and their similarity is underlined by the excuse the Bay elders ostensibly gave for not catechizing their children during the first decade. According to Lechford, *Plain Dealing*, 53, one reason was "because when people come to be admitted, the Church hath tryall of their knowledge, faith, and repentance." Even as he was writing, however, the General Court was directing the elders to instruct youth "in the grounds of religion," and in the next few years the colony press rattled off many different titles. Nathaniel B. Shurtleff, ed., *Records of the Governor and Company of the Massachusetts Bay in New England*, 5 vols. in 6 (Boston, 1853–54), I, 328 (henceforth cited as *Mass. Recs.*); Wilberforce Eames, "Early New England Catechisms," *Proceedings of the American Antiquarian Society*, n.s., 12 (1899), 87–119.

27. Lechford, *Plain Dealing*, 25–28. The sermon's outline also appears in Cotton, *Treatise of Faith*, 4–9. This version varies from Lechford's in small details of enumeration and content, and it also lacks the statement that incorrect knowledge of church government should not hinder communion with a church.

28. J[ohn] D[avenport], *The Profession of the Faith of that Reverend and worthy Divine M^r. J. D.* (London, 1642); Shepard, *Confessions*, 156–61. John Rogers prints his profession in . . . *Ohel*, 350–53. See also Walker, *Creeds*, 115, n. 1, and the Salem creed recited by the baptized children of church members when they came to present themselves for membership, *ibid.*, 120–21. Because Dunster's statement is the sole example that Shepard took down, Selement and Woolley, "Introduction," 22, contend that Shepard allowed candidates to "merge" their conversion relations and professions into one narrative, but their assertion is dubious on two counts, one logical, the other evidentiary. The absence of other professions does not prove that they were never given. Shepard may have wanted to record Dunster's remarks because Dunster was a particularly knowledgeable person whose profession would be useful to keep (according to Mather, *Magnalia*, II, 181, it was something of a learned man's prerogative to entertain the audience at his trial with his own creedal composition), or (and

orthodoxy on major matters, Puritans tolerated petty errors and divergent opinions about details. Richard Mather maintained that Paul's injunction to receive those who "differ from us in opinion about meates and dayes etc.," meant that contrary ideas about church government did not by themselves exclude a person from membership, and Hooker added that mistakes "wherein pious and prudent men are of a different judgement," do not bar one from the visible church. Richard Goldsmith entered into covenant with Wenham although he challenged a portion of that church's confession regarding the resurrection.[29] Such latitude did have its limits, however. Lechford's speculations about the apostolic succession and the identity of the Antichrist prevented him from ever undergoing the admission procedure he so carefully described.[30]

Along with the recitation of doctrine went a "professed subjection to the Gospel" with the expressed "desire of walking therein, with the fellowship of that Church." Wenham, Chelmsford, and Salem also asked for subscription to a local confession of creed.[31] If necessary, the elder solicited testimony from one or more members, who affirmed the applicant's "Christian and sincere affections," instancing acts of "godlinesse" and declaring their willingness to extend "the right hand of fellowship." Outside witness to the candidate's worth, and a sign that he or she had not kept faith hidden in a closet, these attestations could prove influential. In the case of the Mrs. Greene whose confession appears to have been so brief, "Testimonies carried it."[32] Following such an intense, protracted operation, candidates might have felt

---

this is wildly speculative) because Shepard already had some inklings that Dunster held some heterodox opinions (he resigned the presidency of Harvard in 1654 on account of his Baptist leanings). Furthermore, the relations and professions that exist exhibit identifiably distinct forms. Shepard's relations are quite similar to Fiske's and Wigglesworth's, and markedly unlike the credos. There are no passages in any of the other Shepard documents that warrant supposing they were partial professions.

29. Burg, "Letter of Richard Mather," 92; Hooker, *Survey*, I.vi.61; Fiske, *Notebook*, 68. Cf. Welde, *Answer to W. R.*, 23; "A Relatō," fol. 166vo; John Cotton, *A Letter of Mr. John Cottons . . . to Mr. Williams . . .* (London, 1643; facsimile repr. in *Publications of the Narragansett Club*, 1st ser., I (1866)), 303–4.

30. Lechford, *Note-Book Kept by Thomas Lechford, Esq., Lawyer, in Boston, Massachusetts Bay, from June 27, 1638, to July 29, 1641*, in *Transactions and Collections of the American Antiquarian Society*, 7 (1885), 45, 48–50, 89–90, 274–76, 287–88, 435; *idem, Plain Dealing*, 144–46, 152–53, 156–57; Cotton, *Way of Congregational Churches*, 265. Cotton denies that Lechford was refused fellowship "for maintaining the authority of bishops." Were that Lechford's only error, he implies, Lechford could have joined other members who "indifferently allow" episcopal, presbyterian, or congregational church government.

31. Cotton, *Way of the Churches*, 55 (quotation); Mather, *Church-Government*, 24; Fiske, *Notebook*, 10, 29, 37, 45, 61, 104, 174; Walker, *Creeds*, 108, 112–15, 119–22, 153–56.

32. Cotton, *Way of the Churches*, 55; Welde, *Brief Narration*, 9; Cotton, *Coppy*, 5 (quotation); Lechford, *Plain Dealing*, 21–22 (quotation); Shepard, *Confessions*, 118 (quotation). The testimonies might come at almost any time during the meeting until the vote.

relieved to hear the elder finally call for a show of hands from those members who consented to admission; the decision was supposed to be unanimous, church business being governed by Christ's will rather than human pluralities, but in some congregations majority vote sufficed.[33] All that then remained was to formally receive the individual into the fold, which took place either immediately or a few days later, generally on Sunday. Demanding *"whether you be willing to enter a holy Covenant with God,"* the elder pronounced the terms: submission to Christ, subjection to the Gospel ordinances, and association with the church in *"mutuall edification and succor according to God."*[34] After the candidate's assent, vocal or tacit, the elder stated the church's reciprocal responsibilities, establishing the covenant, and another lamb joined the flock.[35]

The successive tests through which applicants passed exposed the full range of their religious experience to interested observers. Congregations apprehended how each new individual's sorrows and joys at overcoming the flesh mixed with his or her intellectual grasp of the Spirit's motions, and how the soul's regenerate changes corresponded to the body's right walking. Central to the procedure was the conversion relation, the "rocke and foundation of a visible Church," whose stated purpose was to ensure that "Such as have onely a *forme of godlinesse, and deny the power of it,"* did not enter into church society.[36] The narratives served another purpose too, unmentioned by defenders of the practice but discernible from descriptions of it. Puritan preachers laid down in their sermons the course of the new birth, but this understanding would have remained merely an exercise in hermeneutics and haranguing had it not met with a popular response. By having conversions, men and women acted out the program of experience that the clergy sanctioned, thereby attesting to its utility. Finding in themselves the same motions of the Spirit that they had heard described, they validated the acuity of the preachers' analysis by finding it personally meaningful. The church admission system in New England provided for another level of assent. A congregation which agreed that an applicant's relation had demonstrated the presence of saving faith at the same time acquiesced in the ministry's paradigm of grace, hence the vote to approve a person for membership also ratified the cultural definition of conversion experience. Guardians of the gates to the church as well as the subjects in whom the Spirit worked, the laity helped confirm the applicability of the conversion model their preachers wrought.

33. Mather, *Church-Government,* 60–62; Lechford, *Plain Dealing,* 28, 38, and n. 37; Welde, *Answer to W. R.,* 19; Winthrop, *Journal,* II, 281.

34. Lechford, *Plain Dealing,* 29; Fiske, *Notebook, passim;* Cotton, *Coppy,* 6 (quotation). Cf. Welde, *Brief Narration,* 9; *Winthrop Papers,* IV, 170.

35. Lechford, *Plain Dealing,* 29; Welde, *Answer to W. R.,* 24; *idem, Brief Narration,* 9.

36. Cotton, *Way of the Churches,* 57.

II

The procedures for entering a church were set down by numerous observers, but since the actual happenings were not so dutifully transcribed, their reconstruction is necessarily partial.[37] When candidates met a congregation to advertise their grace, the expectations of each party influenced the course of events. Churches anticipated that applicants would, or at least should, live up to a well-articulated ideal that combined both subjective and objective notices of regeneration. Visible Saints, the "matter" of a particular church, "haue not only attained the knowledge of the principles of Religion, & are free from gros & open scandals, but also do together with the profession of their faith & Repentance, walk in blameles obedience to the word."[38] Accorded more than "common gifts," Saints "by calling" have been "subdued" by the Spirit to perform God's commands; their tongues declare their faith, and their deeds bespeak the presumed reality of an inner change.[39] This characterization necessarily stopped short of equating all confessors with God's Elect, for hypocrites in gracious guise could infiltrate any church, and some who advertise their faith "do it but *feinedly*." Since it is not the "inward being" but [rather] the outward profession" of belief that constitutes the church on earth, taking an individual into covenant "does not testify that the person admitted is actually faithful, but that he is faithful to the church." A Visible Saint is someone who, to all intents and purposes, appears to have received saving grace and who behaves accordingly. The ignorant, false, and notorious do not qualify.[40]

The definition of a Visible Saint begged the question of recognizability. Witnesses could vouch for a candidate's background, and the community could observe his or her demeanor, but by what criterion could one determine the existence of saving grace, imperceptibly implanted by the Spirit? Although preachers offered a few specific observations—Shepard advised paying close attention to candidates' speech and heeding if they were not "grappling with sin and temptation"—ministers held that the posture with which one should approach the task was more important than any specific

37. Tantalizingly, *Ded. Recs.*, II, 14, states that "p'ticular p'fessions of ye most of them wth notes of ye churches p'ceedings wth them remaine in private notes, & were too large heere to be inserted."

38. "Cambridge Platform," 205. Cf. David D. Hall, ed., *The Antinomian Controversy, 1636–1638: A Documentary History* (Middletown, 1968), 236; Fiske, *Notebook*, 141.

39. John Davenport, *The Power of Congregational Churches Asserted and Vindicated* (London, 1672), 14; "Cambridge Platform," 205. Davenport originally completed his work in the early 1640s, but the printer's copy was lost at sea. He rewrote it, and the text circulated in manuscript for more than twenty years until it was finally published.

40. Davenport, *Power*, 14; Allin and Shepard, *Defense*, 189; Norton, *Answer*, 40–41; John Cotton, *Of the Holinesse of Church-Members* (London, 1650), 19–20.

scrutiny.[41] Applicants should be assessed according to the "judgment of charity," a term that in traditional Christian thought had dual significance. Broadly, it intended the willingness in a doubtful situation to judge people favorably; more narrowly, it connoted the attitude by which one placed the best possible construction on a person's spiritual estate and admitted the impossibility of coming to a sound evaluation of another's inward grace. New Englanders contended that they took notice of the phrase's second sense, but since they also argued the necessity for probing a prospective member's soul, they actually fused the two meanings.[42] By "judgment of charity," New England Puritans understood the readiness to appraise a person's faith, both internally real and externally apparent, with an open mind that, in the presence of "favorable evidences," inclines "to an approving estimate" and takes the individual "for the better." In theory, one was to grade candidates by a divine standard tempered with reasoned compassion, *"rationall charity"* directed by the Word, Christ's "compleat rule" of faith and love. These prescriptions urged that where the church could discern "the least true breathing of Christ, though but as smoaking flax," the candidate had passed the test. We do not exact "eminent measure" of knowledge or holiness, Cotton claimed, but "willingly stretch out our hands" to the weak in faith, "for we had rather 99. hypocrites should perish through presumption, th[a]n one humble soul belonging to Christ, should sinke under discouragement or despaire."[43] Absolute certainty about an applicant's estate was unnecessary, and fractious criticism without any "rule or convicting argument from the word," was "rigour" to be shunned.[44]

In practice, nevertheless, one person's rigor was someone else's charity. Shortly before Shepard warned his flock to be "very careful" in receiving members and admonished them to "take heed of thinking elders or churches are strict," Hooker, the man whose pulpit he took over, left Massachusetts because, rumor had it, the colony's church admission procedures were so harsh. The Cambridge Platform intoned that "Severity of examination is to be avoyded," but in a book published the same year the Platform was finished, Hooker complained that "curious inquisitions and niceties," brought on by "the pride and wantonnesse of mens spirits[,]" too often disturbed churches and prejudiced "the progresse of God's Ordinances."[45]

41. Shepard, *Works*, II, 190.

42. Baird Tipson, "Invisible Saints: The 'Judgment of Charity' in the Early New England Churches," *Church History*, 44 (1975), 460–66.

43. Norton, *Answer*, 39–40; Hooker, *Survey*, I.ii.14; Allin and Shepard, *Defense*, 189; Welde, *Brief Narration*, 9; Cotton, *Way of the Churches*, 58.

44. Allin and Shepard, *Defense*, 189; cf. Cotton, *Holinesse*, 42.

45. Shepard, *Works*, II, 450; *Winthrop Papers*, III, 390; "Cambridge Platform," 222; Hooker, *Survey*, III.i.6.

Reports about the severity of different congregations circulated among the colonists. One letter accounted Davenport, then at New Haven, "the strictest man for the church covenant, and admitting of members in N. England." Martha Collins told her Cambridge hearers that she thought the Boston church too close in their examinations, and Anne Fiske informed her husband's congregation that the practices of Watertown had militated against her joining.[46] Presumably, these two women found their own congregations more charitable. The plenitude of manifest grace a church required depended on how minister and members interpreted what the judgment of charity implied. Expectations surrounding the appearance of Visible Saints varied from place to place.

For their part, candidates anticipated how a church would receive them. Knowledge of the elders' reactions to the preliminary screening, plus familiarity with both the membership—one's neighbors—and the congregation's collective reputation, suggested how the assembly might respond. With what emotions applicants approached the narrative is impossible to know for certain, but a good number must have worried about its pitfalls. Critics then and now have charged that the relation kept many from entering church covenant. William Rathband, an English presbyterian, supposed that the practice would render the timid "afraid to offer themselves to triall, because they know not whether they shall be judged fit or no," an inference Lechford confirmed. Writing to defend the system late in the seventeenth century, Increase Mather admitted that "unjustifiable severity" had indeed discouraged "some truly gracious souls" from offering themselves, and his son Cotton recognized that opponents thought the test "a scare-crow to keep men out of the temple." One modern researcher avers that the relation posed a "formidable" obstacle.[47] Indisputably, the prospect of baring one's soul to a possibly unfriendly group induced anxiety among some prospective members, but another source also contributed. The church admission test was hardly the first time that candidates had confided their experiences to others. Family and friends played important roles in a Saint's spiritual development, and many recounted a timely conversation that pricked the conscience, resolved a doubt, or extended loving encouragment. Some of William Manning's friends, denying his own uncritical self-appraisal, accused him of scandalizing the Gospel, "so that I had much grief and trouble and so was

46. G. H. Turnbull, "Robert Child," *Publications of the Colonial Society of Massachusetts*: 38: *1947-1951* (1959), 50; Shepard, *Confessions*, 131; Fiske, *Notebook*, 7.

47. W[illiam] R[athband], *A Briefe Narration of Some Church Courses Held in Opinion and Practise in the Churches lately erected in New England* (London, 1644), 9; Lechford, *Plain Dealing*, 21, 150-51; Mather, *Magnalia*, II, 67, 244; Wilford Oakland Cross, "The Role and Status of the Unregenerate in the Massachusetts Bay Colony 1629-1729," (Ph.D. dissertation, Columbia University, 1957), 150.

beaten off from it." William Ames, son of the theologian, worried that he had committed an unpardonable sin, until someone counseled him. The support of Roger Haynes's parents "was a great deal of God's goodness."[48] Puritan Saints found their faith as much through social communication as through introspective wrangling. Sometimes, however, an especially oppressive sense of sin led them to retreat from talk. Disheartened by a sermon on Lam. 3.40, Ann Errington refused to tell her husband, "fearing he would loath me if he knew me," and conversed with him two months later only on condition that he not tell a mutual acquaintance. While a teenage apprentice, Manning concluded his condition was "lamentable" yet felt "ashamed to make it known."[49] Giving a relation placed individuals in the troublingly familiar position of having to admit their sins to others—and to themselves—except that now the audience was larger and the stakes higher. The dismay attributed to New Englanders can be ascribed to their own shamefulness too.

But in the end, those wishing to belong to a holy community triumphed over their embarrassment. Nicholas Wyeth worried that he would "not be able to speak the truth," for he had been "very unprofitable," yet because he "desired to enjoy [the] society of God's people," he publicly aired his regret. Moreover, people faced the ordeal with hope as well as alarm. More than a hint of jubilation rings from John Stansby's opening, "'Tis a mercy I have long begged and waited for . . . I bless God for this," and from Manning's closing invitation for his audience to marvel that "such a poor creature should be provided for as I am."[50] The hubbub over the recitation's baneful effects has overshadowed positive aspects that could make it a desirable experience. For Ann Kemp, who "made her relation with great breaking of affection" remembering "her former sins" and the unregenerate nature of her parents, the opportunity to confess may have proved abreactive, long-festering thoughts finally purged in Wenham's forgiveness. Beyond catharsis, the ceremony granted solace to applicants by allowing them to advertise their distress at sin and petition the auditory for support. Admitting he had "cause to take shame to myself," an anonymous Cambridge Saint called on "the

48. Shepard, *Confessions*, 94, 211, 169.

49. Shepard, *Confessions*, 184–85, 94; see also 90, 104, 119–20, 141. The contention of Selement and Woolley, "Introduction," 5, that Errington's remark and a similar one by Mary Sparrowhawk (*ibid.*, 66) disclose how "seventeenth-century women were generally subservient to their husbands and fathers in most matters," is beside the point. (Sparrowhawk's remark, in fact, does not substantiate such subservience, for she said that she "could not speak to anybody," female as well as male relatives.) These statements manifest embarrassment over past transgressions, a sentiment shared equally by men. See the Manning quotation, above, and *ibid.*, 167, 168, 179, 200, 201; Wigglesworth, *Diary*, 428, 442; Thomas Shepard, "The Autobiography," in Michael McGiffert, ed., *God's Plot: The Paradoxes of Puritan Piety* ([Amherst], 1972), 43.

50. Shepard, *Confessions*, 195–96, 86, 98.

people of God to help me," and Elizabeth Hincksman "beg[ged]" Chelmsford's prayers for the Lord to "more and more manifest Himself unto her."
Such solicitations indicated a person's willingness to seek the "watch of the
church[,]" inaugurating the relationship between candidate and congregation
that would soon flower into fullfledged fellowship.[51]

Another benefit inhered in the power of congregations to strengthen weak
faith and enhance assurance by accepting relations as signs of grace. An
affirmative vote announced that an entire population had certified one's faith,
a circumstance that must have prompted great satisfaction. John Rogers of
Dublin pointed to the benefit of exposing "*all* to *light*," in a public scrutiny:
"you have their *assurance* or *pleonasmes* of *joy* and *love*, and *light and all*
brought out; so that they being *openly attested* and *approved*, the *Saints* are
thereby often *advantaged* for future *attempts*, and *troubles* and *suits* in
Law."[52] Validation from peers heartens the Elect for future trials. Citing for
proof Ps. 40.10—"I have not hidden thy righteousness from the great congregation"—the Cambridge Platform advanced a similar argument: a person
must be ready to exhibit one's repentance, faith and calling because "these
are the reason [*sic*] of a well grounded hope." Willingness to express one's
faith declares its presence and promotes assurance. Henry Dunster, having
introduced his personal remarks with the same verse, confidently (and pre-
sumptuously) concluded his relation with the caveat "to be careful what
scholars enter to your churches, and pray for humility of spirit"; the chance to
speak in public became an occasion for declaiming his Sainthood.[53] Just as
churches differed in their estimates of sanctity's signs, applicants came to
examinations with a variety of expectations.

A well-prepared candidate who met a congregation's standards breezed
through admission as if following a script. Having stood propounded for
three weeks without anyone speaking against him, Jonathan Barge publicly
reaffirmed his desire to join with Chelmsford. Standing at the altar with his
two sons, he defended the "use and lawfulness" of giving a relation, then

51. Fiske, *Notebook*, 95; Wigglesworth, *Diary*, 439; Fiske, *Notebook*, 151, 52. The anonymous
confessor must be a man, because the narrative reads (438), "God called me to be master of a
family. . . ."

52. Rogers, . . . *Ohel*, 372.

53. "Cambridge Platform," 223, and see the Chelmsford church's defense for instituting
conversion relations, Fiske, *Notebook*, 145; Shepard, *Confessions*, 161, 164. The passage cited
from the Cambridge Platform conflates the first and last clauses of the verse. Dunster quotes
from the last clause. Tipson, "Invisible Saints," 469–71, suggests the relation's function as a
means to assurance. Caldwell, *Puritan Conversion Narrative*, 86–87, 107–8, allows that
relations may have served this function (though she finds the New England examples much
more anxious than assured), but she argues that their original intention was to link the
Invisible Church to the Visible one, grounding the gathered body of Saints in the communal
dialogue about experience.

"orderly and distinctly" recounted his spiritual doubts, comforts, temptations, and blessings. After testimony from Pastor Fiske, members silently ratified the address, and Barge consented to the church's creed and covenant. Jonathan had come from another church, and in such cases, congregational doctrine prescribed that the person's former brethren release him or her from their discipline by sending a letter of dismission to the new church. Fiske read the requisite notice, which endorsed Barge's behavior, and Chelmsford extended the right hand of fellowship.[54] Bridget Fiske, John's sister-in-law, had nearly as easy a time. The preliminary inquiries found her "reservedness" to speak about "heavenly matters" objectionable, but members recalled that she normally uttered "few words in company," and she confessed the fault. Someone vouched for her, and Wenham agreed to hear her relation. Bridget's taciturnity seems not to have troubled her further, for she gave her narrative "to good satisfaction."[55]

More serious complaints extended the process beyond its usual time span and even passed beyond the town's confines. Edward Kemp lay under "suspicions of drunkenness," and his disclaimer—that it was the bad cheese he had eaten after a day of fasting rather that the several quarts of beer with which he had washed it down that precipitated his attack of vomiting and "wind"—left Wenham "variously inclined." The church delayed for over half a year until the Essex County Quarter Court dismissed the charge as "groundless surmise." Then they accepted him within a fortnight of the verdict, though not without "some little consideration and agitation."[56] Occasionally, a case took on more than local significance, entrapping an applicant in controversy that had nothing to do with his or her personal qualifications. Thomas Parker and James Noyes organized the Newbury church along presbyterian lines, allowing their membership little administrative responsibility. When Hannah Fiske requested them to dismiss her to Wenham, Parker and Noyes signed the letter solely in their own names and addressed it to Reverend Fiske alone, thereby insinuating that only the officers had jurisdiction in the business. This violation of congregational protocol and polity called the missive's acceptability into question. Hannah waited while Wenham debated, until the church concluded that the "substance" of the reply sufficed but that its "form" deserved open rebuke. Some nine months after

---

54. Fiske, *Notebook*, 173–74. Asking Barge to subscribe to the covenant before the church voted him in (cf. *ibid.*, 29, 61) contradicts John Winthrop's assertion (*Winthrop Papers*, IV, 171), that the churches did not do this. On letters of dismission, see "Cambridge Platform," 224–26.

55. Fiske, *Notebook*, 24, 29.

56. Fiske, *Notebook*, 93–95; George Francis Dow, ed., *Records and Files of the Quarterly Courts of Essex County, Massachusetts*, 8 vols. (Salem, 1911–21), I, 285.

she first asked permission to remove, Goodwife Fiske took Wenham's covenant.[57]

The most extreme examples witnessed individual and congregation suffering through charge and countercharge, disclosure and rebuttal. The early reports on Sarah Fiske, by marriage John's first cousin once removed, levelled two accusations: she had publicly maligned her husband Phineas, "saying he loved another woman better than his wife &c.," and she had misbehaved during a Sabbath service. Unwilling to proceed until they settled matters, the membership delegated two brethren "to show her the church's mind," and receive what they probably thought would be a repentant response. Instead, Sarah recriminated, charging Phineas with "false witness bearing." Depositions given during a church meeting, strings of she-said-that-he-said, reduced the affair to a petty misunderstanding and exonerated Phineas. Resolving the issue of her public insults, however, injected into the affray the ugliness that ensues when intimate bitterness becomes common knowledge. Sarah complained that Phineas did not take her side in her troubles, that he failed to pray for and sympathize with her, that he behaved cruelly towards her and said "he would break her heart." The church adjudged him innocent of three "of these so sad accusations"; a letter from his cousin in Watertown took care of the fourth. Having ascertained that the husband needed no correction, the church turned to the wife. Urging everyone to tell her "plainly" that she had to recognize the wrongdoing of her accusations, it encouraged them "to pray for her" and "to walk exemplarily before her." Months elapsed while Wenham waited for solicitude to take its course. Sarah admitted some fault, but insufficiently; patiently, they purposed "to attend her and observe her spirit and conversation to see if any good fruits of repentance might further appear." Eventually, some did. Hoping "to satisfy the church," she "acknowledged she did evil in these particulars." Both spouses conceded their failings, Pastor Fiske wishing that their reconciliation would establish, "if possible, a sweet accord betwixt them," and the church agreed to hear her conversion relation.[58]

Omitting the anguish of her human relationships, Sarah rehashed the familiar Puritan argument with God and self. Inspired by a sermon about the Last Judgment, she prayed God "to show what sin was and whether the Lord spoke to her." Convinced that God had indeed spoken but doubting the

---

57. James Noyes, *The Temple Measured* (London, 1647), 10–49; Fiske, *Notebook*, 15, 17, 18, 22, 23–24, 31, 32–34, 37. Fiske refers to Hannah (née Pike) as Anne, but she is here called Hannah to distinguish her from his wife Anne (née Gibbs or Gipps). On the name Hannah, see David W. Hoyt, *The Old Families of Salisbury and Amesbury, Massachusetts,* 3 vols. and supp. (Providence, 1897–1919), I, 286. Hannah married James Fiske, John Fiske's cousin.

58. Fiske, *Notebook*, 22, 25–29, 32, 34, 35, 40–42.

effect, she besought the Lord to "show her condition," only to discover herself worse off "than any toad." Eventually she took hold of Christ and, gaining a measure of assurance, "went forth rejoicing and praising God, desiring the Lord to go on further with her." Troubled by the direction of the Anglican Church under Archbishop William Laud, she emigrated to Massachusetts. No doubt animated by their own dealings with her, the church subjected Sarah to one of the most withering interrogations on record, a barrage, however, that targeted her religious experience exclusively. What evidence did she have of God? Had the Lord helped her see her failings? Asked "whether they were satisfied?" the examiners demurred, concerned about the way she interpreted the movement of grace in the Bible and her life. How did "the word and work suit," they wanted to know; could she support her experience with proper texts? She could, and did. Following an exchange over whether a verse she had cited rightfully referred to her preparation or to effectual vocation, the church was again asked "if more had aught further to query or object." Finally persuaded, they asked for intelligence of her conversation. The account of one person was challenged, but "he stood to it." The pastor and her husband spoke in her behalf. The church requested her to confess in front of the entire congregation her "miscarriages," which included insinuations that Reverend Fiske had suppressed information favorable to her; she obliged. Sticking closely to prescribed procedure, Wenham demanded that Sarah satisfy each requirement. At long last, everyone's perseverance paid off. A year of trial ended with her acceptance. Refusing to compromise its standards of Visible Sainthood, Wenham had guided an exceptionally querulous—and vulnerable—individual into covenant.[59]

If any person underwent Sarah Fiske's ordeal futilely, the records of early New England are mercifully mute about it. The archives' silence suggests that few who reached an advanced state in the proceedings failed to achieve membership.[60] The earlier screening procedures eliminated clearly unsuitable applicants, and self-selection weeded out persons who, for one reason or another, might well have stumbled along the way. Those who presented themselves as candidates did not constitute a random sample; the scoffers, apathetic, and disaffected did not register. Lechford explained that "I have not received the Sacrament these two yeares, nor am yet like to doe," because he disparaged the "confessions, and professions," as "not tending to the

59. Fiske, *Notebook*, 43–45, 47, and see 27–28.

60. Pope, "Introduction" to Fiske, *Notebook*, xvii, alludes to occasional incidents of rejection after the confession and profession had been given, but does not cite them. Sadler, "Account," 424, claimed that sometimes "the rigider sort" would refuse admission to people whose confessions were "scanty," a waspishness more recently tempered by ministerial "discretion." Cf. Coolidge, *Pauline Renaissance*, 65; Caldwell, *Puritan Conversion Narrative*, 46, n.7.

propagation of the Gospel in peace." Irritated by many New England practices, he declined to apply.[61] In addition, there may have existed an informal
mechanism that encouraged likely or attractive candidates to offer themselves. One zealous pioneer desired a recruiting program of international
scope. Advocating a grandiose policy to import only Saints, he entreated his
former minister to ensure that "all such as you shall advise to sit down with
us," be "fit to be received into church fellowship." The plan points up the
selective and friendly pressures that did operate within communities. Jonathan Barge referred cryptically to "one that named him to join with this
church in fellowship," and the Dedham faithful had "divers loving conferences" with Jonathan Fairebanke that led ultimately to his admission,
"notw'standing he had long stood off fro' ye church upon some scruples about
publike p'fession of faith & ye covenant." Sarah Fiske's familial connections—in the circumscribed world of Wenham, she was the wife of one
member, mother of another, and a cousin of two more, including the pastor—may have contributed to the persistence with which the church reviewed
her case.[62] Puritans believed that grace often runs in families, and her
relationships made her someone worth pursuing.[63] Those in whom a church
presumed especial interest enjoyed the maximum of attention and support.

　　Still, some people at first did not measure up to expectations, and
Rathband feared that those "repulsed" would "hardly offer themselves
againe, but rather live they and theirs out of Church all their dayes."[64] The
surviving evidence, however, projects an alternative development. Rebuffed
once, people who had dared to put their faith on the measuring block tried
again. At an attempted establishment of a church in Dorchester, which by
New England practice required a group of neighboring ministers and magistrates to judge the founders' conversion relations, onlookers ruled that the
majority "had builded their comfort of salvation upon unsound grounds,"
and put off the ceremony. A chagrined Richard Mather rehearsed his companions, and a second attempt to establish the church succeeded. A similar
experience befell Thomas Morse. One of the eight prospective pillars about
whom the incipient Dedham church entertained its "best hopes" of "soundnes

61. Lechford, *Note Book*, 274; *idem, Plain Dealing*, 150–52, and see 129–43.

62. Everett Emerson, comp., *Letters From New England: The Massachusetts Bay Colony,
1629–1638* (Amherst, 1976), 141; Fiske, *Notebook*, 173; *Ded. Recs.*, II, 29; G. Andrews
Moriarty, contrib., "Genealogical Research in England Communicated by the Committee on
English and Foreign Research: The Fiske Family," *New England Historical Genealogical
Register*, 88 (1934), 270–73.

63. Edmund S. Morgan, *The Puritan Family*, rev. and enlg. ed. (New York, 1966), 174–86;
Gerald F. Moran and Maris Vinovskis, "The Puritan Family and Religion: A Critical Reappraisal," *William and Mary Quarterly*, 3d ser., 39 (1982), 35–36.

64. Rathband, *Briefe Narration*, 9.

of grace & meete guifts for such a worke," Morse appeared "so darke & unsatisfying in respect of yᵉ worke of grace" that "thay had not grounds to imbrace him into this society except thay should see further." In time, they did. Two years later, possessing more proof of his carriage and grace, "& upon his renewed desyres of joining to yᵉ church he was received." An extraordinarily plucky individual could even provoke a congregation to reverse its decision on the spot. John Rogers chronicled the fortunes of a candidate who, "answering at first very *fearfully*, and *uncertainly*," caused the Dublin church to reject her. Weeping, she cried that "the *Word* hath called me, and *Christ* hath called me, and bid me *come*, and I must come, without any *worthiness* in my self; and shall I now be put by?" Misty-eyed themselves, the church reconsidered.[65] Then (as even now) a well shed tear could wash away the hurdles in a woman's path.

III

Did anyone purposefully falsify a narrative? The question may be approached from two frames of reference. In Puritan terms, the query strikes to the heart of Saints' quest to keep the Visible Church pure. New Englanders designed the conversion relation so that "harlotts may not bee thrust into christs [*sic*] bosome, for his spouses."[66] One can, nonetheless, imagine a clever individual turning the procedure against itself. Conceivably, a person who learned the proper phrases by attending membership examinations could pass as a Saint. Either the desire to gain the voting privileges associated with freemanship, which in Massachusetts from 1631 to 1664 was available only to male church members, or the thought of gaining "sundry outward and worldly advantages" through membership, may have tempted some to fake regeneration. Richard Sadler, like Lechford an observant critic of congregationalism's genesis, made just such a charge.[67] On the other hand, the responsibilities of freemanship forced many eligible men to refuse it, and the drudgery of godly routine may have made Visible Sainthood an uninviting prospect to all but a few hardy frauds. A fleeting remark by John Brock, a Saint attending Harvard in the 1640s, hints that dissembling may have been its own reward: hypocrites join "our Churches to their own Ruine." If Thomas Welde exaggerated when he claimed that God had often exposed

65. Winthrop, *Journal*, I, 177; and see B. Richard Burg, *Richard Mather of Dorchester* (Lexington, Ky., 1976), 36–37; *Ded. Recs.*, II, 5, 6, 23; Rogers, . . . *Ohel*, 291–92.

66. Burg, "Letter of Richard Mather," 91.

67. *Mass. Recs.*, I, 87; William H. Whitmore, ed., *The Colonial Laws of Massachusetts. Reprinted from the Edition of 1672, with the Supplement through 1686* (Boston, 1887), 56; Davenport, *Power*, 17; Sadler, "Account," 423–24.

hypocrites "in the very act of their triall," cannot be known, but one suspects that people seldom invented stories in order to enter a church.[68] A few of the narratives do bear witness to the opposite phenomenon, a scrupulous regard for veracity. By the time applicants reached the point of speaking to a congregation, they had had ample time to perfect their performances. Still, some allowed that they could not remember details whose absence could have jeopardized their admission. Nathaniel Sparrowhawk conceded that he had forgotten "many things which I cannot now express myself." Jane Willows, née Palfrey, failed to enunciate the specific sins that had cast her down, and Henry Farwell could not "call to mind" the "many scriptures" that had eased his doubts of salvation. John Rogers of Watertown failed to adumbrate his experience with proof texts for a reason that speaks volumes about the seriousness with which candidates approached the relation: he desired "to speak the very truth and not to colour aught."[69]

From a more detached perspective, to ask if hypocrites took the covenant is to state, in the interrogative, how much the events surrounding admission involved the entire church. Digesting every word to discover signs of grace, audiences participated in the confessions along with the speakers. While concentrating on the candidate's trials, exponents of the procedure also pointed out the narrative's effects upon the broader populace. The Chelmsford church explained that "a pious attendance upon this way in admission of members may tend to edification of others to consider God's way with a poor soul," and that the practice "tends not to the hurt or prejudice of any soul but rather to its greater benefit for the future." Increase Mather added that personal accounts sometimes catalyzed conversion in a listener. John Rogers of Dublin adduced yet another effect: "By their *Experiences* you will learne how various God is in his *wayes* and *workings*," for He comes to one like a lamb, to another like a lion.[70] That the narratives did serve to inspire unregenerates is attested to by Roger Clap, one of Dorchester's founders. In an autobiography both historical and hortatory, he reminded his descendants that many people told "their Experiences of the Workings of God's Spirit" to

---

68. Darrett B. Rutman, *Winthrop's Boston: Portrait of a Puritan Town 1630–1649* (New York, 1972), 159–60, 198; Clifford K. Shipton, ed., "The Autobiographical Memoranda of John Brock, 1636–1659," *Proceedings of the American Antiquarian Society*, n.s., 53 (1943), 100; Welde, *Answer to W.R.*, 22.

69. Shepard, *Confessions*, 64, 150; Fiske, *Notebook*, 146, 100. A candidate could, if pressed, present forgetfulness as evidence of lingering corruption. To the query, "Why do you forget things, brother?" Nicholas Wyeth responded that "I see cause enough in my own heart why [the] Lord should deny me. I know many things in my practise. I have not so meditated on the word," Shepard, *Confessions*, 197. This last admission may indicate that Wyeth had not prepared himself adequately to cite compelling proof texts during the relation, but it may also call attention to a more general failure to study the Bible.

70. Fiske, *Notebook*, 143; Mather, *Magnalia*, II, 72; Rogers, . . . *Ohel*, 366.

the churches of the early Bay Colony, and that "many Hearers found very much Good by, to help them to try their own Hearts, and to consider how it was with them." Confessors and auditors, he maintained, flooded the meeting houses with their tears.[71] Clap himself carefully attended to others' confessions. Reacting in the fashion that John Rogers predicated, he discovered in listening to public testimonies that the Lord works "upon some more sensibly, and upon others more insensibly[.]" Comparing his experience to accounts that pinpointed the time and manner of conversion more exactly than he could educe caused him "much Sadness of Heart, and Doubtings how it was with me," until God soothed him through a John Cotton sermon.[72] The dramatic increase in new admissions to the Boston church following Cotton's ascension to its pulpit may also have been fueled by public testimonies of regeneration, for Governor John Winthrop recorded that "the Lord gave witness to the exercise of prophecy, so as thereby some were converted, and others much edified."[73] Church-goers shared with applicants the impact of the narratives.

Occasional confessors even dared to recommend subjects for audiences to ponder. Like preachers spinning out the applications of a doctrine, they drew uses from the texts of their lives. Having recounted how some godly acquaintances had once listened when he needed to talk about his troubled estate, William Manning counselled "all that desired communion with God to make their wants known to ministers." Henry Dunster exploited both the relation and the profession of faith to educate the Cambridge church in grace's ways. From his own "adieu" to self-righteousness, he advised them that "though you do believe the promise, stay for the Spirit till he seals the promise etc.," and he took time during his statement of faith to comment on the errors of Antinomians and Catholics. The former hold that believers "may live dissolutely," the latter "think to be saved by their own doings," and he hoped that Cambridge would be "pestered" with neither.[74] In these cases the conversion relation became a vehicle for a kind of lay exhortation.

The exchange between candidates and congregants in the New England churches points up the fact that Puritan religious experience was not, could never be entirely a private affair. Sainthood entailed constant intercourse with God's other elect children in societies gathered through the love that

71. Clap, *Memoirs*, 5. Alexander Young, ed., *Chronicles of the First Planters of the Colony of Massachusetts Bay* (Boston, 1846), 343–67, reprints the piece in an edited and chronologically rearranged form that deletes Clap's extended account of his own religious experience. Johnson, *Wonder-Working Providence*, 218, makes the point in reference to the admission procedure as a whole.

72. Clap, *Memoirs*, 5, 8.

73. Winthrop, *Journal*, I, 116; Morgan, *Visible Saints*, 98–99.

74. Shepard, *Confessions*, 95, 163–64, 160.

conversion generates. As noted previously, the perception of God's love to oneself that then inspires a reciprocal ardor towards Him and a renewed affection for other worldlings lies at the heart of conversion psychology, and among all classes of humanity, Saints occupy the niche to be most esteemed. "Doest thou love the Lord?" asked Preston, "then thou lovest the Saints," and John Rogers of Dedham directed that the true people of God "are to be loved in the greatest degree of all other men."[75] This feeling for one's fellow regenerates expressed itself in desiring their company; one outcome of conversion was for Saints to affiliate themselves with each other. From the late sixteenth century on, the self-pronounced godly formed small bands of the devout amid the carnal multitudes of English parishes "for the continuance of love, and for the edifying one of another." These consociations, in the words of one participant, "did knit them in that loue, the bond whereof could not be broken, either on their part which now sleepe in the Lord, whiles they here liued; nor in them which yet remaine."[76] Coming together strengthened the cords of affection that were supposed to exist among the brethren, but as long as the Saints had to covenant on the sly, their mutual love lacked official recognition in the church. The freedom of establishing a new ecclesiology on the American strand allowed Puritans there to invent another method to initiate affiliation. The church admission process, particularly the conversion relation, developed into a ritual for incorporating new Saints into the body of the faithful and for encouraging emotional ties between the godly.[77] What was at stake can be glimpsed in the reasons put forward to sanction the

75. *Supra*, 124–32; Preston, *Onely Love*, 66; Rogers, *Treatise of Love*, 145.

76. Patrick Collinson, *Elizabethan Puritan Movement*, 374–82; *idem*, "Towards a Broader Understanding of the Early Dissenting Tradition," in C. Robert Cole and Michael E. Moody, eds., *Essays for Leland H. Carlson: The Dissenting Tradition* (Athens, Ohio, 1975), 20–22; Stephen Foster, "New England and the Challenge of Heresy, 1630–1660: The Puritan Crisis in Transatlantic Perspective," *William and Mary Quarterly*, 3d ser., 38 (1981), 627–28; Cotton, *Way of Congregational Churches*, 198; David D. Hall, ed., "John Cotton's Letter to Samuel Skelton," *William and Mary Quarterly*, 3d ser., 22 (1965), 484; Rogers, *Seven Treatises*, 477, 478 (quotations). Cf. the remark of an anonymous Saint, Wigglesworth, *Diary*, 439: "Seeing so much of God in his people at private meetings my heart had dearly loved the people of God."

77. The implication here is that the conversion relation took over a function that had been less formally performed in England. There, the godly recognized each other in their dissent; in the (for them) freer air of America, they needed a permanent institutional method to identify true believers. Caldwell, *Puritan Conversion Narrative*, 81–116, is an insightful exposition of the relation as the means whereby American Puritans hoped to fashion experience into community and of why America made a new type of religious expression necessary. For her, it is a "literary" phenomenon bonding the Saints together through discourse; for me it is a psycho-cultural one gathering them affectively. To the extent that the relations formalized an aspect of congregational affiliativeness desirable but unattainable in England, Raymond Phineas Stearns and David Holmes Brawner, "New England Church 'Relations' and Continuity in Early Congregational History," *Proceedings of the American Antiquarian Society*, ser. 2, 75, pt. 1 (1965), 13–45, are right that the relations did not constitute a radical innovation, but see Tipson, "Invisible Saints," 467–68, and Caldwell, *Puritan Conversion Narrative*, 83–85, 114.

system. It tends "often times to make the more room for [applicants] in the hearts of the brethren," argued the Chelmsford church, for it occasions "a sweet closure and union of their spirits together." By virtue of relations, intoned Cotton Mather, speaking as an avatar of John Eliot, "younger converts are thereby exceedingly edified; and the souls of devout Christians are hereby very much ingratiated one unto onother." Public conversion statements did more than identify Visible Saints; they kindled the affections which bound together a society that conceived itself the embodiment of God's love.[78]

78. Fiske, *Notebook*, 144; Mather, *Magnalia*, I, 554. Cf. Stephen Foster, *Their Solitary Way: The Puritan Social Ethic in the First Century of Settlement in New England* (New Haven, 1971), 41–64. King, *Iron of Melancholy*, 44–45, recognizes the impact that a public recitation of religious experience could have in bringing an "often disparate church body together," but he goes too far in maintaining that the spiritual relation "never functioned as a test," a congregation being "obligated" to accept the testimony and tender membership in return. No congregation was ever so obligated.

6

Echoes of the Preachers' Call

Puritan religious experience took shape by way of conversations with God, oneself, other people, and ministers. The dialogue with God was ultimately the most significant, of course, but in daily practice, contact with the clergy took on more importance. A preacher acted as God's sounding board; from his lips the Word passed through the ear and entered the mind. Puritan dogma linked the mechanics of regeneration to attendance at sermons. God could convert by using other means, but He chose not to. A prerequisite for salvation, the minister also served a pastoral function; his learning and, one hoped, his charity equipped him to answer parishioners' puzzlements and tide the distracted over shoals of anxiety. Explicators of the *ordo salutis*, promulgators of doctrine, heralds of the Word and doctors of the soul, Puritan preachers guided their congregants' conversions.

Puritanism, then, can be described as the gift of a distinctive religiosity and piety conferred by the clergy upon a band of faithful adherents; but framed this way, the formulation ignores the laity's contribution.[1] They accepted preachments and counsel partly on their own terms. This is not to

1. Darrett B. Rutman, *American Puritanism: Faith and Practice* (Philadelphia, 1970). Rutman approaches the question of how the laity received and responded to what preachers were saying, but never discusses the matter using evidence from the congregants themselves. Cf. the perspective on the laity's contribution to spiritual life taken by Natalie Z. Davis, "Some Tasks and Themes in the Study of Popular Religion," in Charles Trinkaus and Heiko Oberman, eds., *The Pursuit of Holiness* (Leiden, 1974), 307–36, esp. 309, 313.

say that the average listener, the Thomas Hincksmans and Ann Erringtons, offered substantial modifications to the prevailing model of religious experience. Although some might grumble about the severity of admission procedures, and others dissent from points of theology, most people in early seventeenth-century Massachusetts did not question the rudiments of Puritan religion.[2] What is at issue is how individuals incorporated what the preachers told them into their own experience. Hearing about the order of grace, and then absorbing that information into one's life was a complicated business in which no single input had an absolute influence. Ministers had much to say about the course of conversion, but the laity always punctuated their remarks.

I

To achieve their purpose of "preserving, propagating, and restoring the Church," Puritan ministers considered one activity the *sine qua non*: to further these ends, "preaching of the word doth excell, and so it hath beene alwayes of perpetuall use." The significance of sermonizing in Puritan theory derives from the evangelical imperative to publicize the righteousness to be grasped in Christ, and from the minister's own position as the "instrument" through which grace breaks in upon the soul. The Lord's "messenger," his calling commits him to speak.[3] What Puritans called a *"plain and powerful"* ministry was *"the only Ordinary means to Prepare the heart soundly for Christ,"* and to be accounted thus "painfull" (i.e. painstaking, hence movingly effective) was an accolade which acknowledged that one had accomplished the fundamental task.[4] Beyond the pulpit, however, lay a continuous round of private communications with individuals in regard to their spiritual health. Commended as a way of improving the pastor's ability to "confesse his peoples sinnes" to God, such conferences also allowed a person to "disburthen his conscience of such sinnes as disquiet him, and craue [the minister's] godly assistance, and holy prayers."[5] The invitation to convert and, once converted, to secure the sense of assurance pressed people to examine themselves for signs of grace and produced anxious questions from those who doubted their regenerate status. The attention Puritan preachers gave to

2. For those who did, see Philip Gura, *A Glimpse of Sion's Glory: Puritan Radicalism in New England, 1620–1660* (Middletown, 1984); David S. Lovejoy, *Religious Enthusiasm in the New World: Heresy to Revolution* (Cambridge, Mass., 1985).

3. Ames, *Marrow*, I.xxxv.9, 11; Perkins, *Works*, III, 429, 430.

4. Hooker, *Application*, I-VIII, 205. See the caption to the woodcut of Perkins in Thomas Fuller, *The Holy State*, 4th ed. (London, 1663), 80.

5. Perkins, *Works*, III, 446.

promoting the new birth coincided with their interest in casuistry. The "greatest" case of conscience, William Perkins thought, concerned "How a Man May Know Whether He be the childe of God, or no," and he urged the distressed to consult their ministers, the individuals "best able" to advise and solace.[6] Many preachers, Perkins included, were memorialized for their skills in instructing "the weake and wounded conscience."[7] Almost by definition, then, the Puritan clergy had to be affecting speakers and effective counselors. Attending upon the people of early Massachusetts in these dual capacities, they profoundly influenced the religious experience of their flocks.

The conversion relations testify to the ministry's impact. Interactions with clergy easily outnumber any other kind of reported event.[8] In keeping with Puritans' perception of the spoken word as the usual vehicle for grace, references to either ministers in their role as preachers or to sermons alone predominate. A few of the narratives, in fact, survive as little more than staccato recollections of sermons and responses.[9] A sinful place could be

6. Breward, "William Perkins and the Origins of Reformed Casuistry," 3–20; Richard A. Muller, "Covenant and Conscience in English Reformed Theology: Three Variations on a 17th Century Theme," *Westminster Theological Journal*, 42 (1980), 308–11; Perkins, *Works*, I, 421; II, 2.

7. For a few, see Thomas Fuller, *The Church History of Britain, from the Birth of Jesus Christ until the year MDCXLVIII*, 3 vols. (London, 1842 [orig. 1655]), III, 133; *idem, Holy State*, 82; Mather, *Magnalia*, I, 346.

8. "Interaction" defines an event in which a person engages oneself with another individual or with oneself. For example, Jane Champney's statement that "I heard there was hid and healing, and overcoming mercy in Christ, and so I thought there might be mercy for me" (Shepard, *Confessions*, 191) counts as an interaction between her and an (unnamed) minister. In this case, an encounter has led to a recorded reaction, but an interaction would have been counted even had no response been taken down. Every single engagement has been counted as an interaction, but repeated references to the same occurrence are tallied only once. Interactions in the conversion relations divide into four major categories: with ministers, with people other than ministers, with oneself, and with God. The first two are self-explanatory. Interactions with oneself include meditations, prayers, and references to Scripture not explicitly accounted for by other input (for instance, the first line of Elizabeth Batchelor's relation (Fiske, *Notebook*, 8), "Gen. 6:3, my spirit &c., conviction at it," a rumination on that particular verse). Interactions with the Lord consist of incidents in which God is said to work some effect on the individual, but are counted as such only if no other category is applicable. William Ames's statement that "the Lord stirred up my heart to seek after Him, when Mr. Nor: [Edward Norris or John Norton] was preaching out of Revelation . . . " (Shepard, *Confessions*, 211), is considered an interaction with a minister. This procedure has been adopted because, in Puritan thinking, every event could be construed as a manifestation of God's Providence, an idea that, if followed here, would allow for no differentiation of incidents at all. The totals give a rough indication of the ministerial presence, and, simultaneously, note other not inconsiderable influences. Interactions with: Ministers, 467; Others, 116; Self, 246; Lord, 161.

9. See, in Shepard, *Confessions*, the relations of Brewer, Cane, Barbara Cutter, Fessenden, Griswald, Joan Moore, Parish, Joanna Sill, John Stedman, Usher, and Winship. Those of Brewer, Cane, and Usher are especially condensed.

defined as one "where no sermon [was] preached," and since numbers of Puritans in England inhabited such locales, they took to the roads to ensure that carnal ears captured saintly speech.[10] Enjoying no sermons "at home" and desiring "to hear them that were most suitable to my condition to stir up my heart," Nicholas Wyeth traversed his neighborhood on ever-lengthening jaunts. For about a year he forayed four miles to hear Robert Selby, which "did somewhat profit" him and encouraged him "much still to go and hear other good men." Later, feeling sinful but still loving "the word" and the society of "God's people," he frequently travelled sixteen miles to hear Jeremiah Burroughs. When Burroughs' remarks on Gal. 6.7 persuaded Wyeth that he was still in his "natural condition," he "went twenty miles off" to pursue insight from yet another source.[11] The magnetism of certain preachers helps account for Wyeth's perambulations, and for Richard Eccles's move to settle under a "powerful ministry" that provided "better means to bring my soul to God." Having benefitted from the preachings of Jose Glover and "in a doubting condition" when he left, Joanna Sill "followed him and lived under his ministry four years." Conversely, an inadequate speaker might lose his audience. Although his own abode boasted an "orthodox minister," Edward Collins preferred to hear William Greenhill and others at Dedham, where "God carried on His work by Himself and wrought peace." Ann Errington came to New England "thinking one sermon might do me more good than a hundred [in England]."[12] Puritans' eager attendance on sermons, a touchstone of righteous behavior, afforded the ministry countless opportunities to affect them.

Conferences about cases of conscience, although mentioned far less frequently in the relations than were sermons, provided another forum for ministerial influence.[13] Singly or, on rare occasions, in concert,[14] preachers considered the laity's personal problems and determined appropriate courses of action. Most complaints questioned the authenticity of the individual's estate or cried the desperation of thinking oneself permanently lost. Jane Willows imagined that she possessed only the "form" of holiness and lacked its substance, while John Collins, conceiving himself cursed, concluded at Satan's urging that his "time was past. God had left me a long time and therefore there was little hopes [sic] he would return to me again." Pastors countered their congregants' misperceptions by applying basic tenets of Puri-

10. Shepard, *Confessions*, 144.

11. *Ibid.*, 193–94.

12. *Ibid.*, 115, 51, 83, 185. Joanna was John Sill's wife.

13. 18 interactions fall into this category, and there are three mentions of catechizing.

14. Shepard, *Confessions*, 47. Cf. *ibid.*, 120, 151, for references that may indicate ministers meeting together or successively with a person.

tan theology in a practical manner. Thomas Morton told Jane that if she "hated that form it was a sign [she] had more than a form," and when she revisited him wondering about the necessary extent of her humiliation, he explained that those properly humbled "would not think they had enough" but would hunger after Christ "the more." Goodwife Willows asked only for Morton's knowledge; Collins demanded all the learning, patience, and strength that Thomas Shepard could muster. Shepard seems to have thought that the young man, though despondent about salvation, had not properly given himself into God's care, for he advised him to be "constant in private prayer" and "willing to lay down at God's feet that he might do with me as he would." Collins nevertheless went on to commit a "gross disobedience to my parents," and when the Lord in punishment "inflicted the greatest affliction that ever I had," Shepard returned to "wrestle with God for my life." Examining his charge's carriage and former sins, Shepard reiterated his earlier recommendation "to *wait* on God and to part with every sin, to resolve again constantly to follow God and to seek him." In these and other instances, ministers sought two goals. Since people in distress craved support, Morton "encouraged" Willows, and Shepard "somewhat comforted" Collins. But comfort was not an end in itself; sympathy was the handmaid of instruction. Ease could be achieved only by living through a particular experience that the minister had to outline, at which point the central concerns of Puritan theology directly touched the lives of men and women. Advising their congregants how to replace natural self-control with God's direction, Morton and Shepard guided Willows and Collins to the experience prerequisite for grace.[15]

The minister's supportive and didactic functions emerge clearly in Elizabeth Hincksman's account of her close relationship with Peter Bulkeley. No other narrative mentions a specific minister more often than does hers, confirming Cotton Mather's account of the "winning, and yet prudent *familiarity*," that enabled Bulkeley to exercise "the part of a faithful pastor" even when indisposed by chronic illness.[16] A close follower of his preaching since the time "God met her soul" in one of his sermons, Elizabeth related that she first "repaired" to Bulkeley fearing that she did not really have a part in Christ and asking how to recognize the "beginnings of grace in truth." His delineation of the signs "brought her some comfort," but it did not last. Elizabeth was an individual who rode the Puritan pendulum of relief and

15. Shepard, *Confessions*, 150–51 (Willows); Wigglesworth, *Diary*, 429 (Collins). John's affliction was a "wound by a fall, which had like to have cost him his life," according to Mather, *Magnalia*, II, 139. Mather goes on to re-create Shepard's participation in John's recovery using terms that strongly suggest familiarity with the account in Wigglesworth's diary.

16. Mather, *Magnalia*, I, 401.

disquiet in a way that was no less discomfiting for all its clockwork regularity. She would come away from a sermon refreshed only to plunge into new doubts. Tempted to believe herself a hypocrite, she solicited Bulkeley's help, and he told her "to commit her soul in sincerity unto God in the use of all His means and He would never leave her. This encouraged her," but soon "untoward afflictions" and "inward griefs" crowded in again. This time, however, Elizabeth departed from her habitual response to anxiety through a method that signalled success for Bulkeley's teaching. Where before she had sought solace in sermon or conversation, now she began to rely on her own resources as well: the Lord "stirred up her heart to seek more diligently after Him . . . And pondering upon her condition she hoped that she had given up herself to God." Interest in sermons did not flag, and they continued to succor and inform her, but Elizabeth had learned a critical lesson in godly self-reliance that sustained her when first a few miles and then eternity separated her from her pastor. She allayed fears instigated during her move from Concord to Chelmsford by meditating on Song of Sol. 1.2, and she overcame the "discouragement" she felt on visiting Bulkeley during his terminal illness by considering that "though the stream be cut off yet the fountain remains." Doubts still bothered Mrs. Hincksman—given her disposition and Puritan teaching that the flesh survives to worry Saints, she could hardly have acted otherwise—but she professed to the Chelmsford church near the close of her narrative that "she still finds God merciful to her in supplying fresh encouragement and receiving."[17] An understanding of Ro. 8.30 grounded the assertion. As one who had labored to bring her to this realization, Bulkeley would have approved the verse and its application.[18]

To make their points, preachers broached any subject, no matter how intellectually demanding. After a particularly abstruse excursion through the complexities of vocation, faith, and sanctification, Shepard apologized for being "thus large in less practical matters," but excused himself on the grounds that "there is much wisdom of God to be seen not only in his work, but in his manner and order of working."[19] Candidates reported hearing sermons on a variety of weighty topics, including the existence of God, His attributes, and Christ's human nature, potentially arcane matters that

17. Fiske, *Notebook*, 148–50.

18. Ro. 8.30 reads: "Moreover whom he did predestinate, them he also called: and whom he called, them he also justified: and whom he justified, them he also glorified." It is cited in the relation as "whom he predestines them also he called in." Arguing in the *Gospel-Covenant*, 277, for the doctrine of perseverance, Bulkeley contended that to suppose Saints could fall away from grace "would shake the foundation of Gods election," for "those onely whom he knew before, those onely doth he sanctifie: . . . our calling and sanctification is according to his purpose, *Rom.* 8.28.30. 2 *Tim.* 1.9."

19. Shepard, *Works*, I, 170.

preachers always made immediately relevant.[20] A sermon on God's all-sufficiency led Edward Shepard to an important realization. Hearing "when a
poor creature was in a lost condition and knew not what to do yet that the
Lord was sufficient," Shepard discovered that God's being enables Him to
give any unregenerate "a humble heart" and concluded that he might therefore entertain "some hope" of salvation.[21] Ministers commented on the entire
range of their theological concerns. Some decried sins, whether traditional
(sloth), anti-social (offending brethren), heretical (disbelief), or mundane
("using many words in bargaining").[22] Others delved into anthropology,
laying open humanity's "acursed condition in the state of nature" or the will's
"enmity" against God.[23] In the dance of the affections preachers descried
salvific significance and alerted their congregations to the manifest signs of
true sorrow, repentance, and love to Christ.[24] Pressing their evangelical
mission, they warned the ungodly to repent, "else they could not be saved,"
and propounded the good news that "Christ came to save sinners[.]" Alter-
nating between the Law and the Gospel, they spoke "terror to all that were
out of Christ" while promoting the hope that those who "come to Christ
might have comfort."[25] Sermons that moved the Elect covered every facet of
life.

Preachers hoped that every listener would, like Alice Reade, be "something affected" by their words. The reactions of those who were moved range
across the entire sequence of events in conversion. Many people related how
they took notice of their natural corruption. A "good teacher" opened to
Reade "the evil condition of the ungodly man as an apple that outwardly
shows &c. but yet at the core is rotten," whereupon she recognized her own
rotten heart.[26] Called on to become more "enlightened," Golden Moore saw
the extent of his "evil nature in pride and passion." Transgressors also
confronted their specific sins. Goodwife Champney "stood convicted" of
neglecting prayer, John Stedman was "found guilty" of drunkenness, a "fearful sin," and Edward Shepard owned up to having broken the Sabbath.[27] As
preachers called the tune of human depravity, would-be Saints responded
with a threnody of self-vilification, lamenting that "there was not such a vile
heart in hell as mine"; that "I was a prisoner and kept by Satan"; that they

20. Shepard, *Confessions*, 95, 107, 183.

21. *Ibid.*, 174. Edward was not related to Thomas (*ibid.*, 172).

22. *Ibid.*, 101, 166, 137, 176.

23. Fiske, *Notebook*, 61; Shepard, *Confessions*, 67.

24. Shepard, *Confessions*, 121, 109, 59.

25. *Ibid.*, 161, 134, 148, 40.

26. Fiske, *Notebook*, 8.

27. Shepard, *Confessions*, 123, 191, 73, 173.

had appropriated "self principles" from the Devil in thinking they could do good works on their own.[28] The doctrine that one cannot achieve salvation on one's own merits, a corollary to the fact of defective human nature, sometimes startled those who heard it. Having been complacently "performing duties," William Andrews was taken aback by John Carter's comments that even the most godly are saved with great difficulty, "as if an eel should go through a hole and leave her skin behind her." The revelation "did mightily strike me, although before I thought my estate good." The way to change one's nature, ministers maintained, began with preparation. William Ames bore his famous father's name but could not inherit his grace, and it took a sermon by Hugh Peter to demonstrate to him the necessity of legal preparation. "I took that to myself," Ames allowed, acknowledging he had never "had that work of law[.]" Richard Cutter was similarly impressed. A sermon on John 13.30 revealed that the unreadied do not enjoy Christ, "and very sad it was."[29]

Cutter's mournful remark was typical. Preachers meant to unsettle their audiences by driving home the enormity of sin. Learning of the world's "enmity with God," Roger Haynes became increasingly "shaken" as the lesson was pressed "one Sabbath after another," until he "could not see any way of recovery out of this." Smitten by the word, people suffered "spiritual agonies and false fears," or lay under "many troubles and much confusion of spirit." In a gesture not entirely comprehensible but unambiguously plaintive, Cutter responded to the declaration of his separation from Christ by standing "behind the meeting house." Often sermons produced an instantaneous effect, but on occasion their meaning percolated through the mind and elicited a delayed reaction. A warning to prepare for the Lord "did not sit upon me much at first," Nathaniel Eaton admitted, "yet always when I went to my company this chapter and verse was before my eye." When he could stand God's terrors "no longer," he "laid down my sin and set some days apart," presumably for meditation.[30] Ministers did not preach the Law in isolation, a practice that ran the risk of disturbing overly sensitive souls too much. Gospel promises balanced legal threatenings and raised the spirits of the humbled. In a "perplexed condition" on account of secret sins, Richard Eccles heard that "the Lord said he hath saints in [the] worst places," and hoped that He might "bring me to the knowledge of Himself." John Trumbull, "oppressed for God's wrath and sin," was moved by a sermon about God's joy over a repentant sinner to think "there might be mercy." The purpose of terror was

---

28. Wigglesworth, *Diary*, 436; Shepard, *Confessions*, 200; Fiske, *Notebook*, 52.

29. Shepard, *Confessions*, 111, 210, 179. Shepard also recorded the relations of Richard's mother, Elizabeth, and his sister, Barbara (or Barbary, *ibid.*, 178).

30. Shepard, *Confessions*, 167, 92, 199, 179, 54–55.

always to activate, to force sinners into overcoming the perils of damnation by fleeing to God. The strategy succeeded with those who became Saints. Informed of the "soul's preparation for Christ," Martha Collins "was stirred up to seek," and Alice Reade, miserable about her rotten heart, resolved that, if she was to perish, at least she would do so while engaged in using the means of grace.[31]

At each step during their spiritual pilgrimages, people welcomed the preacher's backing; sermons aided the first uncertain strides towards grace. A lecture "encouraged" Mary Parish to seek reconciliation with the Lord, for though she had transgressed, "He would pardon my sins." Having realized that her corrupt nature doomed her to everlasting perdition, Joan Moore was "quickened" when a minister pointed out that Christ came to save sinners, and "supported" upon hearing that the poor in spirit are blessed. A timely word sustained those being hammered for their sins by conscience. Terrified that "the Lord would never accept me more," Mrs. Crackbone "had some hope" from a sermon on Is. 1.18 (" . . . though your sins be as scarlet, they shall be as white as snow . . ."), and Jane Holmes, fearing "night and day" that she was destined for hell because she was not humbled, took heart by learning how she could test her love for the Saints.[32] The regenerate, locked in battle with doubts about assurance, appreciated comments that strengthened their resolve against the flesh. An explanation of how to tell if a Christian has "doffed" Christ "stayed" Parish, and remarks by Bulkeley "did further strengthen and encourage" Thomas Hincksman to draw on Christ. A phrase's profound impression could evoke a surge of relief.[33] From a sermon on "the just shall live by faith"—the watchword of the Reformation—a woman known to us only as Katharine, Mrs. Russell's Maid, had "abundance of comfort from the word" and "blessed the Lord for that condition." Even humiliation could inspire delight in a soul longing to separate itself from sin. Listening to Bulkeley, William Hamlet perceived the proper "spirit of loathing" in himself and "was cheered."[34] The scope and intensity of Puritans' reactions to the spoken word are driven home by this example of a man who rejoiced because a minister had prompted the sensations of degradation.

The importance of the ministry in promoting religious experience stands out in the relations. The most impressive testimony is implicit—the sheer number of references evincing the attention paid to sermons—but voiced

31. *Ibid.*, 115–16, 107, 131; Fiske, *Notebook*, 8.

32. Shepard, *Confessions*, 137, 134, 140, 77. Joan was the wife of John Champney (*ibid.*, 134), and the mother of Joseph Champney, whose relation is given in Wigglesworth, *Diary*, 440–41. After John died, she married Golden Moore. See Savage, *Genealogical Dictionary*, I, 356.

33. Shepard, *Confessions*, 137; Fiske, *Notebook*, 147. Thomas was Elizabeth's husband.

34. Shepard, *Confessions*, 99, 100, 127.

appreciation for the preachers' role is not lacking. Eccles credited the York-shire pastor he had relocated to hear with affording him "more and more light to see into my lost estate every day," and Thomas Hincksman "trust[ed] to profit" from his continued attendance at sermons.[35] The preaching of specific men—John Rogers, William Hubbock, and Jose Glover, to name three—commended itself for mention.[36] Theology sanctioned the clergy's influence, and laypeople accepted the ministry's calling as conduits of the Spirit's activity in the Word. God made John Cotton "instrumental" in discovering Olive Farwell's "miserable condition" to her, while John Collins commenced his relation giving thanks to the Lord for placing him under "glorious living gracious dispensers of the Scripture."[37] The calling did not guarantee influence in and of itself, however, since power did not inhere in the office irrespective of character. Godly comportment was, by puritanical definition, a quality of the ecclesiastic vocation, with consequences Richard Bernard spelled out in a popular treatise: "Common people respect more a good Teachers life, th[a]n his learning, and reuerence the person, and not his preaching so much."[38] William Manning descried the salutary effect of cleri-cal good behavior: he tested himself for hypocrisy by observing "them that did excel in virtue as some ministers." John Furnell seconded the point obversely as he recalled how, while still unregenerate, he had almost passed up some real estate to avoid a minister's morality; though "destitute of a house," he was "loath" to accept one in Mr. Goodwin's parish "because there was not such liberty to sin."[39] Influence also accrued to figures attuned to people's actual circumstances, an ability attributed by Collins to Thomas Hooker, who "certainly knew what a sinner I had been [and] what covenants I had broke." As a result, Collins "thought I was as good as in hell already."[40] Powerful preaching and godly bearing caused emotional attachments to develop. Mrs. Russell's maid said she loved "most" that ministry "which came

35. *Ibid.*, 116; Fiske, *Notebook*, 148.

36. Shepard, *Confessions*, 65, 161 and n. 21, 50–51.

37. Fiske, *Notebook*, 146; Wigglesworth, *Diary*, 426, and see 436, where John Green's re-sponse to the fourth question implicitly recognizes the minister's role. Olive Farwell was Henry's wife.

38. Richard Bernard, *The Faithfvll Sheperd*, rev. and enlg. (London, 1621), 88. Bernard preached in Somersetshire; on the work's popularity, Haller, *Rise of Puritanism*, 137. Ber-nard's emphasis in this quotation on the preacher's setting a good example is somewhat obviated by his primary interest in setting out how ministers should prepare for and deliver sermons. The conversion relations themselves pay much more attention to sermons than to ministers' behavior. On fitness for the ministry, see Ames, *Marrow*, I.xxxv.7.

39. Shepard, *Confessions*, 94, 204. Goodwin could have been either John or Thomas. See *ibid.*, 204, n. 3, 126, n. 4.

40. Wigglesworth, *Diary*, 427. Cf. Jane Greene's comment about an unnamed minister (proba-bly Shepard), who "spake as if known my condition," Shepard, *Confessions*, 154.

nearest to my soul." So abiding was the affection some individuals felt for a favorite pastor that they identified him as the embodiment of grace, and his death, which removed the Word's accustomed mouthpiece, left them momentarily stunned and lost. The demise of Shepard, "that blessed man," struck John Collins "with astonishment as [I] knew my sins had deserved it," and it prompted an unnamed individual to fear that "God might just speak to me now no more."[41] By word and deed, preachers set an example for the laity to follow.

The ministry's influence, however, stopped short of being absolute. A few relations do not refer to preachers or sermons,[42] and others tell how the Elect disregarded lectures. In some instances, polluted nature as yet unchecked by grace explains a refusal to take the word to heart. An anonymous Saint was "carried after the world" so that preaching became " a mere sound," and Robert Holmes in his unregenerate condition preferred to sleep through his parish's monthly sermon.[43] On the other hand, Puritans acknowledged that even a "Childe of God" may be "a fruitlesse hearer of some good Preachers, and yet profit by some other." A minister's impact was never automatic. John Sill refused to take Shepard seriously until, reading over some sermon notes with other people, he saw "there was more in them than I [had] apprehended."[44] That preachers played only feature roles in the drama of salvation also tempered their influence. Puritans conceived the clergy's work in what Henry Dunster called "the Lord's personal dealing with my soul" within the context of God's all-determining will. Divine intention dictates a preacher's success. "*The same dispensation of the word which is powerful and profitable to some is unprofitable to others*," Hooker asserted, because in this way God attains "several ends" and because in doing so He manifests "the soveraignty

41. Shepard, *Confessions*, 100; Wigglesworth, *Diary*, 430, 438. See also Elizabeth Hincksman's remarks on Bulkeley, *supra*, 166–67. Although in the context of the relation Collins seems to be referring to Henry Dunster, he is almost certainly thinking of Shepard. Dunster did not die until 1659 (Jeremiah Chapin, *Life of Henry Dunster* (Boston, 1872), 221), at which time Collins had been in England for at least four and most likely six years. Collins joined the Cambridge church at some point after his graduation in 1649, the year of Shepard's death; see John Langdon Sibley, *Biographical Sketches of Graduates of Harvard University*, I (Cambridge, Mass., 1873), 186. The timing of these events, plus Shepard's "pains" on Collins's behalf (see *supra*, 166) point to the Cambridge minister as the object of John's affection.

42. Those of Daniel, Mrs. Greene, and Nathaniel Sparrowhawk in Shepard, *Confessions*, 60–61, 118, 62–64, and Mary Moulton's in Fiske, *Notebook*, 9. Greene's is highly abbreviated, Moulton's somewhat so, but Daniel's and Sparrowhawk's are of an average length. Elizabeth Batchelor's relation, Fiske, *Notebook*, 8–9, can also be counted if the phrase "The doctrine of original sin handled," is construed as referring to something she thought, read, or heard someone other than a minister discuss.

43. Wigglesworth, *Diary*, 438; Shepard, *Confessions*, 142. Robert was married to Jane Holmes.

44. Hildersam, *CVIII Lectures*, 325 misnum. 305; Shepard, *Confessions*, 47.

of his good wil and pleasure."[45] Henry Farwell, for one, remarked upon the subordination of God's chosen instruments to His supreme direction of regeneration: "Through His goodness by the preaching of His spirit in the word there was wrought in [me] an inward change[.]"[46] God's ultimate responsibility for conversion coupled with the variety of means at His disposal to further grace meant that people often experienced His efforts in the events of the new birth without ministerial intervention. His hand moving in the ripples of the visible world, God "visited" John Collins with a near-fatal case of smallpox that drove him to thoughts of hell, but then "was pleased" to make Collins promise to live "another manner of life than *hetherto* I had done if he pleased to recover me."[47] The Lord revealed and drew Himself to George Willows "by His ordinances," stirred Joseph Champney "to follow him and forsake all" by suggesting to Champney a verse of Scripture, and "let in Himself in a gracious manner" to Nathaniel Sparrowhawk during meditation.[48] Relieved by Protestantism's declaration of the priesthood of all believers from having to rely on human intercessors, Puritans came into contact with God on their own.

Ministers had no monopoly on instructing and counselling; family, friends, and acquaintances of prospective Saints also performed these tasks. The Lord gave Edward Collins the "privilege" of being raised by "godly parents" who looked out for his spiritual welfare. When, following his father's death, Edward was bound out to "a profane house," his mother, hearing about "the ill family," speedily turned him over to the care of Richard Rogers. Mrs. Russell's maid "went on in ignorance" until an aunt enlightened her. Parental guidance shines forth in the account of an unknown individual tempted by Satan "from opening my mind to God."[49] At a family conference, the person's mother opined that perhaps her offspring feared to give Satan "occasion to set on sin," to which the father rejoined that "a soul should make it known to God else [it] would be under more slavery and bondage." The discussion left their child readier to "make my mind known." Barbara Cutter's friends set a silent example for her; the more she observed their holy carriage, "the more she thought ill of herself." Feeling that she hated the Lord, Jane Willows asked a church elder and a friend "if any had such a heart

---

45. Shepard, *Confessions*, 161; Hooker, *Application*, IX–X, 283, 284.

46. Fiske, *Notebook*, 145; cf. Shepard, *Confessions*, 125–26; Wigglesworth, *Diary*, 442.

47. Wigglesworth, *Diary*, 427.

48. Shepard, *Confessions*, 43; Wigglesworth, *Diary*, 441; Shepard, *Confessions*, 63. The verse Champney cited is either Mat. 19.29 or the parallel in Mark 10.29–30, and it is misquoted. Champney allows the faithful follower of God a thousandfold recompense; the Gospels reduce the figure by a factor of 10. George Willows married Jane Palfrey (*ibid.*, 42), and Joseph Champney was the son of Joan Moore (formerly Champney), see *supra*, n. 32.

49. Shepard, *Confessions*, 82, 99, 206.

and such temptations. And they said, yes."[50] Some of the people who came to New England had been in contact with the Puritan prayer and study associations that honeycombed the English church. Impressed with the gracious bearing of some "Christian" youth, Edward Collins "endeavored to get into private Christian meetings at London"; admitted to "private societies of saints," John Stedman found "much sweetness."[51] These bands proselytized as ardently as any preacher. Living in the house of the town vicar though he was an Arminian openly hostile to Puritans and she a sympathizer who enquired "after that way," Jane Holmes conversed with a member of one such group about the "new birth" and decided to pursue it. Casual acquaintances might offer a vital observation. A cattle herder whom John Jones sometimes met in the fields taught him how contrition and humiliation break the soul from sin, which emboldened him to hope that "the Lord might bring me off self unto the Lord Jesus."[52] The army of unregenerates who paraded through the lives of the Elect were not so solicitous of the Saints' salvation, of course, but even they could catalyze the conversion process. John Trumbull's friends warned him he "would go mad as other ministers with study," and Edward Shepard's companions at sea "laughed" at him for not breaking the Sabbath by drinking, but derision only strengthened both men's resolve to plot their puritanic way. Any human being could prove the counterweight that thrust a sinner godward.[53]

50. *Ibid.*, 89, 152.

51. *Ibid.*, 83, 74.

52. *Ibid.*, 76–77, 201.

53. *Ibid.*, 107, 173. The nature of confessors' interactions with others can be further broken down:

INTERACTIONS WITH OTHERS ACCORDING TO THEIR IDENTITY AND ESTATE

Identity	*Estate*			
	Godly	*Ungodly*	*Unclear*	*(Totals)*
Family	21	1	2	24 (21%)
Friends	12	3	0	15 (13%)
Acquaintances	48	17	2	67 (58%)
Unidentified	5	3	2	10 (9%)
Total	86 (74%)	24 (21%)	6 (5%)	116

"Godly" defines those whom the confessors so label and those whose described actions are clearly or probably intended to further the applicant's piety. "Ungodly" defines those so deemed and those whose described actions distract or deflect confessors from righteous behavior. "Family" includes relatives by blood and by marriage. "Friends" designates only people who are specifically called friends or companions; others, though acting in a "friendly" manner, are included among "Acquaintances." The simple statistical results suggest that acquaintances were a more important influence on the Saints' religious experience than were family and friends, but this conclusion is questionable. The number of "Friends" is understated, and there are 38 additional mentions of parents, many calling attention to their role as

"Any human being" included oneself. Saints were hardly passive subjects of experience, for they constantly examined themselves, evaluated what they heard, pondered the Bible, and sought God in prayer. The exigencies of the new birth bathed Puritan converts in the glare of accountability, and they responded by closely observing their thoughts and emotions. The admission of an anonymous person that "I have oft called my state in question" could serve as the motto for a Puritan's coat of arms.[54] Individuals brought on themselves the pains of preparation. Meditating on a verse in Proverbs, Elizabeth Luxford saw for the first time the "bitterness" of sin, while Thomas Hincksman's consideration that he was impotent to come to God on his own induced "some perplexedness of mind." Laboring on a treadmill of works— "the more I did strive to keep the law, the more vile I felt myself"—Henry Dunster mused that he had "returned to folly," and took a long look at his corrupted faculties.[55] Personal biblical exegesis played an important role in the events surrounding Bridget Fiske's union with the Lord. Having prayed for God to turn her soul towards Him, she found in going over Ezek. 33.14–16 "some comfortable hopes" that she desired to renounce her sins. Her willingness to repent enervated by a "great fear and doubting considering her own inability to turn," Bridget "at length" perused Mat. 11.28, saw Christ "tendered" to her, and laid hold upon him.[56] Contemplation advanced the conversion process, but sometimes it also disrupted the smooth exercise of faith; casting up dross as well as gold, the mind might vex a person with

religious educators, that do not appear in these calculations (see *infra*, 216, n. 55). Moreover, figures by themselves weigh every interaction identically and cannot evaluate the "quality" of each: chastisement by a parent, for instance, may have had more of an impact than did conversation with a neighbor. The large number of references to acquaintances may mean nothing more than that, for any individual, this category includes a vastly greater number of people than do the others. Exchanges with the godly outnumber ones with the ungodly by about 3 to 1; confessors did interact with unregenerates (being both attracted to and repelled by their sinfulness), but contact with "right walkers" was more important. The more intimate a group was with confessors, the higher is the percentage of interactions with godly people within that group:

INTERACTIONS WITH GODLY AS PERCENTAGE OF INTERACTIONS
WITH PEOPLE IN EACH IDENTITY GROUP

	Family	Friends	Acquaintances
(Without "Unclear")	95	80	74
(With "Unclear")	88	80	72

Interactions with family members were almost invariably with saintly people; contacts with other groups were less often with the pious. These results intimate the Puritan attitude that grace runs in families, associations holier than the bulk of the population.

54. Wigglesworth, *Diary*, 437.

55. Shepard, *Confessions*, 40; Fiske, *Notebook*, 147; Shepard, *Confessions*, 162.

56. Fiske, *Notebook*, 30.

temptations. Bridget Richardson faced a bevy of troublesome thoughts, including the fear that she had sinned against the Holy Ghost, but overcame them by applying appropriate scriptures. John Sill doubted that Christ was the son of God but refuted his skepticism with the Bible.[57] The laity's habits of introspection and independent reflection prepared them to profit from sermons more fully. Having pored over Zech. 13.1 and had the Lord "refresh my heart with that place hoping that he spoke to me," Mary Wigglesworth, wife of the *Day of Doom*'s future author, attended a Sabbath lecture on the same text and had her hopes confirmed: the Lord "was pleased much to refresh my heart so that I took myself spoke to in it." William Hamlet thought to recover himself from his "sinkings," but prayer only made him "the more vile in my own eyes." Hamlet's melancholy put him in the proper state to benefit from Peter Bulkeley's sermon on Jer. 31.18, for "finding that frame of spirit of loathing myself I was cheered."[58] The activities of individuals on their own behalf could amplify the force of the ministry's words; private exercises enriched public pronouncement. At the same time, the discourses laypeople held with God, their friends and themselves marked out an activity that was uniquely theirs. In facilitating their own experiences, the laity were never a quiescent majority in the face of a loquacious few. Against the pre-eminent role of preachers in guiding the experience of conversion must be admitted the influence of the rest of the community in what was always a multifaceted affair.

II

Plain and powerful preaching, said Thomas Hooker, overpowers corruption "and sets an aw upon the Spirits of such to whom the Word is spoken and

---

57. *Ibid.*, 202; Shepard, *Confessions*, 45–46.

58. Wigglesworth, *Diary*, 443; Shepard, *Confessions*, 127. Hamlet quotes Bulkeley's text as "Ephraim like an untamed heifer." Selement and Woolley see this referring to Hos. 10.11, "And Ephraim *is as* an heifer *that is* taught, *and* loveth to tread out *the corn*; but I passed over upon her fair neck: . . ." Despite Hamlet's use of the word "heifer," however, the sense of Jer. 31.18 more clearly fits into the context of the relation, Hamlet's downcast state, and his desire to escape it: "I [the Lord] have surely heard Ephraim bemoaning himself *thus*; Thou hast chastised me, and I was chastised, as a bullock unaccustomed *to the yoke*: turn thou me, and I shall be turned; for thou art the Lord my God." There is another consideration. Bulkeley loved the Geneva Bible: he cites Zech. 9.11, the text for the *Gospel-Covenant*, in the translations of both the King James Version and of "our *Geneva*," (p. 1), and citations from GenB crop up throughout the work. Jer. 31.18 in GenB reads in part, ". . . I was chastised as an vntamed calfe . . . ," the only use of "untamed" in the two texts under discussion by either Bible. It is possible that Hamlet took "untamed" from Bulkeley's using the GenB text of Jer. 31.18 and conflated it with "heifer" from Hos. 10.11 (KJV or GenB). Bulkeley's attraction for GenB, incidentally, questions Harry Stout's assumption, "Word and Order in Colonial New England," in Mark A. Noll and Nathan O. Hatch, eds., *The Bible in America* (New York, 1982), 31, that, during the Antinomian Controversy, the Hutchinsonians spoke from GenB while the elders used KJV. Bulkeley was one of Hutchinson's leading critics.

blessed."[59] Hooker knew whereof he spoke, for he had watched his words strike home hundreds of times, a perspective modern observers cannot duplicate. Time's passage has all but rubbed out the evidence connecting specific utterances to their attendant impressions. The preceding analysis examined the effects of sermons in the aggregate: preachers covered a range of topics to which congregants responded in a variety of ways. How individuals understood what a preacher meant in a particular sermon, and whether they reacted to the message as he intended, are questions nearly impossible to answer with the available material. Assuming that audiences in each of the eighteen churches enumerated by Thomas Lechford heard two Sabbath sermons every week, Massachusetts ministers in 1640 let fly 1872 discourses, a total that omits works produced for weekday lectures, fast days, thanksgiving days, and other special events.[60] Consider that figure as a rough yearly average for the period 1630–1650, multiply it by twenty, add the indeterminate sum of sermons preached in Connecticut and elsewhere, compare the result with the number of contemporary sermons extant, and the heavy odds against one of the some 400 pieces mentioned in the conversion relations having survived quickly become apparent. However, in a handful of cases, the match can be made, and the sermon's text compared with the narrative's rendition. What remains in the relation is a distillate of the sermon refined by memory and processed according to personal needs, a residue of the interplay between the minister's argument and the listener's perception. These examples afford a rare opportunity to study in detail how preachers influenced discrete moments of a person's conversion.

One of the people whose spirits displayed the proper awe was Roger Haynes. On Feb. 6, 1638/9, Haynes was in Hartford listening to Hooker preach one of the sermons that would become part of *The Application of Redemption*.[61] Lecturing on the doctrine "*There must be a true sight of sin, before the heart can be truly broken for it,*" Hooker had previously dissected the means by which God effectuates the sight of sin, and the extent of the sinner's participation in the process. Now, after alluding to these earlier

59. Hooker, Application, I–VIII, 214–15.

60. Lechford, *Plain Dealing*, 81–86. Lechford omitted Concord from his survey.

61. Henry Wolcott, who abstracted the sermons of several Connecticut preachers, gives the date. See Douglas Shepard, "The Wolcott Shorthand Notebook Transcribed" (Ph.D. dissertation, State University of Iowa, 1957), 124–25 (henceforth cited as Wolcott, *Notebook*).Haynes (Shepard, *Confessions*, 167) spoke of Hooker preaching "old England sermons"; twice before, at Emmanuel College, Cambridge, and at Chelmsford, Essex, Hooker had run through his soteriology (Mather, *Magnalia*, I, 347). Wolcott's account is very similar to that of Haynes. Both quote the doctrine, and both make fragmentary allusions to topics previously covered that Hooker briefly reviewed at the start of this sermon. Each lists two of the three subheadings within the two categories, sin in reference to God, and in regard to "ourselves." For reasons unknown, Haynes presents the first two subheadings in each division, while Wolcott gives the first and third of each. Wolcott's notes testify to the reliability of Roger's account.

topics, he exposed how to see sin clearly in "his naked hue," first as it gain-says the Lord, then as it affects oneself. Sin threatens to disenfranchise God, for it would dispossess Him "of that absolute Supremacy which is indeed his Prerogative Royal." In fact, it seeks to utterly deny Him: the sinner desires "not only that God should not be supream but that indeed he should *not be at all*, and therefore it would destroy the being of Jehovah." Iniquity upsets the harmony of the universe: it "crosseth" Providence, "perverts" the agency of every being, and "defaceth" the "orderly usefulness the Lord first implanted in the order of things." The dismemberment of the divine arrangement ruptures the relationship between God and humankind. Sin "breaks that Union and Communion with God for which we were made, and in the enjoyment of which we should be blessed and happie, *Isai.* 59.1.2." Debility results, for sin renders one incapable "to receive good," while an "obstinate" refusal to repent "maintains an infinit and everlasting distance between God and the soul." The damage transgression wreaks on the created order leads inexorably to Hooker's concluding estimation of sin, *"the greatest evil in the world, or indeed that can be."*[62]

Hooker touched a man already dubious about the quality of his spiritual performances and cognizant that he "could not see" Christ—a man, in short, who questioned the genuineness of his faith. The sermon confirmed Haynes's doubts, and in his narrative he recalled that upon hearing that there must be a true sight of sin, he "could not find" that he had ever had it. Concerned to apprehend sin's real nature, he focused on Hooker's treatment and synopsized it in his relation. Sin "oppose[s] the God of heaven" and "nullif[ies]" His deity. The wicked hate His very "being." Here Haynes stopped to interpolate his reaction. Recently he had balked at renewing his griefs, but "now whether I would or not I must be cast into new sorrows." Roger's disquietude deepened as he heard that sin makes man "separate from God" and "incapable of receiving good," until at last "I saw I saw not sin." This realization collapsed the fragile rationalizations with which he had fended off contrition, releasing a torrent of pain and remorse. The Lord "pressed in upon me and all former truths came in to aggravate my misery." Soon "slavish fears of the devil" tormented him and he feared to do anything lest his actions "aggravate [the] misery" he believed his due. The sermon Haynes attended is tamer in its denunciations of evildoers than are other portions of *The Application of Redemption*, and it lacks a climactic exhortation to drive unregenerates to grace. Nevertheless, in the urgency of passages like "Prosperity without God will be my poyson, Honor without him my bane," Hooker hoped to nudge the consciences of people like Haynes, who, poised to accuse themselves of terrible crimes, might be won away from sin could they but see its character

62. Hooker, *Application*, IX–X, 35, 54, 55, 57–58, 59, 60, 63.

more surely than perhaps they had.[63] Hooker's words plunged Haynes, already primed to examine his deeds, into the despair that Puritans accounted the foremost sign of preparation.

By speaking of Christ's Passion, Shepard made Richard Cutter more aware of sin. In a sermon to prepare Cambridge Saints for taking the Lord's Supper, an opus whose skeleton remains in his manuscript notebook of works preached around 1640, Shepard expounded Mark 14.34 ("And [Christ] saith unto them, My soul is exceeding sorrowful unto death, tarry ye here, and watch") to develop how Christ's "bearing the sins of the elect" burdened him with "intollerable grief brought on by four particulars.[64] Christ beheld and took on all the Saints' transgressions: he "had all the sins of [the] Elect set before him, which he was to answer for," and hence he was "every way sorrowfull, [he] saw sins every way about him." He grieved for the affront sin gives to God, its wrongfulness "exceeding heauy" on the heart. Sacrificed for man's misdeeds, Christ was cast "into the abysse and horrible pit and gulfe" of God's wrath, "an infinite majesty suffering infinite misery." The Son's special intimacy with the Father intensified the anguish of separation: he who had embraced God more closely than had "all angels and Saints" now endured a sorrow "greater than all [the] sorrows of all the Elect for ever."[65] The necessity for the Son's agony cried for comprehension, so Shepard explained how God's justice, Christ's glory, and the church's condition as recipient of Christ's succor required such pain. In treating the nature of and reason for Jesus' suffering, he touched upon some of the most profound questions in Christian theology, but he steered the bulk of his remarks away from these troublesome issues in order to confront his audience with the applications of his doctrine. Christ's sorrow "to the death" foreshadows the doom of the wicked; conversely, it brings "maruelous comfort" to the Saints, for since Christ has borne God's wrath, He "hath not on[e]

63. Shepard, *Confessions*, 167, 168; Hooker, *Application*, IX–X, 60. The Feb. 6 sermon corresponds to *ibid.*, 52–63. It comprises part of an excursus on the doctrine that starts on p. 35, and extends to p. 192. The uses begin on p. 90. Hooker preached what became the following section in the book on Feb. 13, Wolcott, *Notebook*, 126–27.

64. The notebook is an untitled collection of sermon notes in Shepard's hand deposited in Houghton Library, Harvard University (call number bMS Am 1671(2)). The sermons recorded, some 49 in all, cover at least the period 1638–40. This document is henceforth cited as Shepard, *Sermon Notes*, followed by the text of the specific sermon being quoted. The quotation appears in *ibid.*, "Mark 14.34," 1. Since the original is unpaginated, page numbers refer to a sequence in which p. 1 of each sermon is the page on which the opening biblical text appears. The notebook has been transcribed according to the following procedure: All superscriptions and abbreviations (including thorns [y = th] and ampersands) have been expanded. Capitalization and punctuation have been slightly modernized. Spelling, however, remains unchanged.

65. Shepard, *Sermon Notes*, "Mark 14.34," 2, 3.

drop to powre out vpon thee."[66] Saints and sinners alike should mourn for their wrongdoing and let grief "separate your hart from sin." Shepard pressed his audience to remember the Lord's love, "which is the end of a sacrament," and reminded them of Christ's boundless capacity, demonstrated through the Passion, "to pardon, to comfort, to keepe and carry thee, to loue and feed thee."[67] The Lord's example should compel Saints to heighten their own godly sorrow and stun the unregenerate with the danger of their unconcern.

Richard Cutter had been ruminating about sin for some time before he heard these words. Bewildered—"I knew not which way to go"—and spurred on by a friend's advice to "take heed you do not keep the devil's counsel," he dwelled upon "the bitterness of sin." In this frame of mind, he was most impressed by the list of causes why Christ sorrowed, the only portion of the sermon that he mentioned. As Richard remembered them, they were: "(1) Christ saw all the sins of them, (2) he saw the wrath due to them, (3) [he] felt the intolerable[ness] of wrath, (4) he had felt the presence of the Father." There is a discrepancy between this account and Shepard's notes: the narrative replaces the sermon's second point, that Christ grieved for sin's great offense to God, with the formula that Christ sorrowed because he apprehended the coming punishment for sin. Cutter's sensitivity to the imminence of divine wrath, so graphically portrayed in Shepard's third point, led him to magnify its importance within the overall argument. The relation does not reveal the process through which Richard applied these teachings to himself. By "thinking thus," he allowed, in a phrase tantalizingly curt, "sin became bitter unto me." Perhaps Cutter meant that he identified with Christ, that he saw what the Son saw and suffered what Jesus suffered. Possibly he took to heart the sermon's first use, which promised the wicked no escape from God's anger. The evil invent evasions and excuses for themselves, Shepard said, but to no avail. "I stand confounded," he admitted, at the "fearelesness that takes no care to escape" God's wrath.[68] Cutter was not so inclined, and his concern for the harrowing effects of the Father's ire, underscored by his rendition of the second cause of Christ's sorrow, sharpened his perception of sin. Whatever the precise train of thought, Richard tasted sin's gall more sharply because Shepard's message reinforced his predisposition to do so.

While Hooker was spinning out the pattern of the *ordo salutis* and Shepard was delving into the mysteries of the Passion, Bulkeley was forging a sermon sequence on Zech. 9.11 (". . . by the blood of thy covenant I have sent forth thy prisoners out of the pit wherein *is* no water") that became *The*

---

66. *Ibid.*, 3, 4.
67. *Ibid.*, 5, 6.
68. Shepard, *Confessions*, 180; *idem, Sermon Notes*, "Mark 14.34," 4.

Gospel-Covenant.[69] Explicating the text early in the cycle's course, he typologically linked the fate of the Jews under the Babylonian captivity with the bondage that fastens upon everyone in their natural estate. The pit is the "spirituall captivity" in which all reside, the water represents joy or comfort, "so that the meaning is, that as the *Jewes*, so we, one and other of us, we are shut up as prisoners in the dungeon and pit of the Prison, where there is no water of comfort to refresh our souls withall." The deliverance augured in the verse comes about through Christ's blood ratifying the Covenant of Grace. Though the human condition is "miserable and comfortlesse," freedom and peace obtain for those who take Christ in the covenant. In the course of his lectures, Bulkeley reviewed the covenant's nature, dispensations and benefits, finally turning his attention to the issue of its conditionality.[70] There is a condition, he maintained, the act of faith generated by a supernatural, implanted habit, faith "working towards the promise, and from the promise, and causing us to live by faith in the promise." Granted the capacity to enter into a covenant, man completes the agreement by receiving grace. God proffers the covenant, "and we take hold of it," faith closing with grace by "steps and degrees." At first, the heart esteems grace but lightly, which makes "us seem unto selves as undone men, lost, wretched, miserable," and which begets a "longing desire" for it. Craving God's favor but "dismayed" by a sense of sin, faith "stands like the poor *Publican afar off*, as one afraid to come neer into the presence of the holy God." In time, the spirit of faith, "like fire in the bones," compels the soul to open itself to the Lord, and it resolves "to go to the throne of Grace." Pleading for life, the soul waits expectantly until it receives a gracious promise. Then, it "comes by little and little to touch the top of the golden Scepter," and establishes the covenant.[71]

These sermons were quite popular in Concord where the congregation had entreated Bulkeley to repeat his earlier series on the subject and "importun[ed]" him, Cotton Mather claimed, to "fit it for the press."[72] John Jones was one of the attentive listeners. He first heard Bulkeley while afflicted by what he imagined was melancholy. After attempting to cure his ills by socializing, "which did me much hurt," he encountered Bulkeley contending that "everyone by nature was a prisoner in a pit and dungeon with no comfort to be found," and that the "greatest part of [the] world" lies captive to

69. Michael McGiffert, "The Problem of the Covenant in Puritan Thought: Peter Bulkeley's *Gospel-Covenant*," *New England Historical Genealogical Register*, 130 (1976), 107.

70. Bulkeley, *Gospel-Covenant*, 25, 26, 27, and *passim*.

71. *Ibid.*, 332, 337, 338, 339, 341, 344. Part 5, a summation of the covenant's properties, concludes the lectures.

72. Mather, *Magnalia*, I, 402.

Satan.[73] The Devil's role as warden of the doomed does not figure in the printed versions of *The Gospel-Covenant*, but the published editions leave out sections of the original text. Bulkeley suppressed material he had "handled publikely" as the treatise grew "bigger th[a]n I thought in the beginning."[74] Measuring himself by the minister's remarks, Jones discovered a damningly perfect fit: "this the Lord made me to consider of and to open my eyes to see I was a prisoner and kept by Satan." The knowledge depressed him. Conceiving no way out of his predicament, he lapsed into "a sad and miserable condition."[75] John drew his sorrow upon himself. Bulkeley was explicating a doctrine, not exhorting to contrition, and his purpose in tolling out the desperate state of the unregenerate was to contrast it with the promise of redemption in the covenant: "though our condition be thus miserable and comfortlesse, yet there is both freedome from this bondage, and comfort to be obtained by the bloud of the Covenant."[76] Jones, however, could not yet embrace the good news; with his base condition confirmed, he despaired.

For a "pretty while" Jones was "bound up" in fears about his estate, but by "living daily under [the] word" he was "persuaded to attend upon those means wherein I might find Him." He entertained "no hope of helping myself out of my condition," but later, another sermon tempered this pessimism. Bulkeley asserted, Jones recalled, that the means of deliverance consists in "laying hold on Christ." God "had made a covenant with all His and the condition was faith." The best of faith's degrees was "when a man saw himself in his misery and not knowing what way to go but to fly to God." Jones construed Bulkeley's paradigm of how faith seizes the covenant through the miasma of his own remorse, for the preacher did not exalt one "degree" above another. The use of the superlative is John's alone. Bulkeley insisted, continued Jones, that it was "best when a man could see nothing in himself nor favor in God to draw him to Him."[77] In his book, Bulkeley compared

73. Shepard, *Confessions*, 199-200. By going "to company" to remedy melancholy, Jones was practicing an accepted form of therapy (cf. Elyot, *Castell of Helth*, 69[vo]; Burton, *Anatomy*, II.2.6.4), one that Puritan preachers, always ready to detect an aroused conscience blowing about the vapors of black bile, distrusted. Cf. Greenham, *Works*, 175: "Some men are pricked, and to put away their sorow, they will goe sleepe, they wil goe play, they wil goe sport, they will get to merie companie, and passe away the time, and so, as they terme it, they will purge and driue away the rage of melancholie: they neuer goe to any preacher, to aske of the Lorde, or at the mouth of his spirit: they neuer respect prayer, nor seeke any comfort in the word of God." Listening to Bulkeley convinced Jones that he suffered from a spiritual, not a psychophysical affliction.

74. Phyllis M. Jones and Nicholas R. Jones, *Salvation in New England: Selections from the Sermons of the First Preachers* (Austin, 1977), 27; Bulkeley, *Gospel-Covenant*, 27.

75. Shepard, *Confessions*, 200.

76. Bulkeley, *Gospel-Covenant*, 27.

77. Shepard, *Confessions*, 200, 201.

faith so weak that it cannot as yet address God as it would like to "the poor weake Babe which lyes in the Cradle," that "can only look towards the Mother for helpe, the cast of the eye (after a sort) expressing and signifying what it would say." In Jones's narrative, this statement becomes the assertion that God "could with infant [i.e. could draw an infant to Himself] though it could not cry, yet [it] could cast an eye upon the nurse."[78] At this moment, Bulkeley was articulating John's most personal sentiments, and Jones was sympathetically reverberating to the chords of the preacher's call. A mute babe himself until he heard Bulkeley—"loath I was to make my state known to any that might have helped me"—Jones clutched after the thought: having heard "the free grace and mercy of God could cast any eye after Christ, though [I] could not cry after, I considered of this." Still unsure he warranted God's offer—"I could not see any such invitation to me who had despised grace"—he nonetheless dared to believe that he might be saved: "so long as means did last and my life not cut off there was some hope."[79] The nearly perfect congruence of John's state as he perceived it with the model Bulkeley erected buoyed Jones during a troubled time, and it was the layman, not the minister, who applied the sermon in this way. The conclusions Jones drew, while reasonably inferable from the text, were his own.

It is instructive to investigate multiple reactions to the same preacher, even though the only opportunity to do so is muddied by the circumstance that two sermons are involved and that only their framework exists. During 1639 Shepard offered a pair of sacramental lectures on Is. 38.14 (". . . O Lord, I am oppressed; undertake for me"), part of King Hezekiah's petition for life when he lay dangerously ill.[80] Both sermons come to grips with the matter of the Saints' sufferings, and when joined together they provide a unitary vision of an elect soul's progress from spiritual malaise to sweet recovery. The first work opens the character of Hezekiah's "pressures." He was afflicted in body, for his "sicknes was extreame," and in soul, where the Lord was like a "lyon rending and tearing." The King's fate, Shepard observed, gives notice that "the dearest of the Lords servants" undergo "most bitter soule pressures." At their first conversion and later, sorrow and sin lie "heavy upon them."[81] Posing the obvious question of why God should so exercise His people, Shepard answered that He wants to try them, pull down their pride, and raise their esteem for Him in the ordinances. God is an

78. Bulkeley, *Gospel-Covenant*, 339; Shepard, *Confessions*, 201. The printed text of the *Confessions* reads: "Yet [he] could with infant . . . ," but the lower case "h," which refers "he" to Jones, does not make sense. What could Jones do with an infant? In its own terms, and in light of Bulkeley's parallel passage, the missing pronoun must refer to God.

79. Shepard, *Confessions*, 200, 201.

80. The sermons are distinguished as I and II. II is dated Dec. 8, 1639.

81. Shepard, *Sermon Notes*, "Is. 38.14," I, 1, 2.

exacting ruler, but He is not a sadist; counsel on how to overcome such distress occupies the remainder of this sermon and most of the next. God's people may "expect and seek for refreshing from the Lord." This doctrine promotes trusting in God for solace. It exposes "the misery and euill of a hard hart," comforts "poore bruised souls," and encourages gracious hearts to anticipate mercy from Christ "this day."[82] Shepard affirmed the classic Puritan opinion that humiliation is the antidote to suffering.

The second sermon takes up the method by which Saints escape despondency: "The best way for a distressed soule to get deliverance out of his pressures of spirit is to goe and fly vnto the Lord to undertake for him." The chance for the Elect to achieve peace depends on Christ realizing his role as their surety, an office that entails four tasks. Christ intercedes with the Father, entreating Him to forgive the sinner's debt and not "to try his strength in crushing a poore woorme." The Son promises to satisfy the Father for all the covenants the Saints have broken and to "see the debt payd." Jesus is absolutely reliable. At the appointed time he makes his promises good, performing the Covenant of Grace and keeping it "in and by his people." Finally, he answers "all their enemies and accusers," staving off sin and Satan. Christ can and will act for the regenerate, but only when, "helpless and hopeless in itself," the soul desires him to plead its cause.[83] To fly to Christ the soul must be properly "oppressed" like Hezekiah was, and the whole man must yearn after God, going to Him not only with "the mind and some light desires but with the hart and deepe longings." Only Christ entreated with due submissiveness remedies the source of "all trouble and pressures," God's "fearfull anger and wrath" for sin. Laying out the doctrine's uses, Shepard again drummed home the proper posture for imploring the Son. One "great cause" of soul pressures issues from people's failure to ask Christ to act for them. Whether one "bow[s]" to fears, "swallow[s] them down" to ignore them, combats them without divine aid, or gives in to "sin and Satan and selfe," any hesitation to throw oneself upon the surety fails to relieve the soul.[84] The next use follows automatically: labor to feel "vtterly vnable" to perform either covenant "so yow may goe to the Lord to undertake for yow." A final observation completes the study. How sweet it is to an "oppressed soule" to have the Lord undertake for it, Shepard sighed.[85] Everyone should test themselves for signs of God's refreshing, and Saints should take comfort since God cares for His own.

82. *Ibid.*, 3, 4, 5.

83. Shepard, *Sermon Notes*, "Is. 38.14," II, 1, 2.

84. *Ibid.*, 3, 4, 5.

85. *Ibid.*, 6, 8.

Shepard preached these discourses at the same time he was recording some of the earliest narratives in the *Confessions*, and it is not surprising that at least four people who joined the Cambridge church around 1640 mentioned one or the other.[86] The briefest citation belongs to Jane Winship, whose relation intersperses cryptic allusions to her state of mind between numerous references to sermons. Jane wondered how she would know that she had taken the Lord "as king," and when a minister asked out loud if his congregants were "ready for Christ at His appearing," she "had fears"—though of what is impossible to say. Winship gained some sustenance from one of Shepard's talks on Is. 38.14. The transcript says simply: "Hearing—oppressed undertake for me—eased." That one word, "eased," stands for a multitude of hopes that we can never unearth, but if any single term can capture the thrust of what Shepard intended his listeners to experience, "eased" is it.[87] Robert Holmes was more expansive. In England a sermon had "melted" him, but upon coming to New England he found his "heart and all ordinances dead." Holmes considered himself a backsliding Saint even though he had not yet entered into communion with a church; he complained not of his bondage to sin or to natural corruption, but of a decline in his former responsiveness and of dissatisfaction with the spiritual exercises he used to enjoy. Shepard's sermons about Hezekiah were designed to revivify a Saint, and one of them inspired Holmes to pray to God "to help me and reveal Himself to me." Hard-hearted regenerates were supposed to throw themselves on Christ, and Robert obliged; "melted" during the entire sermon and especially affected because it was "sacrament time," he "went home and

---

86. Three other possible references have been excluded. Mary Parish's relation ends: "and so Jeremiah [*sic*] 38—I am oppressed, Lord encouraged me" (Shepard, *Confessions*, 138). The narrative, however, is devoid of any indication that she heard this verse from the pulpit (as opposed to having read it, meditated on it, or heard a friend speak it). Parish's reaction cannot be analyzed as a response to a sermon, though her sentiment—"[the] Lord encouraged me"—is that of people who were clearly reacting to sermons. Ann Errington mentioned that "on Sabbath day on sacrament day Hezekiah was humbled and I thought I was not humbled" (*ibid.*, 185), which matches the occasion of the Isaiah sermons, but the reference draws on 2 Chron. 32.26: "Hezekiah humbled himself for the pride of his heart . . . so that the wrath of the Lord came not upon them in the days of Hezekiah." This, and her response that "I thought I was not humbled"—one more appropriate to the quotation from Chronicles than to either Is. 38.14 or Shepard's treatment—seems to indicate that Errington had in mind a sermon on the former text. However, she also said that "in the latter end [of] that sermon there was obedience of sons and servants," a remark similar to one John Fessenden recalled having heard in a sermon on Is. 38.14 (*infra*, 186). Perhaps Errington did recount one of the sermons in question, but the evidence is too tenuous for a close analysis. Brother Jackson's maid said that "from Hezekiah's example some report I had that I might live [to make my calling sure]" (*ibid.*, 120), but so vague a reference does not necessarily point to having heard the sermon in question.

87. Shepard, *Confessions*, 149.

cried to Him." Holmes's iterated use of "melted" suggests that he underwent a reconversion in which he relived his initial yielding to Christ. Reconversion did not bring him full assurance, but it did leave him more confident about his own course: "Still I am doubting but I know I shall know if I follow on[.]"[88]

Like Winship and Holmes, John Fessenden mentioned a sermon on Is. 38.14 towards the end of his relation, after some experience of grace. Fessenden had already approached God "for justification and sanctification," but mounting "sadness of heart" heartened him "to come to the light, etc." John remembered a discourse on Hezekiah that depicted the "pressures of a son and a slave, the one in regard of a son." He was thinking, most likely, of the first sermon, for he reflected that "sin was it which did oppress," an idea twice expressed in the notes for that work. The phrase "pressures of a son and a slave" does not appear in Shepard's draft, and Fessenden may have imagined that he heard it. The sermon fortified him against evil; he "found some mercy and strength against sin."[89] Roger Haynes also enjoyed God's mercy. Subject to "many fears" despite having listened to Hooker speak "something to them that were wounded," Haynes wondered if God would indeed "undertake" for him: "I found I might say the same words but I knew not whether the Lord would." Certain that he desired Christ but trepid that God would not relieve him, Roger gave particular heed to Shepard's four-fold analysis of what a surety does. He recalled two of the points. A surety "interced[es] and promis[es] to discharge all debts, and pursu[es] and answer[s] all accusers." The shift of a word reveals how strongly Haynes wished to triumph over his feelings of discouragement. Shepard said that Christ intercedes so that the debtor "may not be pursued for the debt or the offense," but Haynes imagined the surety "pursuing" his accusers. No longer the hunted, Haynes in his mind turned the tables on his foes. "Now I thought with myself," he went on, "this was God's great goodness"; his spirit "was much affected and fresh hopes of mercy were let into my soul." Anxiety abated. Doubts still hedged him in, "the Lord stayed my heart yet not without fears," but Roger continued to "hope the Lord might be a surety for me."[90]

Any appraisal of the impact specific sermons had on people should first assess the exactitude with which the laity rendered them. The conclusion must be that their references were essentially accurate. To be sure, a few statements are unsupported by the texts, or are demonstrably incorrect. The

88. *Ibid.*, 143.

89. *Ibid.*, 177; *idem, Sermon Notes*, "Is. 38.14," I, 1, 5.

90. *Idem, Confessions*, 169; *idem, Sermon Notes*, "Is. 38.14," II, 1. Haynes is a graphic example that even superior preachers (and in this case, one who had already affected him) often failed to carry their points.

extant records provide no basis for Fessenden's allusion to the pressures on a son and a slave or Jones's evocation of Satan. Roger Haynes cited Shepard's text from Isaiah incorrectly.[91] On the other hand, Haynes did reproduce Hooker's doctrine almost flawlessly, duplicating 13 of its 17 words.[92] But tracking down such literal correspondences as proof of congregants' accuracy is a misplaced enterprise. The existing narratives are, after all, recordings by ministers that leave out or alter details. Some, like Jane Winship's, refer to sermons in a stilted fashion far removed from normal speech; any information that she might have aired has disappeared through abbreviation. In the accounts just discussed, only the relations of Haynes and Jones provide enough words to afford legitimate comparison with the originals. The surviving texts themselves, whether manuscript or printed, are not necessarily verbatim accounts of what preachers actually said.[93] Since, in addition, the church admission procedures did not require faultless replications, a fitter test of accuracy is to ascertain how faithfully people summarized sermon

91. He cited it as Is. 38.9, Shepard, *Confessions*, 169; one must, however, allow for the possibility that the error was Shepard's, not Haynes's.

92. Wolcott, *Notebook*, 125, gives all seventeen words in the printed version, and adds two more. On p. 120, he gives a variant reading.

93. Manuscript notes like Shepard's give merely the outlines of the argument, which the minister expanded during his address. Puritan preachers favored memorizing either notes or a complete draft of the sermon and then speaking without written aids. Sermon notes, therefore, may more accurately reflect what the minister intended to say than what he really did. Printed works also depart from what was actually said. Since most preachers did not write sermons out fully, many books owe their existence to some indefatigable stenographer, whose labors did not always do the preacher's meaning justice. There was no seventeenth-century equivalent of a tape recorder. Authors reworked pieces before publication, and unauthorized editions, sometimes of dubious reliability, also circulated widely. On these matters, see: W. Fraser Mitchell, *English Pulpit Oratory form Andrewes to Tillotson: A Study of Its Literary Aspects* (New York, 1962 [orig. 1932]), 14–38; John Sparrow, "John Donne and Contemporary Preachers: Their Preparation of Sermons for Delivery and for Publication," *Essays and Studies by Members of the English Association*, 16 (1931), 144–78; John Rechtien, "The Visual Memory of William Perkins and the End of Theological Dialogue," *Journal of the American Academy of Religion*, 45, 1, supp. (1977), D: 86–93; Babette May Levy, *Preaching in the First Half Century of New England History* (New York, 1967 [orig. 1945]), 81–85; Jones and Jones, *Salvation in New England*, 17–20. This does not mean, however, that the discrepancies between the relations and the sermon texts here under discussion are better understood as variations between a person's entirely accurate reproduction of the spoken sermon and a written version, somewhat different, of the same piece. In the case of Cutter's rendition of Shepard's second "cause," Cutter misrepresents the thrust of that entire particular as it appears in Shepard's notes; it is not a question of mistaking a word, but of changing the import of a paragraph. Cutter's other summary statements did conform to Shepard's drift. The same thing holds true for Haynes's shift of the word "pursue." Given the nature of the sources, perhaps no explanation of the discrepancies can be definitive. However, the references' general conformity to the sermon texts they purport to describe increases their credibility and lessens the chance that textual variants are involved. Furthermore, the discrepancies are congruent with their context; they amplify, rather than disturb, themes conveyed in the narratives. Thus a psychological rather than a textual explanation is preferable.

contents. The evidence presented above shows few gross violations of the letter or the spirit. Candidates' ability to re-create bits of sermons probably represents a feat of memory, although many may well have looked over notes while they prepared to tell their spiritual histories. Haynes's résumés, especially his extended recapitulation of Hooker's thinking, and Jones's summation of Bulkeley's "third degree of faith" suggest that these men had studied outlines or transcripts.[94] The preponderance of evidence, however, points to memory working unaided. Individuals seem to have abstracted and recounted the gist of sermons rather than trying to recall them precisely. Cutter paraphrased the four causes of Christ's sorrow, and Jones retained the timbre of Bulkeley's language without maintaining the preacher's exact wording. It should be recalled that Haynes and his fellows were calling to mind sermons that they had heard within a few years. How well they remembered sermons from their more distant pasts is unknown.

Fundamentally accurate in their recollection of sermons, the laity nevertheless introduced small changes reflective of individual preoccupations into their accounts. Haynes moved a word in expressing the wish to be free of his spiritual accusers, and Cutter's concern with God's wrath led him to alter slightly Shepard's analysis of Christ's sorrow. John Jones elevated one degree of faith over others because Bulkeley's treatment of it had special importance for him. Each of these changes adapts the minister's purpose to the hearer's needs. The very appearance of a sermon fragment in a relation testifies to a personal act of choice, for every selection represents a talk plucked out of oblivion and accorded peculiar importance. Once a sermon left a preacher's mouth it belonged to the congregation and was subject to their interpretations. Its impact depended in part on the perceptions of its receivers, a phenomenon illustrated by the differential responses to Shepard's two sermons on Is. 38.14. Four people experienced a lessening of "oppression," which accords with what Shepard was trying to accomplish, but each expressed the reduction of tension in different ways. Where Winship was eased and Holmes made more confident, Fessenden spoke of gaining strength against sin and Haynes dwelled on God's mercy. It is incontestable that ministers directed how people should respond and that to an appreciable extent they dictated the schema through which the sensations of conversion were to be evaluated. At the same time, the laity helped fashion their own

94. It is tempting to speculate that they may have held notes while reciting, but no observer ever commented on such a practice, nor does anyone seem to have recorded how people prepared to give the relations. One slight piece of evidence suggests that people recited verses from memory. Mary Wigglesworth commented on "reading 3 Romans about 19," a locution that sounds as if she were trying to remember the exact verse. The quotation she gave is in fact Ro. 3.12 (and her rendition reverses the position of the two clauses), Wigglesworth, *Diary*, 443.

religious experience, adding personal touches to the categories that the preachers made.

III

Another index of the clergy's relationship to the laity's religious experience is the degree to which the two groups harmonized their readings of the Scriptures, and the extent to which individuals in their devotions acted upon the texts as the preachers thought they should. Considering that the word *Puritan* is likely to conjure up a free association to "Bible" (along with "grim" and "scarlet A"), surprisingly little is known about the routine workings of their textual interpretations. What connotations did ministers ferret out? Did ordinary men and women invent their own meanings? What impact did the communication of the ministry's ideas have on conversions? To answer these questions involves comparing how preachers and congregants comprehended a number of biblical passages, and to what uses they put them. This procedure necessitates returning to a macroscopic analysis, for it is virtually impossible to connect a reference's appearance in a narrative to the influence of a specific preacher. Instead, the meanings and applications that the laity attached to four of the most popular texts mentioned in the relations may be compared to the ministry's discussion of those verses. What results is an indication of how farmers and housewives, apprentices and maids located themselves within the contours of clerical exegesis. Amid the larger consensus of Puritan hermeneutics, personal variations emerge.

Placed after an oracle denouncing false worship, Is. 1.18 holds out a prospect of redemption. "Your new moons and your appointed feasts my soul hateth," the Lord proclaims through His prophet, "when ye make many prayers, I will not hear: your hands are full of blood" (vv. 14, 15). Ceremonies and prayers are vain without righteous living. "[C]ease to do evil," Isaiah implores, "Learn to do well," and he sounds off the community's obligations to itself: "seek judgment, relieve the oppressed, judge the fatherless, plead for the widow" (vv. 16, 17). He then calls the society to court in the legal language of ancient Israel. "Come now, and let us reason together, saith the LORD" (18a); God asks Judah to plead its case.[95] The indictment of empty ritualism, the summons to social activism, and the calling of Judah to trial set the stage for deliberating on the nation's fate, but the remainder of v. 18

---

95. A. S. Herbert, *The Book of the Prophet Isaiah, Chapters 1–39* (Cambridge, 1973), 29; R. E. Clements, *Isaiah 1–39* (Grand Rapids and London, 1980), 34; RSV note to Is. 1.18; but see Edward J. Young, *The Book of Isaiah*, 3 vols. (Grand Rapids, 1965–72), I, 76.

momentarily halts the thrust to judgment. In a passage that brings to mind
the bloodstained hands of v. 15, the prophet offers a vision of transgressors
reclaimed: "though your sins be as scarlet, they shall be as white as snow;
though they be red like crimson, they shall be as wool" (18b). The image is
arresting both for its interruption of the thematic flow and for its depiction of
heinous sins made pure. Verse 18 can be read as a triumphant declaration of
the divine capacity to forgive, but some commentators have opined that
Isaiah may have intended it sarcastically.[96] The two succeeding verses return
to consideration of Judah's course, setting out the consequences of its actions:
"If ye be willing and obedient, ye shall eat the good of the land: But if ye
refuse and rebel, ye shall be devoured with the sword" (19–20a). Redemption
is clothed in national and material terms; Judah shall prosper if it worships
God correctly, and be ravaged should it refuse. Trumpeting the power of the
Lord to pardon, v. 18 stands out amid the pericope's demand for ethical
behavior.

To Puritans, Is. 1.18 spoke clearly of individual redemption. Overlooking
the appeal to the nation and the invitation to social reform, they became
totally absorbed in the majesty of forgiveness and its capacity to effect a
spiritual transformation. They would have had no truck with suggestions of
sarcasm. Richard Sibbes stated their foundational understanding of the
verse. People in love, who see "no issue, no supply," can claim the promise of
the covenant: "Thou hast said, 'At what time soever a sinner comes to thee
with a repentant heart, thou wilt forgive his iniquities; and though his sins
were as scarlet, thou wilt make them as snow, and white as wool,' Isa. i.18."
The verse proves that God will remit the sins of "such as truely repent,"
whether unregenerate or regenerate, and was cited by preachers both to
evangelize the unconverted and soothe the Saints.[97] No sinner stands beyond
God's ability to redeem. Although one's sins are "bred in our Natures," hence
no more removable by human efforts than is scarlet "twice dyed in the Wool,"
yet, Hooker averred, "the Lord hath undertaken it, and he will do it." Cotton
agreed, with a vengeance: God sometimes pours out the Spirit *upon the
most bloody, most haynous, and most desperate, and most prophane, and
most abominable sinners."*[98] The promise of redemptive grace also comforts
the godly. They find great happiness in justification, since God pardons *"all
their sinns & trespasses* whatsoever." When tempted by Satan *"to despair"* for
their *"great sins,"* they should consider that Christ satisfied God's justice and
cleanses them from iniquities, "'though they be as red as crimson,' Isa. i.18."

---

96. Herbert, *Isaiah*, 30; George Buchanan Gray, *A Critical and Exegetical Commentary on
the Book of Isaiah, I–XXXIX*, I (New York, 1912), 27; Clements, *Isaiah*, 34.

97. Sibbes, *Works*, VI, 122, 123; Perkins, *Works*, I, 465, 458.

98. Hooker, *Application*, IX–X, 21–22; Cotton, *way of Life*, 111.

Faith scatters the darkness that obscures assurance of justification by applying a promise as old as the Hebrews but as current as the Saints: "Israel was
not forsaken, no more shall I [be]"; though "my sins were as Scarlet of a
double dye . . . yet there is a power in the blood of Christ, to make them
white as snow."[99] Doubts of assurance dissipate in the knowledge that God
never forsakes His own.

But it was to palliate the shafts of preparation that the verse appealed to
the laity. It eased Bridget Richardson when she feared that people who do not
turn from "worldly worries" to Christ "shall be turned out with dogs." The
tenet promoted by Hooker and Cotton that God may save the worst offenders attracted persons struggling with feelings of worthlessness. Mrs. Crackbone was "terrified and out of hope," but upon hearing a sermon on the text,
she "had some hope."[100] Brother Jackson's maid seems to have enjoyed a
similar experience. Mourning that she had caused Christ to suffer for her
sins, she prayed for pardon, "But little I got and [so I went to] 1 Isaiah—let
us reason together."[101] The narrative does not disclose the woman's immediate response, but the next sentence reveals how a sermon helped her to part
from sin, so that her rumination on Is. 1.18 may have given her an inkling of
grace. Confident that the Lord could forgive her sins but questioning if He
would, Mrs. Russell's maid sought Him "In public and private," reviewing
the life of Manasseh and thinking about "the scarlet sins of Isaiah" made
"white as snow." Katharine's experience typified the rhythms of preparation,
bouts of sorrow and fear mingling with efforts to find surcease from doubt.
According to the preachers' ideal scheme, God would sustain the sinner just
enough to keep him or her from becoming numbingly depressed, while
simultaneously intensifying the burden of sin. Katharine's course exemplified
this pattern. The verse appears to have comforted her momentarily, but the
terror continued and she remained "doubtful of what would become of
me."[102] Despite the clergy's pledges that God would pardon the contrite,
individuals had to convince themselves of the possibility, and the process
took time. Why Is. 1.18 did not figure in the quest for assurance is not clear.
Nothing in the verse itself prohibits such an application, and the ministry
certainly encouraged this use. Nevertheless, the laity employed it to help them
bear the Spirit of Bondage and sought assurance from other passages.

99. Mather, *Summe*, 33; Sibbes, *Works*, V, 244; Cotton, *way of Life*, 328 misnum. 329.

100. Fiske, *Notebook*, 202; Shepard, *Confessions*, 140. There is some justification for including
a verse used as a sermon text in this analysis, even though the person may have been
responding to the body of the sermon rather than to the text itself. Sermons were referred to by
their texts, and in many cases, such as this, the text is the only recollection of the sermon. As
such, it begins to acquire a significance independent of what the preacher said.

101. Shepard, *Confessions*, 120.

102. *Ibid.*, 99, 100.

The situations in which congregants referred to Is. 55.1 varied more widely. Chapter 55 climaxes a series of poetic prophecies assuring the Jewish exiles in Babylon that they remain in God's care, promising the restoration of the godly community in Zion, and heralding the reconstruction of Jerusalem. Verse 1 invites Israel to a feast: "Ho, every one that thirsteth, come ye to the waters, and he that hath no money, come ye, buy, and eat; yea, come, buy wine and milk without money and without price." The passage richly describes God's relationship to His own. He asks people to come, leaving them the responsibility to do so. God's gifts are great, but one must bestir oneself to enjoy them. The Lord offers His graces to all, even to those who have nothing; the sole requirement is that they truly desire them. He nourishes the hungry: "eat ye *that which is* good, and let your soul delight itself in fatness" (v. 2). The bounty is literally priceless. God's mercy is free to all who thirst, and it cannot be purchased. Commencing the envoi of the Second Isaiah's message,[103] verse 1 opens into God's pledge to re-establish His people and end the exile. "I will make an everlasting covenant with you" (v. 3), He swears, later disclosing that "ye shall go out with joy, and be led forth with peace" (v. 12). At the same time Israel's salvation charges it to witness God's redemption to the world: "Behold, thou shalt call a nation *that* thou knowest not, and nations that knew not thee shall run unto thee[.]" Is. 55.1 speaks to Israel as individuals who compose the nation, but the covenant is consummated with the holy community.

Puritans followed up the multiple implications of Is. 55.1. No single interpretation dominated their exegesis, although they did emphasize the verse's call to grace. "Christ our gain calls us to buy 'without money,'" said Sibbes, "and invites us that are laden with sin to come to him, Isa. lv.1; 2 Cor. v.20." John Preston made the same point while remarking the individual's obligation to avail oneself of the opportunity. God offers the righteousness of Christ, compared in Scripture to "Wine and Milke," and "it matters not what your person is, onely you must take it." Also raising the issue of responsibility, Ames linked the necessity for active human participation with the gratuitousness of God's offer: though "God doth fully bestow life upon us, and receive nothing at our hands in lieu of it, *Esa.* 55.1.2. Yet we ought to forsake all unlawful things actually," otherwise "we cannot obtaine the grace of God."[104] John Norton too acknowledged the freeness of grace, "God will either not justifie at all, or justifie for nothing," and he explained why the Bible beckons people to buy: "the sinner parts as hardly with his righteous-

103. Modern biblical scholarship usually divides the book of Isaiah into three parts: chs. 1–39, 40–55, 56–66. Otto Kaiser, *Introduction to the Old Testament*, trans. John Sturdy (Minneapolis, 1977), 261–62, 268–70.

104. Sibbes, *Works*, V, 90; Preston, *Breast-Plate*, I, 14; Ames, "Conscience," II.v.15.

ness, as the covetous man doth with his mony, *Isa.* 55.1." Norton comprehends "buy . . . without money" in regard to the sinner's state of mind—he or she wants to purchase salvation with deeds—but the more common reading, exemplified by Richard Rogers's dictum, understands the phrase in reference to the invaluableness of grace: "this precious pearle is not bought with money."[105] God invites all to Christ, but Hooker raised Is. 55.1 into a hedge against universalism. The fullness of grace and comfort are "freely offered to those, and only to those that thirst."[106] By thirst, Puritans meant "a desire of comfort against God's wrath," the soul's "gasp[ing]" after a draught of Christ's blood when it "clearly apprehends it selfe to be under the fierce scorching wrath of the Almighty."[107] The promise of redemption inspired an obvious pastoral use. To those on the "anvill" of preparation who yearn for the Lord, John Rogers held out hope of relief. "Be of good comfort," he urged, God cannot "deny thee thy part in mercy and salvation," for He has proclaimed that "the price is not money, but a thirsting soul[.]" Richard Rogers cited the verse to strengthen wavering Saints in the confidence of their assurance.[108] All of these interpretations take the verse as pertaining to individuals, but at least one minister applied it more widely. Contending that God's commandments, in addition to His promises, call us to faith, Bulkeley maintained that they "make the Nation so called to come to Christ."[109]

Some people employed Is. 55.1 for purposes that John and Richard Rogers would have recognized. With Is. 1.18 it helped sustain Bridget Richardson during her traumas of contrition, and Alice Reade used it while searching for a firm sense of God's promise.[110] More frequently, in the absence of explicit ministerial directives, people interpreted the verse in ways that were similar to its handling by theologians, but applied it after their own fashion. Humiliated souls grappling with incipient faith most often had recourse to this text. Thomas Hincksman had had "some sweet encouragement" to seek God but believed that "there was nothing in him" capable of executing his intention until the Lord opened Is. 54.7, 43.25, and 55.1, each of which stresses the divine largesse. In order to counteract his paralysis, Thomas had to discover that God would pardon him in spite of, indeed because of, his debility. Confronting the quintessential crisis in conversion's course, Hincksman surmounted it; the texts "set him a work to go afresh to God." The verse had a similar effect on Ann Kemp, though her relation,

---

105. Norton, *Orthodox Evangelist*, 312; Rogers, *Seven Treatises*, 1st p. 20[vo].

106. Hooker, *Spiritual Thirst*, 5.

107. Hildersam, *CVIII Lectures*, 42; Hooker, *Spiritual Thirst*, 9.

108. Rogers, *Doctrine of Faith*, 177, 178–79; Rogers, *Seven Treatises*, 39.

109. Bulkeley, *Gospel-Covenant*, 378.

110. Fiske, *Notebook*, 202, 8.

severely condensed, reveals little more than that she saw "her duty to believe," and that "in the pressing of Isa. 55:1 her soul was drawn to close with Christ &c." The narrative of Roger Haynes, on the other hand, registers in detail how the verse instigated the climax of his first conversion. Having some time since worked through his despair, Haynes ran afoul of "many proud thoughts," but God "let in new thoughts of mercy which stayed my heart, Is. 55:1—all that thirst come and live." Cognizant that the Lord saves all who long for Him, Haynes questioned if he had "that thirsting frame, which I found I had in some measure." Looking over Is. 55.2 as well, he "considered what need I had of Christ." When Roger realized that only ignorance of his longings kept him from God, grace burst into his soul: "the Lord witnessed I did thirst and so the Lord did draw my heart to Himself and then I had manifest light of my estate." The Word illuminated his mind and penetrated into the whole man. Amidst "the sweetness," Haynes heard the Lord saying "buy without money," which "affected my heart."[111] A fragment of Is. 55.1 translates the secret language of the Spirit, reminding Haynes, at the moment of union, that God's grace is incalculable because He donates it to the indigent and undeserving. In the cases of Hincksman, Kemp, and Haynes, Is. 55.1 triggered effectual vocation, an application that no preacher voiced.

John 6.37 also figured in congregants' experience of taking Christ. This text forms part of a speech that occurs during a dialogue between Jesus and people who followed him to Capernaum. Not manna, he tells them, but the Christ is the staff of life, "For the bread of God is he which cometh down from heaven, and giveth life unto the world" (v. 33). Jesus then discloses himself as the Christ—"I am the bread of life" (v. 35a)—and affirms that "All that the Father giveth me shall come to me; and him that cometh to me I will in no wise cast out" (v. 37). He ends by announcing the resurrection of the faithful (v. 40). Each of verse 37's clauses proclaims a major soteriological principle. Emphasizing the priority of God's direction in salvation, the first pontificates that the Father wills whom the Son shall save. The second publicizes God's generosity: everyone who seeks salvation in the Son shall have it, and will not lose it. The faithful will not be "cast out." Mixing universalism and predestinarianism, John 6.37 challenges theologians to identify precisely to whom "All" refers, and to determine the extent of human freedom to believe.

Those who had cut their teeth on Reformed dogmatics knew well how they stood on these issues. In the phrase "All that the Father giveth me," the master of Geneva discerned God distinguishing the Elect from the reprobate, and Puritans likewise detected the divine hand skimming the cream from the milk. Christ "gives himself for none but those which God hath first given

---

111. *Ibid.*, 147, 95; Shepard, *Confessions*, 170.

him," stated Sibbes. He saves only the selected few, "for redemption, in regard of efficacy, is no longer than God's election." John Rogers put the doctrine in Christ's mouth. The first cause of faith is God's predetermination, hence "it is called Faith of Gods Elect. So our Saviour sayeth, *Iohn* 6.37."[112] Into the verse's declaration that all whom Christ calls do in fact come to him, ministers projected their insistence that in each elect soul God's will infallibly consummates the work of conversion. According to Preston, a "certaine, prevalent and irresistible working" characterizes "quickening Grace," which "doth alwayes attain its need in those to whom it is communicated. *John* 6.37." Ames and Norton seconded the thought.[113] The verse gave rise to two major practical applications. Preachers played up the evangelical implications of Christ's promise to take in all who seek him. The Gospel "encourageth the poor lost soul to come to Christ," they advertised, God wants one to "take this mercy." The certainty that the Son "will never cast thee away" should inspire confidence in coming to him, Shepard said, and Bulkeley quoted the verse to underline God's "willingnesse" to establish "a gracious Covenant."[114] Besides extending the good news to sinners, preachers interpreted the verse's second clause to comfort Saints with faltering faith. One may be in covenant "and knows it not," Shepard wrote to a friend in England, but if you find yourself yearning "to cleave unto Jesus Christ by fervent and ardent desire," know that God gives this spiritual thirst "as the first fruit of eternal election, and which kind of people he will never cast away. (John 6.37)." Bulkeley sustained weak faith similarly in Concord.[115]

The laity avoided spinning subtle webs of election and predestination from John 6.37, interesting themselves solely in what it could tell them about the process of gaining faith. Although it quieted Thomas Hincksman's spirit during preparation and helped solidify George Norton's feelings of assurance, the verse, like Is. 55.1, appeared most prominently in descriptions of union.[116] Mary Goldsmith's "closing with Christ came especially in that of John 6:37," and Bridget Richardson received a "Promise of comfort" from it. Unfortunately, the skeletal nature of their relations forbids any insight into what particular effect the verse had on them, but Elizabeth Cutter's narrative does

112. John Calvin, *Commentary on the Gospel According to John*, trans. William Pringle, 2 vols. (Edinburgh, 1847–60), I, 251; Sibbes, *Works*, V, 388; Rogers, *Doctrine of Faith*, 51.

113. Preston, *Position*, 14; Ames, *Marrow*, I.xxvi.28; Norton, *Orthodox Evangelist*, 213–14. Preston claimed proof "by many places of Scripture," but cited only one other, Jer. 31.18 (which is misnumbered 31.23). These authors did not believe their analysis contradicts human freedom or responsibility. Cf. *supra*, 90–93.

114. Mather, *Summe*, 4; Hooker, *Sovles Vocation*, 330; Shepard, *Works*, I, 235; Bulkeley, *Gospel-Covenant*, 51.

115. Shepard, *Works*, I, 320, 321, 322; Bulkeley, *Gospel-Covenant*, 339–40.

116. Fiske, *Notebook*, 147, 37.

afford a peek into her psyche. For a time, she "Durst not seek nor call God Father nor think Christ shed His blood for me," but several of Shepard's sermons plus a conversation with "servants of the Lord" changed her mind, "so I sought the Lord the more." During another sermon, the Lord "rejoiced" her heart "by sundry places," a number of verses clustered around the central theme that Christ came to save sinners and that he invites them to himself. "I thought I had no repentance," she worried, "yet I was encouraged to seek the Lord and to be content with His condemning will to lie at [the] Lord's feet." Measuring a desire for redemption against the results of her self-evaluation, Elizabeth concluded that hard-heartedness tipped the balance against her aspirations. Then, in contemplating the verse, she realized the strength of her commitment: "[I] desired [the] Lord to teach me and desired to submit." John 6.37 convinced Elizabeth that Christ appreciated her spiritual thirst more than he despised her failure to repent, and it may be hazarded that the implications of the second clause (quoted in the account as "he that comes to me I'll not cast away") prompted her to reassess her condition.[117] Verse 37b states that Christ accepts anyone who seeks him. "Coming" is the sole condition; the clause makes no mention of one's sinfulness or the state of one's heart. Only one's longing for Christ matters, and this Cutter knew she had. Suddenly, one suspects, her obduracy weighed less heavily. The relation ends with Elizabeth desiring to submit to God, proof enough, to the Saints of Cambridge, that John 6.37 had brought her to conversion.

The relations cite Mat. 11.28 more frequently than any other scripture.[118] The verse occurs in the middle of a pericope in which Jesus first thanks the Father for revealing His truths "unto babes [i.e. the disciples]" (v. 25), proclaims his own intimacy with Him, and beckons "the multitudes" (cf. v. 7) to "Come unto me, all ye that labour and are heavy laden, and I will give you rest" (v. 28). Like John 6.37, Mat. 11.28 announces the good news of salvation in Christ, but features of the presentations differ. Phrased in the imperative, Christ's invitation appears more forcefully in Matthew than in John, where it takes the form of a declarative statement. Christ appeals to "all" in John, whereas in Matthew he speaks to a more restricted audience, those made weary by the demands of Pharisaic observance. To answer the call brings certainty of acceptance in the former verse, and the unburdensome tasks of discipleship in the latter. The remainder of the passage amplifies the

117. *Ibid.*, 61, 202; Shepard, *Confessions*, 145, 146.

118. Reference to this verse, as well as to John 6.37 and Is. 55.1, seems to have been a widespread phenomenon within Puritan churches, for Owen Watkins, *The Puritan Experience: Studies in Spiritual Autobiography* (New York, 1972), 41, discovers that in a collection of testimonies attributed to members of a London congregation, these three verses "are by far the most popular, the first being quoted twenty-four times." Cf. Caldwell, *Puritan Conversion Narrative*, 21, 29.

themes in verse 28. Accept my teachings, Jesus says, "Take my yoke upon you," and, contrasting the fulfillment of serving him to the supposed onus of satisfying Pharisaic legalism, claims that those who do "Shall find rest unto your souls. For my yoke *is* easy, and my burden is light" (vv. 29–30).[119] In John, Christ summons the faithful to believe; in Matthew, he calls them to obey.

Sibbes promoted the verse's call to duty, but few ministers followed him, nor did they show great interest in its potential for promulgating doctrine. While touching on a variety of subjects—Christ's bountiful mercy, the efficacy of his sacrifice for the Elect alone, the applicability of certain spiritual promises to some but not all Saints—their usual interests were pastoral, covering three primary concerns.[120] Preachers took advantage of the hortatory tone to proselytize. "Christ calls thee to *come to him if thou be heavy laden, and weary of thy sins,*" so why, John Preston asked rhetorically, "shouldest thou then fear any thing, when he can make all things easie to thee?" Grace excludes none from its "Fellowship," John Davenport averred, "unlesse you exclude your selves, Matth. 11.28."[121] Other preachers used the verse to dilate on the difficulties of preparation. A man "can never come to Christ that is not burdened with his sinne," William Fenner maintained, and only when he "cannot sleep for it" will Christ "*ease*" him."[122] This interpretation of what constitutes the burden, standard in Puritan hermeneutics, translates the verse from its historical context to a personalistic one. Christ's audience was "laden" with the yoke of the law, but Puritans identified iniquity as the cumbrance Christ eases. Shepard cited the passage to articulate how the Spirit humiliates unregenerates:

> I take this to be the true meaning of Matt. xi. 28, "Ye that labor," i.e., you that are wearied in your own way, in seeking rest to your souls by your own hard labor or works, (as the word κοπιωντες signifies,) and are tried out therein, and so are now laden indeed with sin and the heavy pressure of that, finding no ease by all that you do.[123]

He came close to the sense of modern commentators, for he criticized the futility of self-righteous endeavor (just as Christ excoriated the ineffectiveness of Pharisaic obligations), but he never let sin's "heavy pressure" wander from

---

119. David Hill, ed., *The Gospel of Matthew* (London, 1972), 207–9; W. F. Albright and C. S. Mann, *Matthew* (Garden City, 1971), 146; Alexander Jones, *The Gospel According to Saint Matthew* (New York, 1965), 141.

120. Sibbes, *Works*, VI, 123; Preston, *Remaines*, 291; Perkins, *Works*, I, 108; Rogers, *Doctrine of Faith*, 458.

121. Preston, *Riches of Mercy*, 169; Davenport, *Knowledge of Christ*, 87.

122. Fenner, *Souls Looking-glasse*, 127; cf. GenB, note to Mat. 11.28.

123. Shepard, *Works*, I, 179.

the center of his attention. Ministers also applied the promise of ease to the godly craving assurance. No "bruised reed" should "except himself, when Christ doth not except him," Sibbes counseled, " 'Come unto me, all that are weary and heavy laden,' &c." Demonstrating how faith brings assurance of justification, Cotton explained that a Saint who discovers oneself "*weary and heavy laden*" can "claime the promise for my comfort[.]"[124] As with the other verses under discussion, Mat. 11.28 served both unregenerates and Saints as the preachers saw fit.

The laity's application of Mat. 11.28 derived from those of the clergy, conformed, as always, to personal exigency. John Collins agreed with the preachers that humbled sinners should seek Christ, but at first he doubted that he himself was properly chastened. Instructed by Henry Dunster that "it was the duty of poor heavy laden souls under their sins to come to Christ for [rest,]" Collins could not estimate his "measure of being laden." Many sermons, Sabbaths, and strivings later, he met the verse's standards: "I thought I could see myself in some measure weary and heavy laden and therefore I was called to come to him that he might give me rest[.]"[125] Several people credited Mat. 11.28 with promoting their effectual calling. Having resolved that, even if she should "perish" she would "perish with Christ," Tryphean Geere was brought up short by a temptation to which Puritans' biblical literalism rendered them particularly prone. Tryphean could not find her name in the Bible (scarcely surprising, in her case) and wondered if the promises included her. She was answered "from Mat. 11:28, come then to me, then Thomas, Mary, or whatever thy name is every burdened soul invited." John Rogers of Watertown thought this text important because it demonstrated to him the "all sufficiency" of throwing himself upon the "free tender" of grace in Christ "(and the insufficiency of all other ways)." Bridget Fiske also emphasized the invitation's gratuity: "in private, from Mat. 11.28 she saw Christ tendered to her and Himself offering Himself freely could she by faith lay hold of Him," whereupon she did. Bridget's relation indicates that ministers prompted new scriptural meanings to the laity. She heard an unnamed preacher "applying that place in Mat. 11:28 as to know whether a soul was in Christ or no," and when she "was full of fears" about her estate, God "brought this to mind in Mat. 11:28 with that in John 13:1." Bridget learned how to apply the verse to gain assurance. Like her, George Norton had recourse to the text at different stages in conversion. Having once employed it to help him escape the "spirit of bondage," he later found it contained the

124. Sibbes, *Works*, I, 70; Cotton, *way of Life*, 323.
125. Wigglesworth, *Diary*, 431, 432.

"Best promise" to promote assurance.[126] The verse could serve an individual in various ways.

In drawing meanings from verses that were central to the development of their religious experiences, the laity did not depart from the clergy's hermeneutics. Both ministers and congregants shared certain assumptions about how to interpret the Bible. Holy Scripture is the Word of God, which is "compleate" and "inviolable," inscribed in "a language fit for the Church"; it is eternally true, and therefore defies any historicizing or relativizing analysis. What God said to Moses, Puritans believed, means the same thing to John Cotton, and to Bridget Fiske. Puritans also discarded the multiple senses dear to medieval exegetes; they "must be exploded and rejected," Perkins fumed, "*There is one onely sense*," the literal.[127] The preachers shunned allegory and anagogy, and the laity followed suit; at no point did they depart from the prescribed techniques. In the practical application of biblical texts to their own experiences, however, congregants did innovate to a limited degree. They might prefer a different use than the one most preachers supported, as happened with Is. 1.18, or they might develop one without clerical direction, as some individuals did with Is. 55.1 People did not automatically repeat what they heard; they chose to mention certain verses in their relations, and to explicate them as they did, because those texts had personal relevance. That the significance had usually been propounded by some minister does not detract from the layperson's independent act of choosing the verse, or from the creative process that adapted it to fit the circumstances of one's life. Ministers might hew the stones, but individuals had to sculpt them.

IV

The Puritan laity helped shape their religious experience. Whether listening to sermons, talking with ministers, conversing with their fellows, or reading the Bible, they interpreted everything they took in and applied it as they thought fit. Having said this, the nature of their activity should be put in perspective. Their emendations to the preachers' message were minor changes, personal adjustments to an accepted system of ideas. The discrepancies between sermons and responses occurred because people tried to adapt what they heard to their own situations as well as they could, not because they were

---

126. Fiske, *Notebook*, 10, 100, 30, 37. For a scruple similar to Geere's, see Shepard, *Confessions*, 91–92.

127, Perkins, *Works*, II, 646, 647, 651.

attempting to develop new approaches. The ways in which lay Puritans talked about what they felt did not depart from what the preachers expected.

This agreement can be explained, of course. When Anne Hutchinson dared to formulate an alternative to the prevailing theory of experience, she was banished. Seventeeth-century Massachusetts did not tolerate its deviants lightly, and anyone audacious enough to depart in any significant particular from orthodoxy risked following her, Roger Williams, Samuel Gorton, and assorted Quakers into exile. The church admission procedure also acted as a brake on heterodoxy; no one wishing to enter into covenant could afford to question what a congregation determined as the mean. The definition of what constitutes true religious experience, articulated from the pulpit and sanctioned by the community at large, blanketed the possibilities for alternatives. To break out of these constraints required courage, the will to challenge entrenched orthodoxy, and an alternative vision, a combination most people, not merely the Puritan masses, do not possess. But there is an additional explanation for the laity's reluctance to move beyond these limits—satisfaction with the *status quo*. Perhaps it is easier to measure discontent than its opposite. The Hutchinsons occupy a great deal of space in the Massachusetts records, while the anonymous individuals who joined churches in Watertown, Dedham, Roxbury and Dorchester take up very little, but surely their silent continuance in seeking regenerative experience and joining churches counts for something. As long as preachers spoke to the spiritual needs of most inhabitants and expounded a meaningful soteriology, individuals were not likely to challenge the system.[128] The laity accepted the ministry's gift because they had no incentive to exchange it.

128. At the end of a brilliant exploration of the linguistic issues severing Anne Hutchinson from the New England elders ("The Antinomian Language Controversy," *Harvard Theological Review*, 69 [1976], 345–67), Patricia Caldwell wonders how satisfactory part of that soteriology was. Noting that the circumstances of the soul's union with Christ was a subject so "inexpressible" (364) that Puritans seldom treated it (cf. *infra*, 208–9), she argues that those who did papered over their inadequate presentations with formulae that the conversion relations reproduced. The articulation of banality prompted Hutchinson's radical elaboration of the Spirit's witness, and it offered the less daring a prescription that "squeeze[d] the individual, the empirical, the spontaneous into a Procrustean bed of formulaic language and weaken[ed] the vital connections between outer words and inner meaning" (365). Parroting an ersatz description, the relations compromised experience; in the standardization of language, their connections with the wellsprings of faith were lost. Caldwell's thesis helps explain Hutchinson's attempt to enhance the vocabulary of grace, but other points are debatable: is it necessarily true, for instance, that a ritualized phraseology cannot gratify the longing for an authentic portrayal of the encounter with the Godhead? Caldwell, herself, has subsequently concluded that the relations were not mere formulae; see *Puritan Conversion Narrative*, 39, n. 66, and *passim*, for her further thoughts on the problem of expressiveness.

7

Tales of Grace

In language as unadorned as their meetinghouses, Puritans told their tales of grace. The ministry might decorate a doctrine with stylish flourishes or exhort a congregation with imaginative imagery, but few laypeople did or could emulate their artistry. The relations feature a limited range of expression and the repeated use of stock phrases to display common incidents; time and again, confessors declared how their sins "troubled" them, how they "resolved" to "seek" Him, how He "encouraged" or "stayed" them during some trial. The narratives give little notice to the technical vocabulary of divinity; for instance, candidates seldom spoke of making a covenant. The infrequent use of this term does not derive from pastors' heterodoxy, for both Thomas Shepard and John Fiske, the two ministers most involved with the applicants here examined, taught the covenant in orthodox ways; nor does it demonstrate an uninformed audience, for several people noted that they had heard sermons on the subject.[1] The absence of *covenant* conforms to the laity's practice of describing what happened to them without giving it a name. They rarely referred to faith, although its permutations form the substance of

---

1. On Fiske's and Shepard's orthodoxy, see their catechisms: Shepard, *Short Catechism*, 15–16; Fiske, *The Watering of the Olive Plant in Christs Garden* (Cambridge, Mass., 1657), 11–12. *Watering* is Fiske's only surviving doctrinal work: some poetry also remains. For reports of preaching on the covenant, Wigglesworth, *Diary*, 443; Shepard, *Confessions*, 74, 105, 177, 199–200, 201.

every account. The inelegance and unsophistication of the confessions in no way imply, however, that they lack either fervor or understanding; they convey the spirituality of conversion with rude intensity, and though less abstract than formal theology, they are no less pointed. The dictions of sermons and relations are the polished and unpolished sides of one coin.[2] The same holds true for their contents. Accounts of actual experience depart from the carefully conceived canons of the doctors. Some items are overemphasized, others left out, and the operations of the *ordo salutis* blur together or are indistinctly defined. The narratives are imprecise versions of the ministry's ideal, discrepant because translating constructs into reality always mars the perfection of vision. The laity did adhere to the models preachers gave them.

A shared style and dogmatic stance cast the relations in a singular mold, and a number of historians have emphasized their stereotypic, formulaic quality.[3] This observation is true to the extent that they are artifacts created in a uniform setting for an identical purpose by people holding mutual ideas, but the obvious similarities should not obscure the variations. Each narrative combines the standard elements of conversion in a unique fashion; each bears the idiosyncratic impress of its author and displays its own personality. They are not rote recitations of some prefabricated scheme, but autobiographies charting the vicissitudes of people's lives.[4] Members of the same family, they mix consanguineous with personal traits, a heredity which would be best displayed by an analytical cubism that could show full-front likenesses of the entire clan simultaneously with individual profiles. Print being a linear medium, this chapter presents sequential portraits; the first section re-creates a composite confession, the second discusses themes common to many of the pieces, and the third reviews four accounts in depth. Combined, these studies reveal the range and limits of Puritan religious experience.

I

Conversion begins with the soul's initial conviction of sin, an event that usually took place before an individual reached twenty-five. Anne Fiske

2. Cf. David D. Hall, "The World of Print and Collective Mentality in Seventeenth-Century New England," in John Higham and Paul K. Conkin, eds., *New Directions in American Intellectual History* (Baltimore, 1979), 175; George Selement, "The Meeting of Elite and Popular Minds at Cambridge, New England, 1638–1645." *William and Mary Quarterly*, 3d ser., 41 (1984), 32–48; *idem*, *Keepers of the Vineyard: The Puritan Ministry and Collective Culture in Colonial New England* (Lanham, Md., 1984).

3. Pope, "Introduction" to Fiske, *Notebook*, xvi; Morgan, *Visible Saints*, 91; Cross, "Role of Unregenerate," 152; *supra*, 200, n. 128.

4. Another statement of this view is Watkins, *Puritan Experience*, 37–49, 55–56.

discovered her "misery" at the tender age of twelve, Thomas Hincksman was "seized" by the Lord when he was about fourteen, and Sarah Fiske first took note of her sins at twenty-two. Henry Dunster was exceptionally precocious (and arrogant) in locating his earliest recognizance of preaching when he was four or five, but he admitted that he had waited another seven years before the Lord gave him "an attentive ear and heart to understand."[5] With a few exceptions like Henry Farwell, whose "first work was more insensible and gradual," Saints remembered a specific incident that had ushered in God's saving work.[6] Whether they had been complacent, sincerely convinced of their own rectitude, or carnally unconcerned with grace, something arrested their attention and forced them to reconsider their ways. Comparing herself to others and finding her condition "very good, being civil," Martha Collins felt "no necessity" to change it until she realized that merely a "paper wall" separated her from hell, which "somewhat affected" her heart. George Willows carried on "in a civil course a long time," but having broken the Sabbath and then hearing a sermon denouncing that sin, he "saw nothing but hell due to him."[7] Virtually half of the extant conversion relations credit ministers with instigating preparation, a percentage consistent with Puritans' recognition of preaching as the primary means of grace, but introspection, divine inspiration, and the promptings of other people also made unregenerates aware of their sin.[8] Ruminating on Christ's judgment led Mary Griswald to "some sad thoughts of that condition"; the Lord convinced Frances Usher that she had "done nothing else but dishonor Him"; and a sister's speech led Elizabeth Luxford to conclude that her conversation was "condemned." Convicted of some special sin or, like John Stedman, confronted with the "woeful estate of men," sinners discovered that transgression placed them in mortal danger.[9]

Not everyone immediately welcomed or sustained this revelation. Wondering what would be the result of many continued iniquities if just one

5. Fiske, *Notebook*, 6, 146, 42–43; Shepard, *Confessions*, 161. It is impossible to determine the ages at which most of the confessors studied here gave their relations and when they began their conversions, but the suggestion of John Demos, *A Little Commonwealth: Family Life in Plymouth Colony* (New York, 1970), 146, that many Puritans experienced conversion "well before puberty" is unfounded; see also Moran, "Religious Renewal," 247, n. 29. A reasonable generalization would put the onset of conversion in the period from ages 10–25 (Selement, "Means of Grace," 90), a longer time than envisaged in Natalie Davis's *en passant* remark ("Some Tasks," 325) limiting it to the teen years.

6. Fiske, *Notebook*, 145.

7. Shepard, *Confessions*, 130, 43.

8. The first conviction of five of the 78 people studied is unclear, either because the narrative does not permit a precise determination, or because it is fragmentary and its opening segment has been lost. Of the remaining 73, 35 (48%) involve a minister, 14 (19%) the Lord, 12 (16%) the individual, and 11 (15%) other people. One (1%) mentions the influence of both Bible and friends.

9. Shepard, *Confessions*, 187, 182, 39, 73.

sufficed to separate a person from Christ, Richard Cutter was "affected much for the present but not much." John Furnell's appreciation of his unregenerate nature "presently died" and he went on "in the same [dead] frame." For most, however, the sudden sense of sin prompted a thoroughgoing assessment of their relationship to the Lord. Concluding she could "do nothing else but sin against God," Frances Usher understood that He "would cut me off." Apprised by a Hugh Peter sermon that he had not yet undergone preparation by the Law, the younger William Ames "was miserable and thus I was enlightened."[10] Ames's "enlightenment" points to the didactic function that preparation served. Comprehending the full extent of one's sinfulness, Puritans thought, required a reorientation to the world and a re-education in its mysteries. An individual awakened to humanity's guilt under Adam has to learn more about sin and grace, a need enunciated by Tryphean Geere, who, after "discovering the fearful state of unbelievers" during a sermon, asked her father "what faith was."[11] Divine illumination comes about through repeated encounters with the Word and meditations upon its significance; the process is one of continual inquiry rather than instantaneous insight. Edward Hall profited from listening to a succession of preachers and pondering some biblical texts. First awakened to his "undone condition" by Jose Glover, then spurred by a passage from the Synoptics to return himself to that pastor's charge after he had left Glover's ministry, Hall eventually "saw more evil in himself" through the agency of Thomas Jenner. Later, Thomas Shepard preaching from John 3.3 "concerning the new birth" furthered Hall's instruction, for "by this text he saw himself no new creature but only a mended man." Joan Moore walked a similar path. Through a series of sermons she conceived that she was "carnal" and not subject to God's will, that her natural corruption served to "condemn" her forever, and that she was empty and poor in spirit.[12]

Apprehending transgressions exposed one's culpability. Lectured by John Rogers of Dedham that he should "slay his dearest sins," William Andrews "knew I was guilty of some sins and hence it did lay hold on me." Disobedience to God's commands rendered sinners subject to His retributive anger, and, having been brought to acknowledge their liability for sin, numerous confessors noticed the Lord's ire directed at them. John Sill saw himself "lying under the wrath due to such," while his wife Joanna perceived "nothing but death and wrath." God levelled His anger at Roger Haynes through the person of Thomas Hooker, who sounded out "most terrible expressions of wrath" as, in the cadences of Mark 9, he warned offenders that "they should

---

10. *Ibid.*, 179, 204, 182–83, 210.

11. Fiske, *Notebook*, 9.

12. Shepard, *Confessions*, 33–34, 134.

go where the worm never dies out."[13] Divine rage called forth a variety of affections, with fear and sadness among the most common. Robert Daniel lay "under a spirit of bondage and fear of God's wrath," while thinking about her condition made Hannah Brewer "saddened and sick."[14] In some people fright and dolor merged: Alice Stedman and Jane Winship each complained of "sad fears." Discouraged, stunned and mournful, Puritans might feel, with Ann Errington, that a text had "struck" their hearts like "an arrow."[15]

Conviction could extend for quite some time, six or seven years in the case of Elizabeth Cutter, "many years" in that of Robert Daniel.[16] However, not even people so ready to bear the Lord's anger had to submit to unremitting terrors. God stands with the Elect throughout their trials, upholding them despite their anguish and mitigating their severest despair. "Christ will not 'break the bruised reed,'" Sibbes reminded, and, expanding the point, counseled, "Let this stay us when we feel ourselves bruised." Carrying the now archaic sense of 'to sustain' or 'to comfort', to "stay oneself" meant to resist despair.[17] Mary Parish was "stayed" when thoughts of the Lord's willingness to cleanse her overrode reflections on her own obstinacy, and protracted use of means "did stay" Golden Moore, keeping him from his former ways. During preparation an individual could expect to alternate between depression and refreshment, a process illustrated in the narrative of Richard Eccles. "[A]ffected" first by a sermon, then again by reading devotional and doctrinal tracts, he reformed, "which did stay me and so I rested." As his life wore on, Eccles came to see "more of my condition," which touched off another cycle of fear and revival. Distressed by his estate, admitting the necessity of "better means to bring my soul to God," and laboring in a "perplexed condition," Eccles established himself under a convenable preacher, by one of whose sermons he had "some hopes the Lord might in time bring me to the knowledge of Himself."[18] A pattern of pervasive anguish tempered by spells of relief characterized incipient Saints' awareness of their sins.

Contrition was salutary only insofar as it forced individuals to grapple with their inherent corruption, for awareness of particular sins was supposed to occasion an encounter with one's innate disfigurement. Confessors lent their voices to the anthem of human depravity. Upon hearing Robert Jenison preach, Ann Errington reported, "I saw my heart had been so vile," a sentiment echoed by a number of her peers. No one recounted the efficacy of

---

13. *Ibid.*, 112, 45, 50, 166.
14. *Ibid.*, 60, 141.
15. *Ibid.*, 102, 148, 184. Alice was John's wife (*ibid.*, 102).
16. *Ibid.*, 144, 60.
17. Sibbes, *Works*, I, 45, 46; *OED*, s.v. "stay," verb 2, def. 1b.
18. Shepard, *Confessions*, 137, 123, 115–16.

the Law's preparatory function more succinctly than did Dunster: "the more I did strive to keep the law, the more vile I felt myself."[19] Some Saints appear to have come by their consciousness of corruption quickly or without much ado, but most reached that point after increasing acquaintance with other transgressions. After one sermon had opened to Brother Jackson's maid that she was "one of [the] world," a second exposed her Sabbath-breaking. "I remembered this sin," she recalled, and, as the sermon progressed, "I saw that sin and so saw my original corruption." John Stansby led a merry course, "rejoicing when I could make others drink and sin," but having been "greatly affected" from time to time even though he valued his "lusts and haunts" more dearly "than God and Christ and mercy and heaven," he came to recognize his "hellish, devilish nature opposite to God and goodness." Such insight elicited the wish to rectify one's estate. People like Martha Collins who saw their "original corruption and miserable condition" responded by "hungering after means which were most searching."[20] Seeking to alleviate the sense of sinfulness, Saints prayed, attended sermons, and attempted to live godly lives, but in their haste to turn to God they usually overlooked a fundamental problem with their activity. What happened to Mary Norton was paradigmatic. Feeling herself "lost and condemned," she "set upon reformation with what she could do in her own strength," until disabused of her efforts by Hugh Peter. The works of the Devil, Peter said, were "first, self principles; secondly, secrecy;" and Mary realized that she had "settled on self principles."[21] The damage to the faculties brought about by Adam's sins doomed any reliance on human efforts unaided by grace to achieve salvation. Corruption must frustrate the best intentions, a truth Puritans learned from Paul and relived over and over. Though he attended sermons, feared the divine wrath, sought God for mercy and abjured his Sabbath-breaking, Robert Daniel "found my will exceeding contrary to the will of God, though I have seen more of my own enmity than before." Mary Wigglesworth read Ro. 3.12 (which she quoted as "there is none that do good they are together become unprofitable") and concluded herself "one unprofitable that could do nothing that was good."[22] The deepening sense of humanity's flawed nature reveals the fact of one's inadequacy. Over against God, the rightful judge, dispenser of mercy, and source of all strength, lies the helpless human being.

The humbled readily admitted their debility. John Jones resolved to "manifest my desires" for grace by attending on means although he entertained "no hope of helping myself out of my condition." A willingness to turn

---

19. *Ibid.*, 185, 162.
20. *Ibid.*, 119, 86, 131.
21. Fiske, *Notebook*, 52. Mary was George Norton's wife.
22. Shepard, *Confessions*, 61; Wigglesworth, *Diary*, 443.

from sin mixed in Bridget Fiske with "great fear and doubting considering her own inability to turn." "The minister showed God would work a new heart," Christopher Cane's relation tersely records, "I saw I was unable."[23] Some narratives omit statements of incapacity, but not one even hints that one's closing with God had benefitted from one's own merit or strength. Other renunciations of self-dependence paralleled the expressions of weakness. Saints submitted to the equity of God's judgment, however damning. Having performed duties without faith, Alice Stedman admitted that "the Lord might justly deprive me and ever withdraw Himself"; John Stansby allowed that, given his profligacy, "just it [would have] been with God to give me up."[24] Unwilling to defend themselves, the godly also acquiesced in the total humiliation of their fleshly self-esteem. Meditating on the glories appropriated for those who love God, a status she accounted beyond her potential, Jane Champney conceived that she had never had "such cause to loathe [myself] as then." Having compared "Ephraim's condition" in Jer. 31.18 with his own, Edward Hall likewise despised himself.[25] At the extreme, humiliation generated thoughts of suicide, the ultimate self-degradation.[26] Some people, however, were spared extensive suffering. John Preston maintained that if a man properly convinced of sin "be at his journies end, it is no matter how hee came there," and Nathaniel Sparrowhawk seems to have been one person for whom, in Preston's words, "that turbulent sorrow, that violent disquiet of the mind" did not ensue. Searching for the Lord "in ordinary and extraordinary means," Sparrowhawk had trusted "in his own strength," and some "warnings of heart and convictions under means" had brought him to "look to the Lord," but no terrors or frenzies appear to have rocked his smooth procession to grace. Instead the Lord periodically revealed Himself "in a gracious manner" during meditation. That Nathaniel had been legitimately humbled was manifested when, on a fast day, wanting "to bewail my condition and there entreating reconciliation," he came closer to God than ever before.[27] What counted was his desire to give himself up.

Recognition of their incapacity in the face of corruption led people to appreciate God's majesty. Frustrated by the insufficiency of their own efforts, they magnified the Lord's power, mercy, love, and the freeness of His grace. She would be lost, Alice Stedman thought at one point, if the Lord "came not with an almighty power to believe." Ro. 5.8–10 persuaded Henry Dunster that God has mercy even on such an enemy as he. When Robert Daniel was at

---

23. Shepard, *Confessions*, 200; Fiske, *Notebook*, 30; Shepard, *Confessions*, 59.

24. Shepard, *Confessions*, 105, 86.

25. *Ibid.*, 191, 134. Jane was married to Richard Champney, a ruling elder, *ibid.*, 190.

26. Wigglesworth, *Diary*, 428, 441; Shepard, *Confessions*, 112, and see 168.

27. Preston, *Breast-Plate*, II, 80; Shepard, *Confessions*, 63.

his "lowest, the Lord held forth some testimony of love," and when heavily afflicted in body and spirit, Mary Moulton "discovered the freeness of grace."[28] These remarks declare a realization critical to Saints passing from unregeneracy into redemption: God is nearest when He is farthest, He grants mercy when the unregenerate is most taken down by sin. The dynamic of Puritan conversion depended on the individual's preserving inklings of God's promise and support while giving up "self-principles," juggling encourage- ment and doubt without letting either crash to the ground through presump- tion or despair. The apperception of God's favor even during humiliation sustained a Saint's spirits and promoted the motivation to persevere. God manifested His "great goodness" to Roger Haynes when Haynes was "almost discouraged [but] still waiting upon Him," a "remedy" that "much affected" his spirit as "fresh hopes of mercy were let into my soul." Anne Fiske's decision "to choose by faith in Christ (whereas before she rested on perfor- mances)," happened "partly from [the] necessity of believing from God's com- mand to believe, partly that He pardons for His own name's sake."[29] This complex of submission and desire propelled Saints to seek God. "I could not but wonder at the freeness of God's grace which did much break my heart," Joan Moore declared, "so I resolved to turn from my sin to the Lord." Moore's statement discloses the activist logic that lies at the heart of Puritan religious experience. Submission engenders the possibility of liberation, for only through conceding the full weight of her insufficiency could Joan make what for her was the free choice to close with God. Reconciliation with one's depravity releases the person from the responsibilities of self-reliance and frees one to pursue the strength of an omnipotent deity. Encouraged by God to "run after Him," John Stansby "went with boldness to [the] throne of grace and was an earnest suitor for pardon and power from Christ."[30]

For some, a discernible event marked their crossing over the great divide between nature and grace. The Lord "came in much" to Alice Stedman as she listened to a sermon, and in similar circumstances her husband realized that God had pardoned him. For others, the moment passed indistinctly amidst the struggles of life's routines, its occurrence registered either by later signs of regeneration or by a mere suspicion of grace. Tryphean Geere was made regenerate at some unmentioned instant between the time she "Desired to know how to come to Christ," and the time she gained the assurance that "the Lord helps not to give over." Hesitantly, William Manning supposed he had "some faith but yet [there was] faintness."[31] The incertitude that could sur-

---

28. Shepard, *Confessions*, 105, 163, 61; Fiske, *Notebook*, 9.

29. Shepard, *Confessions*, 169; Fiske, *Notebook*, 6.

30. Shepard, *Confessions*, 134, 87.

31. *Ibid.*, 105, 74; Fiske, *Notebook*, 9–10; Shepard, *Confessions*, 96. The printed version reads "fainted."

round the happenstance of faith's implantation was symptomatic of a cultu-
rally ingrained inhibition against an iconography of union with God. The
absence of stained glass in the meetinghouse manifested outwardly the plain-
ness of the Puritans' inner world. Refusing to set up what they considered
idols in the church, they removed plastic representations of God from their
minds. Uninfluenced either by the rich imagery of union available within the
Christian tradition, and untouched by the visions of the Old Testament
prophets, Puritans described vocation abstractly. Elizabeth Hincksman "became in some measure persuaded that God was her God," the Lord let
Elizabeth Luxford "feel His love," and Ann Errington "saw [her] heart
changed."[32] Union was perceived not through a grandiose revelation of God
on high, but rather, befitting the Puritan preoccupation with the minutiae of
the self, signified by changes in the whole man. In addition, it was sometimes
celebrated with godly affections. Sarah Fiske loved Christ "might[ily]" when
she received him, while Robert Holmes "melted and I had joy." God blessed
William Andrews with "such a measure of comfort that I could not contain."
Loving God while simultaneously grieving for sin produced in Jane Holmes
the kind of "unnatural" mingling of affections that John Cotton could have
anticipated.[33] A few people closed with God more intensely, exhibiting elements of the mystical piety that surfaced in such Puritans as Sibbes, Preston,
and Francis Rous.[34] The Lord touched Nathaniel Sparrowhawk with "abundance of sweetness of Himself, which rejoicing made me to break out weeping," and He filled Joan Moore's soul "with glorious apprehensions of
Himself."[35] Underlying these several descriptions of union is an impression of
passivity that counterpoises the activism normally so prominent in the relations. Inclusion into Christ's body happens to someone; despite the necessity
for human effort in the process, it ultimately occurs through the operations of
a higher power. Thomas Hincksman "was drawn" to Christ, and Bridget
Fiske "was caused" to lay hold of him, locutions that convey the sense of a
superior force moving the soul to God.[36] Saints described themselves as
alternately passive and active in vocation, dual modes of experience that

---

32. Fiske, *Notebook*, 149; Shepard, *Confessions*, 41, 185. For another view of the Puritan
attitude towards image-making, see Lynn Haims, "The Face of God: Puritan Iconography in
Early American Poetry, Sermons, and Tombstone Carving," *Early American Literature*, 14
(1979), 15–41.

33. Fiske, *Notebook*, 44; Shepard, *Confessions*, 143, 113, 80. Cf. Cotton, *Christ the Fountaine*, 110–24.

34. Wakefield, *Puritan Devotion*, 101–8; *idem*, "Mysticism and Its Puritan Types," *London
Quarterly and Holborn Review*, 191 (1966), 34–45; Geoffrey S. Nuttall, "Puritan and Quaker
Mysticism," *Theology*, 78 (1975), 518–31; Jerald C. Brauer, "Puritan Mysticism and the
Development of Liberalism," *Church History*, 19 (1950), 151–70.

35. Shepard, *Confessions*, 63, 135.

36. Fiske, *Notebook*, 147, 30.

parallel calling's dogmatic division into receiving the habit of faith and closing with Christ in faith's act.

Once in the state of grace, the Elect take up the battle with corruption at a new level. Enervated but not destroyed, the flesh continues to distract them, turning the sweet taste of union bitter. Mary Norton "gave her consent" to the promise of salvation in 2 Cor. 6.2 "and was full of joy &c. Yet afterward she came to question whether this indeed was the time." John Stedman accepted God's pardon only to have "many fears and doubts about my estate" follow hard upon his sense of grace. A single event might shake a person's tranquillity. Martha Collins "blessed [the] Lord that followed me," but when a sermon convinced her that she had committed "the unpardonable sin"—apostasy, for which no forgiveness is possible—she presumed that "surely now [the] gate is shut for me." More diffuse presentiments of unease could also lead to this conclusion. Having enjoyed extraordinary comforts, William Andrews began to doubt whether they were "right" and, like Collins, feared he had sinned unpardonably.[37] Andrews went on to test himself for hypocrisy, a concern that agitated professed Saints as well as individuals who had not yet received grace. Quite some time after he had "evidence" that his nature had "changed," John Stansby rated himself "as devilish a hypocrite as ever lived." Questions about one's estate, which during preparation served to crush self-righteousness, opened for regenerates into reaffirmations of *agape*. Nathaniel Eaton fretted that God had a "controversy" with him until He "cleared [H]is love to me to give me greater experience of it." Similarly, the Lord declared His love to Bridget Fiske when she was "full of fears and dwelling oft about her condition."[38] Saints relived preparation's cycle of despondence and relief, but with a difference; where unregenerates, directed to use every possible means to gain faith, have nevertheless to trust solely in God's sovereign mercy, Saints have within them a spiritual principle that enables them to cooperate with grace in combating the flesh. To be sure, godly self-reliance could edge over into presumption; Mary Norton trusted the means too much, forgetting that "rest came when depending on God only &c."[39] Nevertheless, the Saints do enjoy a capacity to obey the commands. The conversion narratives testify indirectly to church members' sense of power, for the plaints of helplessness that predominate in the narrations of preparation subside once vocation has been described. In a few cases, an individual proclaimed that sense of power, naming its holy source. "I know there can be no living union without daily command to walking with [God and] living to [H]im," John Collins exclaimed, adding, "I know I can't do so

---

37. *Ibid.*, 52; Shepard, *Confessions*, 74, 131–32, 113.

38. Shepard, *Confessions*, 113, 87, 88, 57; Fiske, *Notebook*, 30.

39. Fiske, *Notebook*, 52.

in and of myself but in and by the strength of the Lord Jesus." Thoughts of the Lord's infinite love made "sutch an impreshon" on John Dane that "I thout I could doe anie thing for [G]od." The most striking statement comes from an anonymous man. Asked by the Cambridge church what course he took "When you find your heart dead [,]" he answered, "Why I go to God in prayer and entreat [H]im to take away that dead heart of mine." Queried further if he thought it was in his power to obtain it, he answered in the affirmative.[40]

Every Saint anticipated establishing a sense of assurance, the knowledge that one has irrevocably received faith and salvation, a token of God's "love in Christ." Several sources combined to ground the Elect's confidence in the Lord's abiding *agape*. John Rogers of Watertown trusted to God's all-sufficiency held forth in Gen. 17.1, and Tryphean Geere to the everlasting covenant proclaimed in Jer. 31.31–33. When asked after his relation about his ground for assurance, Nicholas Wyeth replied "Because love began," a phrase that seems to root his belief in the very experience of being loved.[41] Regenerates reached assurance through a variety of means. Wyeth claimed to discern it in his love of the Saints and desire to join them, while Robert Daniel achieved it through mourning, not only because he deserved God's wrath, "but because of my sins to sin against such a God." Sarah Fiske alleged evidence from the Holy Spirit, citing Ro. 8.16 ("The Spirit itself beareth witness with our spirit, that we are the children of God"), a scripture that enjoyed ministerial sanction for this purpose.[42] The perception that one has been unalterably chosen fluctuated and usually did not commence immediately upon vocation. Younger people, still close to the shock of their first conversion and little tutored in the ways of grace, were not expected to enjoy the assurance they might come to in time, and it is not surprising that John Collins, who probably was not more than twenty when he gave his relation, acknowledged that "I can't or dare not say" that he enjoyed assurance of faith.[43] Age and experience, however, did not guarantee certainty. A number of years elapsed between Nathaniel Sparrowhawk's effectual calling and his relation to Shepard's flock, yet he regretted that "the assurance of [the] Lord's love I have not found." The perception of His immutable grace rose and fell with the currents of one's behavior. Cognizant for a while of God's fixed love for him, Francis Moore lost sight of it when he backslid into "loose

40. Wigglesworth, *Diary*, 432; John Dane, "A Declaration of Remarkabell Provedenses in the Corse of My Lyfe," *New England Historical Genealogical Register*, 8 (1854), 155–56; Wigglesworth, *Diary*, 440.

41. Fiske, *Notebook*, 43, 100, 10; Shepard, *Confessions*, 196.

42. Shepard, *Confessions*, 196, 61; Fiske, *Notebook*, 44. Cf. Ames, *Marrow*, I.xxx.15.

43. Wigglesworth, *Diary*, 432. For John's age, see Sibley, *Biographical Sketches*, I, 186; *DNB*, IV, 825.

company" and drunkenness, but recovered it when he returned to God, his heart drawn again "because His love was unchangeable." The hallmark of assurance was not unfailingness, for even veteran Saints intermittently lost their confidence, but a sensation, perhaps at times unconscious, that God was with one notwithstanding. Richard Eccles phrased it best: "I saw although my soul did doubt, yet my soul was a ship at anchor."[44] Tossed about by waves of anxiety, Saints could still hold fast to a bedrock of security.

The composite conversion here sketched out resembles in intimate detail the ideal designed by the ministry. There was some heterogeneity in both theory and actuality, of course, but the correspondence is as close as one would expect. However, the relations do evince some subtle shifts in emphasis. For one thing, they dwell more on preparation than on the life of faith. A few relations even appear to stop before the person has achieved union. John Trumbull's narrative ends with the complaint that "I could not tell whether I had seen sin or no," and Edward Hall's concludes with him being "brought nearer to the Lord," although this remark might have signified emergence of faith.[45] There is also less affectivity regarding union than might be anticipated given the preachers' excited re-creations of it. In particular, not many people openly exalted in profound joy or sublime peace. Several possible explanations can be suggested. Perhaps individuals did not experience these affections; perhaps the evidence has disappeared; but perhaps too some Puritans did communicate their affections by encoding signs of them in the proof texts that footnote their lives. What looks superficially to be a simple declaration of events may convey a message of emotion. "[S]eeing one that had that plague, I asked what promise I had to live on and Isaiah 26—stayed on thee," Robert Holmes reported, a statement that mildly alludes to a feeling of encouragement Holmes enjoyed.[46] Is. 26.3 reads "Thou wilt keep *him* in

---

44. Shepard, *Confessions*, 64, 36, 116.

45. *Ibid.*, 109, 34. Selement and Woolley, "Introduction," 23, note that this phenomenon in the Cambridge church suggests a flexible admissions policy, one which accepted people who could not as yet "demonstrate a personal certainty about their salvation." David Kobrin, "The Expansion of the Visible Church in New England, 1629–1650," *Church History*, 36 (1967), 189–209, accounts for it in terms of the church's changing eschatological role. Defined initially by New Englanders as a body of the demonstrably regenerate, it became by the late 1630s an aid to Saints in the initial stages of conversion, accepting applicants who could prove humiliation but not necessarily justification in the expectation that they would come to grace within it. Though its presentation is flawed in many respects, this thesis does explain why congregations would admit people who could not declare their assurance. Ironically, in judging potential members by this criterion, the churches implicitly accepted Hooker's doctrine of saving preparations, which forecasts that those undergoing proper humiliation are the Elect, even while most ministers derogated it. The policy of admitting the well-prepared was established by 1637 (and possibly earlier, the evidence is hazy), for the synod gathered in that year to confute the Antinomian heresies condemned the opinion that assurance was necessarily prerequisite to admission, Hall, *Antinomian Controversy*, 227 (error 31).

46. Shepard, *Confessions*, 143.

perfect peace, *whose* mind *is* stayed *on thee*: because he trusteth in thee," and Holmes may be saying, in verbal shorthand, that he had enjoyed the peace of conscience that surpasses understanding. Whether this kind of communication represents a deliberate attempt to diffuse a statement's emotional impact, adherence to an unspoken canon of public behavior that limited forensic displays, or a form of discourse engaged in by people whose familiarity with the Bible made such messages easily comprehensible is problematic. The social setting of the conversion relations helps account for other peculiarities in the narratives too. Applicants did not present their acts of obedience, evidence of regeneration that friendly testimonies were supposed to provide. In addition, both candidates and congregants may have taken one's own reports of good works as proof of presumption rather than of sanctification, and suspicions of presumption may also help explain why not many people conceded feelings of assurance. Nicholas Wyeth testified to his assurance only when spurred by questions, and he hedged the statement about with qualifications of his "unprofitab[ility]" and "unfit[ness]," yet still someone demanded, "Have you no fears?"[47] But on the whole, when the adjustments to

47. *Ibid.*, 195, 196. It is conceivable that the absence of many professions of assurance reflects congregations composed of youthful members, but the insufficient evidence for making any kind of reasonable calculations concerning the age composition of the sample, plus the impossibility of determining the elapsed time between the supposed experience of union and the giving of the relation, render this hypothesis untestable. It is not likely that assurance was a subject usually reserved for interrogators to broach. Of the ten people who were asked questions that were recorded, only three were directly quizzed about assurance, and two of them had already treated it in their narratives. Caldwell, *Puritan Conversion Narrative*, has offered the most comprehensive explanation. She finds the American conversion narratives more anxiety-ridden and open-ended than their English counterparts, qualities she explains by adverting to the historical context surrounding the narratives' composition: they were wrapped up in the sea change of emigrating to America, the political circumstances of establishing the New England Way, and the attitudes of ministers towards the possibility of expressing one's experience publicly (35). Coming to America was very unsettling, she argues; the muted tones of the New England Saints testify to expectations shattered and visions of godliness smashed. For confessors, America was emphatically not the land of the covenant. Caldwell marshalls some impressive data for this view, although it should be noted that not everyone felt this way. But even if disappointment was a common experience, why should the English Saints, who had recently undergone the trauma of civil war (20), have been so ready to speak of assurance? Why does dislocation in one instance lead to anxiety, and in the other to comfort? Another reason for Americans' *Angst*, she maintains, lay in the relations' ecclesiological function. In New England they became a fixed requirement for entering a church, part of a "national" religious system delegated to secure the state's moral order. In England, they developed free of centralized control, their purpose to offer evangelical encouragement and comfort. And yet, if New Englanders were trying to establish pure churches on which the health of their polity depended, why did they not demand full assurance from church members, so guaranteeing (as much as possible) churches of the pure? More convincing is her argument that confessors responded to differential evaluations regarding the possibility of expressing their faith; where English ministers instilled the confidence to speak, their American counterparts (particularly Shepard) did not. New Englanders' halting speeches about grace betokened their anxiety about the actual process of verbalizing experience (135-62). I

the exigencies of public presentation are allowed for, the relations do follow the preachers' guidelines faithfully. These Saints had listened to their pastors with care.

II

Within the redemptory framework common to all the accounts, some special features recur consistently enough to deserve attention. One is how the narratives incorporate the contemporary world into their stories of the eternal battle that flesh and spirit wage in the soul's timeless terrain. Stuart England impinges upon this realm in three outstanding ways. The first is through disease. In pre-industrial conditions of poor health care and low life-expectancy, sickness often portended death, and its onset inspired tender consciences to meditate on their precarious state—at least while the malady lasted. Joseph Champney introduced his relation by conceding that "Some-

---

would note a second way in which ministers affected the relations. Although Caldwell downplays the significance of theology in setting standards for them (34, 144), it cannot be entirely discounted; the English relations issued from a different doctrinal milieu. The willing expressiveness of English confessors was a sign of the heightened emotionality typical among radical sectarians, whose ideas of conversion differed from those of more orthodox Puritans. Sectarians permitted dreams and revelations to evidence the Spirit's works, and they esteemed the regenerate's struggle with the flesh less highly than did the mainstream, who tolerated a greater degree of anxiety in Saints after grace. The most extreme "prophets" claimed absolute assurance and publicized their certainty to certify the authority of their personal visions (Watkins, *Puritan Experience*, 157–58). Caldwell draws often on the narratives published by John Rogers of Dublin, an Independent soon to become a Fifth Monarchy Man, who should be classified among the radicals. Rogers accepted—indeed encouraged—dreams and revelations as signs of grace, and his own relation manifests the "extravagant" emotionality and self-assurance characteristic of the sectaries (. . . *Ohel*, 419–39; Watkins, *Puritan Experience*, 93–95). He did not go as far as did the Vulgar Prophets in constituting his church through his own charisma, but he did demand that his candidates have full assurance that they were joining God's people (. . . *Ohel*, 239–53). His personal example was powerful enough that John Taylor, "Some Seventeenth-Century Testimonies," *Transactions of the Congregational Historical Society*, 16 (1949–51), 71–72, has discerned a "Rogers type" of narrative among the Dublin relations. Like some other sectarians, Rogers used the relations for polemical purposes; while the American narratives remained in manuscript until the twentieth century, Rogers's (and the other English examples Caldwell cites) were published in the seventeenth, taking their place in the religious controversies of mid-century. Rogers edited his relations, publishing the best ones and omitting others of "inferior glory" (. . . *Ohel*, 392, 450; cf. Watkins, *Puritan Experience*, 41); one may suspect that he played up those that trumpeted assurance in the strongest terms. In sum, the assurance displayed by the English conversion narratives may be less the product of their "political, ecclesiastical and basic physical" circumstances (35) than of differences in how ministers engaged their congregations affectively and theologically. One might draw the implication from Caldwell's argument that the English conversion relations present the standard from which American examples deviated, but I would suggest that, given the American relations' "fit" with orthodox Puritan theology as it developed from the late sixteenth century, the more assured "English (sectarian) type" evolved as a radical alternative, most notably during the Civil War.

times the Lord has visited me by some *illness* and then I have resolved to seek and follow the Lord[,] but after recovery I have soon forgot my former purposes." John Collins owned up to being similarly fickle. Smitten by smallpox "so strong" that he expected to die and "go to hell[,] remembering how I had backslidden and forgotten God," Collins promised to reform if he recovered, but good health dissolved his good intentions, and his heart became "harder than ever." Since smallpox was one of the most dreaded killers of the era, Jane Holmes's comment that when she "saw others afflicted with pox I thought I wished I were so," registers the depth of her self-disgust at being seduced during her journey to America.[48] Sea-voyages were another hazard, for the frequent threat of sinking provided ample opportunity to face the insecurity of one's estate. During a "sore storm" in which his ship lost its mast, John Trumbull fought off the thought that his Sabbath-breaking condemned him to "die in misery," remembering that "though I was vile yet I did love Sabbaths and saints and so prayed." "When I was at sea the Lord exercised us with storms and then all my sins came to my mind," an anonymous Saint recounted, but in this instance, as with Champney and Collins, God's mercy went initially unappreciated. Having promised to praise the Lord if he survived, this individual soon "hardened my heart from God's fear like Pharoah."[49] English church controversies also figure in the relations. Anglicans permitted recreation on the Sabbath after services, a practice Puritans considered profanatory; Alice Reade, having once succumbed to peer pressure "to see their sports on Lord's day," repented that she should have done evil and grieved her parents. The Church of England prescribed set devotions from the Book of Common Prayer and permitted the reading of homilies in the place of sermons, practices that had "contented" Robert Holmes until he determined upon their sinfulness and "so [was] affected." The Laudian program, which imposed conformity in such matters as kneeling to receive communion, caused Sarah Fiske, who "feared it a way of popery," to flee the country.[50] References in the narratives to plagues, tempests, and an unfavorable religious climate highlighted the providential aspects of one's career by connecting mundane events to the process of salvation, subsuming history to grace's movement in the soul.[51]

48. Wigglesworth, *Diary*, 440, 427; Shepard, *Confessions*, 80; John Duffy, *Epidemics in Colonial America* (Port Washington, N.Y., 1971), 16.

49. Shepard, *Confessions*, 108, 109; Wigglesworth, *Diary*, 437.

50. Fiske, *Notebook*, 8; Shepard, *Confessions*, 142, 143; Fiske, *Notebook*, 43.

51. At the same time, the importance of mundane events should not be overestimated. They usually obtrude only insofar as they bear upon the work of conversion; the inner world, not the outer, interested confessors and their audiences. The relations exclude any event, no matter how personally momentous, that does not figure directly on the progress of salvation, a feature strikingly documented by the absence in Sarah Fiske's account of any reference to the conflict with her husband that so delayed her membership (*supra*, 154–55). See Watkins, *Puritan Experience*, 63–67.

The genius of Puritanism resided by the hearth as well as in the pulpit, and a substantial number of confessors recalled the efforts of their parents to instruct, discipline and comfort them. Nathaniel Eaton began his religious education "from a cradle," and Mary Sparrowhawk's parents "kept her from gross sins." Ashamed of the "woeful deal of sin" in him, Joseph Champney told his father, who encouraged him to continue seeking God.[52] The benefits of such concern did not always appear in future Saints immediately. Richard Cutter "had much opposition of heart against my parents," although, as befitting members of Shepard's church, they had brought him up "in the fear of the Lord." Robert Holmes wilfully disobeyed his parents for over twenty years.[53] In time, of course, Cutter and Holmes did live up to their elders' hopes. Tutelage, example, and concern all contributed to raising a pious child, but in addition to these obvious benefactions, regenerate mothers and fathers might impart a special spiritual confidence. To sooth his "perplexity," Roger Haynes comforted himself with the thought that "I was not so bad because I was under covenant of godly parents." On the other hand, the absence of this persuasion—the result of a "carnal" upbringing—subjected Mary Moulton to repeated fears that her ancestry excluded her from the greater family of God. Once satisfied that He had in fact accepted her, she worried about passing the benefits of the covenant to her own progeny until granted solace from Is. 44.3 (" . . . I will pour my spirit upon the seed, and my blessing upon thine offspring").[54] Godly parents did much to guide their children towards faith, yet Saints credited them with less influence than they did ministers, a valuation explicable in the context of Puritan theology.[55] Unlike preachers, indispensable vehicles of the word, parents had no irreplaceable function. Although they could bring children "externally" into the Covenant of Grace, which in early New England accorded one the privilege of baptism, they could not transmit their regenerate nature;[56] conversely, a person could have carnal parents, like Moulton, and still become a Saint.

The relations uniformly portray Satan as conversion's frustrator, a characterization familiar in Puritan preaching,[57] but they blur their presentation

---

52. Shepard, *Confessions*, 54, 65; Wigglesworth, *Diary*, 442. Mary was Nathaniel Sparrowhawk's wife, Shepard, *Confessions*, 65.

53. Shepard, *Confessions*, 179, 142.

54. *Ibid.*, 167; Fiske, *Notebook*, 9.

55. Parents are mentioned (as both partners in interactions (N=13) and as the subject of remarks) 51 times. Some 32 references call them godly or describe them as acting in a manner that encourages righteousness, 2 call them carnal, and 17 are neutral statements. In addition, one other comment may refer to godly parents, and three more may intend carnal ones.

56. Cf. Thomas Hooker, *The Covenant of Grace Opened* (London, 1649), 20–21; Cotton, *Christ the Fountaine*, 93.

57. Edward R. Trefz, "Satan as the Prince of Evil: The Preaching of New England Puritans," *The Boston Public Library Quarterly*, 7 (1955), 3–22, and "Satan in Puritan Preaching," *ibid.*, 8 (1956), 71–84, 148–57.

of his identity, straining to assimilate contradictory Judeo-Christian traditions. In the Old Testament, the satan (only in 1 Chron. 21.1 does the word indicate a proper name) participates in God's high court as the prosecutor or adversary who verifies human righteousness by inflicting punishment under God's supervision. Influenced by speculations of Jewish apocryphal and apocalyptic literature, the New Testament transformed this figure into a menacing personality operating more or less through his own malice, the "evil one" who seeks to overthrow God and oppress humanity.[58] Elements of the earlier aspect appear in Thomas Hincksman's two uses of the title "the adversary," and in William Ames the Younger's recounting of what happened after he thought himself "enlightened" by a sermon: "Presently the Lord was pleased to let Satan come forth upon me with manifest temptations."[59] In this and other accounts, a now obsolete meaning of "temptation"—'testing,' 'proving'—reinforces the sense of a trial;[60] these temptations are not allurements to sin, but impediments to grace. The concept of the satan as the Lord's tribune who metes out pain and suffering clashes with the idea of Satan the autonomous "Prince of the World" and disposer to sin. Because the former position may imply that God bears responsibility for evil, it could never prevail among Puritans: the Lord's undifferentiated goodness was too obvious, and Satan's malevolence too apparent, for them to imagine otherwise. Hence, they subordinated the first identity within the second. In an anonymous Cambridge Saint's re-creation of a sermon, an unidentified preacher describes Satan "pleading" with Christ against the justice of freeing a sinner who "had been his slave so long"; here Satan no longer argues a judgment for God's purposes, but for his own. This image of the malefic spirit who rules the mundane world to subjugate its inhabitants and who tempts people in order to destroy them dominates the confessions. It surfaces in remarks about natural servility, being "a prisoner and kept by Satan," or "under the lash of Satan's terrors."[61]

Driven by his enmity of God and humanity, the Devil occupies himself by disrupting the person's gracious progress. He attempted to "draw" John Sill's "heart from God," and confronted Jane Holmes so that she "durst not go to prayer." While assaulting unregenerates in hope of forestalling their apprehension of faith, he discomfited regenerates too, exercising Elizabeth Hincksman with "strong temptations" and in John Stedman raising "many fears and

58. Jeffrey Burton Russell, *The Devil: Perceptions of Evil from Antiquity to Primitive Christianity* (Ithaca, 1977), 174–249; John L. McKenzie, S. J., *Dictionary of the Bible* (New York, 1965), 774–75.

59. Fiske, *Notebook*, 146, 147; Shepard, *Confessions*, 210.

60. *OED*, s.v. "temptation," def. 2.

61. Shepard, *Confessions*, 207, 200; Wigglesworth, *Diary*, 428.

doubts about my estate."[62] Satan's favorite ploy was to insinuate the worst about a person's condition, countering every hint of grace with supposed evidence to the contrary. When John Trumbull wanted to make peace with the Lord, Satan accused him of having "no interest in Christ" because he had broken the Sabbath. John Fessenden joyfully anticipated humbling himself for God until the Devil cast "filthy notions into my heart and so I thought I had committed the unpardonable sin."[63] Satan beclouds the mind and un-nerves the heart instead of exciting one's desires; rather than enticing to sin, he dissuades from grace. The Devil did not promise Saints a reward for their apostasizing; Faust could never comprehend how they nearly betrayed them-selves for so little. All the Elect had to rebuff him to win their freedom, and yet, the relations feature him less than one might expect; roughly three-quarters of them do not mention him.[64] A significant but not the essential cause of malfeasance, he occupies a secondary role in promoting the Saints' derelictions. Most impulses to sin, the accounts record, proceed spontane-ously from the individual; the majority of references to distracting tempta-tions omit Satan's name. Corrupt human nature impedes the work of faith quite sufficiently on its own. The real adversary is not Satan, but oneself.

The nature of the sins confessed reveals yet again the concern with which Saints regarded their separation from God and the carnality that occasioned it. Puritan theology divided all sins since Adam's into either original, "the corruption of my Nature," or actual, the "corruption of my Life."[65] Confes-sors did not always label their misdemeanors—the narratives abound with references to innominate evils—but they did name a variety of actual of-fenses.[66] For purposes of analysis, these particular sins can be classified according to a taxonomy William Perkins devised to aid penitents examining their consciences.[67] Perkins listed nearly 200 sins under the headings of the Decalogue, and although some of the entries appear rather forced—hastiness, for example, breaks the commandment against murder—his catalogue has the virtue of completeness. By their own admission, Saints transgressed against God much more frequently than they did against people:[68]

---

62. Shepard, *Confessions*, 46, 77; Fiske, *Notebook*, 150; Shepard, *Confessions*, 74.

63. Shepard, *Confessions*, 108, 176.

64. He appears in twenty-two of the relations (28%).

65. Fiske, *Watering*, 7; cf. Ames, *Marrow*, I.xiii.1–2, xiv.2; Perkins, *Works*, I, 19–23; Norton, *Orthodox Evangelist*, 142–44.

66. The low ratio of identified sins/relation, less than 1.25/1, suggests that people named only their dearest or direst misdeeds.

67. Perkins, *Works*, I, 459–62.

68. This finding agrees with McGee, *Godly Man*, who shows that Puritans were more concerned with breaches of the First Table, Anglicans with breaches of the Second.

ACTUAL SINS AGAINST THE DECALOGUE MENTIONED BY CONFESSORS		
First Table	I (no other gods)	II (no graven images)	
Sins against God	40	7	
	III (not name in vain)	IV (keep Sabbath)	
	4	16	
Second Table	V (honor parents)	VI (no murder)	VII (no adultery)
Sins against people	8	0	13
	VIII (no theft)	IX (no false witness)	X (no covetousness)
	5	1	1

The totals for actual sins tally only the first time a person denominates a sin. There is no limit to the number of different sins that can be counted for one person under the same category. An individual may have broken the first commandment through rebellion and pride, in which case both instances are counted.

The outstanding fact about this distribution is the number of sins against the first commandment—"Thou shalt have no other gods before me" (Ex. 20.3)—a sum roughly 40 percent of the total and greater than that of the combined sins against the Second Table.[69] This grouping encompasses the widest assortment of stated sins: pride, rebellion, worldliness, disbelief, the unpardonable sin, and others.[70] Few people spoke of defying the prohibition against graven images or took the Lord's name in vain. Sins against the former class include engaging in improper liturgical procedures, a charge that, by the 1630s, might have weighed heavily on consciences forced to follow the Laudian reforms. However, though some voiced their resentment at the changes or expressed their satisfaction at reaching New England, these confessors did not gauge their participation in Anglican rites sinful, reflection, perhaps, of the New English clergy's insistence during the 1630s and 1640s that the Church of England was a true church. The impact of sabbatar-

69. The Reformed Protestant enumeration of the Ten Commandments differs slightly from the Catholic and Lutheran versions and the Jewish version. With respect to the first commandment, the former either add the image prohibition to the decree against having false gods or drop it altogether. Jews account the introduction, "I am the LORD thy God . . . " (Ex. 20.2), the first commandment and combine the injunctions against false gods and graven images into the second. McKenzie, *Dictionary of the Bible*, 186.

70. There is a paradox in including the unpardonable sin, for no one who applied for membership in a congregation could actually have committed it. It is recorded here because candidates who confessed to it thought they had committed it at some point in their lives. The unpardonable sin takes in several of the "Sinnes directly against the Gospel" that Perkins designated in an appendix to his list (*Works*, I, 462), but elsewhere (*ibid.*, 107), he grouped it under the First Table, since its nature "is directed against the very maiestie of God himselfe, and against Christ."

ianism, one of Puritanism's most prominent attitudes, accounts for the numerous admissions of Sabbath-breaking. Only three of the final six commandments seem to have posed any problems of compliance. The injunction against adultery in Perkins's arrangement covered a multitude of evils—sloth, drunkenness, fornication, keeping loose company—and its total may reflect in part the category's expansiveness. No more than three people said that they had committed any one of these sins. The same explanation suffices for theft, under which heading confessors admitted to lying, stealing, overcharging, and performing one's calling unfaithfully. Judging by the above tabulation, Saints had the most difficulties in submitting to divine authority. All sins are sins against God in His law, but those against the first commandment especially degrade His person and sovereignty. In addition, the duty to honor one's parents demands respect for all rulers, linking domestic and public obedience with submission to the divine will. Insurrection against the petty governors of family or state was rebellion against the High Lord Himself. However, the most heavily decried sin was not actual, but habitual; original sin, the fountainhead of iniquity, generated the most comment.[71] We cannot help but err, confessors said; corruption makes a life of wrongdoing inevitable. Many more people called attention to their inherent vileness than to any single actual sin. In theory, conversion was supposed to lay the source of degeneration bare. In practice, it did.

Intimations of incapacity could have promoted lassitude among unregenerates, a result preachers warned against. Although good deeds do not merit faith, they exhorted, sinners must exert themselves to prepare for grace. Such appeals prevailed with successful converts. Telling the junior Ames that Christ would not leave a soul that felt "helpless, heartless and strengthless" encouraged him to seek Christ "in means." Aware of her "original corruption" and frightened by an unnamed "affliction," Brother Jackson's maid "prayed and read and frequented ordinances;" the affliction continuing, she "went to means again."[72] Forebodings of predetermined reprobation posed another threat to godly activity; doubts about election might instigate *anomie*. Some people did worry about their scripted fate, but managed to overcome their anxiety. Samuel Foster resorted to the Bible, which advised him "to make out his calling for this country," John Collins was comforted by God's confiding "that it was my duty to wait patiently on him and hope in his word[,]" and Ames, concluding that foreknowledge of election "was a secret to be left with God[,]" resolved "to attend upon Him in His own

---

71. Thirty-seven people confess their corruption in 45 separate references. The most frequently mentioned sin classified under those committed against the first commandment is pride, with 12.

72. Shepard, *Confessions*, 212, 119–20.

way."[73] With Scripture, support, and a little good sense, the Elect could escape the pitfall of pondering the ineffable, but most of them do not seem even to have stumbled into it. The dread of the unalterable reprobation does not often surface in the relations; far more frequent are assertions of God's mercy and the gratuity of His gifts. Waiting for the Lord to "reveal Himself more sufficiently to me," Joan Moore heard a sermon on Is. 55.1, at which she "could not but wonder at the freeness of God's grace which did much break my heart."[74] Those who became Saints did not readily reduce the doctrine of the decree into determinism; they acknowledged the potentially liberating aspects of the Lord's efficiency while declining to draw out the logical possibility that His elective power could also fix their doom. They maintained that predestination intimates freedom, not thralldom, a posture that encouraged autonomous action.

Conversion, preachers said, accomplishes more than knitting the soul to Christ; it also establishes bonds of affection within the holy community. Several relations pronounce the desire to enter into the company of Saints. Ready to abandon the "bad company" with whom he used to consort, William Andrews expected to benefit from righteous companions and "began to cleave to them." The promise of godly society made people willing to emigrate to America. New England drew Joan Moore "because good people came hither[,]" and John Stansby desired to be "where Christ is feeding of His flock in this place."[75] For some, the region immediately fulfilled its promise. "I did much rejoice to see the place and see the people and hear God's servants," Nicholas Wyeth enthused, and Andrews concurred: "when I saw the people my heart was knit to them much and [I] thought I should be happy if I should be joined and united to them." For Sarah Fiske, the advantages of the church covenant took more time to grasp. Upon arriving she found her heart "full of perturbation and distress," but the cause remained a mystery until she heard George Phillips preach from Heb. 10.25, "Not forsaking the assembling of ourselves together, as the manner of some is; but exhorting one another. . . ." In the context of v. 24 ("let us consider one another to provoke unto love and to good works"), the text calls on Christians to band together for mutual edification. Presumably, the sermon informed Sarah that separation from a church was provoking her distress, and she was encouraged "to join in fellowship."[76] Compelling the formation of holy societies, love for the godly also indicated the presence of grace, both preparatory and saving, in the individual soul. Living under contrition's

73, Fiske, *Notebook*, 89–90; Wigglesworth, *Diary*, 431; Shepard, *Confessions*, 211.

74. Shepard, *Confessions*, 134.

75. *Ibid.*, 94; Fiske, *Notebook*, 30; Shepard, *Confessions*, 87.

76. Shepard, *Confessions*, 194, 113; Fiske, *Notebook*, 44.

terror, Mrs. Russell's maid "loved saints dearly," and though dubious about her fate, "to go back, I would not." From time to time Nathaniel Sparrow-hawk had convictions "to look to the Lord and His people with a loving heart, not only rich but poor also." Henry Farwell recognized "the work of a new creation in him" by, among other signs, his inclination "to love these in whom he saw the image of God according to the scriptures."[77] Through conversion, Saints felt they belonged to the Lord and to each other.

A last common theme, so conspicuous that it has thus far gone unre-marked, makes of the relations a single piece. The discussion of every topic has drawn examples from men and women, a practice that, far from acciden-tal, demonstrates the fundamental sameness of the conversion experience for each sex. There are, of course, some divergences. Men's narratives run longer than do women's, though the reason is not readily apparent.[78] Women men-tion their own children more frequently; more men refer to Satan. Men confessed more often to pride, women to sloth.[79] No man expressed his desire to follow a minister with quite the longing that Jane Holmes did: "my heart was so endeared to that man to live with him and so desired my father to live there and resolved to come away whatever came of me."[80] A suggestion of sexual attraction wafts through this statement, an impression that Jane's later flirtation with a Bible-spouting layman does nothing to dispel. Nevertheless, these differences are minor. The smallness of the sample renders any statisti-cal arguments ludicrous—only nine men and seven women in a sample of 78 people speak of breaking the Sabbath. Holmes's remark may raise suspicions about some of the motives underlying female piety, but it is unique. What does stand out in the relations, unverifiable by computation but evident in reiterated readings of the documents, is the uniformity with which men and women phrased their autobiographies. In one tongue they told of their first conviction, the burgeoning awareness of sin and sinfulness, the descent into despair accompanied by yearnings for Christ, release from spiritual bondage

---

77. Shepard, *Confessions*, 100, 63; Fiske, *Notebook*, 145, 146.

78. The most obvious explanation—that women usually delivered their relations privately—is really no explanation at all: 1) In almost every case it is impossible to determine which relations were privately given. 2) Men also gave private relations—how many is unknown. 3) There is no suggestion by Puritans that women's relations in private were or should have been shorter, and no logical reason why they need have been so.

79. REFERENCES TO ASSORTED TOPICS BY CONFESSORS ACCORDING TO SEX:

	Men	Women	Anonymous
Own children	2	4	0
Satan	14	7	1
Pride	8	3	1
Sloth	0	3	0

80. Shepard, *Confessions*, 77.

into Sainthood and the development of assurance. Women do not vent their affections more copiously, nor do men more regularly restrain themselves. This unity of discourse should come as no surprise given the language in which preachers explicated the *ordo salutis*. In all the expositions of grace, no one distinguished between the Spirit's operations in one sex or the other. The practice of later seventeenth-century ministers, who ascribed identical attributes to the pious of both sexes,[81] traces back to this doctrinal postulate. Theologians assumed that a single dynamic of regeneration governs all conversions, an asseveration confirmed in the testimonies of the Elect. The experience of grace submerges the peculiarities of gender.

III

The best way to appreciate the diapason of Puritan religious experience is to feature some solos. Every relation sounds chords of corruption and grace counterpointed by flourishes of individual style; each account develops the fugue's central theme in a new key while retaining the original melody. To illustrate the range and diversity of Puritan conversions, four narratives, whose length and detail give them a complexity that shorter or more compacted confessions cannot match, have been chosen for intensive analysis. The first belongs to a John Green, whose identity cannot be established with any certainty.[82] One of several contemporaries with that name living in or near Cambridge, he provided little information about himself beyond the record of his spiritual growth and some brief references to being catechised by Shepard and to talking with his parents that suggest he was a young man. Perhaps reflecting John's putative youth and inexperience living the life of faith, his relation is, except at the very end, a ballad of preparation wailed out against a *continuo* struck by Jonathan Mitchel's sermons on Psalm 130. John's first inklings of his unregenerate estate occurred during catechism "concerning the dread and terror of Christ Jesus coming to judgment," which exposed his need for grace and "much broke my heart." Green attributed this awakening to God's work, and his periodic assertions of the Lord's activity magnify His influence more than do many other accounts. Led by God to prayer and reading, John purposed "to seek the Lord and follow after him for mercy." A pointed observation deepened sensitivity to his condition. Noticing

---

81. Margaret W. Masson, "The Typology of the Female as a Model for the Regenerate: Puritan Preaching, 1690-1730," *Signs*, 2 (1976), 304-15; Laurel Thatcher Ulrich, "Vertuous Women Found: New England Ministerial Literature, 1668-1735," *American Quarterly*, 28 (1976), 20-40; Leverenz, *Language*, 2.

82. See Savage, *Genealogical Dictionary*, II, 302-4; Wigglesworth, *Diary*, 433, n. 54.

one John French similarly "in a miserable sickness," Green determined that he too was "a miserable creature liable to God's wrath."[83] Consciousness of both actual and habitual sins opened up the extent of Green's alienation. Pondering his disobedience and Sabbath-breaking, he saw he "was far from God and God far from me," while the lesson of "man's misery by nature," framed by Thomas Shepard in catechism, taught him he was God's enemy.[84] Green had thus already assessed his unregeneracy when Jonathan Mitchel underlined it again in a sermon on Ps. 130.2 "showing the miserable estate of all unpardoned sinners," and Green surmised that "I was one of those whose iniquity God would mark if I did not repent." As before, God sent John "aseeking after him."[85] Green passed from initial conviction to the apprehension of original sin through an unusual variety of means.

"God let me see much of the wretchedness of my heart," John went on, "Sore and sad temptations I had[,] evil thoughts against the Lord." Temptations, as we have seen, ordinarily disrupt the advance of grace, but in this instance they served first as additional evidence of Green's nature and as harbingers of humiliation. The above sequence of Green's statements apposed evil thoughts to wretchedness; the existence of temptations proves John's wickedness, for only a base heart harbors malefic intent. Moreover, what John denominates a temptation is also his initial statement of self-reproach. The accumulated insight into real and habitual sins has reached the critical mass that fires a chain reaction of humiliation. No one, Green thought, was "so vile," or had a heart "so proud so stubborn so rebellious," and as he considered "all the mercys that I had despised" he conceived it just for God "never to show mercy to me but forever to loath me and abhor me." John balanced at the lip of despair towards which Puritan culture forced all who sought the new birth. To accept one's inadequacy without recalling God's mercy was to tumble into an abyss; to leap it required trusting to God's clemency on account of, not in spite of, one's vileness. How each Saint came to make this vault is as mysterious to us as the workings of the decree were to them; the relations reveal only the purpose to spring. Seeing himself "a Christless undone creature by nature," John jumped—and hurdled the chasm. "I thought," he continued, in a passage similar to one of Alice Reade's, "whither ever I went if I did not go to Christ I should perish," swearing that "if I did perish I would perish seeking of him."[86]

---

83. Wigglesworth, *Diary*, 433. The John French mentioned may have been the one whose father, a resident of Cambridge, was probably made a freeman in 1644 and died in 1646, Savage, *Genealogical Dictionary*, II, 205.

84. Wigglesworth, *Diary*, 433; cf. Shepard, *Short Catechism*, 18–19.

85. Wigglesworth, *Diary*, 433.

86. *Ibid.*, and see Fiske, *Notebook*, 8.

A Saint might have to execute many such leaps. As resolution faded and doubts reappeared, the cycle of self-abnegation and seeking repeated. Though determined to have Christ, John could not shrug off the weight of "all mine usual sins" added to "heart sins" and "temptations," conceiving it "almost impossible that ever I should find favor with the Lord." Yet, as surely as determination invited doubt, doubt elicited support. God led John to Mat. 7.7—"seek and ye shall find[,] knock and it shall be opened[,] ask and it shall be given"—which made him reconsider how "the Lord might be found" and vow "to follow him and never to leave him."[87] Once more, the cycle turned. Pondering his "wickedness" daily, and realizing that "I had no power to think one good thought [or] speak one good word[,]" that without God's free grace he was "undone forever," Green felt his vitality ebb and for the first time took notice of his debility. The frustration of failing to overcome his innate inclination to sin brought him face to face with helplessness. Having previously bemoaned the impossibility of gaining grace, he now blamed his own weakness. In this predicament, he approached his parents for advice. His mother proferred him a double counsel. Pressing the value of denying self-importance, she told him that the viler he was "the more it was to the honor of God's grace to save me and she did encourage me still to seek him." Her recommendation sponsors activity by demeaning the individual and elevating God, a classic example of how Puritanism's central dynamic aimed to transmute impotence into activity. Further, she warned him that "those poor children that did not now learn to know the God of their father" would "see their parents going to heaven but themselves [be] shut out." This advice strengthened John's purpose—"I saw my help must be only in going to the Lord Jesus Christ"—while subverting any feelings of self-confidence he might have entertained, for he found his heart "empty of all good" and temptations "every day more and more prevailing." His father informed him of three things that signify the presence of grace: a desire to have Christ more than anything, a resolution to wait on God "as long as thou live," and a willingness to believe in God's capacity to save him. John located the first two in himself, but practiced self-deprecation obscured the third, for he could "hardly believe God could have any thoughts of mercy" to one who had "despised" it.[88] Rather than trying to smooth preparation over, John's mother and father abetted his debasement. Pious parents could do nothing else.

Their solicitude succeeded. John had heretofore understood the necessity to trust solely in God's mercy, but conversing with his father seems to have

87. Wigglesworth, *Diary*, 433. The quotation scrambles the order of the text's clauses, which read: "Ask, and it shall be given you; seek, and ye shall find; knock, and it shall be opened unto you."

88. *Ibid.*, 433–34.

refocused his concern. Attributing the process to God, Green took note of the "infinite need of [i.e. for] Christ to save me out of that estate," a sentiment he later iterated when asked by an auditor if he had ever recognized "a need of Christ to reconcile you to the father." Yes, John replied, he saw "an infinite [need]."[89] This admission marks the perigee of Green's humiliation, for the reverse of "infinite need" is his absolute incapacity to save himself, and a reference to Ps. 130.1 ("Out of the depths have I cried unto thee, O LORD") signals John's appreciation of his position. Acknowledging his helplessness, he reviewed the reasons for his impotence: subjection to Satan, enmity to God, the inevitability of his perishing, the lack of "power in myself to look up to God for help." Another admission revealed the frustration of the natural man trying to reach God on his own: "When I should have got nearest to God[,] then I thought I was farthest from him," a predicament that worsened "every day."[90]

Puritan theology promised mercy once humiliation had averted the soul from sin, but the psychological precondition for receiving grace entailed working through an insidious paradox. Worthlessness renders one worthy of grace, but among the properly humbled, to think oneself deserving even by virtue of comtemptibleness was to court presumption and thereby show oneself insufficiently prepared. In Green's case, one of Mitchel's sermons followed by some providentially inspired scriptures enabled him to escape from this vicious circle. Preaching on Ps. 130.4, Mitchel proclaimed that God has mercy on those who desire "to love and fear him though [they have] no power in themselves," a dictum that cuts humiliation's bind by excusing the carnal from their inability to achieve salvation while underlining their responsibility to want it. This argument released Green from his dilemma, and his tone shifts immediately from whines of impotence to assertions of a desire to change. "I thought it were my happiness that I might fear and love him and sin no more," John averred, adding that he preferred "to bear any affliction" than to harbor "such thoughts and corruption as then I found and felt." Mitchel argued that the purpose of God's mercy "was that he might be feared," and John was ready to oblige; mourning for sin, longing for Christ, and conceding that only God's "free and abundant grace and mercy" can promote "salvation and hope," he fully expected the "fear of God's wrath" to break in on him. Instead, God brought to mind three pertinent texts that

---

89. *Ibid.*, 434, 436.

90. *Ibid.*, 434. The text is incorrectly cited as Ps. 130.2. The inspiration for the verse is not altogether clear. John claims to have "thought of" it, which sounds like introspection, but he adds that "He showed a soul in the depth of his misery should cry to the Lord." If "He" refers to the Psalmist, then John did provide himself with the reference, but "He" might also refer to Mitchel, whose sequence of sermons on Ps. 130 Green repeatedly refers to, in which case John's rumination was inspired by a sermon.

charged him with tentative hopefulness. Contemplating a passage from the Synoptics—"Christ came not to call [the] righteous but sinners to repentance" (see Mat. 9.13, Mark 2.17, Luke 5.32)—Green allowed that he was a "poor lost undone creature" and yet "Christ might come to call me though [there was] nothing in me" to cause him to. Only a few lines earlier, this self-perception had prompted a lament, but now that Green had accepted Mitchel's logic, carnality became an asset. Hos. 6.3 and Mat. 11.28 further increased his hopes, the latter inspiring the thought that "Only the Lord could pardon my sins[,] subdue my lusts[,] remove my temptations." In the course of these deliberations, Green maneuvered himself into precisely the position that Mitchel dictated. Confessing his desire to repent, he held fast to his inability to do it; remarking, in the words of Mat. 11.28, that he was "in some measure weary and heavy laden," he also maintained that he had no power against the last temptation."[91] Wanting to repent and failing, he became eligible for grace.

A series of events seemed to confirm that God indeed laid Green "at [H]is feet" and conquered "all my sins and temptations." A Mitchel discourse from Ps. 130.5 about souls that choose "to wait on the Lord whether he showed mercy to them or no" led John to believe that he had "had those resolutions[,] seeing all to be vanity in comparison of [H]im." Seeking God daily, he "found power against those temptations" that "assaulted" him and thought it a "mercy that I was at all enabled to know any good thoughts[,] for of myself I was not able."[92] When Mitchel, replying to a question asked while he was preaching,[93] said that finding "power against sin" signifies its pardon, Green detected that power in himself, "which was an encouragement to me yet to seek the Lord and not to leave him." Later in his lectures, Mitchel taught that a person "willing to part with all sin for Christ should have him," and John fancied himself so willing. The narrative swells with the cockiness of a soul confident that its ritual protestations of impotence insure its good fate. In the event, they provoked disaster. John contracted smallpox, but accounted it "nothing in comparison of the sickness of my soul." Subsequently, "more violent temptations" than ever struck, which had the unusually salubrious

---

91. *Ibid.*, 434–35. Mat. 11.28 is incorrectly cited as 11.29. The phrase "weary and heavy laden" conflates GenB and KJV.

92. *Ibid.*, 435.

93. The practice of asking the preacher questions about the sermon existed with clerical sanction during the first few years of settlement, but the ministry withdrew their approval when Antinomians seized upon it to challenge orthodox doctrine. Having submitted to "halfe a dozen Pistols discharged" in their faces by quarrelsome opponents, the ministry decided that "Though a private member might ask a question publicly, after sermon, for information: yet this ought to be very wisely and sparingly done, and that with leave of the elders." Hall, *Antinomian Controversy*, 209; Winthrop, *Journal*, I, 234. Green's relation indicates that the custom did continue under these guidelines.

effect of destroying his confidence in all other objects save Christ, "in whom I see all my hope all my help was." Practiced by now at submitting for mercy, John summoned to mind three more biblical citations, but the narrative fails to credit the Lord with inspiring them. Perhaps an inadvertent oversight or a scribal lapse, this omission may also indicate Green's habituation to the technique of humiliation; the first episode is a divine revelation, the second a human accomplishment. The verses—Is. 41.16, Mat. 5.3, and Is. 55.1—all voice the theme that God receives the needy, and John surmised that "the Lord might help me," although there was "nothing in me" except what might "cause God [to] loathe me."[94] Green had well learned the procedure of metamorphosing humility into expectation.

John's humiliation let him feel "that poorness[,] hunger[, and] emptiness" ministers denominated "spiritual thirst," indication that effectual calling was either imminent or had just occurred. Corruption and temptations lingered to the last, "much hypocrisy" and a mysterious "night *evil*" bothered him, notwithstanding which "the Lord was pleased to bring my heart in some measure to subjection to him that I desired to choose him as my chief good[,] to forsake all other things and have no portion but him alone." Like most descriptions of vocation, this statement does not call attention to itself. No special declaration sets it off from the rest of the narrative, and no clearly definable incident precedes it; like the movements of the Spirit, Green's pronouncement of his union blends with its surroundings. The lack of immediate clerical involvement bothered one listener, who queried if God had offered Christ to Green "in the ministry of his word" and if Green "did ever take him." This question may strike a modern observer as an overly literal insistence on the doctrine that the Spirit operates through the spoken word, for Green mentioned numerous sermons, and he carefully documented his hopes with appropriate biblical texts. His reply was both evasive and politic: "I hope in some measure I have." Characteristically, the depiction of union avoids any imagery, and it describes a two-fold process: God drew Green's heart (implanting the habit of faith) and John chose God (the soul's act of faith). Also characteristic is the understated celebration of grace, here communicated via a commentary on 1 John 3.14: "That hath been much comfort to my spirit[—]here we know we are translated from death to life in that we love the brethren[.]" This citation introduces John's evidence of regeneration: love for the Saints, more appreciation of sin's bitterness "than ever I saw in any connection," more pleasure in the Sabbath (Sabbath-breaking had been one of his particular sins) and ordinances "than ever I found in any sins." Friendly witnesses presumably testified to John's holy carriage, but confessors were generally expected to produce their own evi-

---

94. Wigglesworth, *Diary*, 435, 436. Is. 55.1 is miscited as Is. 65.

dences that regeneration had occurred. Someone demanded more proof of affection for God's people, since "there may be love for by-ends," and John returned, "I love them for that of God which I see in them and do love their company of all the company I can have in this world." This proclamation asserts the social dimension of Green's conversion, for grace incorporated him into the body of those "whom I loved above any in the world for what of God I see in them." A quiet thrill concludes the tale: those things "once bitter were now made most sweet."[95]

Mary Sparrowhawk also recounted little beyond vocation, probably because her calling could not have preceded her relations by any great length of time. Mary and her husband Nathaniel, who was to become one of Shepard's deacons, migrated from Dedham, Essex, to Cambridge by 1636; he joined the church early in 1639 and, since her relation immediately succeeds his in Shepard's book, she undoubtedly entered covenant in the same year. Since her decision to emigrate occupies the initial portion of Mary's narrative, the record of her spiritual progress must cover recent events. At the time of their admission, Nathaniel was in the midst of a career that would earn him substantial landholdings by his death in 1647, and Mary, whose age is unknown, was in the process of bearing at least six children before her demise in 1644, but these circumstances do not demonstrably figure in her autobiography.[96] Unlike John Green's account, which usually advances specific details, Sparrowhawk's often leaves matters indistinct. Her parents "kept her from gross sins," but what they were is uncertain. John remembered that his first conviction occurred during catechism, but Mary recollected only that the "powerful ministry" of John Rogers convinced her of her "miserable" estate. These convictions "did often wear off," but Mary remained restive even when transported "to a place of more ignorance." Under the impress of some unidentified "powerful means," she "had often stirrings," and though claiming to find "no good" in it, "considering that it was the means appointed to go, she went."[97]

Already conflicted about performing her spiritual duties, Mary anguished over the decision to leave England. The prospects of uprooting oneself from familiar surroundings induced in many Puritans a tenacious ambivalence towards emigrating. Mrs. Russell's maid doubted "whether I had a call to come because I was to leave my friends," Joan Moore refused her father's offer to come, "which the Lord hath made sad to me since," and, once under way, William Manning "would, if possible, [have] returned again," for he

---

95. *Ibid.*, 436. The quotation of 1 John 3.14 cites GenB, which uses "translated" where KJV gives "passed."

96. Shepard, *Confessions*, 62, 65.

97. *Ibid.*, 65–66.

thought he "had not done well" to depart.[98] However gloriously inevitable the Puritan exodus may have seemed to later chroniclers, God's guiding hand was not always manifestly evident to those who had had to move; quitting the country raised fears of deserting the godly at home. On first hearing of New England, Mary "thought if any good here it was," but when Nathaniel "resolved to come, she feared if God should not help all would rise to greater condemnation." On the one hand "unwilling to come from this fear of no blessing," she calculated on the other hand that if her "children might get good it would be worth my journey." The quandary was eased by John Wilson, Boston's pastor, who, having returned to settle some legal business, was recruiting people for the colonies. Maybe, he suggested in prayer, " the Lord thou dost deny to do good to till [thou] come thither," which "gave her more cheerfulness of spirit." The prospect of doing God's bidding in America, sanctioned by a minister fresh from there, decided the case, and Mary "came to the ship thinking to get good."[99]

Removing to a godly place did not make Sparrowhawk a Saint. Hoping "to be better here," she became "worse than ever before." Sermons did not help, she "sat like a block under all means," and, concluding that God "had left her to a hard heart," she proposed to move once more.[100] Mary's willingness to resettle suggests that she was trying to transmute spiritual tensions into an affair of geography and to avoid inner tensions by blaming them on external inadequacies. After some time, however, "continuing under means" began to take effect. The Lord exposed her "sad" condition, and she saw herself "far from humiliation." As often happened when unregenerates discovered their sinfulness, Mary hid beneath a mantle of shame: she "could not speak to anybody and thought also that they would not be plain with her." She kept "her condition close" until a preacher pointed out that some people who did so "were in hell lamenting it," whereupon "she resolved to

---

98. *Ibid.*, 100, 134, 97.

99. *Ibid.*, 66. Twice Wilson returned to England, in 1631–32, and 1634–35, Winthrop, *Journal*, I, 60–61, 80, 145, 160, 164; *Winthrop Papers*, III, 175; Mather, *Magnalia*, I, 309–10. Frank E. Bradish, "John Wilson," *Publications of the Bostonian Society*, VI (1910), 30, asserts a third trip, but without documentation. On the first trip, as Mather tells it, Wilson had to convince his own spouse with a technique reminiscent of the one Sparrowhawk described: "His wife remained unperswadable, till upon *prayer* with *fasting* before the Almighty *turner of hearts*, he received an answer, in her becoming willing to accompany him over an *ocean* into a *wilderness.*" Three years later Wilson was back in England to settle his deceased brother's estate, and brought back to America "four ministers and near two hundred passengers, whereof some were persons of considerable quality." This must have been when Mary contacted him, and perhaps the Sparrowhawks were among the group he shepherded to New England.

100. Shepard, *Confessions*, 66. It is unclear if Mary intended to return to England or to remove elsewhere in the colonies.

make her condition known." Conversation, however, did not arrest her decline. Encouraged by someone to persist in using the means, she nonetheless "grew worse and worse," reasoned that "it was in vain" to continue, and "began to neglect [the] Lord in private." Queried by a concerned neighbor a few weeks later, she confessed to not having sought God privately and rededicated herself to the task, but still "continued worse and worse." To this point, Mary's narration has alluded murkily to unlisted means, unspecified states, and undefined sins, but her neighbor comprehended the situation clearly; "wishing her to leave the Lord to His own ways," this person told Sparrowhawk "that it may be the Lord would let her see her blindness and hardness and God that way work [sic] and that she was God's clay." The reference was to Is. 64.8 (" . . . we *are* the clay, and thou [Lord] our potter; and we all *are* the work of thy hand"), a willing admission to God's supreme creative direction in human affairs that Mary was not yet ready to acknowledge. In light of the counsel to leave God to "His own ways," Mary's frustrated commitment to seeking Him in the means appears to disguise a reluctance to be God's malleable stuff. Trying too hard, she was not trying hard enough. She gained some insight into the nature of her problem through a sermon about "the woman that had the bloody issue," a story, recounted in the Synoptics, that concerns a woman whose belief in Jesus was so strong that touching his clothes cured her hemorrhages. Compared with this lady, Mary discerned that she had no heart to "seek after Christ," and "no faith at all."[101]

This sermon profoundly changed Sparrowhawk's conversion. Complaints about growing worse under means died away, and, since "the Lord did incline her heart hereby to seek help in Him," for the first time she asked God directly for aid. Supported by two texts from Hosea, she "pleaded" with him, while Is. 56.8 suggested that the "Lord might help me." Willingness to attend on God more readily brought in its train a more complete delineation of her sinfulness and its cause. Another sermon disclosed the will's "enmity" against God, a fact that "did lie sad upon her," and it exhorted her "to plead with God to subdue her will, which she did, yet saw her rebellion still exceedingly." The nature and source of her obstinacy laid bare, Mary progressed through the several stages of humiliation. She wakened one morning wondering how she could "eat and drink and sleep and [bear having] no part in Christ," but later the resolution that the "Lord is more merciful than I to myself" stayed her. After she reverted to "as bad a condition as ever," three scriptures "brought me in to submit to the Lord." Through Is. 30.7—quoted as "the Egyptians help in vain but thy strength is to sit still"—Mary "saw I had nothing by quarreling but by being contented." Originally a criticism of a

---

101. *Ibid.*, 66–67. For the Gospel story, see Mark 5.25–34, Luke 8.43–48, Mat. 9.20–22.

projected Judean alliance with Egypt undertaken without the Lord's consent, the verse becomes in Mary's interpretation a promise that quiescence to God empowers the will, while struggling against Him enfeebles it. Acceding at last to the message of Is. 64.8, she agreed that "she was the clay and [the] Lord her potter." Is. 30.15 further calmed her, and yielding produced a "contentedness of spirit" even while Mary uncovered "more sin" than before; once decided upon, the cession of her willfulness proceeded smoothly. Sparrowhawk's humiliation took place much more gently than did Green's, with far fewer exclamations of pain and bellowings of vileness. Still, it led to a similar result, for she came to admit "her insufficiency" to look to the Lord and, entreating Him to "enable her," mused that, in texts like Is. 42.14 and 46.12, He would speak of righteousness and redemption "to such a one."[102]

Sparrowhawk achieved the requisite humiliation and appreciation of God's potency. She observed that if she had not closed with Christ, "the fault was in her," that her "strength was Christ," and that her own power was insufficient to take hold of the promise. As with Green, calling came not with a bang, but a whisper, without overt ministerial agency or a specific precipitating incident. After the admission of her insufficiency, the relation continues merely, "and that other Scripture[—]He had laid salvation on Christ [some five different texts are possible references][—]and she thought now she closed." Again, the statement does not call especial attention to itself, and there is no visual imagery. More clipped than Green's, this account does not mention being drawn to or taking hold of God, and the absence of celebratory affections maintains the generally tepid emotional temperature of Mary's narrative. Perhaps the missing joy reflects the subject's uncertainty that vocation had in fact occurred, for the few remaining lines recount her pursuit of assurance. Asked at some point if she had attained it, she answered "no but some hope." Mary turned to preaching for guidance, but it momentarily failed her; she "feared her estate again, hearing nothing for or against her condition." Resorting to the Bible, she "resolved to look out those Scriptures where [the] person of Christ was set forth," a practice that proved more profitable. From John 1.14 (the Word "dwelt among us . . . full of grace and truth") she saw her own emptiness, Christ's fullness, and "such a suitableness between Christ and me." From John 7.37—quoted as "if any thirst let him come to Me and drink"—she inferred that the Lord's call included her, that only He would satisfy her, and that she desired nothing like Him in heaven or earth. A variety of observations might conduce to assurance, and for Mary, the most promising was the disclosure that she possessed the desires of a Saint. The relation ends, "She thought the Lord called her to

102. *Ibid.*, 67–68.

Himself," not the polished assurance of a mature Saint, but an augury of great confidence to come.[103]

Some relations, like Barbara (or Barbary) Cutter's, treat the regenerate life more extensively than do either Green's or Sparrowhawk's; the final two-thirds covers her struggle with doubt after vocation. In this instance, youth did not preclude such an exposition, for although Barbara would live on into the early eighteenth century and die in her eighties, she was approximately eighteen when she joined Shepard's church.[104] Preparation commenced in early adolescence when "The Lord let me see my condition by nature" from a text in Ezekiel, a perception reinforced by witnessing her friends' holiness: "the more she looked on them the more she thought ill of herself." Her family soon emigrated, and she "embraced the motion to New England," although having to endure "many miseries and stumbling blocks at last removed and sad passages by sea." The phrase "stumbling block" (or "stone") rings with biblical allusions (see esp. 1 Cor. 1.23, Ro. 9.32, 33), and later in the relation it appears in an unambiguously religious context, but whether Barbara here attached any theological significance to it or merely remarked on the normal physical perils of transportation is uncertain. Upon arriving, Barbara "saw my condition more miserable than ever," a not uncommon reaction also reported by Golden Moore and Mary Parish, among others.[105] Like Mary Sparrowhawk, Barbara retreated into shame's isolated silence: she "knew not what to do, and spoke to none[,] as knowing none like me." How long this withdrawal lasted is unclear, but Barbara may have remained quite close-mouthed about her estate; the next conversation she reported took place with a brother after her calling, and she completed her preparation, according to her account, privately reacting to a series of sermons. Preaching engineered Cutter's conversion more obviously than it did Green's or Sparrowhawk's, and the remaining discussion of preparation does little more than summarize a few influential sermons. The thread of Barbara's experience must be teased from the contents she recorded and her brief appended comments. By a discourse on 2 Cor. 5.19 that showed the necessity of coming to Christ for him to remove iniquity, she "saw my vileness," which "discouraged" her. Barbara confessed to the taint of original corruption, but did not reveal any actual sins. The narrative next hints obliquely at the process of humiliation.

103. *Ibid.*, 68–69.

104. *Ibid.*, 89.

105. *Ibid.*, 89–90, 123, 136–37. Landing in New England must have been a shock in and of itself. After the trauma of moving and the dangers of crossing, some people must have wondered if the New World had really been worth all the trouble. William Manning reported that Shepard preached from a text "to encourage them that newly came to land, that it may be had that which I expected not." *Ibid.*, 98. See *infra*, 213, n. 47.

She heard that the soul is "not farther off [from God] when stripped of excellencies," and that to accomplish reconciliation it must "not find a reason why [the] Lord should pity it[,] for if so God would unbottom [it]." To hang on the "good pleasure" of the divine will is precious. The narrative mutely passes by the impact of these doctrines, but when Barbara heard a sermon expounding "the excellency of [the] person of Christ," the Lord "much affected" and "broke her heart at those things." Another sermon inventoried the essential preconditions of salvation—Christ had paid the price for the redemption of even the "vilest," satisfying the Father, hence "God and Christ did tender themselves."[106] This sermon reviewed the knowledge that Cutter had been attaining, and, since the end result of Christ's sacrifice is the offer of grace to those who receive him, its inclusion at this moment in the narrative stands for God's call to her at the conclusion of preparation. Through attending upon the Word, she had readied herself for grace.

Before entering the covenant, Barbara had to overcome one last obstacle. Hearing that to sin against the Gospel "stirred up a two fold anger in God," the Lord "inclined my heart to some secret strife and question in secret whether I would go on and anger [the] Lord or no." Barbara feared that she had consciously rejected the Gospel, thus committing the unpardonable sin, and for the first time she expressed the doubt that her vocation was spurious. Nevertheless, she was ready to accept Christ, and she achieved union, unlike Green and Sparrowhawk, through the instrumentality of the spoken word. Grace inhered in a sermon on Phil. 4.19 ("But my God shall supply all your need according to his riches in glory by Christ Jesus"), a verse that, in this context, advertises God's capacity to pardon. Probably—the relation does not so state it—a sense of God's magnanimity dispelled Barbara's doubts: "hearing [the] Lord would supply wants, cleaved to Him, then questioned whether grace or no."[107] Cutter's narrative identifies the moment of vocation as a more distinct instant than do the two previous relations, and displays less passivity; a dramatic, active verb describes her seizing the Godhead. Immediately, the announcement of union is followed by a question that sets out the central issue of regeneration, the "greatest case of conscience"—does one in fact enjoy grace? The as yet incompletely mortified flesh, which induces the godly to behave in ungodly ways, confounds definitive answers. As Barbara found out by a sermon and by "certain notes," Saints "sometimes took Satan's part if found affection and at other times not." The soul, she learned, may become discouraged if it does not apprehend the sensate feelings of

---

106. *Ibid.*, 90.
107. *Ibid.*

faith.[108] Straining to apprehend them, Barbara "found sweetness," but then, for unexplained reasons, "I lost that which I found in the Lord." A sermon declaring that God bears Christ to all inspired "some affection," and a conversation with her elder brother, who advised her to consider the Gospel promises, invigorated "some hopes again." These in turn evaporated and reappeared with rhythmic inevitability. "[S]unk" under temptation, ignorant of what to do, and once more ashamed to talk of her estate, she heard a minister declaim that "when Satan did most assault, Christ preferred it," a doctrine that gave her "some hopes," informing her that the Devil's manipulations manifest the presence of grace in his intended victims. A reference during the exposition to Ps. 140.7 ("O God, the Lord, the strength of my salvation, thou hast covered my head in the day of battle") reassured Barbara that God's power avails to defeat the Dark Lord's wiles.[109]

Yet the cycle of doubt and relief persisted. Informed that faith can exist even if a person perceives nothing but vileness, Cutter "could say nothing but—Lord I am vile"; then a preachment that faith consists in "cleaving [to] God's justice" supported her. Shepard's lectures on the Parable of the Ten Virgins convinced her that her willingness to join with God and her love to Him distinguished her from the unregenerate foolish virgins, and in addition settled the qualm, also entertained by Tryphean Geere, that God's promises did not apply to her unless she was specifically named. Warned not to pursue the Lord "in [her] own strength," and reminded that Christ gave himself to cleanse the unclean, Barbara thought God "stayed her heart, yet lost that." Nathaniel Eaton's "showing what a sin of unbelief, that [God's] mercy and justice, was [sic] questioned," aggravated her paramount worry, which "set sadly on my soul." The force of Eaton's pronouncement shocked Barbara out of her self-imposed silence, "and so [she] had some resolution to speak of what [the] Lord had done." A sermon at Roxbury, which cautioned that "many went on and smother their doubts," reinforced her intention, "and so I discovered my estate to some." This decision to confide in the group, to tighten the covenantal bonds through private confession, marked a change in how Cutter coped with doubt, and it points to the community's importance in fostering conversion. Barbara's confidants told her that it was a mercy the Lord "let me see my unbelief," and she soon "recovered." To this comfort was added a sermon on Mark 16.7 that interpreted the verse's reference to Peter as indicating God's pity on him for holding a faith weaker than that of the

---

108. *Ibid.*, 91. Barbara's problem was a common one, for preachers constantly had to remind the godly that faith can exist even when it is not felt. Cf. Culverwell, *Treatise of Faith*, 17; Hooker, *Sovles Vocation*, 550; Cotton, *way of Life*, 331; Sibbes, *Works*, I, 137.

109. Shepard, *Confessions*, 91.

other disciples. Sympathetic to Peter's infirmity, she "was stayed" and "wished to beware of sin." Two more sermons helped solidify her emerging sense of confidence. Hearing that a want of feeling, adverse providences, and corruption can arouse "spiritual agonies and false fears," she was convinced of her sin, and God "overpowered" her heart. The second piece counseled the soul to wait on Him in the promise, and since its promulgation the Lord "let me see more of Himself." In so doing, God assuaged Barbara's anxieties. By removing the Saints' "lightness and frothiness," He revealed, doubts keep them "from falling," a reformulation that allows one to entertain periodic disbelief without its existence overturning the foundations of assurance. Drawing Cutter's heart "nearer to Himself," the Lord "answered all doubts from Christ."[110]

Cutter's relation breaks off after she allowed that she saw "somewhat more," so whether she sustained her assurance, which would have been quite an achievement at her age, is problematic.[111] William Hamlet, however, appears to have managed this by his mid-twenties. A carpenter, Hamlet had already experienced regeneration before he arrived in New England during the late 1630s.[112] In his exposition of preparation, the prescribed steps fall into order as neatly as do formations on a parade ground, and the crisp logic of their progression marches him quickly and neatly to grace. Raised "ignorantly," William lived in a "profane and wicked" manner until the Lord "brought me under ministry" where, through a sermon, He "convinced me of my actual sins" and "affect[ed] me with my misery." Enlightened to the awfulness of his demeanor, William "left sins and did duties," conceiving, like all natural men, that he "should do well" by performing in his own strength. The preaching of "Adam's sin," with its corollary that habitual corruption negates human efforts, demanded a revision of William's thinking, so he turned to God. First, the Lord "discovered Himself in regard of His attributes" and "how justly He might require of all creatures power to fulfill His law," persuaded Hamlet that He "would not pass by [the] least sin without satisfaction." Enjoined to obey the commandments perfectly but unable to comply, people cannot come to salvation through the Law. Then, "the Lord discovered Christ and satisfaction and His person and offices," propounding that redemption occurs through the salvific efforts of Christ the Mediator, who performs what mortals cannot. The apprehension of mercy in the Redeemer's person "let forth the glory of Christ into my soul and did draw out my affections out in love to Christ." In one of the most impassioned and christocentric evocations of any confessor's effectual calling, William de-

110. *Ibid*, 91–92.
111. *Ibid.*, 92.
112. *Ibid.*, 125.

lighted in Christ's "loveliness," desired him "for Himself," and longed "that He might be united to me and so satisfy for me," the "greatest happiness" Hamlet could conceive. Less effusive than some in lamenting his humiliation, William emphasized the "beauty" and "glory" of the Savior. Unsmitten with "delight in creatures," he was willing to die "so that I might be found in Christ." Where Green spoke of subjecting his heart to God and Sparrowhawk of yielding to the master potter, Hamlet rejoiced in his submission to the Intercessor: "I endeavored to give up myself to Christ and when I sinned that the Lord would look upon me in Christ Jesus."[113]

Signs of grace soon appeared in "mortification," the withering away of the flesh, and other "fruits" of union. Showed by Thomas Goodwin that Saints mourn "for the sins of others to whom we have no relation" whereas hypocrites do not, Hamlet found that when he saw others sin "I could not endure them but annoyed them."[114] Also informed that genuine Saints love their fellows far more than do hypocrites, he "thought the finger of God in [the Elect] drew my heart to them," further declaring that "I have sought the good of God's people when I could not seek my own." In most emphatic terms, Hamlet avowed that vocation cemented his ties with the greater body of the godly and committed him to advance its welfare. Conversion proved itself in a desire to purge society of sin and constitute a godly community. The twin yearnings of instituting proper worship and joining the holy fellowship moved William to emigrate; grieved by the "evil" of the Laudian "ceremonies," beholding the "sweet people that came hither and seeing the sins and sorrows of the land," he "desired to come." Still, the remnants of his evil nature subsisted. Previously, he had been unable to "close" with the full "abundance of grace in Christ," in London he had "labored" against "the sin of unbelief," and now he scrupled the decision to leave, "considering that when I was farthest from God then my heart was scared from coming. But when it was nearest to God then I did desire to come and [was] content to be a servant."[115] William offered no anecdotes about the crossing, but when he debarked, he felt, like Cutter and others, "decayed and gone and so was dejected." New England, however, lived up to his expectations, for the "sweet order and life of the people of God" gladdened him "though it went ill with me." Hamlet's trials after vocation represent a different process from Barbara Cutter's, who suffered recurrent bouts with the same temptation. William turned away from God and then attempted to recover by recapitulating his former actions—by reconverting. Awash "in my own sinkings" he sought

113. *Ibid.*, 125–26.

114. *Ibid.*, 126, 127.

115. *Ibid.*, 126, 127. The phrase "content to be a servant" probably refers to a condition of indentured servitude, although it might have a purely spiritual signification.

God in prayer, but the loss of accustomed "expressions and affections" rendered him "the more vile in my own eyes." Rehumiliated, he heard Bulkeley preach about "Ephraim like an untamed heifer," and "finding that frame of spirit of loathing myself I was cheered." Abandoning himself to God, he was supported. William had to resubmit, but his regenerated spiritual strength permitted him to participate in repentance. Every Sabbath brought answers to one objection or another, and he "thought the Lord could do for me no more and hence studied to believe." Through such diligence and by God's command, "the Lord much filled my heart with much love to him." Wondering at His "patience and goodness," William "gave up my soul to the Lord again."[116]

The flesh returned. Overconfident about his faithfulness—his spirit was lifted "above man and in some things above God"—William "grew frothy and unsavory."[117] At the same time, he suspected that God would "afflict" him, a word that, in such contexts, usually intended a physical chastisement. God did inflict an unnamed punishment, "which was light," but William suspected that if he persisted God "would come out with seven worse plagues." He prayed "that I might be more heavenly in prayer," but again backslid into "my old evil trade of life" despite premonitions about what would ensue. This time retribution took the form of a gunshot wound in the hand, an ill "seven times worse" than the previous one, yet William considered it a blessing. Though "brought very low," he "never had such consolations as then"; acquiescing to divine justice, he "was quieted." Infection set in, raising a fever, and William "thought I should die. Yet I regarded not that[,] commending my soul to Him." In this echo of Christ's last words, Hamlet accepted humiliation as never before, and, as his health improved, so did the spiritual tenor of his life. The vestiges of presumption crushed, he alleged that "I found and do find the Lord helping me to walk more in the sense of my own vileness and I can bear now what I could not bear with." The demise of carnal self-esteem ushered in a renewed life of faith:

> I find myself also helped more in my conversation and watchfulness and finding the spirit of God helping me in my spiritual and temporal calling, what to do in this and that duty and so more love to God's ordinances more in word and more in prayers.

Relinquishing his pride, he gave himself over to God's potency, receiving divine assistance in all his deeds. Since this incident, Hamlet recognized God's presence "in assurance or affliction," and he hoped to maintain the posture of submission that guaranteed his continued obeisance: "I desire to walk under

116. *Ibid.*, 127–28.
117. *Ibid.*, 129, 128.

the feet of God and His people and all men, being more vile than any."[118] Few Puritan utterances can reproduce as succinctly as these last sentences the boulversement of strength and weakness through which conversion resurrected the power of the Saints.

IV

Puritan conversion turned on the question of power. Preachers harped on human inadequacy, rectifiable through grace. The laity decried their impotence and sought to embrace God's might. One interpretation of seventeenth-century New England places this "search for power" at the heart of Puritan culture. Positing a "widespread insecurity extant in Calvinist society," it depicts Puritans "[p]reoccupied with their powerlessness before God, nature, the English authorities, contemporary status arrangements, and the anxieties of life in a New World." This pervasive malaise poisoned relationships between the sexes. Wishing to surmount their weakness, men "tended to exaggerate prevailing notions of male superiority," and exercised their mastery in such unlovely ways as rape and wifebeating. Women attempted to redress the balance by becoming Antinomians or witches.[119] The endemic feeling of helplessness that nagged all members of Puritan society derived from early experiences aggravated by religious dogma. Child-rearing predisposed people "both psychologically and intellectually, to think in terms of their own virtual powerlessness before God and their own sinful nature. . . . a theology of ultimate powerlessness almost certainly had a profound effect on the psychological well-being of individuals." Conversion offered no palliative. Debilitated in youth, boys and girls were not "magnificently transformed by the conversion experience, by the grand feeling of God's grace operating upon their own souls. The manifest tensions and frustrations, agitated by innumerable sermons and by the disquieting complexities of Puritan theology, continued to fester like spiritual sores, defining and constricting the Puritan's inner life."[120] Puritanism destroyed opportunities for individuals to develop autonomy, leaving them psychically crippled and bereft of any systemic mechanism to relieve them of their woes.

This interpretation calls attention to the feelings of helplessness that, as the relations attest, Puritans inevitably confronted, and it appreciates the impact that the idea of human debility had on Puritan society, but it entirely misconstrues the phenomenon's significance. At best a half-truth adverting to

118. *Ibid.*, 128–29.
119. Koehler, *A Search for Power*, 79, 441, 28, 92, 140, 224, 278, 294.
120. *Ibid.*, 15.

a fundamental issue for the culture, the argument ignores theology and devalues the estimation in which conversion was held.[121] Because this thesis includes no systematic treatment of doctrine, it misses how explicitly the preachers established that conversion combats true powerlessness by transferring one's trust from self to God. Letting go of its own abilities, a task accompanied by feelings of profound weakness, the soul attaches itself to a surer source of strength. The confessors who listened to those "innumerable sermons" do not seem to have been bothered by the "disquieting complexities" of dogma. To infer that they were, without citing any evidence, demeans their intelligence by supposing that they could not have comprehended what they heard, and mistakenly locates the source of anxiety in their incomprehension. The relations testify to the laity's ability to understand at least the essential doctrines of their creed (they did, after all, have to make a profession of faith as well), and no one complained of being hindered from grace because he or she could not fathom what a preacher was saying. If Puritanism be blamed for the "tensions and frustrations" that "continued to fester" (and the intense scrutiny to which Saints subjected themselves did occasion them grief), it should also be credited with providing an antidote. The Elect can come to assurance of salvation, preachers said, and put their souls to rest. Doubt is the Devil's plaything, a fruit of sin, but the godly have in them a principle inspirited through faith that can and will prevail. Conversion provides not only a way to overcome one's initial helplessness, but a method for maintaining a sense of capacity during times of discouragement; reconversion reconfirms a regenerate's vitality. The Elect *were* "magnificently transformed," and they said so. After vocation the cries of insufficiency subsided, and when voiced, presumed the strength to correct it. Conversion was a responsive mechanism for instilling a sense of potency in everyone who submitted to God. The search for power ended in the arms of the Lord.

The other issues this interpretation raises lie beyond the scope of this work, but perhaps some brief observations may be allowed. Puritan ideology had elements to assuage as well as to exacerbate the discord between men and women. Conversion integrated both sexes within the bonds of Sainthood, melded by a love that was regeneration's natural outgrowth and in which a number of confessors delighted. At the societal level of human functioning, Puritanism did mete out disparate gender roles and accorded men the scepter of command. But on the psychological level, it offered women equal access to power, their own and God's.[122] The strength energized by conversion did flow

---

121. Menckenism redivivus, *A Search for Power* is as one-sided in its portrayal of Puritans as it accuses them of being.

122. Malmsheimer exaggerates their subordination, "Daughters of Zion," 486: "women were effectively excluded from the priesthood of believers, and in a society which placed so high a

into separate behaviors; what a woman endeavored with her spiritual strength differed from what a man did. How people regarded and used the power so gained in daily life the relations, unfortunately, do not disclose, nor can we know how "productive" and "assured"—in the widest meanings of those words—conversion made Mary Sparrowhawk as opposed to Nathaniel. That Mary's new birth did not give her the vote, like Nathaniel's did, is an important datum about Puritan society; that it did tender her, like him, entree to God's power is no less consequential.

---

value on the religious condition of its members, women were at a psychological disadvantage." Leverenz, *Language*, 140, acknowledges that Puritanism could sponsor assertiveness in women. A very perceptive study of women's roles and the powers that did, and did not, inhere in them is Laurel Thatcher Ulrich, *Good Wives: Image and Reality in the Lives of Women in Northern New England 1650–1750* (New York, 1982).

8

The Application of Conversion

Puritans knelt before God so that they might stand by His strength. They aimed to catch divine power through conversion's willing surrender, transforming helplessness into potency and energizing activity. The process did not end with one's translation into grace. Human corruption assured that Saints would periodically lapse into spiritual torpor, necessitating their rejuvenation by reconversion (or as it was sometimes called, "renewing the covenant"). Repeating the steps of conversion, rehumbling oneself for God, was meant to recapture lost feelings of strength. In times of duress, Saints using this method should be able to summon up the power to persevere. The discussion thus far has presented the preachers' model of conversion and the laity's response but has not considered the issue of whether reconversion did in fact stimulate godly work in the way that ministers supposed. By themselves, the confessions do not yield the answer. Delivered on ceremonialized occasions and designed to project an overview of salvation's course, they are static pictures, unrelated to the bumps and grinds of daily existence, that seldom touch on reconversion. Rarely did confessors speak of recapitulating their original experiences or disclose the occasion that inspired this behavior. However, John Winthrop did. The first governor of Massachusetts Bay was voluble (or self-obsessed) enough to put down some of his most intimate religious musings, among which are numerous mentions of renewing the covenant. Winthrop's private writings allow one to test if reconversion ever did function to invigorate enervated Saints. The impact of Puritan theology on behavior can be established in one instance at least.

This sort of case study always runs the risk that the subject's uniqueness makes him or her unrepresentative of the group and therefore an unsuitable example from which to generalize. Admittedly, Winthrop was exceptional. He is one of only two men in American history to have had a passage from the Gospel of Matthew so closely associated with one of his declarations that the real author's identity has been forgotten.[1] He was arguably the most important person in newly settled Massachusetts, hardly a typical status. But singularity has its assets for an historian; Winthrop's scribbled introspections provide information about his inner life, his eminence has helped ensure that these documents were preserved, and his behavior is easily observable because he was so often in the public arena. These conditions make it possible to relate his thinking to his performance during a critical time in early New England's history. Moreover, John's piety was not singular at all.[2] Like any Puritan yeoman or housewife, he magnified his corruption, strove to overcome the flesh, sought to satisfy God in all things, and alternated between enjoying the comforts of grace and suffering the horrors of sin. Rank separated him from Robert Daniel and Barbara Cutter, but belief did not.

Two principal sources exist for the re-creation of Winthrop's religiosity. The first is his spiritual diary, a series of meditations staggered over twenty years but concentrated primarily during 1611–13 and 1616–18. The diary varies from the format of the relations. An account of a conversion in progress, it is less teleological, conveys the emotions of the moment more excitedly, and recounts certain incidents at length. The second item, his so-called "Christian Experience," is a consideration of his conversion authored at a single sitting years later. A set piece, it orders events as do the relations, but it was intended for his eyes only.[3] Together, these pieces depict Win-

1. The other is Abraham Lincoln. Cf. Mat. 5.14, 12.25.

2. Cf. Morgan's judgment, *Visible Saints*, 71–72, echoed by Daniel Shea, *Spiritual Autobiography in Early America* (Princeton, 1968), 101. William McKinley Runyan, *Life Histories and Psychobiography: Explorations in Theory and Method* (New York, 1982), 121–25, explores the value of case studies.

3. Winthrop, *Life and Letters*, II, 164–65. J. William T. Youngs, Jr., "The Puritan Conversion Experience: Image and Reality," Paper Read at the Annual Meeting of the American Historical Association (1978), 12, 19, 33, n. 57, asserts that the "Christian Experience" is actually Winthrop's relation to the Boston church sponsoring his full membership, but there is no evidence to support this view, and some objections against it. Why would Winthrop, a founder of the congregation in 1630, have to qualify for full membership in 1637? The church records do not show that he entered into covenant at this time; in fact, no one joined it from Jan. 8, 1636/37 until Dec. 30, 1638. It is inconceivable that Winthrop could have made a relation and failed of admission; certainly, his *Journal*, which records many of his private actions and much of public importance in the Boston church, gives no hint of such an action. See Richard D.

throp's developing spirituality, and, when analyzed with reference to their historical context, show how external events triggered the psychological reactions that Winthrop's culture predisposed its members to have. Such an essay closes the gap studies sometimes leave between how people thought and what they did.

I

Surveying his "lewdly disposed" youth from the vantage of godly maturity, John Winthrop remembered entertaining "notions of God" when he was about ten, but his spiritual diary opens nearly a decade later, the child having since assumed the responsibilities of an adult. Sole son of Adam and Anne Browne Winthrop, lord and mistress of Groton Manor, Suffolk, John spent his adolescence routinely enough for the heir of a prospering country gentleman: a few terms at Cambridge, lessons in estate management, betrothal to the daughter of another well-heeled squire. In 1605, at the age of seventeen, he married Mary Forth, of Great Stambridge, Essex; ten months later, with barely legitimate haste, she bore John Jr., future governor of Connecticut.[4] The diary begins the next year,[5] but except for John's attachment to Mary,

---

Pierce, ed., *The Records of the First Church in Boston, 1630–1868*, in *Publications of the Colonial Society of Massachusetts: 39: Collections* (1961), 12, n. 5, 21–22. Youngs also alleges that the "Experience" simplifies and idealizes the account in the spiritual diary, an instance of how the necessity of public conversion relations damaged the "sense of the connection between piety and day-to-day life"; for another assessment, see *infra*, 260–61, 269–70. Winthrop also authored a journal/history, indispensable for revealing his own and the Bay Colony's activities, but it is devoid of introspection. Richard Dunn, "John Winthrop Writes His Journal," *William and Mary Quarterly*, 3d ser., 41 (1984), 185–212, details the circumstances of its composition.

4. *Winthrop Papers*, III, 338; Morgan, *Puritan Dilemma*, 3–7; Richard S. Dunn, *Puritans and Yankees: The Winthrop Dynasty of New England, 1630–1717* (New York, 1971), 4.

5. The two editions of Winthrop's writings disagree about when the diary begins. Winthrop, *Life and Letters*, I, 64, n. 1 claims that John was eighteen years old at the time, which puts the first entry in 1606. The editors of *Winthrop Papers*, I, 161, opt for 1607. The diary is headed with the date "2 Februarij: 1606," but since Winthrop normally employed Old Style, the year could be reckoned as 1606/7 (i.e. 1607). However, this assertion is confounded by a later entry dated April 20, 1606, which might be a mistake for 1607, but might also suggest that the February date is really February 1605/6. In addition, the diary's second entry (undated) includes the phrase "In that weeke that my wife was delivered . . . ," which might refer to the birth of John Jr. on February 12, 1605/6. However, the later year is preferable. In context, the remark about Mary's deliverance more appropriately relates to her recovery from an ague. Moreover, the diary's content favors 1607. Winthrop sometimes noted the health of family members as it affected him, witness the reference to Mary and his later observations of births and providences. It is almost inconceivable that he would not have mentioned feeling disquieted about his wife's sickness when she was about to bear their first child, or relieved when the birth was accomplished. The diary begins in 1607, when John Jr. was one year old, and John nineteen.

the external circumstances of his life do not influence the early narrative; his soul was universe enough to fill the pages of his book. The initial entry announces a pre-eminent concern, "Worldly cares" compounded with "a seacret desire after plesures and itchinge after libertie and unlawfull delightes" that wearied him of good duties, "whence came muche troble and danger." The shattering of his conscience's "perfect peace with God" left him susceptible to Satan's influence and unprepared to cope with "a smale triall," an illness to Mary inflicted by the Lord, "whereuppon I promised to be prepared better." Incapable of prayer and "wholy unable to raise up my selfe," John eventually mustered the wherewithal to confess his sins, "which I did with much comforte, [and] I found mercie and grace to amende." An attempt to salve a conscience made guilty by embracing mundane affairs more enthusiastically than the Lord's work, this episode epitomizes much of what follows, for the world continued to allure him. Stricken with an ague, he indulged in "negligence and idlenesse," which ushered in "many other sinnes as caringe for this worlde etc." Then, while he attended a sermon, a thought of a journey so delighted and distracted him that in a flash—"I knowe not how"—the world "so possessd" him that he could "hardely recover." In the face of recurrent backsliding, renewing the covenant was a means of reasserting one's spiritual purpose, and soon after these lapses, John re-established his pact. The agreement conforms to the standard Puritan type, spelling out mutual conditions grounded in explicit recognition that mortal compliance depends on God's enacting pleasure. Winthrop prayed to reform his sins, which included love of the world, sloth, and unpreparedness to hear sermons; God compacted to give him "a new heart, joy in his spirit, that he would dwell with me, that he would strengthen me against the world, the fleshe, and the Divell, that he would forgive my sinnes and increase my faith." John closed the ceremony by soliciting the Lord's aid in performing his promises, never doubting that God would undertake His pledges.[6]

For reasons indiscernible, Winthrop ceased his jotting at the end of 1607, and resumed it three years later. In the interim, he had fathered two more boys and, having attained his majority, was permitted to officiate at the manorial court for the first time.[7] As duties increased, so did opportunities to displease God and inaugurate the cycle of guilty discomfort, contrition, and repentance. In January 1611, Winthrop passed through this sequence three times in rapid succession. Pursuing "idle and vaine pastymes" unsettled him, but God "drewe me to repentance and showed me sweet mercye." Almost immediately, John's "rebellious wicked hearte" yielded to "the slaverye of sinne," and again God "mette me in his fatherly love and brought me into his

6. *Winthrop Papers*, I, 161–63.
7. *Ibid.*, 97, 178, 103. A daughter, Mary, was alive by 1613, *ibid.*, 173.

favour." Once more, John "lost the former freshnes of my affections," stumbling into idleness and vain habits; perceiving that "God was angry with me[,] I had no harte to any dutye," until, upon reading a passage from Job, "the Lord moved me to come to him againe, so I returned and found favor." These statements all locate the source of John's activity in God; the man desires to repent, but it is the Deity who transforms His anger into love and who moves Winthrop to accomplishment. Disease sometimes led Puritans to reckon with their condition, and during a "sore sickness" God recalled to John's mind "many of my bould runninges out against conscience," which he had previously glossed over and which now precipitated a "searious and speedye turninge to God."[8] Fascination with the self's precious sins can blind a person to others' troubles, but Winthrop was never so self-involved that he lost sight of his fellows' pains, and one night, having "afforded muche comforte" to a "faithfull servant" of Christ, John enjoyed his initial feeling of assurance. In a dream, a most unusual vehicle for grace, he saw himself "with Christ upon earthe," and had his sins pardoned. So "ravished with his love towards me" that he awoke, John "was forced to unmeasurable weepings for a great while." The effects of this extraordinary incident soon faded, however, as delight in some vanity led him "to make shipwracke of a good conscience and the love of my father." Unable to repent and grown "wearye of myself, unprofitable to others," he wondered if he would ever recover his lost estate. From these experiences he concluded that he must avoid grieving the Spirit, that transgression obstructs repentance, and that sin's profit "can never countervaile the damage of it."[9] Illumination about the ways of grace came through reflecting on his misdeeds.

Another of Winthrop's conclusions concerned a familiar temptation, earthly joys that "deminishe the ioye of my salvation."[10] Worldliness remained the greatest enemy to felicity of conscience, a problem he chose to combat by controlling his desires through resolutions "occasioned throughe the ofte experience of my weaknesse in such things." When appetite for a pleasure grew too insistent, he pledged to check it. He gave up tinkering, content "with such things as were lefte by our forefathers." He gave up shooting; it offends people, wastes time, brings no profit, and, besides, John was a terrible marksman. He vowed to cease card-playing and to "represse it" among his servants. Fond of scraping the trencher clean, he promised "not to eate of more th[a]n 2 dishes at any one meale."[11] The climax to resolution-making, though, came in response to God's beneficence. When he was sick,

8. *Ibid.*, 164.
9. *Ibid.*, 166, 167.
10. *Ibid.*, 167.
11. *Ibid.*, 163, 165, 166, 167.

encumbered, and poor, Winthrop noted, "I prayed often to the Lorde for delivrance," and now that God had provided health, freedom, and a "liberall maintenance" by the death of his father-in-law, he was willing "to give myselfe, my life, my witt, my healthe, my wealthe to the service of my God and Saviour." Listing twelve propositions, he committed himself to a quintessentially Puritan regimen: discharging his calling, promoting familial education and devotion, diligently observing the Sabbath.[12] Thus John sought to bank the fires of worldliness by acts of will, disarming conscience with godly comportment, but morality by resolution did not succeed. In a passage that prefaces this section of the diary, he admitted that he had had to repent his "unadvisednesse" in making vows, "consideringe that they have proved snares to my Conscience, and (in others of them) my wretchednesse and sinne in not carefully observing them." Three years of effort culminate in a warning that "Securitie of heart ariseth of over much delighte in the things of the world."[13]

Again the diary breaks off, resuming three years later under unhappy circumstances. Mary Winthrop died in 1615, and within six months John wed Thomasine Clopton, daughter of a neighboring gentry family. Two days after their first anniversary, she expired from the complications of bearing their first child.[14] Possibly desirous of eulogizing her piety, certainly aware of God's providential hand in the event, Winthrop logged the minutiae of her passing in his book and, holding up her death as a mirror to his life, recommenced his ruminations. Thomasine was "never so adicted to any outward thinges" that she could not "bringe hir affections to stoope to Gods will in them," he wrote, whereas he, of course, was always fending off the world's blandishments. The opening sentence of the entry that follows her memorial exhibits a familiar lament, comfort in God and delight in heavenly things broken off by "entertaininge the love of earthly things."[15] Winthrop noted his wife's fortitude in confronting her fate, her exhortations to everyone present "to prepare for death," and he meditated on her example: readiness to die well "is a signe of more strength of faithe, and Christian courage," than is a wish for victory. Tragedy, like illness, called to mind forgotten sins and aggravated a conscience possibly burdened with assumed responsibility for Thomasine's demise or wishing to square accounts before its own extinction. In "everye affliction, especially in this last," Winthrop remembered having stolen "2 small bookes" as a boy and rationalized his guilt by promising himself he would eventually undo the wrong; only now did

12. *Ibid.*, 168.

13. *Ibid.*, 163–64, 169.

14. Winthrop, *Life and Letters*, I, 63, 75, 79, 88, n. 1.

15. *Winthrop Papers*, I, 190–91.

he "make satisfaction which done, I had peace."[16] Introspection alerted him to the dangers of his estate, and it also helped him cope with sorrow; though he had buried a spouse, he could not so easily inter his pain. Her loss "a grievous thinge," he was comforted by God drawing him "from beinge too intentive upon it, by givinge me cause to looke into myselfe."[17] Thomasine's death initiated a fourteen-month span during which John wholeheartedly examined his estate. Judging by the tenor of the entries and his later valuation of this period, it was the most critical time of his religious growth.

Winthrop's central concern was to control worldliness, the chief of his transgressions. "I conclude that I cannot serve 2 masters," he reckoned, "if I love the world, the love of the father can have no abidinge in me." The most tempting mundane pleasures were idleness and gluttony, "the 2 maine pillars of the fleshe." One abetted the other. Overeating made his carnal nature "growe iollye & slouthfull," intent on earthly things; idleness, in turn, brought "shame and guiltinesse." The world disrupted the exercise of John's calling, obstructiveness that particularly bothered him. Reviewing a day "misspent in the service of the worlde" unnerved him: "Disuse in any good thinge causethe the greatest unwillingnesse and unfitnesse[.]"[18] Every good Puritan wanted to perform his or her vocation satisfactorily, but the increasing attention Winthrop paid to the problems of carrying out his calling may also have resulted from the duties he assumed at about this time. Besides the responsibilities of overseeing the care of his children, John by the beginning of 1617 was serving as a Justice of the Peace, and by the end of the year (if not before) he had taken over Groton Manor from his father.[19] God, state and family expected diligence in executing these tasks, and Winthrop discovered an additional reason for throwing himself into his work. "I plainly perceive that when I am not helde under by some affliction," he averred, "then I must make my fleshe doe its full taske in the duties of my callinge, or suche other service wherein it takes no pleasure." Industry in his vocation was a means of subduing the flesh. Beyond this, it comprised part of the Lord's mandate for a godly life, "the only sweet life."[20] Committed to engaging in holy work, Winthrop searched for the requisite strength.

To be productive, John had to master two inveterate foes. The flesh, "most madde after his wonted baits of pleasure," constantly urged him to "lusts and follies." Satan obstructed the course of grace, as he did with all Saints, taking advantage of John's weaknesses by confounding his medita-

16. *Ibid.*, 188, 193.
17. *Ibid.*, 191-92.
18. *Ibid.*, 191, 194, 197, 206.
19. *Ibid.*, 195, 230.
20. *Ibid.*, 206, 200.

tions "and then enticinge me to delight in worldly thoughts."[21] Winthrop's earlier attempts to master these adversaries had involved trusting his own strength; only in the wake of Thomasine's death did he fully come to grips with the reality and the implications of God's omnipotence. Prefacing his description of his wife's passing, he wrote that "God will have mercie on whom he will have mercie, and when and how seems best to his wisdome and will." Nothing occurs without His superintendence, and no good transpires without His involvement: "there was never any holye meditation, prayer, or action that I had a hand in, that received any worthe or furtherance from me or anythinge that was mine." God's sovereignty was the supreme fact of existence, and until he accepted His absolute pre-eminence in enabling human endeavor, John acknowledged, "I could never have true comfort in God or sound peace in mine owne conscience in any the best that I could performe."[22] The admission of God's self-sufficiency precluded humiliation; the Lord "shewed me mine owne nakednesse and unworthinesse, and thereby sett me on woork to follow him unweariably in prayer." The frustration of doing works by one's own means opened up the opportunity of achieving them through God's gracious assistance. "I neither hope nor desire," John came to conclude, "to stand by mine owne strengthe, wisdome etc: but onely by faithe in Christ Jesus[.]" Faith apprehends the power of the Deity and calls for it in prayer: "Lord strengthen mee, O strengthen me my God and father[.]"[23] Winthrop had properly construed an essential lesson of Puritan belief: submission to God prepares one to receive His power.

Submission did not, however, entail passivity; although no merit accrues to human actions, preachers warned, a person must apply oneself for grace. The injunction to perform works that have no salvific efficacy posed a conundrum in practice; at what point does the legitimate effort of an individual acting as an instrumental second cause pass over into effort motivated by specious self-esteem? Sometimes, Winthrop alleged, when "my heart hathe been but weakly prepared to prayer so as I have expected little comfort," God nevertheless "filled me with suche power of faith, sense of his love, etc: as hath made my heart mealt with ioye, etc." Yet at other times, when he had labored "in greater fervency th[a]n ordinary" to strengthen his faith, God loosed on him "rather more doubtings and discouragements, etc." Given this apparent inconsistency, on what behavior could one rely to maintain the sense of power needed to rule the flesh? The answer to the puzzle, John observed, lay in trusting to God's "free love, and not to the power of

21. *Ibid.*, 194, 197.
22. *Ibid.*, 182, 183.
23. *Ibid.*, 192, 194, 195.

selfeworthe of my best prayers."[24] The sense of potency connects to the perception, engineered by faith, that one is loved by God entirely of His own volition. Winthrop revealed his appreciation of *agape* in a meditation occasioned by his perusing some correspondence between him and his first wife, "and beinge thereby affected with the remembrance of that entire and sweet love that had been sometymes between us." As he read over Mary's letters, observing "the scriblinge hande, the meane congruitye, the false orthog[raphy,] and broken sentences," he found himself "not onely acceptinge of them but delighting in them." The experience suggested a divine parallel. If Mary's crabbed efforts could enflame John's affections, would not Christ, "whose love surpassethe knowledge, and is larger than the ocean[,]" accept his poor testimonies of love and duty? The Saviour "lookes not at the forme or phrase" of a work, but at the doer; he accepts even the "weakest services" if offered by "one in whom he delights."[25] Love is blind, and *agape* is blindest of all, ignoring human inadequacy. It relieves Saints of the necessity to perform perfectly; they need only want to do so, and try their best, to be accepted. They may express this wish through "true" and "humble" prayer, which, casting itself onto God's love, "shall never be unregarded."[26]

Through effort compounded with self-denial, Winthrop could bring the flesh to bay. An exemplary instance occurred soon after he claimed that he could "truely loath my former folly in preferringe the love of earthly pleasures before the love of my heavenly father." Before a week had passed, he complained of losing his former affections: "I uphelde the outward dutyes, but the power and life of them was in a manner gone[.]" He prayed, but "could not finde that comfort and feelinge which I had;" he plied his calling, "but not so cheerfully and fruitfully." Struggling to recapture his previous joy, John relapsed into the fallacious practice of trying to please God through his own achievements, yet "the more I prayed and meditated, etc: the worse I grewe." Frustrated by failure, ready to "frett and storme against God" because He did not levy the blessings he expected, Winthrop realized at last that the flesh and Satan had undone him. The world "had stollen away my love from my God," and John himself had turned from trusting the Lord to depending upon "my prayers and outward dutyes, and so not diligently observing my heart, as I should have done." Relinquishing self-reliance provided the remedy. Avowing his "unfaithfullnesse and pride of heart," Winthrop "humbled" himself before God, "and he returned, and accepted me." What Winthrop called "renew[ing] my Covenant of walking with my God," is the epitome of reconversion, the process of recapitulating humilia-

---

24. *Ibid.*, 193.
25. *Ibid.*, 202, 203.
26. *Ibid.*, 193.

tion to reclaim the feeling of grace.[27] Reconversion sustained John's labors in his godly work.

By this time, re-establishing the covenant was not a new technique; we have seen how Winthrop was already practicing it some years earlier. But in the aftermath of Thomasine's death, John displayed a greater promptitude and facility in self-humiliation. He had, it seems, more fully comprehended the significance of the process and could apply it more expeditiously. A Puritan would say that the Spirit had carried the gracious meaning of conversion into his innermost faculties, an assessment with which John probably would have agreed. Just prior to the incident described above, he "sawe playnely" that many Christians live "uncomfortable" lives because their consciences force them to quit some "unlawfull libertie" before they are totally prepared to forsake it, "whereas if we could denye our owne desires and be content to live by faithe in our God, the Christian life would be the only merrye and sweet life of all." Conscience can direct behavior, but it cannot change the heart. For himself, John found "the Godly life to be the only sweet life," and he discovered "a change in my heart and whole man, as apparent as from darknesse to light."[28] These words can be construed as a declaration that he had undergone conversion, and even if John himself did not single out this particular moment as the instant of his effectual calling, it must have happened during these months.[29]

Symptomatic of his translation into the company of the blessed are the expressions of unbounded joy that echo through these passages. After one meditation on the "presence and power of the Holy Ghost" he could express neither the "understandinge which God gave me in this heavenly matter," nor the "ioye that I had in the apprehension thereof." At another time, thoughts of the love between Christ and him "ravished my heart with unspeakable ioye." Winthrop was a passionate man, and contemplation of union with God released the rapture of silent astonishment that Puritan ministers said accompanies the realization that God has saved one's soul. No one could sustain such ecstasy for long. Following the "gleame of any speciall ioye," he observed, succeeds "a storme of dumpishnesse and discomfort" that abolishes the former pleasure. Still, that was to be expected, and from the succession of cheer and gloom, the repetition of strength and weakness, he concluded that "the life which is most exercised with tryals and temptations is the sweetest,

---

27. *Ibid.*, 200, 201. Similarly, God strengthened Richard Rogers in a time of weakness and made him keep his "covenant of wary walking with the Lord" more constantly, Marshall M. Knappen, ed., *Two Elizabethan Puritan Diaries* (Chicago, 1933), 61.

28. *Winthrop Papers*, I, 200, 201.

29. Cf. *Ibid.*, III, 342, where John puts the climax of his "Christian Experience" at "about thirty yeares of age," i.e., 1617–18.

and will prove the safeste." It is better, he thought, "*to arme and withstand them* th[a]n to avoide and shunne them." To overcome the world meant combatting it, relying on God for strength. The final paragraph of this section trumpets the summation of his creed: "Resist the Devill and he will flee from you."[30]

With this climactic pronouncement, Winthrop put the diary away. Two months later, he married Margaret Tyndal, daughter of a recently assassinated knight;[31] their mutual affection, manifested in numerous surviving letters, could only have confirmed John's conclusion that human love does imitate *agape*. John reopened the diary on March 24, 1619 to record the birth of Stephen, their first child, and to thank God for having spared Margaret after a monstrously painful delivery, "above 40 houres in sore travayle, so as it beganne to be doubtful of hir life[.]" He entered a few more remarks during the next two years, but with neither the frequency nor the intensity he exhibited during 1616–18. Some familiar conflicts still appear. Noting that his zeal was cooled, his comfort in heavenly things gone, and his joy in prayer or Sabbath fleeting, he realized that "I had againe embraced this present worlde," and again resolved to "renounce" it. Satan, he reminded himself, discourages the faithful from their duty "by settinge before us great appearances of danger, difficulty, impossibilitie," that vanish when challenged.[32] These latter entries, however, do not display the perfervid entanglement with the flesh that mark earlier sections; less self-involved, Winthrop widened his scope of interest. Two themes, both present before, become more apparent. John noted events *en famille* more readily. On April 7, 1620, Margaret bore Adam, their second son; while she labored, John "humbled my selfe in earnest prayer [as well he might]," and as he arose, "I heard the child crye." Examining Deut. 6.7, "of talkinge with their children etc, about God," he thought about improving familial devotions.[33] He also evinced more interest in God's governance of the greater world, remarking on a special providence he had experienced and pondering the perfect execution of God's decree. One day, while he, his son Henry, and some others were riding in a coach, the horses bolted and dragged it through Boxford until it smashed upon a "caus[ewa]ye right against the Churche," but fortunately "by Gods most mercifull providence we were all safe." Perhaps with this incident in mind, Winthrop contemplated the provenance of miracles. It may seem that providence does not guide things outside "the ordinarye course of nature[,]" but in

30. *Ibid.*, I, 196, 202, 207, 209, 215.

31. *Ibid.*, 218. Sir John Tyndal, Master of Chancery, was shot by a litigant he had ruled against, *ibid.*, 179–80.

32. *Ibid.*, 235, 236.

33. *Ibid.*, 237, 236.

fact the Lord so orders these phenomena "that the course of naturall causes should concurre at the same tyme." God's greater glory appears in the conservation of normal causality and in His efficiency. The death of a wicked man may occur by natural means, but it occurs at God's direction; similarly, the death of the righteous fulfills His intent.[34] Winthrop's thoughts had strayed from his own narrow battle with the flesh to seek the deeper meaning in events.

The reasons for this shift may be guessed at. Winthrop was now a mature adult who had already outlived two wives, fathered six living children, and taken responsibility for running the Manor. He had committed himself wholeheartedly to vanquishing a host of spiritual enemies, and, through grace and perseverance, had learned how to check his recurrent lusts. He had laid the foundations of his piety with care, and he nestled onto the framework with the assurance of one who had stared Satan in the eye and made him blink. Margaret was probably an important influence too; since she shared his Puritanism completely, he may have confided to her thoughts that he formerly whispered to his book. The diary seems to have served its purpose; having witnessed to his conversion, its testimony was no longer needed.[35] After the comment on God's efficiency, only four more notations appear. Two were entered in 1628, by which date Margaret had borne two more sons, Deane and Samuel, and their father had been awarded a job as a common attorney for the Court of Wards and Liveries in London.[36] The first notes familial providences, the escape of Adam, Stephen, and a friend from a wayward arrow shot by their brother Forth, and Deane's fortune to survive pitching backwards "from a high stoole" unscathed. The second elaborates on Winthrop's victory over "the immoderate use of and love of Tobacco," the love towards him manifested by the "earnest prayinge" of many friends while a "hote malignant feaver" threatened his life, the "assurance [God] gave me of my salvation," and the providential timing of his sickness, which began after he had completed his legal business and ended before the following term.[37] No relationship can be demonstrated between these entries and some concurrent circumstances ominous for Winthrop's future. His financial position was deteriorating, sapped by the depression that plagued Suffolk's textile industry, and the elevation of Puritanism's bane, William Laud, as Bishop of London augured religious hardships as well.[38] There is, however, a clear

---

34. *Ibid.*, 237, 238.

35. Cf. Watkins, *Puritan Experience*, 23–24.

36. *Winthrop Papers*, I, 279, 357, n. 37; Winthrop, *Life and Letters*, I, 214–15.

37. *Winthrop Papers*, I, 405, 412–13.

38. *Ibid.*, I, 379; II, 59–61, 67, 126; Morgan, *Puritan Dilemma*, 21; Claire Cross, *Church and People, 1450–1660: The Triumph of the Laity in the English Church* ([London], 1976), 177–78. Laud became Archbishop of Canterbury in 1633.

connection between these trends and the next entry. By the summer of 1629, Winthrop was no longer serving at the Court of Wards, and was considering emigration. On July 28, he met with some members of the Massachusetts Bay Company at the house of Sir Isaac Johnson to discuss the matter.[39] On the way, his horse fell into a bog "so as I was allmost to the waiste in water; but the Lorde preserved me from further danger. Blessed be his name."[40] The next time he logged an entry, he was in New England, burdened with greater cares than soggy trousers.

The spiritual diary demonstrates how totally a Puritan Winthrop was. His constant concern with sin and his compulsion to carry out his calling, his desire to glorify God and his readiness to submit to God's will, sound the same themes as do the conversion relations. The diary is more inwardly centered than the narratives: Winthrop's meditations are almost invariably described as arising from his own thoughts, not from contacts with others. Ministers do not figure often, although they are mentioned; John did note his attendance at a few sermons, and he credited treatises by some leading divines with having helped his sanctity develop.[41] Friends and relatives play only a minor role, though on at least one occasion he and "a Christian friend or 2" conferred, disdaining "doubtfull questions to exercise our witts" in order to conduct "a familiar examination of our owne experiences."[42] Because the diary records the progress of his regeneration as it happened, the process does not break down into neat stages as often happens in the confessions; the general drift is clear enough, but no single incident stands out as unarguably critical. The extended nature of the narrative does make reconversion a more prominent feature than it is in the shorter pieces. Over and over, Winthrop reversed his backsliding by rededicating himself to work through submission. Reconversion became an ingrained habit, a way of revitalizing himself when the flesh's stress became too overbearing. In this respect, too, he was following a puritanical course. The preachers urged Saints to renew their covenants readily and modeled how humiliation revivifies waning strength. Good Puritan that he was, John obeyed their exhortations.

II

In January 1637, Winthrop took some time from his labors as the Deputy Governor of Massachusetts to record some private thoughts. During the past

39. *Winthrop Papers*, II, 94, 99–100, 102–3; Winthrop, *Life and Letters*, I, 304. Whether Winthrop resigned his office or was dismissed is unclear.

40. *Winthrop Papers*, II, 103.

41. Attendance at sermons: *ibid.*, I, 198, 200; mention of treatises: *ibid.*, 164, 169, 199, 211.

42. *Ibid.*, 202.

seven years he had spearheaded the migration to New England, served four consecutive terms as the Bay Colony's first governor, chronicled the growth of the region's fledgling settlements, and promoted his vision of a godly society ruled by the Elect, but he looked past these recent accomplishments to survey the panorama of his conversion. He kept the spiritual diary handy to aid his memory, but the "Christian Experience" is an original effort.[43] It includes reminiscences of childhood that the diary lacks, and it organizes its material more coherently. The finished product offers another rendition of a Saint's fall and rise, commencing with the youngster's groping efforts to appreciate God. Winthrop did not mention having been reared by pious parents, but his father was paying a vicar "for scholinge" when he was seven, and the tutelage made an impression.[44] John portrays himself as a youthful hellion, inclined to "all kind of wickednesse, except swearing and scorning religion, which I had no temptation unto in regard of my education," but he protested too much. This story of a licentious past is rendered improbable by the reference to his respect for sacred belief and by other displays of early religious sentiment. At ten, John prayed to God "in some great frighting or danger." At twelve, he "began to have some more savour of Religion," and fancied he had "more understanding in Divinity th[a]n many of my yeares." These accomplishments went to his head. He was pleased that he had expanded his knowledge of doctrine through ratiocination, that his "naturall reason" restrained him although he was "still very wild, and dissolute," and that he had achieved the facility to write letters "of meer vanity" or "of savory and Godly counsell" as required. When a "lingring feaver" and a bout of homesickness at Cambridge robbed him of his "youthfull joyes," Winthrop recalled, he sought God for consolation, believing He "would welcome any that would come to him, especially such a yongue soule, and so well qualifyed as I took my self to bee."[45] For some time John believed that God's "manifest answer" to his prayers portended His love, and now that he was "affected with my sins," he was "willing to love God, and therefore I thought hee loved me." But lusts returned with health, and though God "preserved" him from some "foule sins," the goal of satisfying his "voluptuous heart" subverted his "good moodes."[46] Already Winthrop was developing a different thematic emphasis than he had in the diary. Pride rather than worldliness was the besetting sin; as a child, John maintained, he was enamored of his accom-

43. Similarities of wording in parallel passages suggest that Winthrop had the spiritual diary in front of him. Cf., for instance, the remarks about the reigns of Solomon and Ahaz (*ibid.*, III, 343 with I, 210), the man awakened from a dream (III, 343 with I, 214), and the weaned child (III, 342 with I, 205).

44. *Ibid.*, I, 58.

45. *Ibid.*, III, 338, 339. The document is also printed in *ibid.*, I, 154–61.

46. *Ibid.*, III, 338–39.

plishments and expected God to love him accordingly. In the "Experience," conversion revolves around this attitude of carnal confidence, natural man's malignant egotism that impedes potency and subverts assurance.

Marriage to Mary Forth brought Winthrop under the ministry of Ezekiel Culverwell, rector of Great Stambridge, a leading Puritan divine, and a "painful" preacher.[47] For the first time the word came "home to my heart with power," after which he "found the like" in other ministries. With the ardor of an adolescent who has found someone to look up to, John "honoured a faythfull minister in my heart and could have kissed his feet"; with the devotion of the newly won over, he developed "an unsatiable thirst after the word of God and could not misse a good sermon."[48] Thanks to Culverwell's impact, no longer could he "dally with Religion." The spiritual diary begins at about this time, its inception confirming Winthrop's boast that he was taking his piety seriously. Its entries attest to what in 1637 he claimed was happening thirty years before. Fitfully, he "began to come under strong exercises of Conscience." The flesh "would not give up her interest," but God stayed with him until he could ask with Paul, "Lord what wilt thou have mee to doe?" Working through Culverwell's sermons, the spirit blew the sparkles of first conviction into the fires of contrition. The flames flared and subsided—his affections were "very vnsetled"—but meanwhile John's knowledge and his "great striving in my heart to draw others to God" earned him a reputation as a spiritual counselor. People approached him to adjudicate cases of conscience, and "If I heard of any that were in trouble of mind I usually went to comfort them[.]" Success "did not a little puffe mee up," he admitted, and he considered entering the ministry until some friends "diverted" him.[49]

Flushed with congratulations, Winthrop slackened the vigilant introspection that could have warned him of pride's takeover. The "generall approbation of good ministers and other Christians, kept mee from makeing any great question of my good Estate." Eventually, shaken by "secrett Corruptions, and some tremblings of heart," he perceived "a great decay in my zeale and love." Suddenly aware that his seeming security rested on the bubbles of worldly fame, he craved the "better assurance" that the Spirit bestows on believers, but he "could not nor durst say that ever I had it." Searching out the reason in the tomes of William Perkins and other Puritan notables, he read that a "reprobate might (in appearance) attaine to as much as I had done." This negative appraisal shocked and saddened him. Like others cowed by their inadequacies, he felt "ashamed to open my case to any minister that knew mee," for fear "it would shame my self and religion also, that such an

47. *Ibid.*, I, 88, n. 34.
48. *Ibid.*, III, 339, 340.
49. *Ibid.*, 339–40.

eminent professour as I was accounted, should discover such Corruptions as I found in my selfe, and had in all this time attained no better evidence of salvation."[50] Suspecting himself of hypocrisy, he flirted with the notion that he had committed the unpardonable sin.[51] Shame and doubt were common reactions in preparation, as was John's intermittent melancholy. Sometimes he felt God sustaining his prayers or his love for the Saints, as admittedly imperfect as that love was, but the sticking-point, he realized, lay with his failure to give himself over totally to Christ. His conceit had wrapped him up. Conversant with the doctrine that Christ justifies freely, having "often urged it upon my owne soul and others," he yet could not "close with Christ to my satisfaction," and though he had tried by argument to "lay hold upon Christ in some promise," he had failed. John comprehended dogma, but he did not apprehend the Messiah: "I have thought I had received some power to apply Christ unto my soule: but it was so doubtfull as I could have little comfort in it, and it soon vanished."[52] He lacked faith that empowers the soul, and his sense of weakness dissipated any hint of assurance.

Preparation proceeded routinely. Unable to attain a "sure and setled peace," he wrapped himself in a legal straightjacket, concluding that his only chance lay in "walking more close with God and more strict observation of all dutyes." Like Paul, he thought to lose his doubts in the indefatigable performance of God's commands, only to find the exercise futile. The Apostle called the Law a "schoolmaster" (Gal. 3.24), and to Puritans it was a pedagogue who wielded the rod; pride must shatter against its inexorable demands. "I was held long under great bondage to the Law," Winthrop said, recalling the quotidian lessons that corroded his self-esteem—"sinne, and humble my self; and sinne, and to humiliation againe; and so day after day." The effort to obey the Law, to fulfill the Covenant of Works, achieved none of his aims; he "neither got strength to my sanctification nor betterd my Evidence [of salvation]." Instead, he determined that he had to give up even lawful recreation "for fear of breaking my peace." This decision, which again induced melancholy, consummated in absurdly logical fashion the attempt to perform by his own power. In theory, the Puritan psychology of work balanced fear of

---

50. *Ibid.*, 340–41.

51. "It was like Hell to mee to think of that in Hebr. 6," he wrote, *ibid.*, 341. The passage referred to is Heb. 6.4–6, which warns that it is "impossible" for those "once enlightened," who have "tasted" of the "heavenly gift" and the "good word of God," to "renew" their repentance should they fall away. Imagining that he resembled those reprobates who Perkins said "may seeme for a time to be planted in the Church," but who "cannot apply" the promise to themselves, John feared that he had blasphemed grace. Perkins cited Heb. 6.4 to support his contention that reprobates may enjoy "*a taste*" of God's mercies, but, unbidden to the feast of grace, "must not eate and feed of them." See *Works*, I, 358.

52. *Winthrop Papers*, III, 341.

God's anger with desire of His love, but in their lives individuals often focused on one affection or the other. John worried about breaking the Law, but he was less exercised by terror of punishment than by his failure to meet his expectations of performance and to gain the security growing out of the feeling that one can indeed obey. His "greatest troubles were not the sense of God's wrath or fear of damnation, but want of assurance of salvation, and want of strength against my Corruptions." The dull, gnawing ache that one has not measured up to a loved authority's standards dominates the first half of the "Experience": "faine would I have been united to Christ but I thought I was not holy enough." John yearned for *agape*, but felt he did not deserve it.[53]

Winthrop's account is a textbook example of humiliation. Repeated failure disabused him of the idea that works conduce to salvation. Grace, he came to see, can be obtained only by submission, by accepting Christ's free mercy. The learning process progressed through "many intermissions," in which the flesh shook off "this yoake of the law" for a time. At other moments, the confidence that God had "given mee a hungring and thirsting soul after Christ" passed into "secret murmurings that all my paines and prayers etc. should prevayle no more," thoughts he "soon rebuked." As a result, John finally began to trust in God's mercy without relying on his own endeavors. Willing to "Justify God," he "was perswaded I should love him though he should cast mee off." This assertion marks a critical juncture in the conversion, for it admits that, before grace, a would-be Saint must come to grips with the possibility of damnation. The doctrine of works avoids raising the tension implicit in this idea; maintaining that merit may accrue to effort, it assuages anxiety by making redemption an ever-present possibility contingent on good performance. To admit the contrary, that salvation depends on events entirely outside one's efforts, is terrifying, but this terror can be subdued by the belief that God holds out redemption to those who will have it. Faith demands the possibility of grace. Conversion is in part the mastery of anxiety induced by the realization that one's fate does lie out of one's hands, prowess facilitated by believing that the existence of grace bodes well for the future. Winthrop had arrived at this understanding, one of Puritanism's most profound insights. During a family devotion, God showed him "the difference between the Covenant of Grace, and the Covenant of workes"; the former "began to take great impression in mee and I thought I had now enough." At last he grasped the distinction between earning salvation and having it granted, and it was "very sweet to mee."[54] As yet, however, he could not say he had actually been regenerated.

53. *Ibid.*, 341–42.
54. *Ibid.*, 341, 342.

Some twelve years had elapsed since Culverwell had bored into his heart; John "was now about 30 yeares of age [c. 1618]," and "the time [had] come that the Lord would reveale Christ." First, however, God had to strike one final blow to sever John's soul from sin, an unnamed "sore affliction" that "laid mee lower in myne owne eyes than at any time before, and shewed mee the emptines of all my guifts and parts, left mee neither power nor will, so as I became as a weaned child." Completely humbled, Winthrop felt himself reduced to the helplessness of an infant. "I knew I was worthy of nothing for I knew I could doe nothing for [Christ] or for my selfe," he recalled, "I could onely mourn, and weep to think of free mercy to such a vile wretch as I was." Degradation could hardly go further, but at the same time, he added, solace mingled with the self-disgust. "I could now no more look at what I had been or what I had done nor bee discontented for want of strength or assurance," for although he had "no power" to apply free grace, "yet I felt comfort in it." The loss of self-sustained power did not, in the end, result in despair, but in relief that the soul had relaxed its grip on an untenable hope. As self-esteem died, grace subvened: "I did not long continue in this estate, but the good spirit of the Lord breathed upon my soule, and said I should live." The throes of the new birth were a supreme delight: "every promise I thought upon held forth Christ unto mee saying I am thy salvation." The effusion of *agape* overwhelmed John, for he was "so ravished with [Christ's] Love, as I desired nothing nor feared any thing, but was filled with joy unspeakable and glorious and with a spirit of Adoption."[55] The allusions to sublime affections scattered in the spiritual diary implode into a single celebration of the love that John had worked for but had now been given free.

The benefits of grace soon multiplied. Previously at odds with God, Winthrop "could now cry[,] my father, with more confidence." Sanctification proceeded as the Spirit "mortifyed" his corruptions and "quickened" the new man. Christ, the object of faith and desire, "would oft tell mee he loved mee," becoming John's constant companion: "If I went abroad hee went with me, when I returned hee came home with mee." Since the Savior attended him everywhere, "I could goe into any company and not lose him: and so sweet was his love to me, as I desired nothing but him in heaven or earth." The bond of union links believers with the Godhead, transforming Christ from an abstract embodiment of grace into a spiritually substantial entity who dispenses *agape*. He does not physically unite with the Saints, but he makes himself forever accessible to them and irradiates their souls with love. Christ the loving companion surceased the loneliness that Winthrop's isolation from the Godhead had engendered. A holy intimate to whom John could turn for

55. *Ibid.*, 342–43.

the power and consolation that the divine bond generates, Jesus accompanied him in all his business. The estate of regeneration brought Winthrop "much spirituall strength" and "comfort in Christ," the two gifts he wanted most.[56]

Commonly, preachers explained, the exhilaration of first conversion crests soon after effectual vocation, and for "divers months" following his transcendent encounter with Christ, Winthrop enjoyed an unaccustomed euphoria. "The world, the flesh, and Satan, were for a time silent," and if "my comfort, and joy slackened awhile, yet my peace continued, and it would returne with advantage." Slowly, ecstasy ebbed. The "Love of Temporall things" would steal John's heart from Christ, who would withdraw his "sweet Countenance." The rifts, however, were always temporary, and easily mended. Some word, affliction, prayer, or meditation reminded Winthrop of his impropriety, and the chastened Saint repented. These falls disturbed him, but conversion had so bound him with Christ that he never despaired of Christ's return. John cared "not so much to get pardon," but " to mourn for my ingratitude towards my God, and his free and rich mercy." A residue of *agape* remained to activate Winthrop in any trial; if one of the "continuall conflicts between the flesh and the spirit" erupted, or if Satan took advantage of "dead heartednesse, and presumptuousnesse," to "wind mee into other sinnes," he could draw sustenance from the security that God loved him. When "put to it by any suddaine danger or fearfull Temptation," the Spirit never failed to comfort and embolden him. Even in the worst times, with John's spirit paling before the onslaughts of the flesh, the Lord "would yet support mee that my fayth hath not fayled utterly."[57] A Saint in stress could draw on inner resources of love and strength provisioned by God through faith. The capacity to rebound from adversity and to challenge one's spiritual foes was conversion's legacy.

The "Christian Experience" tells a story of weakness and doubt transformed by love into resilience, strength, and assurance. In numerous matters Winthrop departs from the perspective he took in the spiritual diary. His involvement with family disappears, unheralded save for a brief mention of the exercise during which he comprehended the difference between the covenants. All reference to his marriages, his children, and Thomasine's death vanish. So does his interest in providence. Free grace occupies his attention; fortuitous escapes from misfortune and ruminations on the character of God's efficiency do not. The narrative builds to a climax, union with Christ, and then winds down; the twenty years since vocation receive less attention than the twenty years preceding. The world, John's nemesis in the diary, plays a much reduced role in the "Experience." There is nothing contradictory in

56. *Ibid.*, 343.
57. *Ibid.*, 343–44.

the two accounts, however, and both adhere to the canons of Puritan confessional literature. Winthrop views his regeneration in complementary ways, the first from the trenches of his war against the world, the second from the perspective of conversion as the turning point of his life. The "Experience" does not raise any issue that was not first introduced in the diary, nor does it re-create John's conversion *de novo*. The adult did not falsify the testimony of his youth. The second document does not distort the past or substitute a forged reality for the one true vision of immediate recollection. In the "Experience" Winthrop was doing something else. The significance of his effort inheres in the circumstances that compelled it.

III

John closed the "Christian Experience" with the date (Jan. 12, 1636/37) and a note, "the 49 yeare of my age just compleat."[58] January 12 was his birthday, a likely occasion to take the measure of one's deeds,[59] but Winthrop probably attached no special meaning to the date. In contrast to his father, who recorded in diaries and almanacs the hour of his son's birth, the annual significance of January 12, and John's exact age at the time of his first marriage, Winthrop seems usually to have ignored the anniversary. He registered his narrow escape from injury in the coach crash without commenting that providence had spared him at the very conclusion of his thirty-third year.[60] Perhaps John meant to call attention to his age, the "middle years" that can prompt an assessment of whether one will have lived a satisfying life. This is the season to make peace with mortality, missed opportunities, and the narrowing options available for redirecting one's

---

58. *Ibid.*, 344.

59. Astonishingly, although scholars have extensively researched people's reactions to holidays and anniversaries of various kinds (especially the death of a family member), the impact of one's birthday has received virtually no attention. There is some fragmentary evidence correlating birthdays with depression and suicide, especially among the elderly, but the phenomenon deserves thoroughgoing investigation. See Michael Alderson, "Relationships between Month of Birth and Month of Death in the Elderly," *British Journal of Preventive and Social Medicine*, 29 (1975), 151–56; B. M. Barraclough and D. M. Shepherd, "Birthday Blues: The Association of Birthday with Self-inflicted Death in the Elderly," *Acta Psychiatrica Scandinavica*, 54 (1976), 146–49; Anthony La Bruzza, "Birthdays, Depression, and the Risk of Suicide," *Journal of Psychiatric Treatment and Evaluation*, 3 (1981), 151–52. For one of Winthrop's contemporaries, taking notice of his birthday seems to have signified a recognition that he had finally reached old age. See John Demos, "Old Age in Early New England," in John Demos and Sarane Spence Bocock, eds., *Turning Points: Historical and Sociological Essays on the Family* (Chicago, 1978), S261.

60. *Winthrop Papers*, I, 5, 175, 215, 89, 237.

course, or to fester with regret and the dread of death.[61] Perhaps, looking over what he once was and pondering who he had come to be, Winthrop did calculate the extent of his fulfillment, but it is hard to imagine him writing the "Experience" animated by a midlife crisis.[62] He did not brood over his fate or moan about his family and work; rather, he triumphantly affirmed his sainthood, by far the most rewarding status he could ever wish to achieve. He treated longstanding issues, not recently activated ones. The "Christian Experience" did help him grapple with purely personal concerns, but they arose as he attempted to cope with affairs of state.[63] In January 1637 he had little inclination to evaluate his own predicament in isolation, for a dispute about God's Kingdom was threatening to divide His colony in Massachusetts. The "Experience" forms part of Winthrop's private response to the menace of Anne Hutchinson.

The Antinomian Controversy, which culminated with Hutchinson's banishment and the rulers of Massachusetts, lay and spiritual, heaving a collective sigh of relief that their newly emergent politico-ecclesiastical system had survived a major challenge, started as a cloud no bigger than a woman's desire to share her insights about grace with the people of Boston.[64] During her first year and a half in New England, Anne seemed like a welcome addition to the ranks of the godly, joining the church, serving as nurse and midwife, and promoting a religious study group for women. The gathering

61. Theodore Lidz, *The Person: His Development Throughout the Life Cycle* (New York, 1968), 457–73; Erik Erikson, *Childhood and Society*, 2d ed., rev. and enlg. (New York, 1963), 268–69.

62. Especially since, according to John Demos, colonial Americans did not even conceive of "midlife" as a separate state in the life cycle, subsuming it into a general standard of adulthood. The span between 40 and 60 did, however, bring with it certain unique expectations. It was normally the apogee of a person's wealth, prestige, and responsibility, and its "key element" was "the exercise of power, the use of fully developed capacity." If Demos is right that early New Englanders looked forward to enjoying their maximum authority during these years, then feelings of helplessness aroused by the frustration of this hope may have weighed especially hard on a 49-year-old man accustomed to ruling whose conventional mastery of himself and his fellows was suddenly restricted. John Putnam Demos, *Entertaining Satan* (New York, 1982), 67, 68.

63. Shea, *Spiritual Autobiography*, 102–4, suggests that a debate with Roger Williams, the former minister at Salem and founder of Providence, Rhode Island, may have contributed to its writing. While corresponding on the issues that had led to Williams's exile, Winthrop impugned his old adversary's spiritual estate. Roger's reply, Shea proposes, may have forced John to question his own.

64. This and the following three paragraphs draw on Charles Francis Adams, *Three Episodes of Massachusetts History*, 2 vols., rev. ed. (New York, 1965 [orig. 1892]), 363–578; Emery Battis, *Saints and Sectaries: Anne Hutchinson and the Antinomian Controversy in the Massachusetts Bay Colony* (Chapel Hill, 1962), *passim*; Gura, *Glimpse of Sion's Glory*, 237–75 and *passim*; Hall, *Antinomian Controversy*, 3–20 and *passim*. Stoever, *'Faire and Easie Way'* is magnificent on the theological issues, though see also Foster, "New England Heresy," 631, n. 16, and 649, n. 55.

proved so popular that a second was instituted to include men, and by 1636, scores of people clustered in her home each week to hear her dissect the latest sermon and to discuss the ways of grace. The spiritual revival that John Cotton roused in 1633 had spent its force, and he welcomed Anne's efforts to rekindle it. Then reports began to circulate that all was not right at the Hutchinson house, that the participants in her meetings rejected fundamental tenets of orthodoxy, and the rumors were well founded. The Hutchinsonians believed, among other things, that only an immediate revelation of the Spirit, not signs of sanctification, can evidence justification, that union is accomplished by merely the passive receiving of Christ, that the believer is justified by the habit of faith alone without the act, and that the Spirit personally dwells within the regenerate. The orthodox positions, they maintained, sully free grace by making salvation conditional on the performance of duties. To hold that humans participate at all in the infusion of grace is to promulgate a Covenant of Works, and, unhappily, as Anne toured the colony sampling sermons, she found that only Cotton was preaching sound doctrine. The rest, including her own pastor, John Wilson, were leading the churches astray by mistakenly promoting salvation through adherence to the moral law, and this made them unfit to dispense the Word. Upsetting the equipoise between grace and works in orthodox Puritanism, the "opinionists" contested the adequacy of virtually every minister in Massachusetts, and the virulence of their assertions threatened to subvert the founders' goal of a harmoniously functioning community united in its pledge to carry out the Lord's design.

Heresy unleashed the dogs of social discord, polarizing the populace. By the fall of 1636 the Hutchinsonian faction, centered in the Boston church, faced a hostile majority in the outlying towns. Almost to a man the ministry fulminated against the doctrines of the "erronists," but their chorus did not include John Cotton, the colony's most eminent theologian, whose thinking was a subject of much interest and dispute. The Hutchinsonians claimed that they believed nothing more than what he taught, though in fact, many of the eighty-two theses collected by a synod the next year showed that at least some of them had advanced to positions far beyond the limits of his speculations. But Cotton did depart from the orthodox synthesis, denying that sanctification offers primary evidence of justification, that assurance may be grounded in conditional promises, and that regeneration is a progressive renewal of the original Adamic perfection. His precise concurrence with the dissenters' tenets was not easily demonstrable, for his hairline distinctions were at times so refined that they were exceedingly difficult to comprehend. The elders of the Massachusetts churches wanted to determine precisely where he stood, for it was crucial that the clergy solidify their ranks. Meeting with the ministers and the General Court in October, Cotton appeared to agree with them "in the point of sanctification," but skepticism persisted. In December, offended by "some opinions, which some of his church did broach, and for he seemed to have too good an opinion of," they entreated him to answer sixteen questions. "Some doubts he well cleared," they allowed, "but in some things he gave not satisfaction." The year ended with the desired consensus unachieved and the Hutchinsonians still claiming that Cotton's authority supported their ideas.[65]

Meanwhile, the General Court was failing to restore social harmony. Charged with prosecuting the peace of the churches, it could hardly police itself. Prospects for direction from the government faded as the colony's leaders, unable to arrive at a concerted plan of action, took to blaming each other for the turmoil. In a melodramatic outburst on December 7, Governor Henry Vane, an ardent Hutchinsonian, tearfully tendered his resignation. Forecasting the "inevitable danger" of God's judgments on New England "for these differences and dissensions," and distressed by "scandalous imputations" that *he* bore the responsibility for fomenting discord, he begged to retire. Many on the Court would have been pleased to wish him godspeed, but while it adjourned for a few days, some of Vane's fellow Bostonians, who did not need the Spirit to reveal the utility of having a friend in high places, persuaded him to stay. When the Court reconvened, Vane expressed his pique that the ministers had interrogated Cotton "without his privity," whereupon Hugh Peter, the pastor of Salem, surmised that the "scandalous imputations" were justified. Before Vane arrived, he recollected, "the churches were in peace." Wilson capped the session with "a very sad speech of the condition of our churches" that fingered his own congregation and, by insinuation, his partner in the pulpit.[66] The Court's attempt to "freely declare" their differ-

---

65. Winthrop, *Journal*, I, 196, 207; Larzer Ziff, *The Career of John Cotton: Puritanism and the American Experience* (Princeton, 1962), 106–48; Jesper Rosenmeier, "New England's Perfection: The Image of Adam and the Image of Christ in the Antinomian Crisis, 1634 to 1638," *William and Mary Quarterly*, 3d ser., 27 (1970), 435–59; George Selement, ed., "John Cotton's Hidden Antinomianism: His Sermon on Revelation 4:1–2," *New England Historical Genealogical Register*, 129 (1975), 378–94. Foster, "New England Heresy," 647–48, 650, 653, 658, points out that the Hutchinsonians usually denied holding the most extreme opinions charged to them, and, noting that most of the evidence for their holding such tenets comes from their accusers, minimizes their innovativeness. Sharing the nightmare of established churches that sectarian dissent portended a descent into the libertinism and carnage of Munster (where the reign of militant Anabaptists in 1534–35 had sanctioned polygamy and had terrorized the city until they were overthrown and massacred), the New England elders imputed to their adversaries doctrines that the Hutchinsonians did not share and miscast them as English sectarians. However, it is likely that the ferment did inspire creative speculation among some of the Hutchinsonians; at her trial before the Boston church in March 1638, Anne propounded that the soul is mortal and that the natural body is not resurrected (errors not reported by the Synod), Hall, *Antinomian Controversy*, 354–65; James F. Maclear, "Anne Hutchinson and the Mortalist Heresy," *New England Quarterly*, 54 (1981), 74–103.

66. Winthrop, *Journal*, I, 202, 203, 204.

ences resulted in the usually irenic Cotton rushing to "admonish" his co-worker for defamation.[67]

The spat between Wilson and Cotton underscored how little respect Wilson commanded among his own flock. For the Hutchinsonians, nothing better epitomized the contrast between legal and godly preaching than the chasm between their pastor's deadness and their teacher's sublimity. With the arrival of John Wheelwright, a relative of Anne's by marriage driven from his vicarage by Laud, they saw their chance to demote or even remove their *bête noire*. In October, after Wheelwright had exhibited a congenial preaching style and a theology similar to Cotton's, they proposed that the church hire him as an assistant teacher. Wilson's dwindling band of supporters barely deflected the motion, and Wheelwright ultimately accepted a call to a nascent church in Mount Wollaston, but tensions in Boston did not abate. Incensed by reports that Wilson had disparaged Cotton and themselves in his speech to the General Court, the Hutchisonians excoriated him at a special church meeting on December 31 and demanded his censure. Cotton, more temperate, opposed the motion, pointing out that the church lacked the necessary unanimity to carry it, but he nonetheless gave Wilson "a grave exhortation."[68] Momentarily chastened, Wilson delivered a sermon the next day that Vane publicly applauded, but any rapport he had enjoyed with his congregation was, for the time, gone. When he took to the pulpit for sermon or prayer, many congregants, most of them women, walked out.[69] The Hutchinsonians ruled supreme in Boston.

Always near the center of events stood Winthrop. As the Deputy Governor, he participated in the wranglings of the General Court, and as a member of the Boston church, he witnessed the accelerating influence of the woman he dubbed the "*American Jesabel.*"[70] The tumults troubled him. A practical politician, he understood that reports of unrest in the Puritan commonwealth would play into the hands of Archbishop Laud, who headed a committee of the Privy Council that was seeking to vacate the colony's charter, and he also knew that internal dissension would weaken resistance should the Crown

67. *Ibid.*, 203, 204.

68. *Ibid.*, 205.

69. For interpretation of this phenomenon, see Lyle Koehler, "The Case of the American Jezebels: Anne Hutchinson and Female Agitation during the Years of Antinomian Turmoil, 1636–1640," *William and Mary Quarterly*, 3d ser., 31 (1974), 55–78; Ben Barker-Benfield, "Anne Hutchinson and the Puritan Attitude Toward Women," *Feminist Studies*, 1, 2 (1973), 65–96. These pieces tend to overstate the feminist significance of the affair; see the "Communication" of Sidney A. Hart and John Walter Putre, *William and Mary Quarterly*, 3d ser., 32 (1975), 164–69, and Koehler's "Reply," *ibid.*, 170–78; Ann Fairfax Withington and Jack Schwartz, "The Political Trial of Anne Hutchinson," *New England Quarterly*, 51 (1978), 228–29; Foster, "New England Heresy," 641, n. 38.

70. Hall, *Antinomian Controversy*, 310.

attempt to impose a governor-general by force.[71] A magistrate, he easily calculated the Antinomians' threat to civil stability, for they might disobey any official they thought under a "Covenant of Works" and who was thus a minion of Antichrist.[72] Devoutly orthodox, he shuddered at their heresies, and he too feared divine retribution for disorder. But Winthrop also had more personal reasons to feel oppressed by the crisis than almost anyone else in Massachusetts. The man whose credo for society insisted that "wee must delight in eache other, make others Condicions our owne[,] reioyce together, mourne together, labour, and suffer together, allwayes haueing before our eyes our Commission and Community in the worke, our Community as members of the same body," found himself in December 1636 an outcast in his own church.[73] The Hutchinsonians failed to secure Wheelwright's appointment because Winthrop contested it singlehandedly, arguing that the church was "well furnished already with able ministers, whose spirits they knew," and that calling someone with heterodox views about the nature of the union between Spirit and believer hazarded its welfare. He "thought reverendly" of Wheelwright's "godliness and abilities," but the man's propensity "to raise doubtful disputations" compelled him to oppose the appointment. Next day, "Divers of the brethren" chastised their stubborn comrade for treating Wheelwright badly on several counts, including misrepresenting his theology. Winthrop rebutted them, delivering a dissertation on the implications of Wheelwright's ideas and offering to "impart" his reasoning at length to anyone who asked. No one did. At the church's humiliation of Wilson, only Winthrop and "one or two more" stood by him.[74] Winthrop corresponded with Cotton about the case, but his characterizations of Cotton's answer as "very loving and gentle" and the manner of his own reply as "loving" fail to mask his alienation from his congregation's teacher, whose

71. Dunn, *Puritans and Yankees*, 30–34. The Laudian threat was serious enough that both sides took pains to put the best possible face on their divisions for the benefit of the English audience. On Feb. 3, 1636/37, Cotton told some passengers about to sail that "all the strife amongst us was about magnifying the grace of God." Reducing the imbroglio to a quibble, he bade them assure "our countrymen" that Massachusetts was merely carrying on the Lord's work, and that "if there were any among them that would strive for grace, they should come hither." Wilson followed, declaring that he knew of no one who was doing anything but "labor to advance the free grace of God in justification, so far as the word of God required." The success of this masquerade may be doubted, since some of Wilson's remarks "offended those of Mr. Cotton's party," Winthrop, *Journal*, I, 209.

72. Mather, *Magnalia*, II, 509; Ronald D. Cohen, "Church and State in Seventeenth-Century Massachusetts: Another Look at the Antinomian Controversy," *Journal of Church and State*, 12 (1970), 475–94.

73. *Winthrop Papers*, II, 294.

74. Winthrop, *Journal*, I, 197, 198, 199, 205.

judgment of Wilson, Winthrop felt, was "not without some appearance of prejudice."[75]

Winthrop's inability to control the colony's government as he had during its first four years must have frustrated him, but he had forfeited the governorship in 1634 because he did not favor a more representative assembly, and his popularity had not entirely recovered. "He hath lost much of that aplaws that he hath had," asserted one critic in 1635. "He is indeed a man of m[e]n: but he is but a man: & some say they have idolized him, & do now confesse their error." A year later he was second to Vane, whose rank and family connections—his father was a privy counselor—commanded respect, John's included. Winthrop probably would have assumed the governorship had Vane stepped down in December, but the incumbent's change of heart left John still without sufficient authority to act as he wanted.[76] Stalemated in the General Court, he was checkmated in Boston. Though powerful enough to block Wheelwright's appointment, he could hardly disperse the Hutchinsonians by force, and so he sought to win them back to orthodoxy by reason. At every opportunity the divinity-student-who-was-to-have-been picked over their errors. Following his public pronouncements over Wheelwright's interpretation of the Spirit's indwelling, Winthrop "wrote his mind fully, with such scriptures and arguments as came to hand, and sent it to Mr. Cotton." He joined Wilson in engaging Cotton and Vane in written disputation over the same issue. As the Hutchinsonians' reliance on personal revelation urged them to ever more extreme positions, he "wrote against them," and, with Wilson and their tiny rump of supporters in Boston, "bore witness to the truth."[77] His campaign failed. Cotton was hardly to be swayed by a lone amateur when the combined talents of his professional peers could not convince him. The disputation with Cotton and Vane agreed on nothing more controversial than "that the Holy Ghost is God, and that he doth dwell in the believers." The Boston church ignored him. Perhaps it was well for him that they did, and well, too, that he sent some of his epistles to Thomas Shepard to review before publicizing them, for John was no Paul. Hutchinson's doctrines, he later observed, "tended to slothfulnesse, and quench all indevour in the creature," but in his earnest desire to restore a modicum of human initiative to regeneration, he avoided Antinomianism, Shepard judged, only

75. *Ibid.*, 206, 205.

76. Morgan, *Puritan Dilemma*, 111–14; Dunn, *Puritans and Yankees*, 16; Israel Stoughton, "A Relation concerning some occurrences in New England," *Proceedings of the Massachusetts Historical Society*, 5 (1860–62), 141; Timothy H. Breen, *The Character of the Good Ruler: A Study of Puritan Political Ideas in New England, 1630–1730* (New York, 1974), 54. See Winthrop, *Journal*, I, 161–62, 180, 202–3.

77. Winthrop, *Journal*, I, 199, 201, 206.

to foul himself with "Arminianism, which I beleeue your soule abhors."
Dogmatic controversy is tricky business, the Cambridge preacher admitted
—he himself had once had problems avoiding "the dint of Armin[ian] arguments" until William Twisse had straightened him out—and, with steely
gentleness, he counselled that, "it being an easy thing for a subtill adversary
to take advantages at woords," Winthrop might best serve the cause if he
limited himself to transcribing their opponents' positions, refrained from
"priuate duells," and "forb[ore] wrighting for a while."[78] Shepard's advice
denied Winthrop another means to engage his foes.

Puritanism prompted the devout to link public providences with signs of
grace in themselves. Although the correspondence was never automatic—like
Lot's family in Sodom, righteous people might inhabit a land profaned—the
temptation to equate public misfortune with personal malfeasance was hard
for the godly to resist. It is scarcely surprising that, beleaguered by the
Hutchinsonians and maddened by his incapacity to deal with them, even a
Saint with Winthrop's fortitude should question his salvation. Sometime in
December, he wrestled with his doubts, and for the first time in over seven
years, charted the proceedings in his spiritual diary:

> Upon some differences in o^r Churche about the waye of the Spirit of God
> in the worke of Justif[ication,] myselfe dissentinge from the reste of the
> brethren, I had occasion to examine mine owne estate, wherein the Lord
> wrought marveyloysly upon my heart, revivinge my former peace & conso-
> latiõ wth muche increase & better assurance th[a]n formerly; & in the
> middest of it (for it continued many dayes) he did onc tyme darte a beame
> of wrathe into my soule, wch strucke me to the heart, but then the Lord
> Jesus shewed himselfe & stood betweene that wrathe & my soule.

The reference to his isolation in the church discovers a cause of his unsettled-
ness. Did the Lord support him in his lonely stand? Self-scrutiny raised his
assurance to a new pitch, but first he had to bear God's anger. Then Christ
interceded, and the magnitude of Winthrop's release gauges the intensity of
his former discomfort: "Oh how sweet was Chr^t then to my soule. I thought I
never prized him before, I am sure never more, nor ever felt more need of
him." *Agape* poured through the breach in his uncertainty, sweeping away
the miseries of the past months: "Oh how I was ravished wth his love! my
prayers could breathe nothinge but Christ & Love & mercye, wch continued
with meltinge & teares night and daye."[79] The procession of doubt and
trembling followed by rapture and prayer evinces the familiar pattern of

78. *Ibid.*, 201; Hall, *Antinomian Controversy*, 264; *Winthrop Papers*, III, 328, 329, 327.

79. Winthrop, *Life and Letters*, II, 161. The *Winthrop Papers* omit this passage, which
explains why Shea, who used them exclusively, thought Winthrop made no entries later than
1629, *Spiritual Autobiography*, 102.

reconversion. Despondent over the Antinomian affair, Winthrop retraced his spiritual steps to find sustenance.

Within a few weeks, he penned the "Christian Experience," which reveals why God had darted His wrath into his soul. John had "defiled the white garments of the Lord Jesus[,]" staining justification by "undervalueing the riches of the Lord Jesus Christ and his free grace," and soiling sanctification "by many foule spotts which Gods people might take notice of, and yet the inward spotts were fouler than those."[80] He had been trusting to his own abilities until Cotton's recent preaching shocked him into appreciating the gravity of his situation. "The Doctrine of free justification lately taught here took me in as drowsy a condition, as I had been in (to my remembrance) these twenty yeares," he admitted, "and brought mee as low (in my owne apprehension) as if the whole work had been to begin anew." God's "voice of peace" that customarily softened such falls "did not speak so loud nor in that measure of joy that I had felt sometimes."[81] Confession of the Spirit's muteness indicates again the depth of his depression, as do the assertions that he had not despised himself so much since his first conversion and that he would have to start again. The "Christian Experience" is Winthrop's effort at his new beginning, or rather a re-beginning, for it marks another incident in a reconversion episode that extended for weeks.

Winthrop did not have to re-acquire faith, but he did need an infusion of spiritual strength. Perusing the spiritual diary assisted his recovery. At one point during his first conversion, the tactic of looking over "some things which I had written heere before, concerninge the manifestation of Christs love unto me, my unspeakable ioye therein, and the advised and cheerful

---

80. *Winthrop Papers*, III, 344. For an insightful reading of the "Christian Experience" with concerns different than those pursued here, see Shea, *Spiritual Autobiography*, 105–10. Shea's judgment on the above lines, however, is debatable: "In a closing paragraph describing how he learned to value both justification and sanctification, the amateur theologian has given way to an autobiographer who is the sole authority for his argument. Shaped to the uses of the present, experience gave the lie to both Antinomians and legalists" (110). It is hard to know if Shea is expressing his own thoughts or summarizing Winthrop's, but the formulation is questionable in either case. Winthrop would not have seen himself "giving the lie" to the "legalists," the party whose lay champion he was, nor would he have employed that name, a Hutchinsonian epithet. If Shea is speaking for himself, he seems to assume that by valuing both justification and sanctification, Winthrop was assimilating both the Hutchinsonians' reliance on revelation and the orthodox emphasis on sanctified works as evidence of salvation into an original mix. The orthodox position, however, never dismissed the admissibility of the Spirit's revelations as evidence of justification as long as they concurred with scripture. See Errors 29, 30, 40, 47, 71 collected by the Synod of 1637 and their refutations, Hall, *Antinomian Controversy*, 227, 230, 232, 238–39. Cotton himself did not deny that sanctification could witness to justification, but he insisted that the Spirit's evidence of justification must precede, *Sixteen Questions of Seriovs and Necessary Consequence* (London, 1644), 7–12. In this respect *he* occupied a middle ground between the orthodox and the Hutchinsonians.

81. *Winthrop Papers*, III, 344.

Covenants that thereupon I had made," led him "to an humble and searious submission, in abundance of teares." His folly revealed, he renewed his covenants with prayer and beseeched God "to incourage and inhable me to performance."[82] Now, wallowing in a similar personal crisis, he repeated those acts. Rereading the spiritual diary reminded him of his history, which he reinterpreted in the "Christian Experience." Focusing on how he had turned helplessness into strength, he called the method to mind. The "Experience" is both a remembrance of strengths past and a plea for strength present that concludes with a prayer for Christ to "wash away all those spotts also in his good time."[83] Casting himself on God's mercy, Winthrop once more yielded to the Lord. In Puritan gymnastics, this posture invited power.

In pursuing strength by these means, Winthrop was a man of his culture. Preoccupied with human impotence, Puritans had devised a technique, conversion, that tapped God's potency. Once learned, a Saint could duplicate the procedure, reconvert, whenever the performance of one's calling suffered.[84] Nearly demoralized by a conspiracy that shattered God's city on a hill, Winthrop conquered his inner impotence by reconverting. Humbling himself, he renewed his trust in God's gracious sovereignty and re-established his claim to share His strength. Reassurance that the Lord still loved him prepared him for further battles against the Antinomians at the gates.

Faith could not be more efficacious.

82. *Ibid.*, I, 211.

83. *Ibid.*, III, 344.

84. Youngs, "Puritan Conversion Experience," derives Saints' renewed efforts to lead the godly life from the energy synthesized in the gap between the ideal image of conversion laid out by the preachers and its experiential reality in converts. The regenerate's failure to live up to the "totally engag[ing]" experience of conversion, far from contributing to despair, stimulated repeated efforts of obedience. Youngs does not define the ideal well, and there is no reason to assume a gap between expectation and actuality. His description of the paradigm contains a number of errors (to cite two: he equates justification with adoption and neglects contrition (3, 4, 12, *passim*)). He implies (5–6) that the ideal depicts an absolutely secure Saint, but he also admits (15) that preachers anticipated periods of spiritual deadness during sanctified life. Saints who missed the feeling of salvation should have been able to foretell their loss from listening to sermons. Reconversion is better understood as a drive to strengthen one's ability to perform, an activity that follows the ministry's blueprint.

Epilogue

Innumerable things can make a human being feel helpless. Some are shadows welling up from forgotten corners of the self; others are real objects bearing down on body and psyche in the material world. Like other people, every Puritan harbored private dreads that never received a name, but this essay has mentioned a few debilitating feelings common to the culture: guilt for sin, fear of God's wrath, and a pervasive sense of incapacity emanating from the anthropological fact of the corrupted faculties. To these internal sources may be added some historical phenomena that are likely to have inspired thoughts of impotence: bishops who quashed attempts to reform the church, pursuivants who hunted down dissident ministers, "neuters" who went to church but did not care, rowdies who did not even go, plain folk who amused themselves on the Sabbath, and, in the 1630s, a king who ruled without Parliament. Behind these two-legged manifestations lurked the disembodied demons of change: enclosures that moved people off the land and made them "masterless men" who disordered the countryside, increasing mobility that disrupted the bonds of traditional village life, a secular trend of inflation. Puritanism became prominent at a time when the habits of medieval English society were breaking up, and the godly dedicated themselves to restoring order, both psychological and social, to what they perceived as chaos. It is impossible to know how helpless Puritans sometimes felt in the midst of these forces, whether they reacted more strongly than did their contemporaries or have other peoples facing unsettled conditions, but the theme of helplessness dominated their preachers' discourse, and the experience of impotence must have been general. To people touched by weakness in a time of social stress, conversion provided a means to gain strength against a hoard of troubles.

All this puts the matter too baldly, of course. If the tenor of English life occasioned Puritans' helplessness and provoked their reforming reply, it determined neither the ideological content of their reaction nor its invigorating mechanism. These were supplied by a theology that highlighted humanity's abject helplessness over against the infinite majesty of an omnipotent God who donated to a predestined few the power of contesting sin, personal and social. Within Reformed Protestantism lay elements of an explosively activistic psychology that could funnel energy into moral purpose. It took some time, however, before Puritan theologians, responding to the fortunes of ecclesiastical politics and to innovations in Reformed dogmatics, fashioned these elements into a consciously coherent system and moved them to the forefront of their program. The earliest Puritan leaders were seriously concerned with liturgical and ecclesiological matters; the task of evangelizing a rag-tag people and imbuing them with a sense of the Lord's potency remained just one item on an agenda that, by the 1580s, called for insinuating presbyterian governance into the English church. Only in the 1590s, after the bishops had defeated the Classical Movement and when the first expositions of the dual covenant scheme were beginning to contribute a new perspective on human reaction to the divine initiative to grace, did regeneration and moral reform emerge as the outstanding Puritan preoccupations.[1] Attempts to master the external world of prayer books and bishops mutated (in the face of superior force) into an impulse to control the inner world of flesh and spirit. In succeeding years, conversion became Puritan preachers' primary concern. The origins of its function as a means of invigorating the soul were first of all theological.

The stated purpose of the new birth was to translate a sinner headed for hell to the Kingdom of God. It was the way of salvation. But it was also an instrument ideally suited to engender in people threatened by social change and by the disfavor of the religious establishment the capability of resisting. Acknowledging a person's innate debility, it promised to transform a weakling into a dynamo and to identify one's activity as being in the best interests of God Himself. In addition, it assured that an individual did not act alone, for the affections stimulated by regeneration encouraged affiliation with

1. George Yule, "Theological Developments in Elizabethan Puritanism," *Journal of Religious History*, I, 1 (1960), 16–25; *idem*, "Developments in English Puritanism in the Context of the Reformation," *Studies in the Puritan Tradition: A Joint Supplement of the Congregational Historical Society "Transactions" and the Presbyterian Historical "Journal,"* (Chelmsford, England, 1964), 8–27; Christopher Hill, *Society & Puritanism in Pre-Revolutionary England*, 2nd ed. (New York, 1967), 501–6.

other similarly engaged people. The Saints' renewed sense of spiritual self-worth as servants of the Almighty Lord promoted group solidarity. The covenanted bodies they organized leaned first of all towards religious rather than political reform; one can overdraw the godly as innovators of radical political cadres.[2] Nevertheless, the enormous potential for political and social activism of people animated by conversion is obvious in logic and in fact. Conversion transformed single unregenerates into members of communities dedicated to opposing ungodliness. What they accomplished depended on the historical situations they faced. In England, although Puritans wished to restore the integrity of traditional society, they helped to promote a revolution, the most discordant of social phenomena. In New England, given the opportunity of cutting commonwealths from whole cloth, they created a society notable for its cohesiveness, stability, and order.[3] The English Civil War and the founding of New England were complex events, molded by many factors but carried out by people energized through a profound religious experience. In its inceptive form, conversion could inspire one to kill a king or build a new world.

By the 1640s, two generations of powerful preachers had taught thousands the gospel of reciprocating *agape* with love and work. The later history of this psychology is imperfectly known. Religious and social upheaval during the English Civil War forced the Puritan habit of self-examination down some little-travelled roads. The march of the more radical sectarians and "vulgar prophets" led in the direction of quietism and enthusiasm; their exaltation of a well-settled assurance much earlier in one's life than the traditional paradigm had it knocked the well-oiled balance of fear and joy awry, while their sometimes indulgent pneumatology overturned the moral scaffolding that structured Puritan earnestness. The older position still survived, now just one voice amid a proliferating chorus.[4] In New England the

2. Michael Walzer's discussion of Puritanism as essentially a political movement devoted to establishing order through repressive discipline ("Puritanism as a Revolutionary Ideology," *History and Theory*, 3 (1963), 59–90; "The Revolutionary Uses of Repression," in Melvin Richter, ed., *Essays in Theory and History: An Approach to the Social Sciences* (Cambridge, Mass., 1970), 122–36; and esp. *The Revolution of the Saints*) should be read in light of David Little's able critiques ("Max Weber Revisited: The 'Protestant Ethic' and the Puritan Experience of Order," *Harvard Theological Review*, 59 (1966); *Religion, Order, and Law: A Study in Pre-Revolutionary England* (New York, 1969), emphasizing the movement's religious character and the voluntary, contractual features of its discipline).

3. Timothy H. Breen and Stephen Foster, "The Puritans' Greatest Achievement: A Study of Social Cohesion in Seventeenth-Century Massachusetts," *Journal of American History*, 60 (1973–74), 5–22.

4. Watkins, *Puritan Experience, passim*, demonstrates the variety of religious sensibility the Civil War called forth. In a world suddenly populated with Ranters, Antinomians, Fifth Monarchists, and Quakers, Richard Norwood, Thomas Goodwin, Richard Baxter, and John Bunyan adhered to older modes of feeling.

orthodox voice more or less called the tune in the seventeenth century, and some evidence suggests that the experience mandated by Perkins and Hooker had not changed much when the revivals of the 1740s swept the land.[5] At first hearing the revivalists' language of sin and redemption, old man and new birth, sounds familiar, but their biblical cadences do not by themselves necessarily prove the continuity of experience, for the religious setting of conversion changed in the intervening century. Although Reformed dogmatics did not entirely succumb to the Arminian challenge, certain aspects, like the covenant, declined in importance. During the awakenings, preachers emphasized the role of religious affections more than their predecessors had, and they detached conversion from a formal doctrinal locus. Any pretense that New England was somehow a holy commonwealth had long since dissipated, no single procedure governed admission to all the churches, and giving a relation had fallen into widespread disrepute. Conversion became less the initiation into a group charged with a holy mission than a private act of supreme individual importance.[6] Social circumstances had shifted too. Mid-eighteenth-century New England suffered its share of disruptions—war, depression, epidemics, competition for land, escalating urban poverty, and the intrusion of capitalist economic relationships into older patterns of exchange—but what effects these alterations may have had on conversion as an empowering and rejuvenating agency are unclear.[7] Certain behavioral changes—increasing punctiliousness in observing the exact moment of regeneration, the adoption of convulsive bodily displays accompanied by groans and shrieks—argue against an easy presumption that the new men and women of the revivals underwent the same experience as did seventeenth-century converts. It remains to be seen how the evangelical psychology of Anglo-American civilization developed from the Puritans' potent fusion of humility and strength, the grace of love transfigured into iron wilfulness.

5. Jerald C. Brauer, "Conversion: From Puritanism to Revivalism," *Journal of Religion*, 58 (1978), 230–33. Grimes, "Saving Grace," implicitly supports this position, though see 8, 17, 22.

6. Brauer, "Conversion," esp. 238–43.

7. Richard Bushman, *From Puritan to Yankee: Character and the Social Order in Connecticut, 1690–1765* (Cambridge, Mass., 1967); Gary B. Nash, *The Urban Crucible: Social Change, Political Consciousness, and the Origins of the American Revolution* (Cambridge, Mass., 1979); James A. Henretta, *The Evolution of American Society, 1700–1815: An Interdisciplinary Analysis* (Lexington, Mass., 1973), 119–46; J. M. Bumsted, "Religion, Finance, and Democracy in Massachusetts: The Town of Norton as a Case Study," *Journal of American History*, 57 (1970–71), 817–31. Bushman's fine book hypothesizes that feelings of guilt over acquisitiveness induced conversion during Connecticut's revivals, but since he never analyzes what converts said about their experience, it is difficult to know how such feelings may have been translated into new births and how (if at all) conversion actually helped people cope.

Elect Bibliography

It is customary, or at least polite, to thank one's fellow laborers in the vineyard, and to declare that, if one sees farther, it is because one has stood on their shoulders. The following bibliography tenders a fervent if incomplete "thank you" to all the authors who have helped me. Fervent, since, though I cannot claim superior vision, I have raised myself on other scholars' backs, which bear much of the foregoing discussion's weight. Incomplete, because it does not pretend fully to encompass a corpus that includes many superlative efforts and that dwarfs the efforts of most mortals to manage it. My intention is to give some sense of how I approached the materials and to provide easy entree into the issues they raise. Specialists will be able to multiply citations; non-specialists may be happy I did not. This list discriminates against articles, includes some materials not mentioned in the notes while omitting many references cited there, and makes some quixotic choices, but it should provide some assistance to people interested in the Puritans whose weight I hope to bear.

"The Call of the Puritans" builds on the familiar (some would say too familiar) expressions of Puritan divinity. William Haller, *The Rise of Puritanism* (New York, 1957 [orig. 1938]), 405-40, opens the English Puritans' sermon literature (and their hagiography too). The most awesome compilation of sources is the 7250-item bibliography in Henry Martyn Dexter, *The Congregationalism of the Last Three Hundred Years as Seen in Its Literature*, 2 vols. (New York, 1970 [orig. 1880]), II, Appendix, 5-286, but even this behemoth does not cover everything. Dexter's interest in ecclesiology rather than soteriology means that many works about conversion do not appear; one will find Hildersam's *Lectures upon the Fourth of Iohn*, for instance, but not Hooker's *The Application of Redemption*. Titles may also be culled from three standard works: A. W. Pollard and G. R. Redgrave, comps., *A Short-Title Catalogue of Books Printed in England, Scotland, & Ireland, And of English Books Printed Abroad, 1475-1640* (London, 1948 [orig. 1926]), vol. 2 of whose

2d edition, revised and enlarged by W. A. Jackson and F. S. Ferguson with Katherine F. Porter, appeared in 1976; Donald Wing, comp., *Short-Title Catalogue of Books Printed in England, Scotland, Ireland, Wales, and British America, and of English Books Printed in Other Countries, 1641–1700*, 3 vols. (New York, 1945–51), the first two volumes of whose 2d edition, revised and enlarged (New York, 1972, 1982), are now available; and Charles Evans et al., *American Bibliography*, 14 vols. (Chicago and Worcester, 1903–59), covering 1639–1800, to which should be added Roger P. Bristol, *Supplement to Charles Evans' American Bibliography* (Charlottesville, 1970). Peter Milward introduces the *Religious Controversies of the Elizabethan Age: A Survey of Printed Sources* (Lincoln, 1977) and the *Religious Controversies of the Jacobean Age: A Survey of Printed Sources* (Lincoln, 1978). Robert Watt, *Bibliotheca Britannica*, 4 vols. (Edinburgh, 1824), a subject bibliography occasionally misleading but always informative, eased the trauma of finding titles in such diverse fields as lexicography and law; it located, for instance, Thomas Wilson's *Christian Dictionary*, a little-known but to me invaluable work. There is no aspirin-free way to collect documents pertaining to early New England, but two extremely useful finding aids help ease the pain: George Selement, "A Check List of Manuscript Materials Relating to Seventeenth-century New England Printed in Historical Collections," *Bulletin of the New York Public Library*, 79 (1976), 416–47, saves much thumbing for sources squirreled away in hundreds of volumes of printed matter, while Harold Field Worthley, *An Inventory of the Records of the Particular (Congregational) Churches of Massachusetts Gathered 1620–1805*, Harvard Theological Studies, vol. 25 (Cambridge, 1970), provides much more information on the New England churches than just the location and contents of their records. Lewis R. Rambo, "Current Research on Religious Conversion," *Religious Studies Review*, 8 (1982), 146–59, tracks relevant work in history, psychology, anthropology, and sociology as well as religious studies.

This study rests on the fundamental premise that divining the *mentalité* of people who regarded the Bible as the ultimate worldly authority means first immersing oneself in Scripture. Fortunately, two superior compilations lead researchers through the myriad editions of the world's most popular book. Thomas Herbert Darlow and Horace Frederick Moule, eds., *Historical Catalogue of the Printed Editions of Holy Scripture in the Library of the British and Foreign Bible Society*, 2 pts. in 4 vols. (London, 1903–11), lists virtually every printed version of the Good Book in every language into which it was translated; and Arthur Sumner Herbert, ed., *Historical Catalogue of Printed Editions of the English Bible, 1525–1961* (London and New York, 1968), updates vol. 1 of Darlow and Moule. Together they cover every English version from the first fragmentary quarto of Tyndale to the NEB NT. Both catalogues contain a wealth of data particularly valuable in tracing textual variants. The sixteenth century was the first great age of English Bible translating, and keeping the versions straight is imperative because Puritans relied on no single one; readings from every English edition (and some from none) crop up everywhere. KJV becomes increasingly dominant as the seventeenth century wears on, but the Puritans' most favorite edition, which underwent over one hundred printings from 1560–1644, is GenB; Lloyd E. Berry introduces *The Geneva Bible* (Madison, 1969), a facsimile of the 1560 edition. The necessity of sitting amidst a stack of rare books and microfilms to compare textual variants has been obviated in part by Luther A. Weigle, ed., *The New Testament Octapla: Eight English Versions of the New Testament in the Tyndale–King James Tradition* (New York, 1962), which includes Tyn., GB, GenB, BB,

Rheims, and KJV. Only the first book of the Hebrew Scripture has received such treatment, in idem, ed., *The Genesis Octapla* . . . (New York, 1965). Neither of these volumes prints the marginal notes, which, especially in GenB, are such an important adjunct to the text. The second great age of English Bible translating is the post-World War II era, and a horde of volumes compete for a reader's attention. Each version has its own peculiar advantages and defects, but in my opinion, RSV most successfully combines KJV's poetry with the accuracy of modern biblical scholarship, and *The New Oxford Annotated Bible with the Apocrypha* . . ., ed. Herbert G. May and Bruce M. Metzger (New York, 1977), has the additional virtue of printing all the apocryphal books used by Christian churches. *The New English Bible with Apocrypha* (London, 1970) intones the Word in a freer translation than RSV.

The Cambridge History of the Bible, 3 vols. (Cambridge, 1963–70), surveys the field completely; S. L. Greenslade, "English Versions of the Bible, 1525–1611," *ibid.*, III, 141–74, covers the relevant English texts. F. F. Bruce has written a good, compact *History of the Bible in English* (formerly *The English Bible*), 3d ed. (New York, 1978). More expanded treatments include Hugh Pope, *English Versions of the Bible*, rev. and amp. by Sebastian Bullough (St. Louis, 1952), and Astley Cooper Partridge, *English Biblical Translation* (London, 1973), rather hard sledding in parts. Charles C. Butterworth, *The Literary Lineage of the King James Bible, 1340–1611* (Philadelphia, 1941), shows how much of Tyndale's wording remained in KJV. Much research has focused on the sixteenth- and seventeenth-century English Bible because of its importance in the Reformation's doctrinal disputes and because its diction has so influenced English literature, but, surprisingly, virtually no one has yet developed the Bible's impact on colonial America. Harry S. Stout, "Word and Order in Colonial New England," in Nathan O. Hatch and Mark A. Noll, eds., *The Bible in America* (New York, 1982), 19–38, takes a first step, educing the scriptural foundations of American exceptionalism.

How Puritans understood the Bible becomes more apparent after examining its composition, vocabulary, content, and theology, and although Anne Hutchinson relied on the Spirit alone to contest the elders' readings of Scripture, to put their hermeneutic into perspective using the letter means committing oneself to a shelfful of exegetical aids. Two good guides to biblical history are Bernhard W. Anderson, *Understanding the Old Testament*, 3d ed. (Englewood Cliffs, N.J., 1975), which avoids reading Hebrew Scripture as merely the overture for the Incarnation while delivering a good sense of the scholarly controversies, and Howard Clark Kee, Franklin W. Young, and Karlfried Froehlich, *Understanding the New Testament*, 4th ed. (Englewood Cliffs, 1983). Otto Kaiser, *Introduction to the Old Testament*, trans. John Sturdy (Minneapolis, 1977) and Willi Marxsen, *Introduction to the New Testament*, trans. G. Burwell (Philadelphia, 1976), open up questions about each book's sources, authorship, composition, and purpose. The best Bible dictionaries are small encyclopediae with abundant cross-references to apposite verses; John L. McKenzie, *Dictionary of the Bible* (New York, 1965) is a good single-volume work, while *The Interpreter's Dictionary of the Bible*, 4 vols. (Nashville, 1962), provides detailed exposition of important terms. The first English concordance dates from 1535, but KJV is the first English version to enjoy a complete compilation of its words. A number of concordances reference it, but I have used James Strong, comp., *The Exhaustive Concordance of the Bible* (New York, 1894), because it contains Hebrew and Greek vocabularies that prove very helpful for making word studies. Solomon Mandelkern, *Veteris Testamenti Concordantiae Hebraica atque Chaldaicae*, 2 vols.

(Graz, 1955 [orig. 1896]), breaks down the Hebrew text, while the Greek text has been compiled by Edwin Hatch and Henry A. Redpath, *A Concordance to the Septuagint and the Other Greek Versions of the Old Testament (Including the Apocryphal Books)*, 2 vols. (Graz, 1975 [orig. 1897]), and Michael Darton, *Modern Concordance to the New Testament* (Garden City, N.Y., 1976). Two dictionaries that link their vocabularies to those of the broader biblical world are Benjamin Davidson, *The Analytical Hebrew and Chaldee Lexicon* (Grand Rapids, 1970), and William F. Arndt and F. Wilbur Gingrich, eds., *A Greek-English Lexicon of the New Testament and Other Early Christian Literature*, 2d ed. (Chicago and London, 1979). The most complete analyses of the original biblical vocabulary lie in G. Johannes Botterweck and Helmer Ringgren, eds., *Theological Dictionary of the Old Testament*, trans. John T. Willis et al., 4 vols. to date (Grand Rapids, 1977–), and Gerhard Kittel and Gerhard Friedrich, eds., *Theological Dictionary of the New Testament*, trans. Geoffrey W. Bromiley, 10 vols. (Grand Rapids, 1964–76). Some of the most important terms receive extended discussion, which details their use in profane as well as sacred literature and the evolution of their doctrinal significance in ancient times.

By highlighting a passage's historical context or unraveling the meaning of an obscure phrase, biblical commentaries can clarify the sense of a text and provide needed perspective on past interpretations. Good modern exegesis exists in abundance, but anyone working on Puritanism ought first to look at *Calvin's Commentaries*. The Calvin Translation Society published a complete English edition, 45 vols. (Edinburgh, 1844–56; repr. Grand Rapids, 1948–59); David Wishart Torrance and Thomas Forsyth Torrance have edited some of his *New Testament Commentaries*, 12 vols. (Grand Rapids, 1960–72). Modern series vary widely, depending on the expected audience and the theological bent of the writers. Both Jewish and Christian scholars have contributed to William Foxwell Albright and David Noel Freedman, eds., *The Anchor Bible*, 38 vols. to date (Grand Rapids, 1964–); each individual translates the particular book under discussion, hence the text conforms to no standard version. Aimed at a general readership, these volumes nevertheless often delve deeply into historical and linguistic as well as theological materials. Much briefer treatments can be found in P. R. Ackroyd, A. R. C. Leaney, and J. W. Packer, eds., *The Cambridge Bible Commentary on the New English Bible*, 53 vols. to date (Cambridge, 1963–). *The Interpreter's Bible*, 12 vols. (Nashville and New York, 1951–57), prints KJV and RSV in parallel columns with a critical commentary and a homiletical guide running underneath; one of the most popular commentaries, it sometimes represents the intellectual climate of the 1950s. Still useful even though it first appeared at the turn of the nineteenth century, Samuel Rolles Driver et al., *International Critical Commentary on the Holy Scriptures of the Old and New Testaments*, 45 vols. (Edinburgh, 1949–59), features a strong interest in philology and is geared for advanced students; its contributions vary greatly in quality and theological viewpoint. A few volumes are being entirely rewritten; for instance, C. E. B. Cranfield, *A Critical and Exegetical Commentary on the Epistle to the Romans*, 6th ed., 2 vols. (Edinburgh, 1975–79), replaces William Sanday's original effort. Other worthwhile series include Ronald E. Clements and Matthew Black, eds., *The New Century Bible*, 22 vols. to date (London, 1967–); Roland Kenneth Harrison, ed., *New International Commentary on the Old Testament*, 7 vols. to date (Grand Rapids, 1965–); and F. F. Bruce, *New International Commentary on the New Testament*, 15 vols. to date (Grand Rapids, 1951–). Not all commentaries travel in groups, and much insight can be gained from, for instance, Bruce Vawter, *On Genesis* (Garden City, 1977).

But the Bible is more than a collection of texts awaiting the interpretation of others; each book advances its own theological reflection. Not everyone agrees that it is desirable, or even possible, to reconstruct the pristine thought of biblical authors, but the effort seems essential, if only to recall that Scripture has a mind of its own. Walter Eichrodt, *Theology of the Old Testament*, trans. John A. Baker, 2 vols. (Philadelphia, 1961–67), and Gerhard von Rad, *Old Testament Theology*, trans. D. M. G. Stalker, 2 vols. (New York, 1962–65), are superior efforts, as is Rudolf Bultmann, *Theology of the New Testament*, trans. Kendrick Grobel, 2 vols. (New York, 1951–55). Since much of Puritan theology looked approvingly to Paul, the Apostle's writings deserve special attention. Herman Ridderbos, *Paul: An Outline of His Theology*, trans. John Richard De Witt (Grand Rapids, 1975), is an exhaustive handbook, D. E. H. Whiteley, *The Theology of St. Paul* (Oxford, 1964), a readable introduction.

Puritanism arose as an attempt to improve institutions and worshippers considered insufficiently reformed. Claire Cross, *Church and People, 1450–1660* ([London], 1976), reviews the creation of the English Church, emphasizing the laity's growing dominance, and Keith Thomas, *Religion and the Decline of Magic* (New York, 1971), explores the considerable extent to which English men and women crossed the bounds of Protestant propriety to cope with misfortune using magic. Dewey Wallace, "George Gifford, Puritan Propaganda and Popular Religion in Elizabethan England," *Sixteenth Century Journal*, 9 (1978), 27–49, reveals one minister's efforts to bring religion to the ungodly masses. What preachers like Gifford were doing did not constitute a clearly definable movement, contend Charles and Katherine George, *The Protestant Mind of the English Reformation, 1570–1640* (Princeton, 1961); their controversial thesis maintains that the characteristics of "Puritanism" permeated the entire English church. The Georges have succeeded in forcing historians to define Puritanism more precisely, although they have not convinced many, myself included, that "Puritanism" is an empty concept. Ian Breward, "The Abolition of Puritanism," *Journal of Religious History*, 7 (1972–73), 20–34, answers the Georges and introduces the extensive literature of definition that this controversy has spawned; for further references see *supra*, 3, n. 1, and 8, n. 12. One special problem concerns the extent to which Puritans can be said to have deviated from the doctrines of John Calvin. R. T. Kendall, "The Puritan Modification of Calvin's Theology," in W. Stanford Reid, ed., *John Calvin: His Influence in the Western World* (Grand Rapids, 1982), 199–214, thinks they did, to their detriment; David D. Hall's broad-ranging review article "Understanding the Puritans," in Stanley N. Katz, ed., *Colonial America: Essays in Politics and Social Development*, 1st ed. (Boston, 1971), 31–50, prefers to view their thinking as the evolution of Calvin's (and other Reformed theologians') ideas. Hall's essay is a convenient window into the research on Puritanism conducted during the 1960s; another is Michael McGiffert, "American Puritan Studies in the 1960's," *William and Mary Quarterly*, 3d ser., 27 (1970), 36–67. Laura B. Ricard reviews "New England Puritan Studies in the 1970s," *Fides et Historia*, 15 (1983), 6–27.

This study treats Puritanism as a form of religious expression rather than as a social movement, but it owes much to the many historians who have traced its political and institutional history. Alan Simpson's fine little overview, *Puritanism in Old and New England* (Chicago, 1955), draws that history back to the experience of conversion. No one has told the story of the laity's importance in defining the Puritan program better than Patrick Collinson, whose *The Elizabethan Puritan Movement* (London, 1967), *The Religion of Protestants* (Oxford, 1982), "Towards a Broader

Understanding of the Early Dissenting Tradition," in C. Robert Cole and Michael E. Moody, eds., *Essays for Leland H. Carlson: The Dissenting Tradition* (Athens, Ohio, 1975), 3–38, and *Godly People: Essays on English Protestantism and Puritanism* (London, 1983), offer superb ecclesiastical history. Collinson's Puritans are the "hotter sort" of Protestants covenanted together as a church within the church to reform their neighbors through righteous zeal and social pressure. His depiction of the godly in local congregations as well as the movement's intellectual and political heads improves on Marshall M. Knappen, *Tudor Puritanism* (Chicago, 1939; repr. Gloucester, 1963), who deals only with the ministry. Knappen is still informative about Elizabethan Puritanism's intellectual program, a subject Collinson sometimes scants. L. C. Richardson, *Puritanism in North-west England* (Manchester, 1972), shows how the laity contributed to the movement's growth in one of the "dark corners of the land." Larzer Ziff, *Puritanism in America* (New York, 1974) presents a highly suggestive, if overly critical, history of the Saints' endeavors in New England, while Darrett Rutman, *American Puritanism* (Philadelphia, 1970), proposes treating this religion as a "gift" from the preachers to the congregation. Rutman is especially insightful concerning the Puritans' sense of themselves as a special people, less so on points of theology.

The ministers' gift of the Word came gift-wrapped in words; Marinus van Beek, *An Enquiry into Puritan Vocabulary* (Groningen, 1969) defines their terms. What English Puritan preachers said in the long decades before the Civil War is recounted in Haller, *The Rise of Puritanism*, an eloquent (if occasionally hagiographic) rendition of their plans for individual and social regeneration. Irvonwy Morgan relates the activities of *The Godly Preachers of the Elizabethan Church* (London, 1965), while Paul Seaver, *The Puritan Lectureships* (Stanford, 1970), explains how lay Puritans set up preaching positions outside the church establishment. W. Fraser Mitchell, *English Pulpit Oratory from Andrews to Tillotson* (New York, 1962 [orig. 1932]), tells how seventeenth-century preachers composed and presented their sermons, as does John Sparrow, "John Donne and Contemporary Preachers: Their Preparation of Sermons for Delivery and for Publication," *Essays and Studies by Members of the English Association*, 16 (1931), 144–78. In *The Art of Prophecying*, William Perkins articulated the techniques of the Puritan "plain style," emphasizing the preacher's duty to "open" a text logically and clearly; John Rechtien examines his method in "The Visual Memory of William Perkins and the End of Theological Dialogue," *Journal of the American Academy of Religion*, 45, 1, supp. (1977), D: 69–99, and "Logic in Puritan Sermons in the Late Sixteenth Century and Plain Style," *Style*, 13 (1979), 237–58. See also Jesper Rosenmeier, "'Clearing the Medium': A Reevaluation of the Puritan Plain Style in Light of John Cotton's *A Practical Commentary Upon the First Epistle of John*," *William and Mary Quarterly*, 3d ser., 37 (1980), 577–91. Babette May Levy, *Preaching in the First Half Century of New England History* (New York, 1945) carries the story to the American strand, as do Phyllis M. Jones and Nicholas R. Jones, *Salvation in New England: Selections from the Sermons of the First Preachers* (Austin, 1977). Phyllis M. Jones, "Puritan's Progress: The Story of the Soul's Salvation in the Early New England Sermons," *Early American Literature*, 15 (1980), 14–28, treats changing presentations of conversion; see also her "Biblical Rhetoric and the Pulpit Literature of Early New England," *ibid.*, 12 (1976–77), 245–58. For the later seventeenth century, a period beyond the scope of this work, Emory Elliott, *Power and the Pulpit in Puritan New England* (Princeton, 1975), offers an intriguing psychological analysis of ministerial rhetoric, noting how the spleen of the aging first generation against the perceived falling-away of its children passed into a more comforting message when those children themselves ascended the pulpit.

The men who made the words took their task seriously, but, according to David D. Hall, *The Faithful Shepherd* (Chapel Hill, 1972), a masterful social and intellectual study of how preachers accommodated the Reformed theological tradition to social and political change, they also closely guarded their prerogatives as spiritual leaders. Yet the ministers did not form an elite removed from the ebbs and flows of daily life, argues George Selement in *Keepers of the Vineyard: The Puritan Ministry and Collective Culture in Colonial New England* (Lanham, Md., 1984); rather, they constituted a group of engaged pastors whose influence dominated the region's cultural style. As individuals, the leading Puritan clerics have commanded a fair amount of attention, although there are some surprising gaps. William Perkins, for instance, has yet to attract a biographer in English; Ian Breward, ed., *The Work of William Perkins* (Abingdon, 1970), furnishes a good introduction. H. C. Porter, *Reformation and Reaction in Tudor Cambridge* (Cambridge, 1958), relates Perkins's role in the intellectual controversies of the 1590s. Perkins has commanded an extensive article literature, which includes Ian Breward, "The Significance of William Perkins," *Journal of Religious History*, 4 (1966–67), 113–28; Gordon J. Keddie, " 'Unfallible Certenty of the Pardon of Sinne and Life Everlasting': The Doctrine of Assurance in the Theology of William Perkins (1558–1602)," *Evangelical Quarterly*, 48 (1976), 230–44; Richard Muller, "Perkins' *A Golden Chaine*: Predestinarian System or Schematized *Ordo Salutis*?" *Sixteenth Century Journal*, 9 (1978), 69–81; and Mark R. Shaw, "Drama in the Meeting House: The Concept of Conversion in the Theology of William Perkins," *Westminster Theological Journal*, 45 (1983), 41–72. Keith Sprunger, *The Learned Doctor William Ames* (Urbana, 1972), is worthy of its subject, Puritanism's foremost systematic theologican, and is richly informative on Puritanism in the Netherlands. Douglas Horton, trans., *William Ames by Matthew Nethenus, Hugo Visscher, and Karl Reuter* (Cambridge, Mass., 1965), covers Ames's theology. Irvonwy Morgan, *Prince Charles's Puritan Chaplain* (London, 1957), shows John Preston wheeling and dealing in the tangled politics of the 1620s; his *Puritan Spirituality* (London, 1973), sketches Preston's thought but fails to evaluate it critically. Preston's mentor fares better in Larzer Ziff, *The Career of John Cotton* (Princeton, 1962); Everett Emerson, *John Cotton* (New York, 1965), is a brief literary study. Sargent Bush, *The Writings of Thomas Hooker* (Madison, 1980), and Frank Shuffleton, *Thomas Hooker, 1586–1647* (Princeton, 1977), ably examine Cotton's archrival. B. R. Burg, *Richard Mather of Dorchester* (Lexington, Ky., 1976), should be read in conjunction with Robert Middlekauff's keenly perceptive intellectual portrait in *The Mathers* (New York, 1971). There is no complete biography of John Davenport, although Isabel M. Calder contributed a sketch to her edition of the *Letters of John Davenport, Puritan Divine* (New Haven, 1937), and the only extended treatment of Shepard is John A. Albro's "Introduction" to *The Works of Thomas Shepard*, 3 vols. (Boston, 1853; repr. Hildesheim, 1971). Shepard warrants a modern appraisal; Andrew Delbanco, "Thomas Shepard's America: The Biography of an Idea," in Daniel Aaron, ed., *Studies in Biography* (Cambridge, Mass., 1978), 159–82, makes a start. The critical literature on Cotton, Hooker, Mather, and Shepard can be found in Edward J. Gallagher and Thomas Werge, eds., *Early Puritan Writers: A Reference Guide* (Boston, 1976).

In the field of American Puritan studies, the name of Perry Miller towers above the rest. *Orthodoxy in Massachusetts, 1630–1650* (Cambridge, Mass., 1933), *The New England Mind: The Seventeenth Century* (New York, 1939) [made more accessible by James Hoopes, ed., *Sources for "The New England Mind: The Seventeenth Century"* (Williamsburg, 1981)], *The New England Mind: From Colony to Province* (Cambridge, Mass., 1953), *Jonathan Edwards* (New York, 1949), and a myriad of essays, many collected in *Errand into the Wilderness* (Cambridge, Mass., 1956), and *Nature's Nation* (Cambridge, Mass., 1967), re-created the field, defined it, endowed it with the prestige of his awesome intellect, and erected a synthesis that, if eroded in countless ways, has not yet been replaced. In breathtaking fashion Miller opened up the subjects here treated in the first three chapters; indeed, he called attention as no one had before to the importance of both the psychology and the covenant to Puritan thought. His spirit, which beckons scholars to the impossible task of emulating his narratives of the mind in action—the best depictions of the thrill of thinking that I know—hovers over these pages; having been tested by genius, I have learned much about humility. Yet Miller is conspicuous here by his virtual absence. He made hundreds of factual and interpretive errors; he focused on the structures of intellect, not emotion (albeit there is fervor aplenty in "The Augustianian Strain of Piety," chapter 1 of *The New England Mind: The Seventeenth Century*); he did not concern himself with popular piety; and he overlooked the single most important text in Puritans' libraries—the Bible. Miller's objectives did not shape my agenda, and I did not think it necessary to add another small voice to the chorus of critics who have so capably demonstrated his failings. Their critiques live in a thousand footnotes sprinkled throughout the vast literature he did so much to inspire; see John C. Crowell, "Perry Miller as Historian: A Bibliography of Evaluations," *Bulletin of Bibliography and Magazine Notes*, 34 (1977), 77–85, and the discussion among James Hoopes, Joyce Appleby, David Hall, P. M. G. Harris, and Margaret Sobczak in *American Quarterly*, 34 (1982), 1–48.

In Part I, I have sought to delineate the preachers' understanding of conversion, an understanding that began in the consideration of God's awesome omnipotence but which essentially concerned itself with the nature of Man—and Woman. Two ancient anthropologies, scriptural and faculty-humoral, mingle in Puritan discourse, and each has attracted an extensive literature. Ernest De Witt Burton, *Spirit, Soul, and Flesh* (Chicago, 1918), introduces the key terminology, as does C. Ryder Smith, *The Bible Doctrine of Man* (London, 1949). Aubrey R. Johnson, *The Vitality of the Individual in the Thought of Ancient Israel*, 2d ed. (Cardiff, 1964), stresses the dynamic perception of human nature embedded in the Hebrew world-view, while I. Cohen, "The Heart in Biblical Psychology," in H. J. Zimmels, J. Rabinowitz, and I. Finestein, eds., *Essays Presented to Chief Rabbi Israel Brodie* (London, 1967), 41–57, explores the significance Hebrews accorded the heart, the seat of psychological as well as physical power. Hans Walter Wolff, *Anthropology of the Old Testament*, trans. Margaret Kohl (Philadelphia, 1974), ably reviews the subject, and J. W. Rogerson, *Anthropology and the Old Testament* (Atlanta, 1979), raises methodological questions about the theories scholars use to understand the mentality of "primitive" peoples. Surveys of the New Testament doctrine include Werner Georg Kümmel, *Man in the New Testament*, trans. John J. Vincent, rev. and enlg. (London, 1963), and Bo Reicke, "Body and Soul in the New Testament," *Studia Theologica*, 19 (1965), 200–212. Much of the controversy surrounding New Testament anthropology centers on Paul's thought, since his innovative, unsystematic, and often cryptic approach has made a consensus about his meanings impossible. Recent scholarship tends to judge his anthropology an idiosyncratic perspective rooted in Hebrew holism rather than in Greek dualism, the argument voiced by John A. T. Robinson, *The Body: A Study in Pauline Theology* (Chicago, 1952), and Walter David Stacey, *The Pauline View of Man* (London, 1956). These works should be compared with Robert Jewett, *Paul's Anthropological Terms* (Leiden, 1971), and Robert H. Gundry, *Sōma in Biblical Theology* (Cambridge, 1976), which revises Johnson's conception of Hebrew holism.

The place of what I have called the faculty-humor psychology in Western thought is covered by Herschel Baker, *The Dignity of Man* (Cambridge, Mass., 1947). E. Ruth Harvey, *The Inward Wits* (London, 1975), details major medieval Arab and European contributions to the theory, while Paul H. Kocher, *Science and Religion in Elizabethan England* (San Marino, Cal., 1958), takes the story into the sixteenth century. Some of the best discussions treat the psychology in the context of Elizabethan literature: Ruth Leila Anderson, *Elizabethan Psychology and Shakespeare's Plays* (Iowa City, 1927); Lily B. Campbell, *Shakespeare's Tragic Heroes* (New York, 1968 [orig. London, 1930]); and E. M. W. Tillyard, *The Elizabethan World Picture* (London, 1958), which sets the psychology within the larger intellectual patterns of the sixteenth century. Puritan appropriation of the psychology forms the subject of Eugene E. White, "Master Holdsworth and 'A Knowledge Very Useful and Necessary'," *Quarterly Journal of Speech*, 53 (1967); J. Rodney Fulcher, "Puritans and the Passions: The Faculty Psychology in American Puritanism," *Journal of the History of the Behavioral Sciences*, 9 (1973), 123–39; and James G. Blight, "Solomon Stoddard's *Safety of Appearing* and the Dissolution of the Puritan Faculty Psychology," *ibid.*, 10 (1974), 238–50. The psychology underlay Puritan discussion of moral philosophy, an area in which Norman Fiering, *Moral Philosophy at Seventeenth-Century Harvard* (Chapel Hill, 1981) is essential.

Studying how the Bible employs the covenant motif illuminates how the Puritans used it. Delbert Hillers, *Covenant: The History of a Biblical Idea* (Baltimore, 1969), traces its origins and meanings throughout Scripture. Moshe Weinfeld, " בְּרִית‎," in *TDOT*, II, 253–79, details the Hebrew term's nuances and proposes that promissory covenants (with Abraham and David) derived from royal grants of favor to deserving servants. In *Law and Covenant in Israel and the Ancient Near East* (Pittsburgh, 1955) and "Covenant" in *The Interpreter's Dictionary of the Bible*, I, 714–23, George Mendenhall argues that obligatory-type covenants like Sinai paralleled Hittite suzerainty treaties; Dennis J. McCarthy, *Old Testament Covenant: A Survey of Current Opinions* (Atlanta, 1972), and Francisco O. Garcia-Treto, "Covenant in Recent Old Testament Studies," *Austin Seminary Bulletin: Faculty Edition*, 96 (1981), 10–19, review the criticisms leveled against this hypothesis. Johannes Behm, "διαθήκη," *TDNT*, II, 106–34, covers New Testament formulations. These works show Scripture raising issues that resonate in Puritan thought; the difficulties of working out precisely what the Bible means are brought out by James Swetman, "Suggested Interpretation of Hebrews 9:15–18," *Catholic Bible Quarterly*, 27 (1965), 373–90, and John J. Hughes, "Hebrews 9:15ff and Galatians 3:15ff: A Study in Covenant Practice and Procedure," *Novum Testamentum*, 21 (1979), 27–96, who contest whether one particularly difficult passage refers to a testament or a covenant, terms fraught with implications about God's dealing with His human partners.

In exalting the Covenant as the "marrow" of Puritan divinity, Perry Miller portrayed it as the instrument with which Puritans bound John Calvin's omnipotent God and forced Him to contract with wilful human beings over the terms of their salvation. The diminution of Calvin's importance as a formulator of covenantal thought has been refuted by Everett H. Emerson, "Calvin and Covenant Theology," *Church History*, 25 (1956), 136–44; Anthony A. Hoekema, "The Covenant of Grace in Calvin's Teaching," *Calvin Theological Journal*, 2 (1967), 133–61; and Paul Helm, "Calvin and the Covenant: Unity and Continuity," *Evangelical Quarterly*, 54 (1982), 65–81. Calvin was not the only significant influence on the Puritans' theology of covenant; as Leonard J. Trinterud, "The Origins of Puritanism," *Church History*, 20 (1951), 37–57, and Jens Møller, "The Beginnings of Puritan Covenant Theology," *Journal of Ecclesiastical History*, 14 (1963), 46–67, have observed, Reformers like Ulrich Zwingli and Heinrich Bullinger also contributed, but differed with Calvin over such points as the conditionality of the Covenant and the circumstances of its fulfillment. In an important review article, Richard L. Greaves, "The Origins and Early Development of English Covenant Thought," *The Historian*, 31 (1968), 21–35, discerned these two traditions threading through English covenantal thought, but the notion that the Genevan and Rhineland/Zurich positions are in fact substantially different has been challenged by Lyle D. Bierma, "Federal Theology in the Sixteenth Century: Two Traditions?" *Westminster Theological Journal*, 45 (1983), 304–21, which suggests that Greaves has overestimated the differences in seventeenth-century English thought. On later developments, see Richard A. Muller, "Covenant and Conscience in English Reformed Theology: Three Variations on a 17th Century Theme," *ibid.*, 42 (1980), 308–34, and *idem*, "The Spirit and the Covenant; John Gill's Critique of the *Pactum Salutis*," *Foundations*, 24 (1981), 4–14.

Bierma's article is especially significant because it recognizes how the Reformers maintained the tension between the Covenant of Grace as both a unilateral and bilateral pact, a conditional agreement that was, in fact, ultimately unconditional. In "The Covenant Theology—A Review Article," *Journal of Presbyterian History*, 44 (1966), 198–204, J. A. Ross MacKenzie could affirm Miller's position that Puritans treated the Covenant as a contract, but Bierma, John von Rohr, "Covenant and Assurance in English Puritanism," *Church History*, 34 (1965), 195–203, Francis Lyall, "Of Metaphors and Analogies: Legal Language and Covenant Theology," *Scottish Journal of Theology*, 32 (1979), 1–17, and Michael McGiffert, "Grace and Works: The Rise and Division of Covenant Divinity in Elizabethan Puritanism," *Harvard Theological Review*, 75 (1982), 463–502, dispute that position, McGiffert demonstrating how the Covenant took on the nature of a testament. As should be evident, covenant theology has recently received a great deal of attention; paradoxically, a number of scholars have reached the conclusion that, *pace* Miller, the Covenant was not the marrow of Puritan divinity. The Puritan theology of covenant deserves full-length investigation in the light of modern research, and, as of this writing, both von Rohr and McGiffert are preparing extensive treatments. McGiffert's thought can be followed in a number of articles, which include "The Problem of the Covenant in Puritan Thought: Peter Bulkeley's *Gospel-Covenant*," *New England Historical Genealogical Register*, 130 (1976), 107–29, "God's Controversy with Jacobean England," *American Historical Review*, 88 (1983), 1151–74, and "The Making of the Covenant of Works: England, 1585–1610," (forthcoming).

The student of Puritan theology is fortunate to have some excellent guides. The best technical discussion, which covers the same period that I have, is William K. B. Stoever, '*A Faire and Easie Way to Heaven*': *Covenant Theology and Antinomianism in Early Massachusetts* (Middletown, Conn., 1978), on almost every count an accurate and insightful presentation of Puritan dogmatics as a unified system. Dewey Wallace, *Puritans and Predestination* (Chapel Hill, 1982), establishes the centrality of the Reformed theology of grace in England during the sixteenth and seventeenth centuries, masterfully expositing its doctrines and the opposition it ultimately aroused. Wallace treats Puritanism as a recognizably distinct current within the larger stream of English theological opinion, whereas John F. H. New, *Puritan and Anglican* (Stanford, 1964), and J. Sears McGee, *The Godly Man in Stuart England* (New Haven, 1976), portray it more as a separate river. New discusses, among other things, the Puritan view of human nature, while McGee contends that Puritans emphasized the individual's duties to God, Anglicans one's duties to man. John S. Coolidge, *The Pauline Renaissance in England* (Oxford, 1970) is one of the few books to examine in depth the Puritans' indebtedness to the Apostle; the Bible's impact on Puritan theology deserves comprehensive examination. The doctrine of conversion enjoys central place in R. T. Kendall, *Calvin and English Calvinism to 1649*, which overemphasizes the Puritans' (or as he would have it, the "experimental predestinarians'") differences with Calvin; J. Sears McGee, "Conversion and the Imitation of Christ in Anglican and Puritan Writing," *Journal of British Studies*, 15 (1976), 21–39; Lynn Baird Tipson, Jr., "The Development of a Puritan Understanding of Conversion," (Ph.D. dissertation, Yale University, 1972); and most especially Norman Pettit, *The Heart Prepared* (New Haven, 1966), which broke new ground by elucidating the development of preparation. I substantially disagree with many of Pettit's readings, but I have always kept the book close at hand. Geoffrey F. Nuttall's *The Holy Spirit in Puritan Faith* (Oxford, 1946) traces the Puritans' theology of experience during the English Revolution, and his *Visible Saints: The Congregational Way, 1640–1660* (Oxford, 1957) details the formation of gathered churches in England.

Pointing out the activist nature of Puritan psychology means running up against one of the monuments of Western scholarship, Max Weber, *The Protestant Ethic and the Spirit of Capitalism*, trans. Talcott Parsons (New York, 1958 [orig. 1930]); see also "The Protestant Sects and the Spirit of Capitalism," in Hans H. Gerth and C. Wright Mills, eds., *From Max Weber: Essays in Sociology*, (New York, 1958), 302–22. The literature on Weber is immense; see the bibliographies in S. N. Eisenstadt, ed., *The Protestant Ethic and Modernization* (New York, 1968), 385–400; David Little, *Religion, Order, and Law* (New York, 1969), 226–37; Robert W. Green, ed., *Protestantism, Capitalism, and Social Science: The Weber Thesis Controversy*, 2d ed. (Lexington, 1973), 191–95; and Benjamin Nelson, "Weber's Protestant Ethic: Its Origins, Wanderings, and Foreseeable Futures," in Charles Y. Glock and Phillip W. Hammond, eds., *Beyond the Classics? Essays in the Scientific Study of Religion* (New York, 1973), 113–30. In Chapter 4, I have demurred to his depiction of Puritan psychology, but my debt to him is obvious. Robert M. Mitchell, *Calvin's and the Puritan's View of the Protestant Ethic* (Washington, D.C., 1979), corrects some of Weber's misunderstandings of Puritan theology, but in turn misrepresents part of his thesis. I have been concerned to explore the psychological origins of Puritan activism more than its sociological manifestations, though I have suggested that conversion grounded the Saints' communalism; other historians have confronted this subject more thoroughly. Michael Walzer, in "Puritanism as a Revolutionary Ideology," *History and Theory*, 3 (1963), 59–90, "The Revolutionary Uses of Repression," in Melvin Richter, ed., *Essays in Theory and History* (Cambridge, Mass., 1970), 122–36, and most especially *The Revolution of the Saints* (Cambridge, Mass., 1965), sees anxious Saints channeling their alienation into an essentially political movement unhesitant to discipline and repress individuals to achieve the goal of an ordered society. To this characterization, David Little, "Max Weber Revisited: The 'Protestant Ethic' and the Puritan Experience of Order," *Harvard Theological Review*, 59 (1966), 415–28, and *Religion, Order, and Law*, has replied that Puritans were first of all concerned to reform the church, not the polity, and that their discipline included many more elements of "voluntary choice, self-initiated behavior and consensuality" than Walzer allows. Thomas Leverenz, *The Language of Puritan Feeling* (New Brunswick, 1980), also sees Puritanism arising as a response to the perceived chaos of English society, though he then concerns himself with their psychological and literary response, while Timothy H. Breen and Stephen Foster, "The Puritans' Greatest Achievement: A Study of Social Cohesion in Seventeenth-Century Massachusetts," *Journal of American History*, 60 (1973), 5–22, argue that, in America, at least, they succeeded in implementing their plans for social discipline. Christopher Hill, *Society & Puritanism in Pre-Revolutionary England*, 2d ed. (New York, 1967), locates the essential sphere of Puritan activity in the realm of economics, the industry of middling artisans and yeomen propelled by religious doctrines that were at bottom an ideology of capitalist entrepreneurialism. Paul Seaver, "The Puritan Work Ethic Revisited," *Journal of British Studies*, 19 (1980), 35–53, sees in the Saints' enterprise less of an effort to maximize profits and more of an attempt to earn the coin of good conscience. Unfortunately, David Zaret, *The Heavenly Contract: Ideology and Organization in Pre-Revolutionary Puritanism* (Chicago, 1985) arrived too late to engage with.

The laity speak out in "The Cry of the Faithful," and the most important sources consist of three collections of conversion narratives, all of which appeared in the *Publications of the Colonial Society of Massachusetts*: "The Diary of Michael Wigglesworth," ed. Edmund S. Morgan, 35 (1951), esp. 426–44; *The Notebook of the Reverend John Fiske, 1644–1675*, ed. Robert Pope, 47 (1974), *passim*; and, most importantly, *Thomas Shepard's "Confessions"*, ed. George Selement and Bruce C. Woolley, 58 (1981), *passim*. Selement and Woolley modernize spelling and punctuation; Patricia Lee Caldwell, "A Literary Study of Puritan Testimonies of Religious Experience from the 1630s to the 1660s . . .," (Ph.D. dissertation, Harvard University, 1979), transcribes the *Confessions* and retains the original spelling and punctuation, a strategy that makes the messiness of the original document more apparent. Discussion of the relations should begin with two outstanding volumes that treat both their context and their content. Edmund S. Morgan, *Visible Saints* (Ithaca, 1963), explains how the Puritans' desire to establish churches of the regenerate led them to create membership tests in which the relations played a key role, and he elaborates on the "morphology of conversion" that the relations were expected to evince. Scholars have contested Morgan's conclusions on a number of points, but the book is an essential introduction to the ecclesiological ramifications of conversion. Patricia Caldwell, *The Puritan Conversion Narrative* (New York, 1983), updates research on the origins of the spoken relations and proposes that they constitute the first vocalizations of a uniquely American expressiveness. I have not been able to indicate all of our agreements and disagreements—in part because her elegant sophistication spins out stimulating ideas on every page—but by any standard this is a major interpretation of Puritan religiosity. One of her British sources is the collections of testimonies printed by John Rogers of Dublin, which are also covered in John H. Taylor, "Some Seventeenth-Century Testimonies," *Transactions of the Congregational Historical Society*, 16 (1949–51), 64–77. Accounts of conversion appear too in personal diaries, journals, and mémoires; Daniel Shea, *Spiritual*

Autobiography in Early America (Princeton, 1968), analyzes a few of the more extended accounts, including John Winthrop's. Owen C. Watkins, *The Puritan Experience* (New York, 1972), is a very important guide to the British literature, mainstream and sectarian; he contends that the self-examination demanded by Puritan religiosity fostered a growing sense of self-consciousness. On the other hand, Sacvan Bercovitch, *The Puritan Origins of the American Self* (New Haven, 1975), sees the self constricted, not liberated, by puritanic introspection, a conclusion that may be granted with the emendation that out of the ashes of the old man was supposed to spring a new self grounded in God's grace and submissive—but liberatingly so—to His commands. I hope that my study will serve as the baseline for further investigations of religious experience beyond the seventeeth century. Any attempt would do well to consider Jerald C. Brauer, "Conversion: From Puritanism to Revivalism," *Journal of Religion*, 58 (1978), 227–43, a pathbreaking argument that sees conversion in the eighteenth century becoming more subjective and less doctrinaire than it had been in the seventeenth. Mary Cochran Grimes, "Saving Grace among Puritans and Quakers: A Study of 17th and 18th Century Conversion Experiences," *Quaker History*, 72 (1983), 3–26, makes some superficial comparisons of Saints and Friends, finding little change of experience within the two traditions.

Puritan piety extended beyond the experience of conversion, and a number of fine studies examine the broader contours of their religious sensibility. Horton Davies, *The Worship of the English Puritans* (Westminster, 1948), discusses their liturgies and forms of worship; the first two volumes of his *Worship and Theology in England* (Princeton, 1970, 1975) compare Puritan practices to those of the Anglicans and Catholics. Gordon S. Wakefield, *Puritan Devotion* (London, 1957), stresses the Puritans' religion of the heart, concentrating on England, but the pre-eminent work in this area is Charles E. Hambrick-Stowe, *The Practice of Piety* (Chapel Hill, 1982), which shows the dynamics of conversion inhering in the structures of devotional and ceremonial practice. Hambrick-Stowe deftly describes how religious sentiment influenced the forms of Puritan culture in New England, and though I disagree with his conclusion that piety subserved contemplation as much or more than it did activism, I emphatically concur that conversion was an experience to be repeated throughout one's life. One man's recapitulation of conversion may be followed in Baird Tipson, "The Routinized Piety of Thomas Shepard's Diary," *Early American Literature*, 13 (1978), 64–80; see also Robert Middlekauff, "Piety and Intellect in Puritanism," *William and Mary Quarterly*, 3d ser., 22 (1965), 457–70. Puritan piety began at home; on this subject see Hill, *Society & Puritanism*, 443–81; Edmund S. Morgan, *The Puritan Family*, rev. ed. (New York, 1966); Gerald F. Moran, "Religious Renewal, Puritan Tribalism, and the Family in Seventeenth-Century Milford, Connecticut," *William and Mary Quarterly*, 3d ser., 36 (1979), 236–54; and Gerald F. Moran and Maris A. Vinovskis, "The Puritan Family and Religion: A Critical Reappraisal," *ibid.*, 39 (1982), 29–63.

The religion of the heart becomes the religion of the psyche in: Howard Feinstein, "The Prepared Heart: A Comparative Study of Puritan Theology and Psychoanalysis," *American Quarterly*, 22 (1970), 166–76; Murray G. Murphey, "The Psychodynamics of Puritan Conversion," *ibid.*, 31 (1979), 135–47; Michael D. Reed, "Early American Puritanism: The Language of Its Religion," *American Imago*, 37 (1980), 278–333; George Selement, "The Means to Grace: A Study of Conversion in Early New England" (Ph.D. Dissertation, University of New Hampshire, 1974), 83–104; and Leverenz, *Language of Puritan Feeling*, easily the most persuasive interpretation. Philip Greven, *The Protestant Temperament* (New York, 1977), is a major work on religious life and the family. I have challenged a number of his arguments in the "Introduction"; here I want to applaud Greven's objectives, the daring of his research, and his recognition of the topic's importance.

John Winthrop makes the perfect candidate for a case study of conversion; a layman who listened intently to the ministry of the Word, he left behind a hoard of documents rich in details of his personal and political lives: the *Winthrop Papers,* ed. Allyn B. Forbes et al., 5 vols. (Boston, 1929–47), the most complete printed collection; Robert C. Winthrop, *Life and Letters of John Winthrop*, 2 vols., 2d ed. (Boston, 1869); and *Winthrop's Journal "History of New England" 1630–1649*, ed. James Kendall Hosmer, 2 vols. (New York, 1908; repr. 1959). Richard Dunn is now preparing what promises to be the definitive edition of Winthrop's "History"; see "John Winthrop Writes His Journal," *William and Mary Quarterly*, 3d ser., 41 (1984), 185–212. Interestingly, Winthrop has never received lengthy biographical treatment. Edmund S. Morgan, *The Puritan Dilemma* (Boston, 1958), touchingly evokes the struggles of a pious, loving man to transcend the world without ever quitting it, but Morgan's generous assessment of Winthrop's liberality as a political leader should be weighed in light of Richard S. Dunn, *Puritans and Yankees* (New York, 1971), 1–56. Robert George Raymer, *John Winthrop* (New York, 1963), is unreliable. One might guess that Winthrop was not the only person to recapitulate his conversion during the Antinomian Crisis, although his prominence and exposed position certainly made him a likely candidate to do so; the brouhaha over the Hutchinsonians shook New England, and continues to shake historians. David D. Hall, ed., *The Antinomian Controversy, 1636–1638: A Documentary History* (Middletown, 1968), and Charles Francis Adams, *Antinomianism in the Colony of Massachusetts Bay, 1636–1638* (Boston, 1894), print important source material; Adams's own account of the affair is in *Three Episodes of Massachusetts History*, 2 vols., rev. ed. (Boston, 1892; repr. New York, 1965), strong on narrative, weak on theology. Emery Battis, *Saints and Sectaries* (Chapel Hill, 1962), weaves an appreciation of the doctrinal concerns into an engagingly written narrative that finds much of Hutchinson's support coming from the nascent commercial community. Stoever, *'Faire and Easie Way'*, is the best guide to the theological debates; see also Jesper Rosenmeier, "New England's Perfection: The Image of Adam and the Image of Christ in the Antinomian Crisis, 1634 to 1638," *William and Mary Quarterly*, 3d ser., 27 (1970), 435–59; James F. Maclear, "Anne Hutchinson and the Mortalist Heresy," *New England Quarterly*, 54 (1981), 74–103; and George Selement, ed., "John Cotton's Hidden Antinomianism: His Sermon on Revelation 4:1–2," *New England Historical Genealogical Register*, 129 (1975), 278–94. Patricia Caldwell, "The Antinomian Language Controversy," *Harvard Theological Review*, 69 (1976), 345–67, finds the nub of the issue in different understandings about how one can (or cannot) communicate religious experience. The crisis is seen as a political affair in Ronald D. Cohen, "Church and State in Seventeenth-Century Massachusetts: Another Look at the Antinomian Controversy," *Journal of Church and State*, 12 (1970), 475–94; and Ann Fairfax Withington and Jack Schwartz, "The Political Trial of Anne Hutchinson," *New England Quarterly*, 51 (1978), 226–40. Hutchinson becomes a protofeminist in Lyle Koehler, "The Case of the American Jezebels: Anne Hutchinson and Female Agitation during the Years of Antinomian Turmoil, 1636–1640," *William and Mary Quarterly*, 3d ser., 31 (1974), 55–78, and Ben Barker-Benfield, "Anne Hutchinson and the Puritan Attitude Toward Women," *Feminist Studies*, 1 (1973), 65–96.

New England Antinomianism connected to larger spheres of seventeenth-century sectarianism, worlds explored by Stephen Foster, "New England and the Challenge of Heresy, 1630-1660: The Puritan Crisis in Transatlantic Perspective," *William and Mary Quarterly*, 3d ser., 38 (1981), 624-60; Philip Gura, *A Glimpse of Sion's Glory* (Middletown, 1984); and David S. Lovejoy, *Religious Enthusiasm in the New World: Heresy to Revolution* (Cambridge, Mass., 1985).

All of the above works, and more, have helped me find answers. A few others, however, enabled me to pose questions, and their influence is adverted to not in the footnotes but in the very structure of the essay. This book may be read as an inquiry into how a society calls up and then channels certain emotions, an attempt inspired by psychological and symbolic anthropologists. Out of many, I would mention four. Anthony F. C. Wallace, *Culture and Personality*, 2d ed. (New York, 1970), showed me how personality and culture combine to determine behavior, Victor Turner, *The Ritual Process* (Chicago, 1969) and *Dramas, Fields and Metaphors* (Ithaca, 1974), how one might interpret meanings implicit in group behavior. What method exists amid the foregoing madness owes much to Clifford Geertz, *The Interpretation of Cultures* (New York, 1973) and *Local Knowledge* (New York, 1983), which have taught a generation of historians to read cultures as texts. Turner and Geertz show how the meanings people appropriate from a culture's institutions and symbols guide their behavior. Most particularly, however, I have drawn on the work of Melford Spiro. In "Social Systems, Personality, and Functional Analysis," in Bert Kaplan, ed., *Studying Personality Cross-Culturally* (Evanston, 1961), 91-127, "An Overview and a Suggested Reorientation," in Francis L. K. Hsu, ed., *Psychological Anthropology* (Homewood, Ill., 1961), 459-92, and "Ghosts, Ifaluk and Teleological Functionalism," *American Anthropologist*, 54 (1952), 497-503, Spiro demonstrated how cultural formations satisfy psychological needs, an insight that lies at the very genesis of my research. The South Seas and colonial Massachusetts are not so far apart after all.

Index

I: PEOPLE, PLACES, SUBJECTS

II: BIBLICAL VERSES

OLD TESTAMENT

NEW TESTAMENT